Lecture Notes in Computer Science 13464

More information about this series at https://link.springer.com/bookseries/558

Mohammed-Amine Koulali · Mira Mezini (Eds.)

Networked Systems

10th International Conference, NETYS 2022
Virtual Event, May 17–19, 2022
Proceedings

Springer

Editors
Mohammed-Amine Koulali
Mohammed First University
Oujda, Morocco

Mira Mezini
Technical University of Darmstadt
Darmstadt, Germany

ISSN 0302-9743   ISSN 1611-3349 (electronic)
Lecture Notes in Computer Science
ISBN 978-3-031-17435-3   ISBN 978-3-031-17436-0 (eBook)
https://doi.org/10.1007/978-3-031-17436-0

This Springer imprint is published by the registered company Springer Nature Switzerland AG
The registered company address is: Gewerbestrasse 11, 6330 Cham, Switzerland

Preface

The aim of the International Conference on Networked Systems (NETYS) is to bring together researchers and engineers from both the theory and practice of distributed and networked systems. The scope of the conference covers all aspects related to the design and the development of these systems, including multi-core architectures, concurrent and distributed algorithms, parallel/concurrent/distributed programming, distributed databases, big data applications and systems, cloud systems, networks, security, and formal verification.

The tenth edition of NETYS received 100 high-quality submissions from around the globe that were reviewed by a Program Committee of 33 international experts covering all branches in the spectrum of distributed and networked systems. Each paper received at least three reviews and underwent a critical discussion of its merits. Based on this, 18 submissions were accepted as full papers and two as short papers (a 20% acceptance rate). The Program Committee also selected one Best Paper and one Best Student Paper. The Best Paper was awarded to Aravind Segu and Wojciech Golab for their paper "Recycling Memory in Recoverable Mutex Locks". The Best Student Paper award was conferred to Viktor Malík, Tomas Vojnar, and Petr Šilling for their paper "Applying Custom Patterns in Semantic Equality Analysis". Viktor Malík was a full-time student at the time of submission.

The COVID-19 pandemic had a serious impact on the organization of NETYS 2022. It was decided not to organize the METIS Spring School that otherwise accompanies NETYS and serves as a social platform for Ph.D. students. The conference was implemented as an asynchronous event and the videos of all presentations are available at the following link: https://netys.net/accepted/.

As the program chairs of NETYS 2022, we thank the authors for their high-quality submissions and the Program Committee for their careful evaluations and the lively discussions. All this occurred under challenging circumstances, and we are grateful to all for making NETYS 2022 happen. Special thanks go to the NETYS General Chair Mohammed Erradi (ENSIAS, Morocco) and the General Co-chairs Ahmed Bouajjani (Université Paris Cité, France) and Rachid Guerraoui (EPFL, Switzerland) for numerous helpful suggestions on the organization. The Organization Committee brought the online event to life, and we thank them for their support. Finally, we thank Springer for their help in assembling the proceedings.

July 2022

Mohammed-Amine Koulali
Mira Mezini

Organization

General Chair

Mohammed Erradi — ENSIAS, Morocco

General Co-chairs

Ahmed Bouajjani — Université Paris Cité, France
Rachid Guerraoui — EPFL, Switzerland

Program Committee Chairs

Mohammed-Amine Koulali — Mohammed I University, Morocco
Mira Mezini — Technische Universität Darmstadt, Germany

Program Committee

Ahmed Khaled — Northeastern Illinois University, USA
Amr El Abbadi — University of California, Santa Barbara, USA
Amr Rizk — University of Duisburg-Essen, Germany
Andreas Podelski — University of Freiburg, Germany
Anis Charfi — Carnegie Mellon University, USA
Bernd Freisleben — Technische Universität Darmstadt, Germany
Carole Delporte-Gallet — Université Paris Cité, France
Carsten Binnig — Technische Universität Darmstadt, Germany
Constantin Enea — École Polytechnique, France
David Mohaisen — University of Central Florida, USA
Erik-Oliver Blass — Airbus Group Innovations
Francois Taiani — IRISA, University of Rennes, France
Guevara Noubir — Northeastern University, USA
Guido Salvaneschi — Technische Universität Darmstadt, Germany
Hajar Elhammouti — Mohammed VI Polytechnic University, Morocco
Hanen Idoudi — ENSI, Tunisia
Imad Benlallam — Mohammed V University, Morocco
Ismail Berrada — Mohammed VI Polytechnic University, Morocco
Karima Echihabi — Mohammed VI Polytechnic University, Morocco
Khalil Ibrahimi — Ibn-Tofail University, Morocco
Maurice Herlihy — Brown University, USA

Michel Raynal	IRISA, University of Rennes, France
Mohamed Elkamili	Hassan II University, Morocco
Mohamed Faouzi Atig	Uppsala University, Sweden
Mohamed Jmaiel	University of Sfax, Tunisia
Mustapha Benjillali	INPT, Morocco
Parosh Aziz Abdulla	Uppsala University, Sweden
Patrick Eugster	Universitá della Svizzera italiana, Italy
Philipp Haller	KTH Royal Institute of Technology, Sweden
Rupak Majumdar	University of California, USA
Slimane Bah	Mohammed V University, Morocco
Wolfgang De Meuter	Vrije Universiteit Brussel, Belgium
Yahya Benkaouz	Mohammed V University, Morocco

Organizing Committee

Khadija Bakkouch	IRFC, Morocco
Abdellah Boulouz	Ibn Zohr University, Morocco
Rachid El Guerdaoui	Mohammed VI Polytechnic University, Morocco
Zahi Jarir	Cadi Ayyad University, Morocco
Mohammed Ouzzif	Hassan II University, Morocco

Contents

Distributed System

A Snapshot-Based Introduction to the Linearizability Hierarchy

Armando Castañeda[1], Sergio Rajsbaum[1], and Michel Raynal[2(✉)]

[1] Instituto de Matematica, UNAM, Mexico City, Mexico
[2] Univ Rennes (IRISA, Inria, CNRS), Rennes, France
raynal@irisa.fr

Abstract. This paper is neither a survey nor a research paper in the classical sense, but an example-based introduction to the linearizability hierarchy. Its aim is to explain it in an "as simple as possible" way. While linearizability is a consistency condition that addresses objects defined by a sequential specification, set-linearizability and interval-linearizability are consistency conditions that have been introduced to take into account objects defined by a concurrent specification. So, they naturally extend linearizability (and its fundamental *composability* property) from sequential to concurrent object specification. The aim of the article is not to present the theoretical foundations of set-linearizability and interval-linearizability, but to explain concurrency patterns allowed by concurrent specifications, and show how these consistency conditions report on them. This is done in a very simple way with the help of three objects that define a family of snapshot objects. In addition to the fact that it constitutes a pedagogical introduction to the topic, this article has also a concurrency-related historical flavor.

Keywords: Asynchrony · Concurrent object · Concurrent specification · Contention point · Contention interval · Crash failure · Interval linearizability · Linearizability hierarchy · Object specification · Modular programming · Read/write registers · Set linearizability · Simultaneity · Snapshot object · Time ubiquity

1 Objects and Concurrency: A Short Historical View

Once Upon a Time. One of the major advances in programming languages and software engineering occurred in the sixties with the notion of *structured programming* [11], that culminated in the introduction of an axiomatic basis for sequential programming [21,22,24] and the introduction of the concept of an *object* [7]. An *object* is a programming abstraction that encapsulates a data structure (e.g. the data implementing a stack) that can be accessed only with specific operations (e.g. push and pop). Hence objects allow programmers to define modularity-based abstraction layers. At the programming languages level, this appeared for the first time in the language Simula that allowed programmers to write programs as a set of computing entities (threads called co-routines) communicating through objects [7][1].

From Sequential Computing to Concurrency: Early Days. Always in the sixties, the operating systems community was confronted to the management of physical resources such as disks, printers, and memory pages. This led to the introduction of both the concept of a *process* and the concept of the *mutual exclusion* object (also called a lock object) that provides the processes with two built-in operations acquire() and release(), which act as control parentheses allowing processes to share physical or logical resources in such a way that at most one process at a time can access the corresponding resource [9,10]. So, mutual exclusion allowed the problem of conflicting operations on a resource to be solved by forcing them to execute sequentially, thereby implicitly introducing the notion of *atomicity* of an object operation.

At the programming level, the concurrency-related notion of a *monitor* was later proposed to be included in programming languages [23]. A monitor allows programmers to encapsulate an object in such a way that the operations on the given object are executed in mutual exclusion and, at the object level, it is possible to use the pre/post condition-based approach to prove the correctness of the encapsulated object and its correct use by the processes.

Concurrent Processes. The advent of multiprocessors, multicores distributed architectures, etc., combined with adversaries such as asynchrony and process failures, asks the fundamental question (posed in [30,31]) of what is *atomicity* from a theoretical point of view. This question and the nature of concurrency are answered in [20,29] which consider a formalism based on the association of two events with each execution of an operation by a process (its beginning/invocation and its end/response) and an associated set of axioms which capture concurrency on operation executions. Considering a *global time frame* defined by an external observer, let us say that two operations the executions of which do not overlap are *sequential*, while two operations the executions of which overlap are *concurrent*.

An example of a queue accessed by two concurrent processes is represented in Fig. 1. The beginning and end events seen by the external observer are denoted $e1, ..., e10$. The main issue is to define which values are returned by the concurrent operations dequeue(). We only know that a precedes b in the queue (because they have been sequentially issued by the same process). Can, for example, a be returned to p_1 and c be returned p_2, or can b be returned to p_1 and a be returned to p_2, or can a be returned to both p_1 and p_2? etc. In the last case, the semantics of the queue must be relaxed.

In such a context, the *atomicity* issue can be intuitively rephrased as follows "Is it possible to totally order all the operation executions in such a way that

---

[1] Co-routines were executed sequentially, their scheduling being managed by the programmer (the built-in operation resume(c) allowed the invoking co-routine to stop its execution while giving the control to the co-routine c).

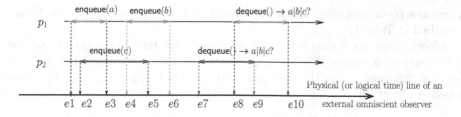

Fig. 1. Time diagram of a concurrent execution

are respected both the sequential order on operations (as defined from the global time frame) and the semantics of the objects?".

What is a Consistency Condition. The notion of a *consistency condition* was introduced in [20], where the reader will find a formal definition. Informally, given a global time frame (which can be physical or logical [33]) and the execution of a program made up of processes accessing shared objects, a *consistency condition* is a *mapping from* the (beginning and end) events generated by the object operations produced by the execution *to* the specification of each object.

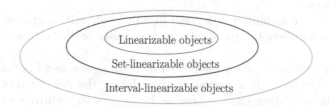

Fig. 2. The linearizability hierarchy for concurrent objects

Content of the Article. Linearizability is a consistency condition introduced in 1990 [20]. Keeping the linearizability spirit, two other consistency conditions have been defined later, namely set-linearizability in 1994 [32], and interval-linearizability in 2018 [3]. In a very interesting way, these three consistency conditions define a strict hierarchy as described in Fig. 2. All these consistency conditions consider that the global time frame of the external observer is the physical time.

As we are about to see, linearizability is intended for objects defined by a sequential specification. Set-linearizability is intended for objects defined by a concurrent specification that allows operations to be seen as being executed concurrently (*simultaneity*). Finally, interval-linearizability is intended for objects defined by a concurrent specification that allows operations to be seen as being executed simultaneously with several other (non concurrent between themselves)

operations (*time-ubiquity*). The main features of the linearizability hierarchy are
described in Table 1.

After a short presentation of the underlying implementation model, the rest
of the article describes this hierarchy with simple snapshot objects, namely,
the base snapshot object [1], the immediate snapshot object [2], and the write-
snapshot object [3][2].

Table 1. Attributes of the three level of the linearizability hierarchy

Consistency cond.	Specification	Implementation	Reference	Example
Linearizability	Sequentiality	Concurrent	[20]	Snapshot
Set Lin.	Lin + simultaneity	Concurrent	[32]	Im.-snapshot
Interval Lin.	Set Lin + time ubiquity	Concurrent	[3]	Write-snapshot

2   Base Underlying Model

The objects are built on top of an underlying system made up of n asynchronous
sequential processes denoted p_1, ..., p_n. Asynchronous means that the speed of
each process is arbitrary, can vary with time, and remains always unknown to
the other processes.

The processes communicate through atomic read/write registers, which are
denoted with identifiers in capital letters. A variable var local to a process p_i is
denoted var_i.

During an execution, any number of processes may crash (a crash is a pre-
mature definitive halt). If a process crashes during the execution of an object
operation, this operation must appear as being executed entirely or not-at-all
(this is ensured with mechanisms such as helping, see [3,16,19,34,35] for technical details).

Let us observe that, due to possibility of process crashes, an object cannot
be implemented with mutual exclusion. This is due to the following observation. Suppose that the operations are executed in mutual exclusion: a process
executes acquire(), then the operation, and finally executes release(). One can
easily see that, if the invoking process crashes after it invoked acquire() and
before it invokes release(), the object is locked forever, which can entail the
blocking of the full application.This results from the net effect of asynchrony
and unexpected process crashes. The interested reader can consult textbooks
such as [19,34,35] for more information on this issue. Object implementations
in the presence of asynchrony and process crashes require specific techniques
where any number of processes can concurrently access the internal representation of a shared object [16,19,34,35]. This has given rise to a hierarchy of
liveness properties designed to cope with asynchrony and process crashes[3].

---

[2] The interested reader will find in [5] an expanded journal version of this introductory
article, including many examples of concurrent objects.

[3] These liveness properties are described in the appendix.

3 Linearizability

What is Linearizability. Introduced by M. Herlihy and J. Wing in 1990 [20], *linearizability* is a consistency condition such that (i) the external observer's time is the usual physical time and (ii) the objects are defined by a sequential specification.

An object execution satisfies linearizability (we also say that an *object execution is linearizable*) if it is possible to totally order all the operations in such a way that are respected both (i) the physical time-defined sequential order on operations and (ii) the sequential specification of the object.

It follows that, despite the fact that some object operations are executed concurrently with respect to physical time, each operation on an object can be *linearized* at a distinct point of the time line (no two operations are linearized at the same point) that respects their physical time occurrence order and, for each object, the projection of its operations issued by the processes is a trace that belongs to its sequential specification.

Example: The Snapshot Object. This object, introduced in [1], provides the processes with two operations denoted write() and snapshot(). It is an initially empty set that will contain at most one pair per process.

When a process p_i invokes write(v), the pair $\langle i, v \rangle$ is added to the object and, if any, the pair $\langle i, - \rangle$ previously written is suppressed from the object. When a process p_i invokes snapshot(), it obtains the current value of the object (a set of pairs) as if this operation had been executed instantaneously.

The sequential specification of a snapshot object is the set of all the sequences that satisfy the previous properties. An example of a linearizable execution of a snapshot object SN is described in Fig. 3. Several fault-tolerant snapshot algorithms have been designed, each with its own features (e.g., [1,27]).

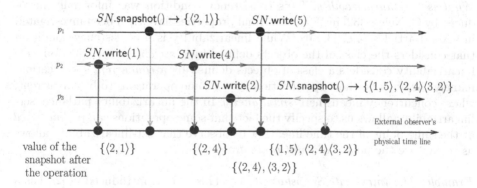

Fig. 3. Example of a linearizable snapshot object execution

A lot of concurrent crash-tolerant implementations of sequential objects that satisfy linearizability have been proposed. The interested reader will find more developments and many examples on linearizable objects in synchronization-oriented textbooks (e.g. [19,34,35]).

A Fundamental Property: Composability. A fundamental property associated with the linearizability consistency condition is *composability* (this property is also called *locality*). Let us suppose that we have a software library containing two independent packages, one containing a linearizable implementation LQ of a queue and another one containing a linearizable implementation LS of a stack. Let us consider a concurrent program P that use both a queue QU and a stack ST whose independent implementations are LQ and LS, respectively. Does the pair of objects (QU, ST) considered as a single object satisfy linearizability? The answer is yes: the fact that linearizable objects are implemented independently the ones from the others does not impact their correctness at the upper program layer which use several linearizable objects.

At first glance the previous question may seem naive, but it is not. It is important to be conscious that the "composability for free" property is not satisfied by all the consistency conditions. As an example, *sequential consistency* [28] is a consistency condition that is not composable. This is due to the fact that, differently from linearizability, the global time notion used by sequential consistency is a logical time that takes into account only the local order on operations inside each process. This means that if, in the previous example, both the implementations of the queue and the stack are sequentially consistent, the pair of objects (QU, ST) is not sequentially consistent when used in the same program (the sequentially consistent implementations of the queue and the stack must cooperate for the pair of objects (QU, ST) to be sequentially consistent).

4   Set-Linearizability

What is Set-Linearizability. This consistency condition was informally introduced by G. Neiger [32] in 1994. Its formal properties have then been investigated in several articles (e.g. [3,14]). While linearizability is a consistency condition that considers the class of the objects defined by a *sequential* specification, set-linearizability considers a class of objects defined by a *concurrent* specification, namely the objects whose specification allows some operations to be concurrent, where concurrency means here *simultaneity*. In the linearizability parlance, set-linearizability allows us to specify the fact that some operations can be *linearized* at the same point of the time line. (Let us observe that set-linearizability allows us to capture the notion of *point contention*).

Example: The Immediate Snapshot Object. This object, introduced in [2], has a single operation that aggregates the operations write() and snapshot() of the base snapshot into a single operation denoted im_snapshot(). It is defined as follows where $view_i$ is the set of pairs returned to p_i. To simplify the presentation and without loss of generality we consider the one-shot version of this object in which a process can invoke im_snapshot() at most once[4]. The object is defined by the three following properties.

- Self-inclusion. If im_snapshot(v) returns $view_i$ to p_i, we have $\langle i, v \rangle \in view_i$.
- Containment. If the invocation of im_snapshot() by p_i returns $view_i$ and the invocation of im_snapshot() by p_j returns $view_j$, we have $view_i \subseteq view_j$ or $view_j \subseteq view_i$.
- Immediacy. If the invocation of im_snapshot(v) returns $view_i$, the invocation of im_snapshot(w) returns $view_j$, and $\langle i, v \rangle \in view_j \land \langle j, w \rangle \in view_i$, then $view_i = view_j$.

The immediate snapshot object is not linearizable but is set-linearizable. Due to the immediacy property, concurrent invocations of im_snapshot() can return the same set of pairs, in which case they are linearized at the same point of the time line (from which follows simultaneity of operations).

The algorithm described in Fig. 4 (from [2]) implements an immediate snapshot object. To this end, it uses two underlying arrays of atomic read/write registers: $MEM[1..n]$, whose entries are initialized to $\perp$, and $LEVEL[1..n]$ whose entries are initialized to $n + 1$. Let us consider the entries of $LEVEL[1..n]$ as being the steps of a staircase that the processes have to descend. Initially all the processes are on the step $n + 1$.

```
operation im_snapshot(v) is                              % code for process p_i
(L1)  MEM[i] ← v;
(L2)  repeat LEVEL[i] ← LEVEL[i] − 1;
(L3)        for each j ∈ {1, ..., n} do level_i[j] ← LEVEL[j] end for;
(L4)        set_i ← {x | level_i[x] ≤ level_i[i]}
(L5)  until (|set_i| ≥ level_i[i]) end repeat;
(L6)  let view_i = { ⟨x, MEM[x]⟩ | x ∈ set_i };
(L7)  return(view_i).
```

Fig. 4. An algorithm that builds an immediate snapshot object on top of read/write registers

When a process p_i invokes im_snapshot(v), it deposits v in $MEM[i]$ (Line L1), and enters a repeat loop, in which it first descends to the next step (Line L2). Then it reads (asynchronously the progress of descending the staircase of all the processes (Line L3) and computes the set of pairs deposited by the processes which are at the same or a lower step of the staircase than its current step (Line L4). Then, if p_i sees less processes at a step lower than its current step, it continues looping (Line L2). Otherwise p_i exits the repeat loop, computes its set $view_i$ (Line L6), and returns it (Line L7). A formal proof

---

[4] The generalization to obtain a multi-shot im_snapshot() operation is easy. It requires a simple adaptation of the containment property.

of this algorithm can be found in [34]. It relies on the following invariant: $\forall\ x\ :$ at most x processes stop descending the staircase at steps y such that $y \leq x$. (if a crash occurs during an operation execution, its pair can be or not added to the object, which depends on the asynchrony of the run).

An example of a set-linearizable immediate snapshot object IS is depicted in Fig. 5.

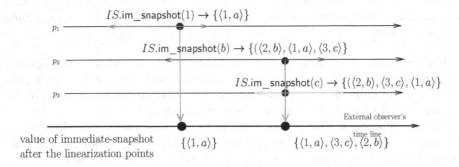

Fig. 5. Example of a set-linearizable immediate-snapshot execution

Relaxed Stacks and Queues. Examples of relaxed stacks and queues, that are set-linearizable, built top of atomic read/write registers are presented in [4]. Several concurrent dequeue() operations can be linearized at the same point of the time line, in which case they return the same value. The other dequeue() operations and all enqueue() operations are linearized at a single point of the time line. And similarly for push() and pop() operations in the case of a stack. (Such objects can be used to implement idempotent work-stealing).

5   Interval-Linearizability

What is Interval-Linearizability. Interval-linearizability, which completes the linearizability hierarchy, was introduced by A. Castañeda, S. Rajsbaum and M. Raynal in 2018 [3]. It considers objects defined by a concurrent specification, where the concerned concurrency is *time-ubiquity*. More precisely, set-linearizability allows to consider operations that can be seen as being *concurrent at different points* of the timeline with several other operations which are not necessarily concurrent between themselves.[5]

It has been shown in [13] that interval-linearizability is *complete* in the sense it captures all the concurrent specifications satisfying a reasonable set of axioms (*reasonable* means here that the axioms capture intuitive notions such as commutativity of operation invocations, prefix closure, etc.). Finally, despite the fact

---

[5] Let us note that while set-linearizability is related to the notion of *contention point*, interval-linearizability is related to the notion of *contention interval*.

it allows to capture non-trivial concurrency patterns, it is remarkable that, as linearizability and set-linearizability, the interval-linearizability consistency condition is composable. (Let us observe that interval-linearizability allows us to capture the notion of *interval contention*).

It is also worth noting that interval-linearizability unifies the notions of concurrent objects and distributed tasks [3], which are two distinct specification styles for distributed systems prone to asynchrony and process crashes. Roughly speaking a *distributed task* is a mapping from a set of input vectors to a set of possible output vectors [15]. The most famous distributed task is consensus.

The size of each vector is the number n of processes. The i-th entry of the input (resp. output) vector represents a possible input (resp. output) of process p_i. (If $n = 1$, the distributed task boils down to a classical function.)[6]

Example: The Write-Snapshot Object. The write-snapshot object was introduced in [3]. It is a version of the immediate snapshot object, which has a single operation denoted write_snapshot(). This operation pieces together the snapshot() and write() operations of the basic snapshot object in a single operation. Differently from the atomic snapshot() and write() operations, the operation write_snapshot() can appear to different processes as executed at different points of the time line (hence time-ubiquity). It is required to satisfy the base self-inclusion and containment properties (but not the immediacy property).

---

operation write_snapshot(v) **is**   % code for process p_i
(W1) $MEM[i] \leftarrow \langle i, v \rangle$;
(W2) $new_i \leftarrow \cup_{1 \leq j \leq n}\{\langle j, MEM[j]\rangle$ such that $MEM[j] \neq \perp\}$;
(W3)   **repeat** $old_i \leftarrow new_i$;
(W4) $new_i \leftarrow \cup_{1 \leq j \leq n}\{MEM[j]$ such that $MEM[j] \neq \perp\}$
(W5)   **until** ($old_i = new_i$) **end repeat**;
(W6)   return(new_i).

Fig. 6. An algorithm that builds a write-snapshot object on top of read/write registers

The algorithm described in Fig. 6 is a simple algorithm that implements a one-shot write-snapshot object. An example of execution is depicted in Fig. 7. In this example, the operations write_snapshot() issued by p_1 and p_3 see, at distinct points of the time line, the operation write_snapshot() issued by p_2, hence the

---

[6] Input/output vectors have one entry per process. An input vector represents a vector of values that can be proposed by the processes for an execution of the task. An output vector defines which are the value decided by each process. For example, all the entries of an output vector of the consensus task contain the same value, which is one of the values present in the corresponding input vector. So, there are at most n possible output vectors associated with a given input vector. For k-set agreement [6,8], an output vector can contain up to k different values, each being a value present in the input vector.

added notion of time-ubiquity that captures concurrency patterns nor allowed by set-linearizability.

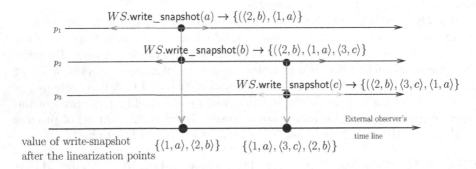

Fig. 7. Example of an interval-linearizable write-snapshot execution

Another (Practical) Example: Lattice Agreement. Let us consider a set L partially ordered by a binary relation $\sqsubseteq$ such that any pair $x, y \in L$ has a least upper bound called *join*.

A lattice agreement object is an object that provides the processes with a single (one-shot) operation propose(v) with input $v \in L$ and returns a value $v' \in L$, such that:

- Termination: if a process invokes propose() and does not crash, it returns form its invocation.
- Validity: If propose(v) returns v', the returned value v' is a join of some proposed values including v and all values returned by previous propose() operations.
- Consistency: The returned values are ordered by $\sqsubseteq$.

It is shown in [12] that, in distributed systems, global state reconciliation is an instance of lattice agreement.

6   Conclusion

This short paper was a guided visit to the linearizability hierarchy which is on consistency conditions that allows us to take into account objects defined by a concurrent specification. While linearizability considers only sequential specifications, set-linearizability allows us to take into account *simultaneity* of some operations, and interval-linearizability allows us to take into account *time-ubiquity* (when an operation is seen as being concurrent with other operations not concurrent between themselves). In a very interesting way, as linearizability, set-linearizability and interval-linearizability are composable, which means that any set of linearizable, set-linearizable or interval-linearizable objects can be composed for free without loosing their linearizability-related properties. This is a crucial property for concurrency-related software engineering.

We hope that this example-based introduction to the linearizability hierarchy can help researchers to relax the specification of objects defined by a sequential specification to obtain concurrent meaningful objects as suggested in [4] for stacks and queues.

Liveness Properties for Read/Write Crash-Prone Systems

The three following properties have been proposed for asynchronous read/write systems in which any number of processes may crash. They define a strict hierarchy (the items that follow start from the stronger to the weaker liveness property).

- Wait-freedom (Introduced by M. Herlihy in [16]). If a process does not crash while executing an operation on an object O, it terminates (whatever the behavior of the other processes which can be concurrently invoking operations on O).
  This is similar to starvation-freedom in failure-free systems.
- Non-blocking (Introduced by M. Herlihy and J. Wing in [20]). (This property is sometimes named lock-freedom or mutex-freedom). If one or several processes invoke an operation on an object 0, and one of them does not crash, at least one process will terminate its operation on O.
  This is similar to deadlock-freedom in failure-free systems.
- Obstruction-freedom. (Introduced by M. Herlihy, V. Luchangco and M. Moir in [17].) If one or several processes invoke operations on an object 0, at least one of them will terminate its operation on O if all the other processes invoking operations on O stop executing for a long enough period of time.

The algorithms described in Fig. 4 and Fig. 6 satisfy the wait-freedom liveness property. More developments on liveness properties in the presence of asynchrony and process crash failures can be found in [18, 25, 26, 36].

Remark 1. Let notice that problems that cannot be solved when the wait-freedom property is required can be solved if it is replaced by the weaker obstruction-freedom property. This is the case of consensus.

Remark 2. Let us also notice that if the number of processes is bounded, and the object that is built is a one-shot object, non-blocking implies wait-freedom.

References

1. Afek, Y., Attiya, H., Dolev, D., Gafni, E., Merritt, M., Shavit, N.: Atomic snapshots of shared memory. J. ACM **40**(4), 873–890 (1993)
2. Borowsky, E., Gafni, E.: Immediate atomic snapshots and fast renaming. In: Proceedings of the 12th ACM Symposium on Principles of Distributed Computing (PODC 1993), pp. 41–51. ACM Press (1993)
3. Castañeda, A., Rajsbaum, S., Raynal, M.: Unifying concurrent objects and distributed tasks: interval-linearizability. J. ACM **65**(6), 42 (2018). Article 45
4. Castañeda, A., Rajsbaum, S., Raynal, M.: Relaxed queues and stacks from read/write operations. In: Proceedings of the 24th Conference on Principles of Distributed Systems (OPODIS 2020), LIPIcs, vol. 184, 19 p (2020). Article 13
5. Castañeda, A., Rajsbaum, S., Raynal, M.: A linearizability-based hierarchy for concurrent specifications. Submitted to Communications of the ACM (2022)
6. Chaudhuri, S.: More choices allow more faults: set consensus problems in totally asynchronous systems. Inf. Comput. **105**(1), 132–158 (1993)
7. Dahl, O.-J., Nygaard, K.: SIMULA: an ALGOL-based simulation language. Commun. ACM **9**(9), 671–678 (1966)
8. Delporte, C., Fauconnier, H., Rajsbaum, S., Raynal, M.: Distributed computability: relating k-immediate snapshot and x-set agreement. Inf. Comput. **258**, 104815 (2022)
9. Dijkstra, E.W.: Solution of a problem in concurrent programming control. Commun. ACM **8**(9), 569 (1965)
10. Dijkstra, E.W.: Cooperating sequential processes. In: Genuys, F. (ed.) Programming Languages, pp. 43–112. Academic Press (1968)
11. Dijkstra, E.W., Dahl, O.-J., Hoare, C.A.R.: Structured Programming, 220 p. Academic Press (1972)
12. de Souza, L.F., Kuznetsov, P., Rieutord, Th., Tucci Piergiovanni, S.: Distributed state reconciliation: accountability and reconfiguration: self-healing lattice agreement. In: OPODIS 2021, pp. 25:1–25:23 (2021)
13. Goubault, E., Ledent, J., Mimram, S.: Concurrent specifications beyond linearizability. In: Proceedings of the 22nd International Conference on Principles of Distributed Systems (OPODIS 2018), LIPIcs, vol. 125, pp. 28:1–28:16 (2018)
14. Hemed, N., Rinetzky, N., Vafeiadis, V.: Modular verification of concurrency-aware linearizability. In: Moses, Y. (ed.) DISC 2015. LNCS, vol. 9363, pp. 371–387. Springer, Heidelberg (2015). https://doi.org/10.1007/978-3-662-48653-5_25
15. Herlihy, M., Kozlov, D., Rajsbaum, S.: Distributed Computing Through Combinatorial Topology, 336 p. Morgan Kaufmann (2014)
16. Herlihy, M.P.: Wait-free synchronization. ACM Trans. Program. Lang. Syst. **13**(1), 124–149 (1991)
17. Herlihy, M.P., Luchangco, V., Moir, M.: Obstruction-free synchronization: double-ended queues as an example. In: Proceedings of the 23th International IEEE Conference on Distributed Computing Systems (ICDCS 2003), pp. 522–529. IEEE Press (2003)
18. Herlihy, M., Rajsbaum, S., Raynal, M., Stainer, J.: From wait-free to arbitrary concurrent solo executions in colorless distributed computing. Theor. Comput. Sci. **683**, 1–21 (2017)
19. Herlihy, M.P., Shavit, N.: The Art of Multiprocessor Programming, 508 p. Morgan Kaufmann (2008). ISBN: 978-0-12-370591-4

20. Herlihy, M.P., Wing, J.M.: Linearizability: a correctness condition for concurrent objects. ACM Trans. Program. Lang. Syst. **12**(3), 463–492 (1990)
21. Hoare, C.A.R.: An axiomatic basis for computer programming. Commun. ACM **12**(10), 576–580 (1969)
22. Hoare, C.A.R.: Proof of correctness of data representation. Acta Informatica **1**, 271–281 (1972)
23. Hoare, C.A.R.: Monitors: an operating system structuring concept. Commun. ACM **17**(10), 549–557 (1974)
24. Hoare, C.A.R.: Programming: sorcery or science? IEEE Softw. **1**(2), 5–16 (1984)
25. Imbs, D., Raynal, M., Taubenfeld, G.: On asymmetric progress conditions. In: 29th ACM Symposium on Principles of Distributed Computing (PODC 2010), pp. 55–64. ACM Press (2010)
26. Imbs, D., Raynal, M.: A liveness condition for concurrent objects: x-wait-freedom. Concurr. Comput. Pract. Exp. **23**, 2154–2166 (2011)
27. Imbs, D., Raynal, M.: Help when needed, but no more: an efficient partial snapshot algorithm. J. Parallel Distrib. Comput. **72**(1), 1–12 (2012)
28. Lamport, L.: How to make a multiprocessor computer that correctly executes multiprocess programs. IEEE Trans. Comput. **C-28**(9), 690–691 (1979)
29. Lamport, L.: On inter-process communications, part I: basic formalism, part II: algorithms. Distrib. Comput. **1**(2), 77–101 (1986)
30. Lamport, L.: The mutual exclusion problem - part II: statements and solutions. J. Assoc. Comput. Mach. **33**(2), 313–348 (1986)
31. Misra, J.: Axioms for memory access in asynchronous hardware systems. ACM Trans. Program. Lang. Syst. **8**(1), 142–203 (1986)
32. Neiger, G.: Set linearizability. In: Proceedings of the 13th Annual ACM Symposium on Principles of Distributed Computing (PODC 1994), Brief Announcement, p. 396. ACM Press (1994)
33. Perrin, M., Petrolia, M., Mostéfaoui, A., Jard, C.: On composition and implementation of sequential consistency. In: Gavoille, C., Ilcinkas, D. (eds.) DISC 2016. LNCS, vol. 9888, pp. 284–297. Springer, Heidelberg (2016). https://doi.org/10.1007/978-3-662-53426-7_21
34. Raynal, M.: Concurrent Programming: Algorithms, Principles and Foundations, 520 p. Springer, Heidelberg (2013). https://doi.org/10.1007/978-3-642-32027-9. ISBN: 978-3-642-32026-2
35. Taubenfeld, G.: Synchronization Algorithms and Concurrent Programming, 423 p. Pearson Education/Prentice Hall (2006). ISBN: 0-131-97259-6
36. Taubenfeld, G.: The computational structure of progress conditions and shared objects. Distrib. Comput. **33**(2), 103–123 (2020). https://doi.org/10.1007/s00446-019-00356-0

Varda: A Framework for Compositional Distributed Programming

Laurent Prosperi[1]([⊠])[iD], Ahmed Bouajjani[2][iD], and Marc Shapiro[1][iD]

[1] Sorbonne-Université, CNRS, Inria, LIP6, Paris, France
{laurent.prosperi,marc.shapiro}@lip6.fr
[2] IRIF, Université Paris Cité, Paris, France
abou@irif.fr

Abstract. A distributed system is made of interacting components. The current manual, *ad-hoc* approach to composing them cannot ensure that the composition is correct, and makes it difficult to control performance. The former issue requires reasoning over a high-level specification; the latter requires fine control over emergent run-time properties. To address this, we propose the Varda language (a work in progress) to formalize the *architecture* of a system, i.e., its components, their interface, and their orchestration logic. The Varda compiler checks the architecture description and emits *glue code*, which executes the orchestration logic and links to the components. The Varda system relies on a generic *interception mechanism* to act upon distribution-related system features in a transparent and uniform manner. Varda also takes into account important non-functional system properties, such as placement.

Keywords: Distributed programming · Language · Distributed system · Composition · Orchestration · Architecture

1 Introduction

The developer of a distributed system rarely implements it from scratch, as a monolithic program. Instead, a common approach is to compose independent components, either off-the-shelf or bespoke. For instance, a sharded key-value store might be composed of shard servers (a and b in Fig. 1a), with a router to direct client requests to the correct shard.

The composed system should both be safe and have good performance. This requires the developer to be able to: (1) formalize the individual components; (2) specify how they communicate [17,25,30]; (3) reason over both the static effects of the composed object [25], and its dynamic effects; and, (4) control and other non-functional and performance-related properties, such as co-location or inlining.

The current approach to compositional programming is *ad-hoc* and mostly manual. It consists of running components as processes that send messages to each others' API [30]. This satisfies in part Requirements 1 and 2 above, but does not express high-level safety [17,30], placement, or performance constraints.

M.-A. Koulali and M. Mezini (Eds.): NETYS 2022, LNCS 13464, pp. 16–30, 2022.
https://doi.org/10.1007/978-3-031-17436-0_2

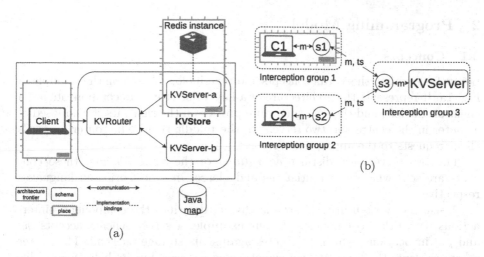

Fig. 1. (a) A key-value store (S-KV) composed of two shards and a router. (b) Adding causally consistent communication (cc) layer to our key-value store: with two client ($c1$, $c2$), one KVServer (kv) and three CC-sidecars ($s1$, $s2$, $s3$). m denotes a message and ts denotes a vector clock.

An improvement is to use an *orchestration engine*, such as Docker Compose, Kubernetes or OpenStack [3,4,15] to automate deployment and to control the topology. This addresses Requirement 4 only. Alternatively, a *protocol language* or an *orchestration language* can express some of the semantics. However, current languages do not satisfy Requirements 3 and 4, as we detail in Sect. 4.

We address these issues with Varda, our framework for compositional distributed programming. A system developer specifies the *architecture* of a distributed system in the Varda language. This enables to formally define the components of a system, their interface, their interconnection, and their placement. In particular, our *orchestration* sublanguage prescribes the run-time interactions between the components. Based on this specification, the Varda compiler performs static and run-time checks, and generates the interaction code between components, called the *glue*.

Note that an architecture description abstracts over issues not related to distribution. In particular, the individual components are imported and linked into the generated glue, but assumed implemented outside of our framework (written for instance in Java).

We claim the following contributions for this work:

- A language for expressing the component architecture and the orchestration of a distributed system (Sect. 2).
- A general *interception* mechanism for imposing orchestration logic and other transformations onto components (Sect. 3).
- As an example, we show how to impose transparently a common pattern: sharding (Sect. 3).

This paper does not yet provide an experimental evaluation, as the implementation is progress.

2   Programming Model

2.1   Concepts

Let us first explain the Varda concepts and terminology, based on the example in Fig. 1a. It represents the architecture of a key-value store. Its components are a client on the left, and the key-value store proper on the right, itself composed of a router in the centre and two servers on the middle right. The router forwards client requests to the appropriate server.

The two servers are distinct *activations* of the same *schema*; these concepts are somewhat to instantiations and classes in object-oriented languages respectively.

A schema, written in the Varda language, describes the component's interactions with other components. In our example, a server schema accepts *get* and *put* invocations, which it executes against its storage backend. The router schema accepts the same *get/put* signature as a server, but its behaviour is different: based on the arguments, it forwards the invocation to the appropriate server activation, awaits the response, and forwards the response to the client.

An activation can link to an *implementation*, a black-box executable component exported as a library. In the figure, the implementation of Activation a stores its data in a Redis implementation [36], whereas that of Activation b uses a custom storage logic.

Finally, the figure shows *places*, i.e., physical or logical locations in the distributed system. In this example, the client is in its own place, and Server a is in the same place as its implementation. Placement is an important consideration, for instance for performance, fault tolerance or physical security.

2.2   Components

Recall that a schema is the code for a class of components. The Varda schema code has several parts, each described in an appropriate sublanguage. Its *signature* declares the names and types of messages it can send and receive, using both classical (declarative) types and (imperative) safety assertions. Its *protocol* describes the sequencing of such messages, expressed in the language of *session types* [14]. *Ports* are communication entry and exit points; a port is described by its name, signature, and protocol.

The *orchestration* logic describes how the component behaves, in a Turing-complete imperative sublanguage. It can specify a callback method to be invoked when a given type of message is received. It also includes specific methods for creating and destroying an activation of the component (called `onStartup` and `onDestroy` respectively). Orchestration logic can maintain local state, can send messages, and can invoke the implementation.

The binding between the component, and its implementation written in some external programming language, is expressed using imperative templates that embed fragments of the external language.[1]

---

[1] Currently our compiler supports only Java bindings.

A component schema may contain sub-components. The scope of a sub-component is the enclosing component, i.e., a sub-component cannot be invoked from the outside.

An instance of a schema at run time is called an *activation*. The activation is the smallest grain of distribution and concurrency. Computation within an activation is sequential. Receiving a message, instantiating the activation or terminating it run the corresponding callback method. A method executes until it terminates, or until it waits for an asynchronous invocation.

2.3   Interaction Interface

This subsection details how two components interact. Activations communicates by sending messages to each other. Programmers group message into protocols. A protocol describes the type and the order of events. Session types [14] directly inspire protocols. Between activations, those messages are flowing through channels. A channel interconnects ports of multiple components. A programmer formalizes components interface by defining *ports*: inport, to communicate with the outside, and outport, to listen for incoming messages.

The interaction should both be safe and have good performance. This requires the developer to be able to: (a) constraints the communication topology to explicitly specify which component is talking to whom; (b) interacting component have to agree on the order and the type of messages they exchange to perform lightweight verification and to drive the code-generation of the networking interfaces; (c) represents the underlying network layer to do specialize the code-generation and to represents assumption on the underlying network in the architecture description; and, (d) (weakly) isolate component functionalities from each other.

Events. To communicate, activations exchange events. Each event is strongly typed and can carry a payload. Its payload should be serializable.

A programmer can manually define an event *key* carrying a string payload with event key of string;. Otherwise, a programmer can send classical serializable types without defining events. The Varda compiler auto-box those types into events and un-box them at reception. Event auto-boxing alleviate the programmer from the burden of defining events for base types (e.g., int).

Varda type system supports type evolution of event through subtyping. Subtyping define a relation of substitutability between data types. Substitutability is a property where code written to operate on the supertype can safely be substituted for any of the subtypes in the subtyping relationship [27].

A component can send a message with more information than expected. For instance, lets assume than Activation b expects messages of type record: {value: string}. An Activation a can send to b a message of type: {checksum: string; value: string;}. At reception, b considers only the field value.

Protocols. Protocols address Requirement b. It constraints communication between activations: programmer attaches a protocol to each channel and each port. A (binary) session represents one instance of a protocol. An Activation i can creates a session s with Activation j by calling `initiate_session_with` (`outport_of_i`, `j`). Let's assume that the protocol of the port is `protocol p_get = !key?value. ;`. Where key and value are event types. The session type implicitly bound to `p_get` guarantees that a communication through s is as follows: i starts by sending a message of type `key` and ends by receiving a message of type `value`.

Varda exposes classical communication primitives managing session [14]: asynchronous message sending `fire(s, msg)`, asynchronous receiving using call-back (ports) or `receive` primitive, non-deterministic branching `branch` and recursive protocol. Each of this operations returns a new session types with the protocol of the continuation and preserves the session identity.

Channels. Channels address Requirement c and their types solves the static part of Requirement a. A channel can interconnect multiple activations, of different component schemas. A channel can represents different communication guarantees, provided by the underlying network primitives. For instance, a channel can be protected by TLS encryption or can guarantee point to point FIFO communication, which is the default guarantee. A channel is compiled directly to network layer code to preserve performance.

A channel definition is asymmetric for communication establishment to statically constrain communication topology. A channel of type `channel<A, B, protocol>` guarantees that only activations of type A can initiate a request to activations of type B. Bidirectional channels can be constructed using union type: `channel<A|B, A|B, protocol>`.

Ports. The set of ports of a schema defines its interaction signature. Ports solves Requirement d. Each port define a functionality of a component: A port only accept communication that follow a given session type. Moreover, ports reduce the complexity of the component code: Ports abstract away the communication interconnection between the component inner logic (statically defined) and the activations interactions over channels (dynamic bindings). For instance, sessions primitives take ports as arguments and not channels.

Ports are static since they define the signature of a component schema: new ports can not be added nor removed at runtime. However, bindings between ports and channels depend of activation identity. Those bindings can evolve dynamically, and transparently for the inner activation logic. Operationally, a programmer binds a channel with port using the initial knowledge provided at activation creation (thanks to parameters) or by exchanging channel identity over existing sessions.

```
1       protocol p_kv = &{ (* non-deterministic choice *)
2           "get": !key?value.; (* send key, receive value *)
3           "put": !tuple<key,value>?bool.; (* or send tuple, receive ack *)
4       };
5
6       (* channel<active,passive,protocol> *)
7       channel<Client, KVServer, p_kv> chan = channel(p_kv);
8       (* start new component at a given location *)
9       activation_ref<KVServer> kv_a = spawn KVServer(chan) @ place_redis;
10      (* start and connect a client *)
11      activation_ref<Client> c = spawn Client(chan, kv_a);
```

Listing 1: The minimal key-value store in Varda.

2.4 Orchestration Logic

The objective of the orchestration is to write executable code doing dynamic interaction whereas the interaction interfaces describes what messages can be exchanged between components.

The main work of orchestration is to spawn activations and to interconnect ports using channels. Inside a component schema, the orchestration logic is in charge of doing the bindings between communication interfaces with procedural ones. For instance, this is the only work of the callback method of Listing 2. A programmer can also write the core behaviour of orchestration schemas (e.g., KVRouter) using the Varda orchestration logic in order to be completely agnostic to the underlying language. The Varda compiler generates the effective implementation.

In addition to component schema description language, Varda proposes a small imperative and Turing-complete language to write the orchestration logic. Varda language contains classical language constructs (e.g., binders, expression, function, control-flow statement and inductive type); communication primitives to exchange between activations using sessions; and, activation creation primitive: spawn Schema(arguments) @ place;.

2.5 Example: A Minimal Key-Value Store

Listing 1 presents the architecture of a warm-up case study: a key-value store composed of one server and one client. This warm-up example is a piece of Fig. 1a: a KVServer (kv_a), without sharding, that serves requests of one client such that the server use a Redis backend and is collocated with it. This example assumes that the Redis server is already running before spawning a KVServer. KVServer serves as a proxy to the Redis server.

In Listing 2, KVServer specifies the interface of a Redis server. Conversely, Client specifies of the interface of an application using the key-value store. KVServer exposes a *communication interface*, composed of its port p_in and the communication handling logic callback method; a *procedural interface* composed of two abstract methods get and put bound the black-box service (resp.

```
1   component KVServer {
2       (* Method triggered at spawn, binds the channel *)
3       onstartup (channel<Client, KVServer, p_kv> chan){
4           this.chan = chan;
5       }
6       (* Communication interface *)
7       channel<Client, KVServer, p_kv> chan;
8       (* Liste on channel [this.chan] for session with
9           (dual p_kv) type.  Upon reception, message is handled by
10          [this.callback]. *)
11      inport p_in on this.chan expecting (dual p_kv) = this.callback;
12      (* Bindings between interaction interface and procedural interface *)
13      void callback (blabel msg, p_kv s) {
14          branch s on msg { (* non deterministic choice*)
15              | "get" => s -> {
16                  tuple<key, ?value.> tmp = receive(s); (* wait for key *)
17                  (* return the value bound to the received key [tmp.0] *)
18                  fire(tmp.1, get(tmp.0));
19              }
20              | "put" => s -> { ... }
21          }
22      }
23      (* procedural interface *)
24      value get(key k);
25      bool put(key k, value v);
26  }
```

Listing 2: KVServer component schema

```
1       target akka;
2
3       impl headers {=
4           (* use the java-redis-client library *)
5           import nl.melp.redis.protocol.Parser;
6       =}
7
8       (* binding for the get method *)
9       impl method KVServer::get {=
10          (* Open a socket to the local redis backend *)
11          nl.melp.redis.Redis r = new nl.melp.redis.Redis(new
              ↪ Socket({{ip(current_place())}}, {{port(current_place())}}));
12          (* perform the GET request on key [k] *)
13          return r.call("GET", {{string_of_ley(k)}});
14      =}
```

Listing 3: KVServer::get bindings for the Akka target. The compiler interprets
Varda {{expression}} strings inside an impl body.

implementation) and no orchestration logic. The compiler specializes the two abstract methods get and put during code generation according to implementation bindings (Listing 3). Moreover, the communication handling logic (here the callback method) is in charge of doing the binding between the communication interface and the procedural interface.

A channel chan, guaranteeing FIFO delivery for point-to-point communication, interconnects the client with the server (Listing 1). Both client and server discover chan as an argument. chan is asymmetric and constrains the communication topology: the left hand side of the channel type (e.g., Client) initiate the communication, the right hand side can not. Moreover, communication follows the protocol p_kv (technically, a session type [14]): a client can choose between two operations put or get. Once client chooses the get (resp. put) case, the communication must follow the pattern: client sends a key and expects to receive a value before the session is closed (resp. put).

3   Interception

At this point, one major remaining question is how to easily and safely enrich (or trim) system's functionalities. For instance, manually sharding the minimal key-value (Listing 1) would be time consuming: a programmer needs to manually (1) create the sharding logic (the router); (2) creates new channels to interconnect the shards (resp. the clients) with the sharding logic; (3) instantiate a router with correct channels interconnections; and (4) for each shards, bind correctly the new channels.

We propose that Steps (2), (3) and (4) should be automatically handled during compilation while followings this requirements: (a) impose arbitrary interception, orthogonal from placement and communication topology, and prevent intercepted activation to bypass the interception mechanism (b) be non invasive and transparent to avoid to the programmer to edit the whole architecture; (c) be generic and modular (d) should be executed efficiently to preserve performance; and, (e) be preserved by composition: multiple alterations could be nested to modularly build a major functionalities.

To address this problem, Varda leverages the interception mechanism as the core Varda primitive used to uniformly apply the orchestration logic. Developers write the interception logic at same abstraction level, and in the same language as the orchestration logic. Then, the Varda transparently and statically rewrite the architecture by adding proxies [38] in between groups of activations.

Varda interception is an architecture construction. This helps preserving the preexisting semantics and formalizing the new architecture. Other approaches work on the network layer and do dynamic interception, as we describe it in Sect. 4.4.

In the following, we review what a programmer can achieve using interception:

- *Message redirection* can be achieved by using the same interception instrumentation as sharding, with a custom routing policy (e.g., round-robin for *loadbalancing* and broadcasting for *replication*).

- *Dynamically constraining topology* (e.g., access control) can be done as long as dropping communication take place at session establishment since sessions can not be discard arbitrarily due to session type guarantees.
- *Encapsulating messages or piggy-packing metadata* between activations can also be done even if it is a bit more tricky: the programmer needs to introduce a new intermediate protocol without breaking transparency.
- *Changing the communication behaviour* can be performed by intercepting the communication and implementing the communication behaviour inside the interception logic. For instance, programmers can transparently replace a point to point communication by a broadcast.
- *Any combinations of those patterns* can be achieved using nested interception contexts.

3.1   What is Interception?

The interception concernes a group of channels in between an *internal* group of activations and the *external one* composed of all the remaining activations. In Varda, the programmer has only to enclose the creations of activations, she want to intercept, into an interception scope (using a `intercept` statement). The interception scope is part of the orchestration code. Therefore, applying interception is orthogonal to defining the logic of the both groups, their interactions and their placement. This solves Requirement a. Whereas, the interception behaviour can depend on those three elements.

Interception concerns both the session establishment and the messages exchanged inside the session. Interception give the ability to the programmer to alter arbitrarily the communications between two groups of activations: message value and session can be alter or delayed. However, the type of the protocol can not be altered arbitrarily, this point will be discussed when detailing transparency.

What is not Interception? Interception is not designed for ensuring security isolation. Interception can no prevent malicious activations to communicate with the external worlds. Indeed, interception works with Varda communication primitives whereas a malicious activation could *bypass it from below* by using arbitrary communication primitives provided by external code (e.g., sockets). Even if activations only communicate with Varda communication primitives, interception isolation could also be *breached by above* if an intercepted protocol allows channel exchange (recall that channels are first-class value) and if the intercepted activation dynamically binds this received channel to one of its ports. Varda compiler does not prevent this: breaching interception could be used to removed interception at some point to preserved performance, for instance once an activation has migrated. However, this kind of breaches can by either *forbidden*: by disallowing channel transmission in the protocol definition: or, *mitigated*: by checking the identity of forwarded channels inside the interception logic.

```
1  intercept<KVRouter, anonymous> interception_policy {
2      activation_ref<KVServer> kv_a = spawn KVServer(chan);
3      activation_ref<KVServer> kv_b = spawn KVServer(chan);
4  }
5
6  activation_ref<Client> c = spawn Client(chan, kv_a);
```

Listing 4: Intercepting KVServer from Listing 1 to support sharding

3.2 Example: A Sharded Key-Value Store

With Varda, transforming the simple key-value store example into a sharded version is a matter of transparently created an interception context containing two KVServer, Listing 4. Such that the interception logic, defined as a component called KVRouter, implements the sharding strategy. The interception_policy instantiates a singleton KVRouter activation for the whole interception context. The KVRouter postpones the establishment of a session between the interceptor and a KVServer until the client give enough knowledge (e.g., the key) to select the right KVServer. Delaying messages can be tricky, since arbitrary long delay between messages of the same session could be trigger a timeout depending of session implementation.

3.3 Expressing Interception

To setup interception context, programmers have three things to do: (1) define the *interception logic* by providing an interceptor component schema (e.g., KVRouter); (2) delimit the interception scope using a *intercept* block statement and (3) describe what interceptor activation is in charge of which intercepted activations thanks to an *interception policy*.

Interception Logic. The interception logic is in charge of processing (alteration, delaying and forwarding) session establishments and messages between internal and external activations. The interception logic is defined as annotated methods to remains generic and not to be specific to a given interception context. That way, programmers do not have to take care of creating the communication interface of the interceptor which depends on the interception context. The compiler is in charge of *specializing the interceptor component schema*, for each context, in order to create the needed ports according to the intercepted bridges. It binds the annotated methods with generated ports based on methods signature: intercepted session type (and message type for @msginterceptor) and the topology of the communication (defined by from and to schemas).

Varda provides three methods annotations: @sessioninterceptor, @msginterceptor and @onboard. @onboard methods are triggered at the creation of an intercepted activation. Interceptor needs onboarding to distinguish internal activations from externals one. To preserve transparency, onboarding must be hidden to the intercepted activation (resp. external activations). Hence, it is up to the activation running the interception context to trigger the onboarding. Interception logic can access the set of in the set of `onboarded_activations`. `@sessioninterceptor` methods are triggered when a session is established, conversely `@msginterceptor` methods are triggered when a message cross the interception border.

Interception Context. Programmers define interception context inside the orchestration logic using a syntactic scope introduce by the `intercept` statement (Listing 4). Activations spawned inside this scope are intercepted, the others are not. Interception context does not behave like a classical syntactic scope. Indeed, to make the interception fully transparent in term of variable bindings, the interception scope exposes its binders. The parent scope, of the `intercept`, contains the variables bound inside the interception context. Activation and channels must process with special care not to break isolation, we only describe the activation case for brevity. Activations variables are exposed with the same type but, outside the interception context, they are references to their interceptor activation. This work transparently since the compiler specialize the interceptor schema into a subtype of any intercepted schema, i.e., communication interfaces are equivalent. Moreover, exposed activations may need to embed additional identity information. There are two different use cases: (1) for sharding, `KVServer` identity (`kv_a` and `kv_b`) are not exposed because a `Client` does not need to distinguish between intercepted activation; whereas (2) to achieve access control with interception, the intercepted activation identity must be exposed since sending a request to `kv_a` differs from sending one to `kv_b`. Identity exposition is managed by using the **anonymous** modifier of the `intercept` statement: `intercept<BaseInterceptor>` preserve identity whereas `intercept<BaseInterceptor, anonymous>` erase identity of intercepted activations.

User Defined Interception Policy. Neither the interception logic nor the interception context can expressed how and where interceptor activations are spawned and what is the relation between intercepted activation and interceptor activation (e.g., one to one or many to one). To achieve this, the `intercept` statement expect a user defined function called `interception policy`. Listing 5 defines a singleton interceptor activation in charge of all intercepted `KVServer`.

Programmers can use the interception policy to (1) define the relation between *intercepted activations* and *interceptor activation* by splitting intercepted activation in groups managed by an interceptor (according to their place, schema and identity); (2) to *reuse interceptor activation(s)* between interception context; (3) to *choose where to place interceptors*; and, (4) to *customize interceptor arguments in a per context basis*.

The policy is called at each spawn of an intercepted activation and it attributes an interceptor activation to each spawned activations. The arguments `intercepted_component_schema` denotes the schema of the intercepted activation and `p_of_intercepted` denotes its place. To make policy generic and

```
1   activation_ref<KVStore> policy(
2       place -> activation_ref<KVStore> factory,
3       string intercepted_component_schema,
4       place p_of_intercepted
5   ){
6       if(this.singleton_interceptor == none()){
7           this.singleton_interceptor = some(factory(current_place()));
8       }
9
10      return option_get(this.singleton_interceptor);
11  }
```

Listing 5: Interception policy for S-KV

strongly typed, the compiler does not pass arguments of the intercepted spawn to the policy.

To relieve programmers of binding the generated ports, of the specialized interceptor, with intercepted bridges (remember that both depends on the context and not only of the interceptor schema). The factory function spawns interceptor's activations to relieve programmers of binding the generated ports, of the specialized interceptor, with intercepted bridges (remember that both depends on the context and not only of the interceptor schema). The compiler provides and specializes a factory function for each context.

4 Related Work

4.1 Programming Languages

Classical programming models for distributed computing are actor model [6,8, 13], service oriented computing [26], dataflow [9] or reactive programming and tierless programming [10]. Recent evolutions tend to focus on easing specific distribution features by incorporating them into programming languages like consistency handling [18,29,32,33], placement aware-computation [37,40] and builtin fault-tolerance with [13,23,34] or without manual control [13]. However, they are not designed to compose black boxes easily and transparently while preserving programmer control on low-level details. This has a high cognitive cost for the programmer and a performance overhead.

4.2 Interface Description Languages

Interface description languages permits to formalize API to some extent and often to derive serialization mechanism and interfaces skeleton. Google's Protocol Buffer [21] and Apache's Thrift [19] provide basic typed specification of exchange messages. Hagar [1] extends the type system with polymorphism and generics. However, all of them tend to be limited on *what they can specify*: they can not reason on values; and, *they must be used manually in combination with other tools* to build a system which implies that they can not capture the orchestration nor the non-functional requirements.

4.3   Composition Framework

Currently composition mostly rely on interconnecting containerized application [5,12,16] or even serverless approach [7,20,22,31]. However, composition frameworks do not achieve safe composition [17,30]. They mostly work at the network layer which hamper reasoning on the semantics of the composition and of working on non-functional requirements. At a higher level of abstraction, CORBA [39] permits to transparently compose heterogeneous components with well-defined interfaces. They all deport the dynamic interconnections description and management into each component implementation without any general plan, except in English written documents. Regis [28] models communications and dynamic interconnection logic. However, this work do not address non-functional aspect of composition and they do not provide the ability to transform the architecture (like our interception mechanism) which means that every patterns must be established by hand.

4.4   Dynamic Interception

Other approaches providing interception mostly focus on dynamic interception. The use network based interception mechanisms: firewall-like features (e.g., iptables [2], mesh-services [11,24]) or service workers [35] embedded in browsers. They all lack the ability to describe the effects of the interceptions on the system's behaviour.

5   Conclusion

We present Varda, an architectural framework designed to build performant and safe distributed systems by composing heterogeneous components. Furthermore, it *discharges the programmer* from bridging the gap between implementation and design architecture; and that simplifies the writing of classical distribution patterns using a language-based interception mechanism. Varda model rests on three principles: (1) strict separation of concern between architecture and component implementation: one architecture can be used to generated multiple distributed systems; (2) interception is the core primitive to uniformly and transparently apply distribution patterns using static architecture rewriting; and, (3) preserve programmer control on distribution by incorporating dynamic aspects of the architecture (orchestration logic) and by embedding low-level details as first class value (e.g., place, bridges).

We are currently working on the evaluation of Varda: we are investigating the cognitive cost of the model and the performance overhead of the generated glue. Futures works can be divide in two branches: a) the first one targets performance, for instance optimizing the architecture using rewriting (e.g., merging components to avoid context switching); whereas, b) the second one explores how to improve the dependability of distributed system using Varda (e.g., enriching the type system or adding dynamic contracts).

References

1. Hagar. https://github.com/ReubenBond/Hagar
2. Iptables. https://www.netfilter.org/projects/iptables/index.html
3. Kubernetes. http://kubernetes.io
4. OpenStack. https://www.openstack.org/
5. Podman. https://podman.io/
6. Akka: Akka. https://akka.io/
7. Amazon: Aws lambda. https://aws.amazon.com/lambda/
8. Armstrong, J.: Erlang. Commun. ACM **53**(9), 68–75 (2010)
9. Bainomugisha, E., Carreton, A.L., Cutsem, T.V., Mostinckx, S., Meuter, W.D.: A survey on reactive programming. ACM Comput. Surv. (CSUR) **45**(4), 1–34 (2013)
10. Boudol, G., Luo, Z., Rezk, T., Serrano, M.: Reasoning about web applications: an operational semantics for HOP. ACM Trans. Program. Lang. Syst. (TOPLAS) **34**(2), 1–40 (2012)
11. Buoyant Inc.: Linkerd. https://linkerd.io/
12. Burns, B., Oppenheimer, D.: Design patterns for container-based distributed systems. In: Clements, A., Condie, T. (eds.) 8th USENIX Workshop on Hot Topics in Cloud Computing, HotCloud 2016, Denver, CO, USA, 20–21 June 2016. USENIX Association (2016). https://www.usenix.org/conference/hotcloud16/workshop-program/presentation/burns
13. Bykov, S., Geller, A., Kliot, G., Larus, J.R., Pandya, R., Thelin, J.: Orleans: cloud computing for everyone. In: Proceedings of the 2nd ACM Symposium on Cloud Computing, p. 16. ACM (2011)
14. Dezani-Ciancaglini, M., de'Liguoro, U.: Sessions and session types: an overview. In: Laneve, C., Su, J. (eds.) WS-FM 2009. LNCS, vol. 6194, pp. 1–28. Springer, Heidelberg (2010). https://doi.org/10.1007/978-3-642-14458-5_1
15. Docker Inc.: Docker Compose. https://docs.docker.com/compose/
16. Docker Inc.: Docker Engine. https://www.docker.com/
17. Emerick, C.: Distributed systems and the end of the API. https://writings.quilt.org/2014/05/12/distributed-systems-and-the-end-of-the-api/
18. Eskandani, N., Köhler, M., Margara, A., Salvaneschi, G.: Distributed object-oriented programming with multiple consistency levels in ConSysT. In: Proceedings Companion of the 2019 ACM SIGPLAN International Conference on Systems, Programming, Languages, and Applications: Software for Humanity, pp. 13–14. ACM (2019)
19. Apache Foundation: Thrift. https://thrift.apache.org/
20. Google: Cloud functions. https://cloud.google.com/functions/
21. Google: Protocol buffers. https://developers.google.com/protocol-buffers
22. Hendrickson, S., Sturdevant, S., Harter, T., Venkataramani, V., Arpaci-Dusseau, A.C., Arpaci-Dusseau, R.H.: Serverless computation with OpenLambda. In: Clements, A., Condie, T. (eds.) 8th USENIX Workshop on Hot Topics in Cloud Computing, HotCloud 2016, Denver, CO, USA, 20–21 June 2016. USENIX Association (2016). https://www.usenix.org/conference/hotcloud16/workshop-program/presentation/hendrickson
23. Hutchinson, N.C., Raj, R.K., Black, A.P., Levy, H.M., Jul, E.: The Emerald programming language (1991)
24. Istio: https://istio.io/

25. Kramer, J., Magee, J., Finkelstein, A.: A constructive approach to the design of distributed systems. In: 10th International Conference on Distributed Computing Systems (ICDCS 1990), 28 May–1 June 1990, Paris, France, pp. 580–587. IEEE Computer Society (1990). https://doi.org/10.1109/ICDCS.1990.89266
26. Lewis, J., Fowler, M.: Microservices. https://martinfowler.com/articles/microservices.html
27. Liskov, B.H., Wing, J.M.: A behavioral notion of subtyping. ACM Trans. Program. Lang. Syst. (TOPLAS) **16**(6), 1811–1841 (1994)
28. Magee, J., Dulay, N., Kramer, J.: Regis: a constructive development environment for distributed programs. Distrib. Syst. Eng. **1**(5), 304–312 (1994). https://doi.org/10.1088/0967-1846/1/5/005
29. Meiklejohn, C., Van Roy, P.: Lasp: a language for distributed, coordination-free programming. In: Proceedings of the 17th International Symposium on Principles and Practice of Declarative Programming - PPDP 2015, pp. 184–195. ACM Press (2015)
30. Meiklejohn, C.S., Lakhani, Z., Alvaro, P., Miller, H.: Verifying interfaces between container-based components (2018)
31. Microsoft: Azure functions. https://functions.azure.com/
32. Milano, M., Myers, A.C.: MixT: a language for mixing consistency in geodistributed transactions. In: Proceedings of the 39th ACM SIGPLAN Conference on Programming Language Design and Implementation - PLDI 2018, pp. 226–241. ACM Press. https://doi.org/10.1145/3192366.3192375. http://dl.acm.org/citation.cfm?doid=3192366.3192375
33. Milano, M., Recto, R., Magrino, T., Myers, A.: A tour of gallifrey, a language for geodistributed programming. In: Lerner, B.S., Bodík, R., Krishnamurthi, S. (eds.) 3rd Summit on Advances in Programming Languages (SNAPL 2019). Leibniz International Proceedings in Informatics (LIPIcs), vol. 136, pp. 11:1–11:19. Schloss Dagstuhl-Leibniz-Zentrum fuer Informatik (2019). https://doi.org/10.4230/LIPIcs.SNAPL.2019.11. http://drops.dagstuhl.de/opus/volltexte/2019/10554
34. Mogk, R., Baumgärtner, L., Salvaneschi, G., Freisleben, B., Mezini, M.: Fault-tolerant distributed reactive programming. In: 32nd European Conference on Object-Oriented Programming, ECOOP 2018, 16–21 July 2018, Amsterdam, The Netherlands, pp. 1:1–1:26 (2018)
35. Mozilla: Service Worker. https://developer.mozilla.org/fr/docs/Web/API/Service_Worker_API
36. Redis: Redis. https://redis.io/
37. Sang, B., Roman, P.L., Eugster, P., Lu, H., Ravi, S., Petri, G.: Plasma: programmable elasticity for stateful cloud computing applications. In: Proceedings of the Fifteenth European Conference on Computer Systems, pp. 1–15 (2020)
38. Shapiro, M.: Structure and encapsulation in distributed systems: the proxy principle. In: International Conference on Distributed Computing Systems (ICDCS), Camchannel, MA, USA, pp. 198–204. IEEE (1986). https://hal.inria.fr/inria-00444651
39. Vinoski, S.: CORBA: integrating diverse applications within distributed heterogeneous environments. IEEE Commun. Mag. **35**(2), 46–55 (1997). https://doi.org/10.1109/35.565655
40. Weisenburger, P., Köhler, M., Salvaneschi, G.: Distributed system development with ScalaLoci. Proc. ACM Program. Lang. **2**(OOPSLA), 129 (2018)

Recycling Memory in Recoverable Mutex Locks

Aravind Segu and Wojciech Golab[✉]

University of Waterloo, Waterloo, Canada
{yasegu,wgolab}@uwaterloo.ca

Abstract. Recoverable algorithms have blossomed recently in the distributed computing community in response to the commercial release of persistent main memory by Intel. In this context, recoverability refers to an algorithm's capacity to meet its correctness guarantees despite crash failures, which affect the memory hierarchy in complex ways: any state written to the persistent memory medium is preserved, but any state held in DRAM and volatile CPU registers is lost, along with the volatile cache on some hardware platforms. Classic synchronization problems suddenly become more challenging and interesting to solve in this failure model. In this paper, we focus specifically on the recoverable variant of mutual exclusion, called recoverable mutual exclusion (RME), which was formalized recently by Golab and Ramaraju (PODC'16). Aiming to make RME locks more practical, we introduce a simple memory management scheme for an important class of RME locks, and discuss how to tune it.

1 Introduction

Recoverable algorithms have blossomed recently in the distributed computing community in response to the Intel's commercial release of Optane Persistent Memory (PMem). In this context, recoverability refers to an algorithm's capacity to meet its correctness guarantees despite crash failures and possible recovery from such failures. Such crash-recovery failures affect the modern memory hierarchy in complex ways since the introduction of PMem does not entirely eliminate volatile media. Namely, any state written to PMem is preserved during a crash, but any state held in DRAM, volatile CPU registers, and in dirty cache lines (on some platforms), is lost. Classic synchronization problems suddenly become more challenging and interesting to solve in this failure model after being studied for decades under the assumption that crashes are either permanent or not possible at all. In this paper, we focus specifically on the recoverable variant of mutual exclusion, called recoverable mutual exclusion (RME), which was formalized recently by Golab and Ramaraju [11] and featured in several follow-up publications. (e.g., [2,3,5,8,9,12–16,18]). RME is a new take on Dijkstra's classic mutual exclusion problem [7] that combines concurrency with fault tolerance in the following sense: a thread that is acquiring, holding, or releasing a mutex lock is permitted to crash and attempt to acquire the lock again on recovery, and must preserve the lock's correctness properties while doing so.

M.-A. Koulali and M. Mezini (Eds.): NETYS 2022, LNCS 13464, pp. 31–36, 2022.
https://doi.org/10.1007/978-3-031-17436-0_3

Prior work on the RME problem focuses almost exclusively on correctness properties and time complexity bounds, as quantified by counting remote memory references (RMRs), and has mostly overlooked fundamental questions pertaining to space complexity. Even the empirical evaluation of RME lock implementations by Xiao, Zhang, and Golab [18] does not discuss memory management explicitly despite dealing with queue-based algorithms that dynamically allocate queue nodes. The only published memory management scheme for RME locks we are aware of is Dhoked and Mittal's [6], which uses $\Theta(N^2)$ space for N threads and incurs constant overhead in terms of worst-case RMR complexity.

In this paper, we advance the state of the art in memory management for RME locks by presenting a simple memory reclamation scheme for queue-based algorithms that allocate one new queue node structure per passage. Our scheme uses $\Theta(N^2)$ space ($\Theta(N)$ per thread), similarly to [6], and incurs $O(1)$ RMRs amortized per passage in the absence of failures. Although the time complexity bound is weaker than Dhoked and Mittal's, mainly due to amortization, our scheme is much simpler. In particular, it requires only one additional array of shared variables, as compared to nine arrays in [6]. Our scheme preserves starvation freedom, and can be tuned by adjusting the size of the circular buffer of queue nodes maintained by each thread. We show experimentally that a buffer size on the order of ten queue nodes per thread yields a good trade-off between throughput and space.

2 Background

Some of the most scalable mutual exclusion locks use queue structures to decide the order of entry into the critical section [1,4]. Variations of the Mellor-Crummey and Scott (MCS) algorithm [17], in particular, have seen widespread deployment in Java monitor locks. One of the attractive features of the MCS algorithm is that a thread t_i can reuse its queue node q_i immediately after releasing a lock, even if the node q_j of the successor thread t_j in the queue still holds a pointer to q_i, because at this point t_i and t_j have already synchronized and the pointer will not be followed again. Memory management is more complex in queue-based RME locks [5,8,13] since additional pointers are maintained to enable correct reconstruction of the queue during recovery.

Figure 1 presents a generic overview of a queue-based RME lock, inspired by [8,13], for threads labelled with IDs 1..N. Pointers to queue nodes are recorded in an announcement array $A[1..N]$, whose entries are all NULL in the initial state. In the absence of failures, a thread t_i omits the body of the recovery section at lines 2–3 since $A[i] = $ NULL at line 1. It then proceeds to the entry section where it allocates a new queue node at line 4 and saves the pointer in the announcement array at line 5. The new queue node is then appended to the tail of the queue at line 6, and t_i waits until its node becomes the queue head at line 7. The node is removed from the queue in the exit section at line 9, and finally $A[i]$ is reset to NULL at line 10. Following a crash that occurs in a state where $A[i] \neq$ NULL, t_i executes line 2 of the recovery section, where it analyzes the pointers recorded in the announcement array and identifies loose fragments of the node queue that need to be reconnected. Queue nodes are not freed explicitly, and it is unsafe for t_i to reclaim its node immediately after line 10 because another thread t_j may be in the recovery section with a pointer to t_i's queue node saved in a private variable. Thus, the fundamental challenge in memory reclamation is to synchronize a thread t_i that is attempting to reclaim its old queue nodes with any thread t_j that may still be accessing such a node during recovery.

Persistent shared variables:

- $A[1..N]$: array of pointers to queue nodes, initially NULL, N is the number of threads
- T: pointer to tail of queue node

```
   // recovery section
1  if A[i] ≠ NULL then
2  |   use state saved in T and A[1..N] to reconstruct the queue
3  |_  A[i] := NULL

   // entry section
4  node := allocate new queue node
5  A[i] := node
6  append t_i to the queue by swapping node into T
7  wait until t_i is the head of the queue
   // critical section
8  ...
   // exit section
9  signal the next thread in the queue
10 A[i] := NULL
```

Fig. 1. Allocation of queue nodes in an RME lock. Code shown for thread t_i.

3 RMR-Efficient Memory Reclamation

Since [8,13] do not explain when and how queue nodes are reclaimed, we propose a simple but effective memory management scheme. Each thread t_i maintains its own pool of queue nodes, and records the number of allocated nodes in a persistent variable. If the pool is exhausted prior to allocation in the entry section at line 4 of Fig. 1, the synchronization procedure presented in Fig. 2 is executed to ensure that other threads have completed any pending execution of the recovery section; this ensures that any references to t_i's queue nodes obtained by reading $A[i]$ during recovery are released. Upon completion of the procedure, t_i reclaims its entire pool of queue nodes, and then allocates a node.

The main feature of the synchronization procedure is a loop in which t_i waits for every other thread t_j to complete any pending execution of the recovery section. This is accomplished primarily by reading NULL from $A[j]$, otherwise by observing a state change in $A[j]$. Since each node maintains a finite pool of nodes, it is possible in theory that the node pointers read from $A[j]$ repeat endlessly even as t_j executes passages infinitely often, and so additional steps are taken to ensure preservation of starvation freedom. Since t_j eventually also calls the synchronization procedure, t_j increments a counter $S[j]$ at the beginning of the procedure, and t_i's wait loop terminates since the value of $S[j]$ increases.[1]

Persistent shared variables:

– $S[1..N]$: array of integer synchronization variables, initially zero

---

```
11  S[i] := S[i] + 1
12  for each thread ID j ≠ i do
13      n_j := A[j]
14      s_j := S[j]
15      if n_j ≠ NULL then
16          await A[j] ≠ n_j ∨ S[j] ≠ s_j

    // entire node pool is free, reset count of allocated nodes
```

Fig. 2. Synchronization procedure for thread t_i, called from line 4 of Fig. 1.

The algorithm in Fig. 2 is guaranteed to terminate as long as the following property holds: if thread t_i is waiting for thread t_j at line 16, then t_j eventually either (i) halts in the non-critical section, which necessarily happens with $A[j] =$ NULL due to line 10 and the assumption that crashed threads are resurrected [11]; or (ii) overwrites $A[j]$ with a different non-NULL value at line 4; or (iii) enters the code in Fig. 2 from line 4 upon exhausting its node pool and increments $S[j]$ at line 11. Deadlock and starvation are ruled out because the reclamation algorithm is always invoked by t_i with $A[i] =$ NULL (see lines 1, 3 and 10 in Fig. 1).

The remote memory reference (RMR) complexity of the algorithm in Fig. 2 for N threads is $\Theta(N)$ due to the for loop. The **Await** statement incurs $O(1)$ RMRs because the values written to $S[j]$ never repeat, and the non-NULL values written to $A[j]$ may repeat only after t_j itself executes the algorithm, which increments $S[j]$. As long as each thread maintains a node pool of size N per thread ($\Theta(N^2)$ space overall), and allocates at most one node per passage, N consecutive node allocations by the same thread incur $\Theta(N)$ RMRs total in a failure-free execution. To analyze the effect on the RMR complexity of the RME lock that uses our reclamation scheme, note that the locks under consideration [8,13] incur $O(1)$ RMRs in any passage where a thread is not recovering from a

---

[1] The algorithm assumes that $S[1..N]$ are unbounded integers, but 64-bit variables are sufficient in practice to prevent overflow.

failure (i.e., one not beginning "in cleanup" [10]), and $O(N)$ RMRs per passage in the worst case. After applying our reclamation scheme, the same asymptotic bounds hold but only in an amortized sense,[2] even in the presence of failures.

Figure 3 demonstrates how the size of the per-thread node pool affects performance in failure-free experiments. The results were obtained using a 20-core Intel Xeon Scalable Processor with Optane persistent memory, configured as in [18]. The horizontal axis uses a logarithmic scale, and shows the number of queue nodes per node pool. The vertical axis shows the throughput, defined as the number of critical sections executed per second, of Golab and Hendler's queue-based RME lock [8] augmented with our reclamation scheme. We observe that 90% of the optimal throughput at each level of parallelism (up to 20 threads) is obtained with a pool of only 4–8 nodes per thread, and that roughly 2/3 of maximum throughput is obtained using a pool of unit size.

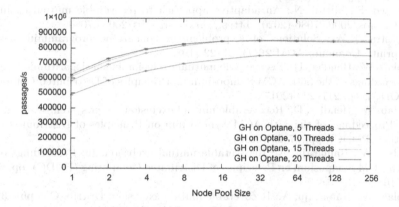

Fig. 3. Effect of queue node pool size on throughput.

4   Conclusion

We presented an RMR-efficient memory reclamation scheme that is applicable to queue-based recoverable mutual exclusion algorithms [8,13], and evaluated its performance using genuine Intel Optane Persistent Memory. We hope that our results will encourage practical adoption of RME locks.

Acknowledgements. We thank Neeraj Mittal and Sahil Dhoked for stimulating technical discussions of the RME problem. This research was supported by an Ontario Early Researcher Award, a Google Faculty Research Award, as well as the Natural Sciences and Engineering Research Council (NSERC) of Canada.

---

[2] In the amortized analysis, the cost of executing the code in Fig. 2 by thread t_i is charged to t_i's most recent $N-1$ passages if they were all failure-free, otherwise it is charged to t_i's most recent passage where it is recovering from a failure.

References

1. Anderson, T.E.: The performance of spin lock alternatives for shared-memory multiprocessors. IEEE Trans. Parallel Distrib. Syst. **1**(1), 6–16 (1990)
2. Chan, D., Woelfel, P.: A tight lower bound for the RMR complexity of recoverable mutual exclusion. In: Proceedings of the 40th ACM Symposium on Principles of Distributed Computing (PODC), pp. 533–543 (2021)
3. Chan, D.Y.C., Woelfel, P.: Recoverable mutual exclusion with constant amortized RMR complexity from standard primitives. In: Proceedings of the 39th ACM Symposium on Principles of Distributed Computing (PODC), pp. 181–190 (2020)
4. David, T., Guerraoui, R., Trigonakis, V.: Everything you always wanted to know about synchronization but were afraid to ask. In: Proceedings of the 25th ACM Symposium on Operating System Principles (SOSP), pp. 33–48 (2013)
5. Dhoked, S., Mittal, N.: An adaptive approach to recoverable mutual exclusion. In: Proceedings of the 39th ACM Symposium on Principles of Distributed Computing (PODC), pp. 1–10 (2020)
6. Dhoked, S., Mittal, N.: An adaptive approach to recoverable mutual exclusion. CoRR abs/2006.07086 (2020). https://arxiv.org/abs/2006.07086
7. Dijkstra, E.W.: Solutions of a problem in concurrent programming control (reprint). Commun. ACM **26**(1), 21–22 (1983)
8. Golab, W., Hendler, D.: Recoverable mutual exclusion in sub-logarithmic time. In: Proceedings of the 36th ACM Symposium on Principles of Distributed Computing (PODC), pp. 211–220 (2017)
9. Golab, W., Hendler, D.: Recoverable mutual exclusion under system-wide failures. In: Proceedings of the 37th ACM Symposium on Principles of Distributed Computing (PODC), pp. 17–26 (2018)
10. Golab, W., Ramaraju, A.: Recoverable mutual exclusion. In: Proceedings of the 35th ACM Symposium on Principles of Distributed Computing (PODC), pp. 65–74 (2016)
11. Golab, W., Ramaraju, A.: Recoverable mutual exclusion. Distrib. Comput. **32**(6), 535–564 (2019). https://doi.org/10.1007/s00446-019-00364-0
12. Jayanti, P., Jayanti, S., Joshi, A.: Optimal recoverable mutual exclusion using only FASAS. In: Podelski, A., Taïani, F. (eds.) NETYS 2018. LNCS, vol. 11028, pp. 191–206. Springer, Cham (2019). https://doi.org/10.1007/978-3-030-05529-5_13
13. Jayanti, P., Jayanti, S., Joshi, A.: A recoverable mutex algorithm with sub-logarithmic RMR on both CC and DSM. In: Proceedings of the 38th ACM Symposium on Principles of Distributed Computing (PODC), pp. 177–186 (2019)
14. Jayanti, P., Joshi, A.: Recoverable FCFS mutual exclusion with wait-free recovery. In: Proceedings of the 31th International Symposium on Distributed Computing (DISC), pp. 30:1–30:15 (2017)
15. Jayanti, P., Joshi, A.: Recoverable mutual exclusion with abortability. In: Proceedings of the 7th International Conference on Networked Systems (NETYS), pp. 217–232 (2019)
16. Katzan, D., Morrison, A.: Recoverable, abortable, and adaptive mutual exclusion with sublogarithmic RMR complexity. In: Proceedings of the 24th International Conference on Principles of Distributed Systems (OPODIS), pp. 15:1–15:16 (2021)
17. Mellor-Crummey, J.M., Scott, M.L.: Algorithms for scalable synchronization on shared-memory multiprocessors. ACM Trans. Comput. Syst. **9**(1), 21–65 (1991)
18. Xiao, J., Zhang, Z., Golab, W.: Benchmarking recoverable mutex locks. In: Proceedings of the 32nd ACM Symposium on Parallel Algorithms and Architectures (SPAA), pp. 583–585 (2020)

Distributed Blockchain Price Oracle

Léonard Lys[1,2]([⊠]) [iD] and Maria Potop-Butucaru[1] [iD]

[1] LIP6, UMR 7606 Sorbonne University - CNRS, 4 place Jussieu, 75252 Paris Cedex
05, France
[2] Palo IT, 6 rue de l'Amiral Coligny, 75001 Paris, France
llys@palo-it.com

Abstract. Blockchain oracles are systems that connect blockchains with
the outside world by interfacing with external data providers. They provide decentralized applications with the external information needed for
smart contract execution. In this paper, we focus on decentralized price
oracles, which are distributed systems that provide exchange rates of
digital assets to smart contracts. They are the cornerstone of the safety
of some decentralized finance applications such as stable coins or lending
protocols. They consist of a network of nodes called oracles that gather
information from off-chain sources such as an exchange market's API and
feed it to smart contracts. Among the desired properties of a price oracle
system are low latency, availability, and low operating cost. Moreover,
they should overcome constraints such as having diverse data sources
which is known as the freeloading problem or Byzantine failures.

In this paper, we define the distributed price oracle problem and
present PoWacle, the first asynchronous decentralized oracle protocol
that copes with Byzantine behavior.

Keywords: Blockchain oracle · Price oracle · Decentralized finance

1 Introduction

Decentralized finance (DeFi) is a term that emerged during the past few years
to describe financial instruments that do not rely on centralized intermediaries
such as brokerages exchanges or banks. In order to implement those instruments, DeFi protocols make use of smart contracts hosted on blockchain systems. Those smart contracts are programs that implement the logic of classical
financial instruments. A wide range of applications is already in production,
from interest-earning saving accounts to lending protocols to synthetic assets or
trading platforms, etc. This industry is quickly gaining in popularity both in
terms of the number of users and in market capitalization.

In order to function, a lot of those DeFi protocols make use of what is called
blockchain oracles and more specifically blockchain price oracles. A price oracle
is a system that provides exchange rates or prices to DeFi protocol's smart
contracts. They gather data from off-chain sources, such as an API, and feed it
to a smart contract on-chain. For example, a popular DeFi application consists

© The Author(s), under exclusive license to Springer Nature Switzerland AG 2022
M.-A. Koulali and M. Mezini (Eds.): NETYS 2022, LNCS 13464, pp. 37–51, 2022.
https://doi.org/10.1007/978-3-031-17436-0_4

in issuing a number of tokens to a user in exchange for collateral that will be locked in a smart contract, until the user pays back his debt. Obviously, for the process to be fair, it is necessary to know the current exchange rate between the token issued and the token locked as collateral. This is where prices oracles come into the picture.

Price oracles can be split into two categories, centralized and decentralized. A centralized oracle relies on the observations of a single trusted entity while decentralized oracles gather information from several sources. In this paper, we focus on decentralized ones, as we consider that DeFi protocols should not rely on a single trusted entity.

Although decentralized price oracles have a central role in designing DeFi applications, there is very little academic literature that addresses fault-tolerant decentralized oracles. To the best of our knowledge, the only academic work addressing this problem is [2]. However, several non-academic reports propose ad hoc solutions practical solutions. In the line of non-academic work, the most interesting contributions are the band protocol [1] and DOS network [6].

Band protocol [1] is a public blockchain network that allows users to query off-chain APIs. It is built on top of the Cosmos-SDK and uses the Tendermint consensus engine to reach instant finality. The oracles in the band protocol are selected pseudo-randomly to produce observations that they gathered from off-chain data sources. Much like in a proof-of-stake-based chain, they have tokens staked on the chain and their chances of being elected to produce an observation are proportional to their share of the total stake. When an oracle produces an observation, this observation is published to the bandchain, and a proof is generated. This proof can be later used by smart contracts on other blockchains to verify the existence of the data as well as to decode and retrieve the result stored. This process obviously requires a bridge contract on the targeted blockchain in order to interpret the proof. While Band protocol's approach is interesting, we think that it lakes interoperability concerns. Indeed a bridge contract has to be implemented for each new integration. Our proposal is integrated by design as it leverages the target blockchain's keys.

Another non-academic work is DOS network [6]. The DOS network leverages verifiable random functions, distributed key generation, and threshold signature scheme to implement their Decentralized Oracle Service. The system is made of a network of oracle nodes connected to off-chain data sources. The time is divided into rounds and for each round, a group of nodes is randomly selected to provide the observations. Each member of the group is given a share of a distributed private key. Members of the group exchange messages containing their signed observations until one of them has received enough signatures to generate the group signature. This node will be responsible for publishing the report containing the group's observations and group signature. The smart contract will then verify the signature and execute the payout. The idea proposed by this scheme is interesting however it has a major drawback. The probability that two or more members of the group are able to construct the group signature at the same time is high. This will result in several nodes publishing the same reports simultaneously. Although this can be resolved on-chain by a proxy that only accepts the first response, the cost of the transaction is permanently lost for the following reporters. Our approach based on proof-of-work can be used in asynchronous settings it allows us to better sample the probability of finding a valid report.

In this paper, we follow the line of research opened by [2]. Differently from their approach, we consider an asynchronous communication model. In [2], Chainlink presents the "Off-chain Reporting Protocol", an oracle system designed, among other goals, to minimize transaction fees. Transaction fees for some blockchains have become quite prohibitive, motivating the need for such systems. The system consists of n Oracles that exchange messages through off-chain communication channels. The Oracles and their respective public keys are listed in a smart contract C. Time is divided into epochs, and a leader taken from the list of oracles is associated with each epoch. Epochs are mapped to leaders through a deterministic function. A simple modulus that can be calculated by anyone in the network. The Oracles make observations (such as price observations), sign them with their private keys, and submit them to the leader. When he received a sufficient amount of observations, the leader builds a report that lists them all, as well as the signatures, and submits it to a transmission protocol. Finally the transmission protocol hands out the report to the smart contract C. A new epoch associated with a new leader starts whenever the oracles think that the current leader does not perform correctly. While this protocol shows good resilience and low transaction fees, they assume a partially synchronous model. Formally, they assume that clocks in the system are not synchronized until a point in time called global stabilization time (GST). Afterward, all correct nodes behave synchronously. Outside those synchronous periods of time, the liveness of the protocol is not ensured. We think that by using proof-of-work for leader election, we could ensure similar properties in a fully asynchronous timing model.

Our Contribution. In this paper, we formalize the distributed price oracle problem in the context of decentralized finance applications. Furthermore, we propose a protocol and prove that it verifies the specification of the problem in asynchronous communication environments prone to Byzantine failures. The protocol combines a gossip module with a light proof-of-work module and incentives oracles via a simple reputation mechanism to have a correct behavior.

2   Model

We consider a similar model as the one used by the chainlink off-chain reporting protocol [2]. The main difference is the communication model which is partially synchronous while in our system it is asynchronous.

Oracle Network. The system consists in a set of n Oracles $P = \{p_1, ..., p_n\}$ that are referred to as nodes. Each oracle node p_i makes time-varying observations over the price of an asset pair. The set of oracles is determined by an oracle smart contract C that records the public keys of the nodes. The owner of the smart contract has administrative powers which allow him to update the list of oracles. As we are working with time-varying quantities, there is no proper way to evaluate if an observation is correct or not. Thus the protocol only guarantees that the report contains a sufficient number of observations signed by honest oracle nodes.

Nodes exchange messages through peer-to-peer, bi-directional communication channels. Nodes are identified by unique identifiers and authenticated by digital signatures. All communications are authenticated and encrypted, which means any node can authenticate any other node based on the oracle list recorded in the smart contract C. We consider an asynchronous communication model, which means that there is no global clock shared among the nodes. Moreover, we make no assumption over the reliability of the network, meaning that messages can be delayed or lost. Furthermore, messages can be delivered in a different order than the order they were sent. In the following, we assume that the network does not partition.

Failures. We consider that any $f < n/3$ nodes may exhibit Byzantine faults, which means that they may behave arbitrarily and as if controlled by an imaginary adversary. All non-faulty nodes are called honest or correct. We consider that these faults can occur adaptively meaning an adversary can choose and control the faulty nodes on the fly.

Cryptographic Primitives. The protocol uses public-key digital signatures. We assume an idealized public-key infrastructure: each process is associated with its public/private key pair that is used to sign messages and verify signatures of other nodes. A message m sent by a process p_i that is properly signed with the private key of p_i is said to be properly authenticated. We denote by m_{σ_i} a message m signed with the private key of a process p_i. In practice, we would use the standard EdDSA and ECDSA schemes for digital signatures. It is assumed that signatures cannot be forged.

Oracle Smart Contract and Report. The goal of the system is to produce reports containing a sufficient number of signed observations from the oracle nodes when a client requests them. Differently from Breidenbach et al. in [2], the reports are submitted to the oracle smart contract C by some node during a proof-of-work inspired cryptographic race. The smart contract C corresponds to a single asset pair (e.g. BTC/USD). When submitted a report, the oracle smart contract C verifies the signatures of each observation as well as the proof-of-work. If they are valid, the oracle smart contract updates its variable $lastPrice$ to the median of observation values contained in the report. Using the median value among more than $2f$ observations guarantees that the reported value is plausible in the sense that malicious nodes cannot move the value outside the range of observations produced by honest nodes. The value $lastPrice$ can then be consumed by the requesting client or by any other user. The requesting client pays a fee for each new report he requests, which will be distributed equally among the observant nodes.

3 Decentralized Price Oracle Problem

In this section, we will define the decentralized oracle problem and review major threats and constraints that must be taken into account when designing a decentralized oracle system.

The blockchain Oracle problem is well known in the ecosystem and the grey literature. It is also described in [4] by Cardelli et al. The oracle problem describes the ambivalence between blockchain systems that are supposed to be immutable through decentralization and oracles that, by definition, input outside world data that cannot be verified by the blockchain itself. A blockchain is a self-contained environment with its own validation rules and consensus mechanism. This isolation is what makes blockchain transactions safe and immutable. However, when data is inputted from off-chain data sources, the said data cannot be verified by the blockchain itself. A piece of software, in this case an oracle, is required to guarantee the veracity of the inputted data. As the safety of a system is limited by its weakest element, in a system where the execution of a smart contract depends on the data provided by an oracle, the oracle may be a single point of failure. This oracle problem has already led to several exploits. In 2019, an oracle reported a price a thousand times higher than the actual price [5], which led to a one billion U.S. dollars loss. Funds have then been recovered but it shows how crucial is it to have reliable oracles. To be best of our knowledge there is no formal definition of the blockchain price oracle problem.

The price oracle smart contract can be seen as a particular single-writer multi-reader shared register. The variable of this particular shared register, $lastPrice$, can be read by any client of the system. This variable can be modified only by the smart contract C, and the modification is triggered each time clients invoke $requestNewPrice()$. We propose below a definition of the blockchain price oracle problem in terms of liveness, integrity and uniformity.

Definition 1 (Decentralized blockchain price oracle). A decentralized blockchain price oracle should satisfy the following properties:

- **Δ-Liveness**: There exist a $\Delta > 0$ such that if a client invokes a price request to the smart contract C at time $t > 0$ then a corresponding report r will be retrieved from C within $t + \Delta$ time.
- **Observation integrity**: If a report with v is declared final by C, then v is the observation of a correct oracle or in the range of the observations of the two correct oracles in the system.
- **Uniformity**: If two clients, c_1 and c_2 read the oracle $lastPrice$ at time $t > 0$ then the same price report will be retrieved by both of them.

The price oracle smart contract can be seen as a shared register. The variable of this particular shared register, $lastPrice$, can be read by any client of the system. This variable can be modified only by the smart contract and the modification is triggered each time clients invoke price requests.

Designing distributed price oracles is not an easy task. In the following, we discuss several difficulties.

Freeloading Attacks. The freeloading attack, also known as mirroring is formally described in [7]. It refers to the technique employed by malicious oracles, that instead of obtaining data from their data source, replicate the data fetched by another oracle. Since oracle systems are often comprised of a reputation system, a "lazy" oracle could simply copy the values provided by a trusted oracle instead of making the effort of fetching the data itself. By doing so, the lazy oracle maximizes its chances of receiving its payout and avoids the cost of requesting data from sources that might charge per-query fees. As explained in [9], this freeloading attack weakens the security of the system by reducing the diversity of data sources and also disincentivizes oracles from responding quickly: Responding slowly and freeloading is a cheaper strategy.

Majority Attacks. Much like in blockchain systems, oracle systems may be threatened by majority attacks. If an entity controls a majority of oracles in a network, it may be able to manipulate the data to provide prices that diverge from the real observable data.

Price Slippage. Price slippage refers to the fact that the price returned by an oracle may differ from the actual price. This may be intentional or unintentional but the result is the same. Price slippage may be the consequence of delays generated by the transaction validation time. Indeed real-world prices evolve continuously while the events on a blockchain are discrete. The state of the chain only changes when a new block is added.

Data Source Manipulation. The source which the data is gathered from might also be a vector of attack. Indeed, if the data source or the communication channel between the oracle and the data source can be altered, the resulting observation will ultimately be altered too.

4   PoWacle Protocol Overview

In this section, we propose first a high-level overview of the PoWacle protocol then propose the protocol pseudo-code.

The goal of the protocol is to publish reports containing price observations from the oracles when a client makes a request. The oracle nodes are connected to external data sources such as a market's APIs where they find their price data. When a client requests a price, the oracles will exchange messages containing hash-signed observations of the asset's price. It is very important to note that the content of the observations exchanged is not readable by the other oracles, as they are hashed observations. This is to avoid the freeloading problem. Each oracle node listens for incoming hash-signed observation messages and much like in a proof-of-work-based blockchain builds a pool of messages in their local memory. The difference with a proof-of-work-based blockchain is that instead of transactions, the pool contains hash-signed price observations, and instead of producing a block of transactions, the goal is to produce a report containing the said observations. To select the oracle that will be responsible for proposing and publishing the report, a proof-of-work protocol is applied. Once they have received hash-signed observations from a sufficient number of nodes, i.e. more than $2f + 1$, the oracles start the report mining process. They try to build a report proposal whose hash value is inferior to some target difficulty number. When a node finds a report proposal whose hash value is inferior to the target difficulty number, he broadcasts the report proposal to the network. On receiving the report proposal, the other nodes return the readable pre-image of their hash-signed observations. For each received observation, the proposer verifies that the observation matches its hash. Once he has collected at least $2f + 1$ clear observations, he submits the report proposal to the oracle smart contract along with the proof-of-work. The oracle smart contract verifies the proof-of-work, the match between observations and their hashes, and the signatures. Once all verifications are done, the smart contract calculates the median of the received observations and updates the price of the asset. The price can then be consumed by the client. The smart contract calculates the payout and updates the reputation of the oracle nodes.

The incentive mechanism is designed such that each oracle that produced an observation will be paid equally. Thereby, the report proposer, the one that won the proof-of-work and published the report to the chain, has not more incentives than the other oracles. This should help to limit the computing power that the oracles will put in the network, and thus the operating cost of the system. In the meantime, the oracles are still encouraged to find valid reports regularly, as this is the way they get paid. The goal is to have an incentive equilibrium between producing reports regularly and having a low operating cost in terms of computing power.

Let us unfold the main steps of the protocol:

1. The client requests a new price to the smart contract C and pays a fee.
2. The oracles pick up the request and gather price data from their data sources. They create their observations, hash and sign them. They broadcast it to the oracle network through gossiping.
3. On receiving the hashed signed observations, the nodes verify the signatures. If they are correct, they add the observation to their local memory. Once they have received a sufficient number of hashed signed observations, i.e., above the $2f + 1$, the oracles sequentially rearrange their report and a nonce until they find a report proposal whose hash value is below a target difficulty number.
4. The first oracle to find a valid report proposal broadcast it to the oracle network via gossiping.
5. On receiving a valid report proposal, the oracles whose observations were contained in the report return the readable pre-images of their hashed signed observations to the candidate leader.
6. Once he has collected enough pre-images, the proposer verifies that they match their hashes. If they do match, he submits the report to the smart contract C.
7. On receiving a report proposal, the smart contract C verifies the signatures of each individual observation as well as the matching between clear observation

and their hash. If everything matches, the smart contract verifies the proof of work. It also verifies that there are at least $2f + 1$ clear observations in the report. Once all checks are passed, the smart contract updates the price, making it available to the client. The report becomes final.

8. The smart contract C calculates the payouts and updates the reputations.

5   Protocol Detailed Description

We provide a detailed description of the protocols using an event-based notation (e.g. [3] Chap. 1).

The protocol consists of an oracle smart contract hosted on a blockchain presented in Algorithm 1 and an oracle network. The nodes in the oracle network react to events triggered by the oracle smart contract C. The oracle nodes can at any time read the state and the variables of C. Protocol instances that run on the same oracle node (instances of Algorithm 2, 3 and 4) also communicates trough events. In the following, Algorithm 1 is the oracle smart contract C, Algorithm 2, executed by every node is a daemon that reacts to events triggered by C. Algorithm 3 is the observation gossip protocol and Algorithm 4 is the report mining protocol.

5.1   The Smart Contract (C)

The protocol Algorithm 1 is orchestrated by an oracle smart contract C hosted on a blockchain. Each oracle smart contract represents a price feed for a single pair of assets, for example, USD/BTC for bitcoin versus U.S. dollars. The oracle smart contract C consists of four primitives; identity, proof-of-work, incentive, and reputation. We will review individually each primitive in this section.

Identity. The oracle smart contract is responsible for storing the identity of the oracles nodes. It maintains a list of oracle nodes and their public keys. The set of oracles is managed by an owner with administrative power. How the administrator curates the list of authorized oracles is behind the scope of this document. The oracle list is used to verify signatures.

Proof-of-Work. The proof-of-work primitive is responsible for verifying the proof-of-work that is submitted along with each report. It verifies the match between hash-signed and clear observation, verifies that there are more than $2f$ clear observations, requests the identity primitive to verify the signatures, and finally verifies the proof-of-work. To do so, it checks that the submitted report header hash value is below the target difficulty number. If so, the report is final and the contract updates the last price value, making it available to the client.

The proof-of-work primitive is also responsible for adjusting the difficulty target number. To do so it uses a system similar to Bitcoin's difficulty adjustment [8]. For each new request, the smart contract C records the time difference between the moment the request was made by the client, and the moment the corresponding report was submitted. Then for every new report, the contract calculates the average report generation time over the last hundred reports. It then adjusts the target difficulty number to have a stable average report generation time. To do so, it multiplies the current difficulty target number by a ratio between observed and desired report generation time. Target report generation time is specified by the owner with administrative power. What value should be chosen is out of the scope of this document and would require further analysis.

Incentive. The incentive primitive calculates and broadcasts the payouts to the oracles. For each final report, the contract C pays an equal share of the total fee to each oracle that produced an observation that was included in the report.

As introduced earlier, the incentive system must be designed to create an incentive equilibrium between producing reports regularly and having a low operating cost in terms of computing power. Thus, the payout received by the report publisher will be equal to the payouts received by the other oracles that produced an observation contained in the report. The only difference is that the report producer gets his transaction fees refunded.

In order to reduce transaction fees, the payout is not automatically transferred at each report. Instead, the smart contract C records the total payout each oracle is eligible to, and they can cash out on request.

Reputation. The reputation system is primarily used by the oracles to prioritize the observation they will include in their report proposal. Indeed, an adversarial oracle could choose not to send back his clear observation at stage 7, thus slowing down protocol execution. To minimize this risk, each oracle is associated with a reputation number corresponding to the number of his observations that have been included in past valid reports. When an oracle tries to find a valid report proposal, it is in his interest to prioritize observations from nodes that have a high reputation number. When a submitted report becomes final, the smart contract increases by one the reputation number of each oracle that produced an observation contained in the said report.

5.2   The Oracle Network

In this section, we detail the algorithms executed by nodes in the oracle network. It consists of three algorithms. Algorithm 2 is a daemon that listens for event triggered by C. Algorithm 3 is instantiated by every p_i for each new request by the daemon. Its role is to propagate and collect observations among the network. Algorithm 4 is the report mining protocol. Its role is to build a report proposal out of the delivered observation and eventually submit this report to the oracle smart contract C. The oracle smart contract C maintains a list of oracles, their public keys, and their reputation. The client makes his request to the smart contract C. The instances of Algorithm 3 and Algorithm 4 can read the state of C at any time. They can access the list of oracles, their public keys, reputation, current request-id, and current target difficulty number. Those public variables are used implicitly in the pseudo-code presented here. We denote by $sign_i(m)$ the function that signs the message m with the private key of process p_i producing

---

Algorithm 1. Oracle smart contract

---

state
 $lastPrice \leftarrow \perp$: last valid reported price
 $reports \leftarrow [\perp]$: table of valid reports
 $oracles \leftarrow [\perp]^n$: list of oracles' public keys and their reputation
 $targetDifficulty \leftarrow 0$: current difficulty target number
 $tergetReportTime \leftarrow 0$: Target report generation time

function $requestNewPrice()$
 $reports[requestID].requestSubmitted \leftarrow time.now$
 Emit event $newRequest()$

function $verifyProofOfWork(reportHeader)$
 return $hash(reportHeader) \leq targetDifficulty$

function $verifySignatures(hashSignObs)$
 return $\forall h_{\sigma_i} \in hashSignObs | verify_i(h_{\sigma_i})|$

function $verifyHashes(hashSignObs, observe)$
 return $\forall o_i \in observe | hash(hashSignObs[i] = hash(o_i))|$

function $submitReport(requestID, [reportHeader, hashSignObs, observe])$
  if $verifyProofOfWork(reportHeader) \wedge verifySignatures(hashSignObs) \wedge$
 $verifyHashes(hashSignObs, observe) \wedge observe.length \geq 2f + 1$ **then**
    $reports[requestID] \leftarrow [reportHeader, observe, hashSignObs]$
    $reports[requestID].requestFulfilled \leftarrow time.now$
    $lastPrice \leftarrow median(observe)$
    $\forall o_i \in observe | oracles[i].reputation \leftarrow oracles[i].reputation + 1|$
    $adjustDifficulty()$
    Emit event $finalReport(requestID)$
  end if

function $adjustDifficulty()$
 $l = reports.length$
 $sum \leftarrow \sum_{i=l-100}^{l} reports[i].requestFulfilled - reports[i].requestSubmitted$
 $averageReportTime \leftarrow sum/100$ ▷ Calculate the average report generation time
 over the last 100 reports
 $targetDifficulty \leftarrow targetDifficulty * \frac{averageReportTime}{targetReportTime}$ ▷ Adjust the difficulty
 by a factor of the ratio between observed and desired report generation time

function $registerOracle(publicKey)$ ▷ Function restricted to administrator
 $oracles.append([publicKey, 0])$ ▷ Register new oracle and set reputation to 0

function $setTargetReportTime(time)$ ▷ Function restricted to administrator
 $targetReportTime \leftarrow time$

---

the signed message m_{σ_i}. Similarly $verify_i(m_{\sigma_i})$ verifies the signature of signed message m_{σ_i} with the public key of process p_i.

The Daemon. Algorithm 2 is a deamon that is executed continuously by every process. This deamon awaits for $newRequest$ events from C to instantiate the observation gossip protocol presented in Algorithm 3. It is also responsible for stopping instances of Algorithm 3 and Algorithm 4 when a $finalReport$ event is emitted by C.

Algorithm 2. Oracle daemon executed continuously by every $p_j \in P$

Upon event $newRequest(requestID)$ from C **do**
   initialize instance $(requestID)$ of observation gossip protocol

Upon event $finalReport(requestID)$ from C **do**
   abort instance gossip protocol $(requestID)$
   abort instance report mining $(requestID)$

The Observation Gossip Protocol. Algorithm 3 is the observation gossip protocol. Its goal is for the nodes to propagate observations messages among the network. It is instantiated by Algorithm 2 upon new request event emitted by C. Oracle nodes gather data from sources, hash and sign their observation, and broadcast it to every $p_i \in P$. Every oracle p_i maintains a list $hashSignObs$ of hashed-signed observations delivered by any $p_j \in P$. When a node p_i has received at least $2f + 1$ hashed-signed observations, he starts the report mining protocol presented in Algorithm 4. For the sake of simplicity and readability, we separated Algorithm 3 and Algorithm 4. In practice, those algorithms will be executed in parallel on a single machine and thus share the same local memory. This means that when Algorithm 3 starts a report mining instance for request $requestID$, the list of hashed observations $hashSignObs$ can still be updated by the observation gossip protocol. The report gossip protocol continues execution even if the report mining process has started. It is in the interest of the nodes to include as many observations as possible in their report proposal to minimize the chances of an adversarial oracle blocking execution. This will be further developed in the paragraph about the report mining process. Yet it must be noted that the abort condition of the observation gossip process is a $finalReport$ event from C.

Algorithm 3. Observation gossip protocol instance $requestID$ (executed by every oracle p_i)

---

state
   $observe \leftarrow [\bot]^n$: table of observations received in OBSERVATION messages
   $hashSignObs \leftarrow [\bot]^n$: table of hashed signed observations received in HASHED-OBSERVATION messages

Upon initialization **do**
   $v \leftarrow$ gather price value from data source
   $observe[i] \leftarrow [time.now, assetPair, v]$
   $hashSignObs[i] \leftarrow sign_i(hash(observe[i]))$
   send message[HASHED-OBSERVATION, $hashSignObs[i]$] to all $p_j \in P$

Upon receiving message [HASHED-OBSERVATION, h_{σ_j}] from p_j **do**
   if $verify_j(h_{\sigma_j})$ then
      $hashSignObs[j] \leftarrow h_{\sigma_j}$
   end if

Upon $|\{p_j \in P | hashSignObs[j] \neq \bot\}| = 2f + 1$ **do**
   initialize instance report mining ($requestID$)

Upon receiving message [REPORT-PROPOSAL, $hashSignObs'$, $reportHeader$]
   from p_l **do**
   if $hashSignObs[i] \in hashSignObs'$ then
      if $\{\forall\ h_{\sigma_j} \in hashSignObs' | verify_j(h_{\sigma_j})|\} \wedge hash(reportHeader) \leq$
   $targetDifficulty \wedge hashSignObs'.length \geq 2f + 1$ then
         send message[OBSERVATION, $observe[i]$] to p_l
      end if
   end if

The Report Mining Protocol. Algorithm 4 presents the report mining process. Much like in a proof-of-work-based blockchain the principle is for the oracles to rearrange the content of the report until the hash value of the report header is below a target difficulty number. Each report maintains a pool $hashSignObs$ of n pending observations that have not been yet included in a report. An observation has three attributes, the target asset pair, the observed price, and a timestamp. To this observation correspond an observation header that contains the public key of the oracle, the hash of the observation, and the oracle's signature. When oracle nodes try to find a valid report, they don't hash the full report. Instead, much like in a proof-of-work-based blockchain, they only hash the header of the report. This header consists of a timestamp a nonce and most importantly the observations hash. The observations hash would correspond in a proof-of-work blockchain to the Merkle root. But because we don't need simple payment verification, building a Merkle tree out of the list of observations is unnecessary. Hashing the concatenated list of observations is sufficient in our case.

    The way nodes rearrange their hash-signed observation list to find a valid report proposal is not explicitly developed in Algorithm 4. Indeed, similarly to proof-of-work-based mining, it is the responsibility of the nodes to find a strategy that maximizes their rewards and reduces their costs. However, we would advise that they rearrange their list according to the reputation of the other nodes. Indeed, the only way for an adversarial oracle to slow down or block protocol execution is not to respond with an OBSERVATION message on receiving a REPORT-PROPOSAL message. In order not to include dishonest parties in their report proposal, oracles should prioritize observations from oracles that have a good reputation. It is to be noted that to be considered valid by the smart contract C, a report does not need to have a clear observation for every hash-signed observation contained in the $hashSignObs$ list. Indeed, the only requirement is that the report contains at least $2f + 1$ clear observations.

6 Analysis

In this section, we prove that the PoWacle protocol satisfies the properties of the oracle problem definition as presented in Sect. 3.

Lemma 1. *The PoWacle protocol satisfies the liveness property of a decentralized blockchain price oracle.*

Algorithm 4. Report mining algorithm instance $requestID$ executed by every p_i that has delivered more than $2f + 1$ hash-signed observation

---

state
   $reportHeader \leftarrow \perp$

Upon initialization **do**
   loop
      $nonce \leftarrow 0$
      $hashSignObs' \leftarrow prioritize(hashSignObs)$ ▷ Create a prioritized copy of the hash-signed observation list
         while $reportHeader = \perp \lor nonce \neq 2^{32}$ **do**
            if $hash(time.now, nonce, hash(hashSignObs')) \leq targetDifficulty$ **then**
               $reportHeader \leftarrow [time.now, nonce, hash(hashSignObs')]$
               send message[REPORT-PROPOSAL, $hashSignObs'$, $reportHeader$] to all $p_j \in P$
               break
            end if
            $nonce \leftarrow nonce + 1$
         end while
   end loop

Upon receiving message [OBSERVATION, o_j] from p_j **do**
   if $hash(o_j) = hashSignObs[j]$ **then**
      $observe[j] \leftarrow o_j$
   end if

Upon $observe.length \geq 2f + 1$
   $C.submitReport(requestID, [reportHeader, hashSignObs', observe])$

Proof. Consider a client request made to C at time t. Every correct node is triggered by this event and broadcasts its observation to every $p_j \in P$. Recall that correct oracles resend every message until the destination acknowledges it. Even if an adversary coalition can choose faulty nodes on the fly, they can not control more than $f < n/3$ process. Thus every correct oracle should eventually deliver a hash-signed observation from every correct node. This also holds for the process where nodes send clear observations to the proposer. Consequently, every correct node should be able to start the mining process. Let $d > 0$ be the difficulty target number. Due to the uniformity and non-locality properties of hash functions (outputs should be uniformly distributed), for each trial, there is a non-zero chance of finding a report whose hash value h is less or equal than the difficulty d. Consequently, there is a finite Δ within which an oracle should find and submit a valid report to C. Because the observations contained in the report are from correct nodes, C should declare the report final. Thus the protocol satisfies the Δ-Liveness property of a decentralized blockchain price oracle.

Lemma 2. *The PoWacle protocol satisfies the observation integrity property of a decentralized blockchain price oracle.*

Proof. Consider a protocol execution where a report with value v has been declared final by C. To be considered final by C, a report must contain at least $2f + 1$ observations that have been individually signed by each oracle. The value v is the median of those observations. Since there are at most f faulty nodes, out of the $2f + 1$ observations, more than half have been produced by a correct node. Trivially, the median of those observations is either the one of a correct node or the one of a faulty node but in the interval between a larger and a smaller value provided by honest nodes. Thus, the protocol satisfies the observation integrity property of a decentralized blockchain price oracle.

Lemma 3. *The PoWacle protocol satisfies the uniformity property of a decentralized blockchain price oracle.*

Proof. Recall that the value *lastPrice* of C can only be updated by the smart contract itself when *requestNewPrice* is invoked by a client. Thus trivially, if two clients c_1 and c_2 read this value at some time $t > 0$, the value they will read corresponds to the same report.

7   Conclusions

Price oracles are at the core of various applications in Decentralized Finance. It should be noted that due to security attacks these oracles are difficult to design in a distributed fashion. In this paper, we propose and prove correct the first distributed price oracle designed for asynchronous Byzantine prone environments. Price oracles have some similarities with classical distributed shared registers however, the presence of smart contracts (pieces of code) that automatically execute on an underlying blockchain make their particularity. In future works, we would like to investigate how price oracles can benefit from the existing distributed system literature. In the same vein, we will like to investigate new distributed abstractions that encapsulate the blockchain technology specificity.

References

1. Bandchain: Band protocol system overview. https://docs.bandchain.org/whitepaper/system-overview.html
2. Breidenbach, L., Cachin, C., Coventry, A., Juels, A., Miller, A.: Chainlink off-chain reporting protocol (2021). https://blog.chain.link/off-chain-reporting-live-on-mainnet
3. Cachin, C., Guerraoui, R., Rodrigues, L.: Introduction to Reliable and Secure Distributed Programming. Springer, Heidelberg (2011). https://doi.org/10.1007/978-3-642-15260-3
4. Caldarelli, G., Ellul, J.: The blockchain oracle problem in decentralized finance-a multivocal approach. Appl. Sci. **11**(16), 7572 (2021)
5. Connell, J.: Sophisticated trading bot exploits synthetix oracle, funds recovered (2019). https://cointelegraph.com/news/sophisticated-trading-bot-exploits-synthetix-oracle-funds-recovered
6. DOS: A decentralized oracle service boosting blockchain usability with off-chain data & verifiable computing power (2011). https://s3.amazonaws.com/whitepaper.dos/DOS+Network+Technical+Whitepaper.pdf
7. Murimi, R.M., Wang, G.G.: On elastic incentives for blockchain oracles. J. Database Manag. (JDM) **32**(1), 1–26 (2021)
8. Nakamoto, S.: Bitcoin: a peer-to-peer electronic cash system. Decentralized Bus. Rev. 21260 (2008)
9. Paradigm: Chainlink: Detailed review on the project (2019). https://medium.com/paradigm-fund/chainlink-detailed-review-on-the-project-9dbd5e050974

FEBR: Expert-Based Recommendation Framework for Beneficial and Personalized Content

Mohamed Lechiakh$^{(\boxtimes)}$ ⓘ and Alexandre Maurer

Mohammed VI Polytechnic University, UM6P-CS, Benguerir, Morocco
{mohamed.lechiakh,alexandre.maurer}@um6p.ma

Abstract. So far, most research on recommender systems focused on maintaining long-term user engagement and satisfaction, by promoting relevant and personalized content. However, it is still very challenging to evaluate the quality and the reliability of this content. In this paper, we propose FEBR (Expert-Based Recommendation Framework), a collaborative recommendation framework based on apprenticeship learning to assess the quality of the recommended content on online platforms. FEBR exploits the demonstrated trajectories of a set of trusted users (chosen to be experts with reliable behavior) in a recommendation evaluation environment, to recover an unknown utility function. This function is used to learn an optimal policy describing the experts' behavior, which is then used in the framework to optimize a user-expert-based recommendation policy with an adapted Q-learning algorithm, providing high-quality and personalized recommendations. We evaluate the performance of our solution through a user interest simulation environment (using RecSim), and compare its efficiency with standard recommendation methods. The results show that our approach provides a significant gain in terms of content quality (evaluated by experts and watched by users) while maintaining an important engagement rate.

Keywords: Recommender systems · Apprenticeship learning · Reinforcement learning · Beneficial recommendations · Expert policy

1 Introduction

Recommender systems (RS) try to provide their users with content matching their interests and preferences. To do so, they use many different approaches: collaborative filtering, content-based approaches, hybrid approaches... [1]. Recent works on collaborative interactive and conversational RS showed promising methods to improve the relevance and the personalization of recommendations [7,13,15]. However, recommendation platforms are often blamed for lacking transparency and accountability for their algorithmic recommendations, that may (for instance) incentivize users to consume addictive, harmful and radical content. Aligning recommendations with human values is actually a complex problem: one should have a good understanding of users' behavior, and one should also optimize the right metrics.

© The Author(s), under exclusive license to Springer Nature Switzerland AG 2022
M.-A. Koulali and M. Mezini (Eds.): NETYS 2022, LNCS 13464, pp. 52–68, 2022.
https://doi.org/10.1007/978-3-031-17436-0_5

1.1   Problem Statement

Indeed, finding beneficial information within mainstream RS is far from obvious. According to *YouTube Official Blog* [14], YouTube recently adopted the concept of "social responsibility" as a core value for the company. In this context, they defined new metrics for quality evaluation (namely, "user watch time" and "quality watch time"). These quality features characterize what we call a *beneficial* personalized content. In addition, Youtube started recommending more videos from official sources, and less "borderline" videos. However, despite these efforts, YouTube's recommendation algorithm, similarly to many large RS platforms, still suggests content containing misleading or false information, as well as conspiracy theories. In such a huge RS, high-quality content is easily "drowned" among low-quality content, making it less visible to users.[1] Nowadays, this problem of ensuring beneficial and personalized content becomes a major concern for all recommendation platforms, impacting the trust and the engagement of their customers.

1.2   Contributions

To address this problem in current recommendation environments, we propose **FEBR** (**F**ramework for **E**xpert-**B**ased **R**ecommendations), the first expert-based Apprenticeship Learning (AL) [9] framework for news (video, articles...) RS. Basically, FEBR is a recommendation framework that consists of two components:

- **Expert AL/IRL component:** It uses relevant quality signals derived from expert behaviors in a customized evaluation environment to learn an optimal expert-like policy. Then, this policy can be used to identify high-quality content to be recommended to users. The novelty in our approach is in the way we measure this quality, and the guarantees we present in terms of importance, accuracy and reliability.
- **User RL recommendation component:** In the user recommendation environment, we propose a Q-learning algorithm to optimize the user's recommendation policy based on the optimal expert policy (provided and updated by the Expert AL/IRL component), which can be used in online user interactions for delivering personalized and beneficial recommendations.

In addition, we implemented our solution as a configurable framework (using RecSim [6]), that can be used for simulation experiments related to our topic. Finally, we empirically validate the performance of our solution through extensive simulations. The results show a consumption of high-quality content that remarkably exceeds baseline approaches, while maintaining a very close total watch time as well as the average clicks of videos (as shown in Figs. 4 and 5 of Sect. 6).

---

[1] For instance, in the context of the COVID-19 pandemic, a considerable number of users are mislead with false information uploaded everyday on Youtube and social networks, inducing dangerous habits and behaviors. Such behaviors have likely increased the propagation rate of the virus in many countries.

1.3   Motivation and Overview of Our Solution

We took inspiration from the WeBuildAI framework [8] to propose FEBR: a participatory system where the RS, experts and users collaborate between each other in Markov Decision Process (MDP) environments, to leverage expert knowledge for a better user experience. We assume that experts are reliable and can get involved in the RS through a trustworthy hiring process (we are aware that they can only evaluate a small fraction of the system's items). Therefore, we aim to push users to mimic these expert's trajectories (i.e., the expert's sequence of visited states within the recommendation environment) as often as possible while respecting their own preferences, since we assume that a reliable expert's behavior across the recommended contents (for a given topic) is different from a layman's one.[2] Thus, unlike classical RL problems, that use well-defined reward functions to learn desired behaviors, we cannot straightforwardly specify this reward to learn complex and multi-intention expert trajectories.

In a personalized expert $MDP\backslash R$ environment, our contribution can be formulated as an AL problem that uses Inverse Reinforcement Learning (IRL) [3, 9] to recover an unknown (linear) reward function (within the expert AL/IRL component), which will be used to learn an optimal expert policy. More specifically, we developed a dedicated expert MDP environment that uses a personalized evaluation mechanism within the response model. This enables experts to evaluate videos and, at the same time, to capture the main patterns of quality and engagement features delivered during this process (which could help to efficiently learn the reward function). In the user RL recommendation component of the same RS, we propose an adapted Q-learning algorithm to optimize the user recommendation policy, based on (1) the (learned) optimal expert policy and (2) a classification state model that matches similar expert-user states. Note that we do not discuss the problem of disagreement between experts, since they all maintain their own evaluations, and the system converges to a unique optimal expert policy.

1.4   Research Scope and Delimitation

This paper presents a first research proposal that mainly focuses on the beneficial aspects of online recommended content with satisfactory personalization performance in today's dynamic RS. Our objective is not to improve the accuracy of the recommendations, but rather to guarantee an acceptable level of safety for the personalized content, in terms of validity, expertise, authoritativeness and trustworthiness, which are encapsulated here in the term "beneficial". In other words, we exploited powerful imitation learning models to achieve our goals in a modular configurable framework, which we put at the disposition of the RS research community as a proof-of-concept to initiate and advance future

---

[2] For instance, a healthcare specialist, when reviewing videos about COVID-19 on YouTube, may carefully select these videos based on their titles, references and descriptions. Then, she can evaluate their quality, according to her expertise domain.

works in this direction. Despite, we clarify the following challenges related to our contribution:

1. This work is based on a selected set of experts, providing evaluations based on well-chosen criteria. The way we find or choose these experts is out of the scope of this contribution, and could be independently investigated at the system management level using convenient procedures (see for instance [26]).

2. Simulation with real dataset is very challenging [28,29] for two reasons. First, the expert on-policy learning using value iteration or policy iteration algorithms (as we propose in the AL/IRL component) is designed for online interaction training with the environment. Therefore, even if we consider adding a off-policy deep Q-learning implementation to learn from logged expert data, it may not be efficient, and may fail to learn [27], especially in a complex dynamic space (as it is the case for RS): indeed, static data do not record the factors and patterns of expert choices and behaviors, which are necessary for efficient long-term policy learning using AL/IRL. Second, even if we decide to train the Expert AL/IRL component with a real static dataset, this would require a specific dataset structure to fit our model, as existing dataset are not adapted. Instead, we choose to perform simulated experiments using synthetic data (as previously done for several RL-based RS [18–20]) using RecSim, a robust interactive simulation environment for dynamic RL-based RS, which has proved to be very efficient to evaluate the performance of RL-based RS [11,20,30].

3. FEBR is implemented and evaluated based on RecSim. However, the choice of RecSim is not a limitation of our approach: each of its components could be implemented by different RL-based recommendation simulators, that could be adapted to FEBR's model design.

The rest of the paper is organized as follows. In Sect. 2, we discuss related works. In Sect. 3, we state basic definitions. In Sect. 4, we describe our proposed framework. In Sect. 5, we describe the design and setting of our experimentation. In Sect. 6, we describe and comment our experimental results. We conclude and discuss future works in Sect. 7.

2   Related Works

The quality of recommendations has long been an important topic in RS research. It is mainly measured from the user engagement perspective, using different techniques and paradigms [7,13,15]. These works often focus on modeling complex user behaviors and dynamic user/item interactions to optimize long/short term engagement metrics, without studying the quality of the content itself. Some previous works have initiated the use of expert knowledge/ratings to improve the accuracy of recommendation. For instance, Amatriain et al. [16] exploits a small dataset of expert ratings (collected from the Web and identified by specific techniques like "domain authority" and reputation-like scores). Anand et al. [24] pay selected influencers (considered as experts) to comment on new items, and use some heuristics to build a social user-expert influence network, in particular to deal with the cold start item and user problems. Similarly, Lin et al. [22] define experts as popular influencers in the news reading community that users follow, and implicitly exploit user news rating/access log to select potential semantic relationships between users and experts. In [17], the authors propose a recommendation process which defines similarity and expertise metrics to propose trusted and personalized recommendation by internally scoring users' profiles based on their rating behaviors. Other works [23, 25] propose personalized recommendation by considering semantic and contextual social network factors to detect and track expert-user relationships. In the context of IRL applications, Massimo and Ricci [10] proposed a POIs (Point Of Interests) optimization approach for touristic RS, which aims to improve recommendations based on policies learned from clustering users' personal trajectories with IRL. However, their method only addresses personalization of user's preferences by exploiting potentially similar user experiences.

To sum up, most of these existing works mainly use a classical algorithmic approaches (e.g. collaborative filtering) to bias their underlying optimization models towards the opinions of these "experts" or "content producers" (that are globally identified based on social influence and relationships with users) or simply "trusted users" (that could be identified using some special interaction activities). Then, they focus on detecting high-quality content producers (or typical trusted online user profiles) to recommend personalized items, which would likely be of high quality. However, this methodology is (1) mostly addressing content personalization rather than content quality, (2) "naively" identifying experts based on algorithmic optimization of user interaction and social metrics of engagement, and (3) not presenting any quality evaluation schemes to justify the beneficial aspects of their recommendations.

Therefore, if we agree that a personalized (attractive) content is not necessarily beneficial, then the quality of recommendation from the beneficial content analysis perspective has not been given a considerable focus from most, if not all RS research works; yet, it is rarely addressed as a crucial research concern. To the best of our knowledge, this paper is the first to propose a content quality-centered recommendation approach which leverages the behavior of a set of selected experts to analyze the beneficial aspects of the recommended content, while ensuring a level of personalization comparable to baseline methods.

3   Preliminaries

RL-Based RS Definitions. A MDP is defined in forward reinforcement learning (RL) by the tuple (S, A, T, D, R, γ), where S is the state space and A is the action space. $T : S \times A \times S \mapsto [0, 1]$ is the state transition function. D is the initial-state distribution, from which the initial state $s_0 \in S$ is drawn. $R : S \times A \times S \mapsto \mathbb{R}$ is the reward function. γ is the discount rate. A stationary stochastic policy (we simply say "policy" from now) $\pi : S \times A \mapsto [0, 1]$ corresponds to a recommendation strategy which returns the probability of taking an action given a user state s_t at timestamp t. Thus, for any policy π, the state value function is defined by

$V^\pi(s) = E[\sum_t^\infty \gamma^t R(s_t, a_t)|D, T]$, where $s_0 \sim D$ and $(s_t, a_t)_{t \geq 0}$ is the sequence of state-actions pairs generated by executing policy π. We call an optimal policy a policy that maximizes the value function such that $V^\star(s) = max_\pi V^\pi(s)$ for each $s \in S$. In general, a typical interactive RL-based RS executes an action $a_t = \{i_t \in I\}$ through recommending a slate of items i_t (e.g., videos, commercial products) to a user who provides a feedback $f_t \in F$ (e.g., skipping, clicking and other reactions) at the tth interaction. Then, the RS recommends the next slate (a_{t+1}) until the user leaves the platform (end of session). Here, I (resp. F) is the set of candidate items for recommendations (resp. set of possible feedback). We model a user MDP state by: $s_t = (user, a_1, f_1, ..., a_{t-1}, f_{t-1})$; then a trajectory is represented by $\zeta = (s_0, a_0, r_0, ..., s_t, a_t, r_t, ..., s_T)$ where $r_t \in \mathbb{R}$ is a reward associated with the user's feedback. in the case of direct RL, this reward is known and explicitly formulated as a function to be maximized by the recommender agent, which will derive its optimal policy.

AL/IRL Definitions. Algorithms for AL problems take as input a MDP with an unknown reward function (MDP\$R$).[3] In a MDP\$R$ environment, we observe an expert trajectory ζ_e through a sequence of state-action pairs $\zeta_e = (s_t, a_t)_{t \in \mathbb{N}}$ such that $s_t = (expert, a_1, f_1, ..., a_{t-1}, f_{t-1})$ where f_i are the expert feedback. We assume that the expert behaves according to an optimal policy π_e, which is assumed to maximize an unknown reward function $R = R^*$. There are many IRL algorithms [2,3] that could be used to approximate this function (with recurrent calls to RL policy optimization loops, using some RL algorithms). At the convergence, we obtain the optimal expert-like policy π_e^*.

4   Proposed Bi-component FEBR Framework

The framework is composed of an AL/IRL component and a recommendation component as shown in Fig. 1. This model is a centralized version of our approach, where the experts collaborate to learn the same policy. In this section, we

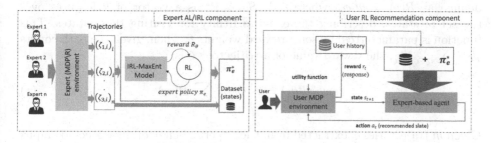

Fig. 1. FEBR model framework.

---

[3] More generally, we can consider a partially observable MDP (POMDP\R), if we are dealing with noisy states.

describe the main components of our framework in the context of video recommendation systems, but the approach remains valid for other types of instructive and informative recommended contents.

4.1   Expert AL/IRL Component

Expert MDP\R Environment. Following the AL/IRL component in Fig. 1, the main objective of the expert environment is to generate trajectories reflecting expert behaviors. The experts are assumed to be reliable and to act in a professional and ethical way. Then, for an expert session, the recommendation task is defined as the sequential interactions between a recommender system (agent) and the expert environment. It uses a finite MDP\$R = (S, A, T, \gamma, D_0)$ environment to model it, where...

- **S** reflects the expert state space that refers to her interest distribution over topics, and her watching history (e.g., watched videos and the interactions they involved: clicks, ratings using evaluation features...).
- **A** is the set of actions that contains all possible recommendation slates of size $k \geq 1$.
- **R** is the reward function when the system takes an action a_t from a state s_t. Basically, this reward is unknown, and it is influenced by the expert's response model (watching information, evaluations...).

We adopt a non-deterministic transitions between states according to the state-transition distribution **T**. In addition, $\mathbf{D_0}$ represents the initial state distribution and $\gamma \in [0, 1)$ is the discount factor. For a given expert, instantiating this environment at timestamp t gives us the state model: s_m^t = [expert state, response state, video state] (which is used to build the state dataset $\mathcal{D}_s$; see the paragraph "state dataset $\mathcal{D}_s$" in Sect. 5 for more details). Thus, s_m^t forms, with previous states (in the same trajectory), the general state model $s_t = (s_m^1, ..., s_m^t)$ of the expert environment within the AL/IRL component.

IRL-MaxEnt Model. For our contribution, we assume that R can be linearly defined as $R(s) = \theta^T \phi_s$, where $\phi_s : S \mapsto \mathbb{R}^k$ is a vector of k features over the set of states, describing the expert's utility for visiting these states. This function is parameterized by some reward weights θ. Then, given the path counts $\phi_\zeta = \sum_{s_t \in \zeta} \phi_{s_t}$, the reward value of a trajectory ζ is:

$$reward(\theta_\zeta) = \theta^\top \phi_\zeta = \sum_{s_t \in \zeta} R(s_t) \tag{1}$$

Given m trajectories $\tilde{\zeta}_i$ extracted from the expert's behavior, its expected empirical feature count is $\tilde{\phi} = \frac{1}{m} \sum_i \phi_{\tilde{\zeta}_i}$. The idea here is to find a probability distribution P over the entire class of possible trajectories respecting the following equality:

$$\tilde{\phi} = \sum_i P(\zeta_i | \theta, T) \phi_{\zeta_i} \tag{2}$$

The matching problem of Eq. 2 may result in a distribution that causes an excessive bias over its trajectories. Therefore, many reward functions may correspond to the same optimal policy, and many policies can lead to the same empirical feature counts, as proven by [4]. This problem becomes more critical in the case of sub-optimal demonstrations, like in our case, where the expert's behavior is often not a perfect one (since she is performing an evaluation work where optimal performance is not always expected). Then, an efficient solution is to choose a stochastic policy that only considers the constrained feature's matching property (Eq. 2) and does not add any additional preferences on the set of paths (other than the ones implied by the constraint of Eq. 2). Thus, we propose to use the Maximum Entropy principle [2] to resolve this problem. Intuitively, this principle would provide the statistically most likely distribution for constructing consistent trajectories based on a non-committal reward function (i.e., a reward function which matches demonstrated feature counts without additional assumptions about the demonstrated behavior). According to [2], the selected distribution (yielding higher total reward) is an exponentially preferable choice, and it is parameterized by the reward weights θ. Then, it turns out to be an optimization problem: $\theta^* = \arg\max_\theta \sum_i log P(\zeta_i|\theta, T)$.

We then maximize the likelihood of observing the expert demonstrations under the maximum entropy distribution P. This can be solved by a gradient optimization method:

$$\Delta L(\theta) = \tilde{\phi} - \sum_i P(\zeta_i|\theta, T)\phi_{\zeta_i} = \tilde{\phi} - \sum_s D(s)\phi_s \qquad (3)$$

where $D(s)$ is the *expected state visitation frequency* of state s, and represents the probability of being in such a state. [2] presented a dynamic programming algorithm to compute $D(s)$. Within the gradient optimization loop, π_e is jointly learned and optimized by a *value iteration* [5] RL algorithm and the IRL-MaxEnt model to derive the expert's optimal policy π_e^*.

4.2   User RL Recommendation Component

The recommendation component presented in Fig. 1 is designed to host the end-user recommendation environment. This component uses $\mathcal{D}_s$ (presented in Sect. 5) and π_e^* (learned by the AL/IRL component) to build a classification model $\mathcal{C}_e$ that calculates the cosine similarity between a given user state s_u and experts' states s_e. Then, in a user finite MDP environment $(S', A', T', r, \gamma, D_0')$, we model $\mathcal{C}_e$ by the function $\alpha : S' \to \{0, 1\}$ such that:

$$\mathcal{C}_e : \alpha(s_t) = \begin{cases} 1, & \text{if } \exists s_e \in \mathcal{D}_s : cosine(s_t, s_e) = \frac{s_t s_e^\top}{||s_u||||s_e||} \leq \delta \\ 0, & \text{otherwise.} \end{cases} \qquad (4)$$

where δ is a fixed comparison threshold. For each user, we define a user recommendation expert-based policy as $\rho_\pi = \alpha\pi_e^* + (1-\alpha)\pi$, where π_e^* is the optimal expert policy (learned by the AL/IRL component) and π is a (stationary deterministic) user local policy followed when $\alpha(s_t) = 0$. Thus, ρ_π's structure enables to exploit the expert knowledge for similar user/expert states and to explore new (non-evaluated) videos, which leads to continuous optimization of the sub-optimal recommendation policy ρ_π^*. Basically, ρ_π^* maximizes the following expected return (sum of discounted rewards):

$$\rho_\pi^* = \arg\max_{\pi \in \Pi} \mathbb{E}_{\tau \sim \rho_\pi} \left[\sum_{t=0}^{\infty} \gamma^t r(s_t, slate_t) \right] \tag{5}$$

where $\tau = (s_t, slate_t, s_{t+1})_t$ denotes a user trajectory; r is the reward associated with the user's feedback when the slate $slate_t$ is recommended at state $s_t \in S'$; $slate_t \sim \rho_\pi(slate|s_t)$; $s_0 \sim D_0'$ and $s_{t+1} \sim T'(s|s_t, slate_t)$. Note that, in this component, we use a well-known user reward function r, to avoid confusion with the AL/IRL methodology. In addition, the user environment must include a quality model to rank items (videos) in the document corpus of each state, based on specific calculated scores (see related paragraph in Sect. 5). Furthermore, the rewards r are used to construct a user's history dataset (for content personalization), which can be exploited by the AL/IRL component to propose new (more viewed) videos to experts for future evaluations.

Recommendation Policy Learning. We propose the Algorithm 1 to optimize our user recommendation policy ρ_π by directly incorporating π_e^*, and optimizing π using a *Q-learning* [5] method (with λ as a learning rate), under the control of the classifier C_e. The training could be done in direct interactions with users, but offline training (using logged session data) would be preferable to minimize risk of recommending problematic content during π optimization process. The value function V^π and action-value Q^π of π are respectively given by:

$$V^\pi(s_t) = r(s_t, \pi(s_t)) + \sum_{s_{t+1} \in S'} T'(s_{t+1}|s_t, \pi(s_t))V^\pi(s_{t+1}),$$

$$Q^\pi(s_t, slate_t) = r(s_t, slate_t) + \sum_{s_{t+1} \in S'} T'(s_{t+1}|s_t, slate_t)V^\pi(s_{t+1}) \tag{6}$$

For each user session (of length T) at state s_t, if $\alpha(s_t) = 1$, the recommender agent returns a slate by executing the expert policy $\pi_e^*(s_t)$. Otherwise, for $\alpha(s_t) = 0$ (i.e., $\rho_\pi = \pi$), the recommender chooses the slate to recommend using an ϵ-greedy policy[4] w.r.t. the approximated action-value function $Q^\pi(s_t, slate_t)$ (see Eq. 6). The agent then receives the reward r (which could be the total watch time or the average clicked videos, as considered in our simulations) in the user history. The cycle continues until the user leaves the session.

5 Experimental Design and Setting

For the evaluation of our solution, we used the RecSim [6] platform to develop the simulation environment of our framework, in the case of a video recommendation

---

[4] That is: with probability $1 - \epsilon$, it selects the action (i.e. slate from the current corpus) with the highest Q-value, and a random slate otherwise.

Algorithm 1: Expert-based recommendation policy optimization

---

1 Initialize s_0;
2 Initialize $Q_0^{\pi}(s_0, slate_0)$ for all possible $slate_0$ from the document corpus;
3 **for** *SESSION=1:M* **do**
4   **for** *t=0:T* **do**
5   Observe the state s_t;
6   **if** $\alpha(s_t) = 1$ **then**
7              $slate_t \leftarrow \pi_e^*(s_t)$;
8   Execute $slate_t$, observe reward r and state s_{t+1};
9   **end**
10   **else**
11             $\pi^{(t+1)}(s_t) \leftarrow \arg\max_{slate \in \mathcal{C}_u} Q^*(s_t, slate)$ (using equations 6);
12             $slate_t \leftarrow \pi^{(t+1)}(s_t)$;
13   Execute $slate_t$ and observe reward r and state s_{t+1};
14             $Q^{\pi}(s_t, slate_t) \leftarrow \lambda \left[r + \max_{slate} \gamma Q^{\pi}(s_{t+1}, slate) \right] + (1 - \lambda) Q^{\pi}(s_t, slate_t)$
15   **end**
16         $\rho_{\pi}^{(t+1)}(s_t) \leftarrow slate_t$;
17   Add $(s_t, slate_t, s_{t+1})$ to the user history;
18         $s_t \leftarrow s_{t+1}$;
19   **end**
20 **end**

---

platform. We highly recommend to refer to our implementation project and to [6,11] for more details about the models used in our framework (response, choice, transition...).[5] In the following, we present the principle models used to develop both expert and user environments:

5.1   Quality Model

In general, we call $q(s_t)$ the quality of the clicked (and probably watched) video related to a given state s_t. The closer $q(s_t)$ is to 1 (resp. -1), the better (resp. worst) quality we get; 0 corresponds to a neuter quality. Typically, as for many practical RS, FEBR algorithmically scores/ranks candidate videos using a DNN by optimizing a combination of several objectives (e.g., clicks, expected engagement, satisfaction) using user/expert context and video features as inputs. These scores are often used to describe the quality of videos in the RS, and they exactly correspond to $q(s_t)$ in our work. In general, $q(s_t)$ is initially set to follow a uniform distribution $U(-1, 1)$ for new videos that have not yet been clicked. Then, it is estimated using the intrinsic engagement metrics of all users who have interacted with the video. Specifically for FEBR, we note that $q(s_t)$ may be differently updated inside (1) the expert AL/IRL environment, when providing evaluations (assumed to be objective) after watching a video by an expert (see Sect. 5.2 for

---

[5] Our source code is available here: https://github.com/FEBR-rec/ExpertDrivenRec.

more details), and (2) the user RL recommendation environment, when the user clicked a video that has already been evaluated by an expert. In the second case, $q(s_t)$ has the value resulting from this evaluation.

5.2 Configurable Evaluation Model

Within the expert environment, we propose a simple model to evaluate the quality of videos based on four quality criteria: $Eval$ = {pedagogy, accuracy, importance, entertainment}. This is a non-exhaustive list, which could be modified and adapted depending on the evaluation procedure of the problem we consider. These features are initially set to 0. Then, when a video is evaluated by an expert (for instance, through a dedicated expert Web interface), an average quality score is calculated: $s_v = (1/4) \sum_{f_i \in Eval} f_i$, and the video is marked as "evaluated" by this expert. In this case, we update $q(s_t)$ (the state quality introduced in Sect. 5.1) by $s_v \times f$ ($f \in [0.1]$ is the expert weight, representing her level of expertise in the topic of the video).

5.3 State Dataset $\mathcal{D}_s$

This dataset is constructed from expert trajectories. The inputs have the form [expert ID, expert state, response state, video state], where: (1) the **expert state** contains the interest distribution vector over topics $e_i \in \mathbb{R}^n$ (n is the number of topics); (2) the **response state** contains the expert behavior on the recommended slate (clicked video, watch time, values of evaluation metrics, engagement rate, new estimated quality); and (3) the **video state** contains videos of the corpus sampled for this expert environment's state. For each video, we store its topic, length and quality.

5.4 Baseline Recommendation Approaches

We compare our approach (that we now call *RecFEBR*) to...

- *RecFSQ*, a standard, full slate, Q-learning based approach. This approach was first discussed in [12], and then implemented by RecSim [6] as a baseline non-decomposed Q-learning method to test new recommender agents.
- *RecPCTR* [11], which implements a myopic greedy agent that recommends slates with the highest pCTR (predicted click-through rate) items.
- *RecBandit*, which uses a bandit algorithm to recommend items with the highest UCBs (Upper Confidence Bound) of topic affinities [21].
- *RecNaive*, which is based on a random agent [11] that recommends random videos from a corpus of videos with high expert ratings, which best match the current user context. *RecNaive* is useful to test the efficiency of our approach for personalizing high-quality content for each user.

These baseline approaches reflect the general performance of popular RL-based RS that seek to maximize a reward function, which leads to optimized learned actions. They essentially optimize video quality to represent topic-independent attractiveness[6] to the average user (without expert evaluations, except for *RecNaive*). To better compare our approach with other methods (that do not use expert evaluations, namely, *RecFSQ*, *RecPCTR* and *RecBandit*), we make the following (conservative) assumption:

Assumption: For these baseline methods, we use the same quality model as FEBR, but without the specific expert updating methodology applied by FEBR components (see Sect. 5.1 for more details). Thus, we implicitly consider that the notion of quality used by these methods reflects the same information as *RecFEBR*, even when *RecFEBR* provides a quality that has been assessed by experts.

This assumption does not concern *RecNaive* because it basically uses expert evaluations. In addition, it is important to note that the considered assumption is an unfair comparison (for our approach), because it may involve the comparison of (1) a video quality estimated to reflect the attractiveness of an element for a given user and (2) a video quality that characterizes the content itself, assessed by an expert. For instance, suppose a video delivered qualities q_1 and q_2 after being watched through *RecFEBR* and *RecBandit* (or *RecFSQ* or *RecPCTR*) respectively. Therefore, our assumption implies the comparison between q_1 and q_2, and even though we get closer results, it remains a very conservative estimate for FEBR.

5.5 Evaluation Metrics

We first investigate the efficiency of our solution for recommending positive contents. Therefore, we analyze the quality of watched videos that are already evaluated by experts (i.e., most likely recommended based on the learned expert policy π_e^*). We denote this quality by Q_e. For the comparison with baseline approaches, we propose to evaluate the performance of FEBR by measuring the average total quality of watched videos $Q_T = \frac{1}{l \times M} \sum_{t=0}^{l} q(s_t)$, where l is the length of a full user recommendation session $\mathcal{S}_u$ (episode) and M is the total number of sessions. We have $Q_T = Q_e + Q_r$, where $Q_r = \sum_t q(t)$ is a system total quality (score) related to items that have been recommended and watched at these states, because the classifier $\mathcal{C}_e$ did not match these states to any similar expert states (as explained by Eq. 4). In addition, we evaluate the total watch time W_T and the average value of clicked videos C_T as two engagement metrics showing how much the user was interested in the proposed content.

5.6 Settings

We consider a global system of 8 categories of video topics. We assume that each video belongs to a single category (note that this is for experiments simplification: it is still possible to consider the assignment to many categories).

---

[6] This attractiveness is based on measuring engagement quality signals to equitably score items regardless of their categories or area of interest, so that it does not influence the feedback of the user.

The size of the set of videos has as an order of magnitude 10^5. For each user state, we sample a video corpus of size 5 (of the best videos that match the state context in term of user interests), and the recommended slate is of size 2 (small values are chosen for technical constraints). We conducted extensive simulations to confirm our findings.

AL/IRL Training. We consider a sub-system of 100 experts. For each expert, we generate 100 trajectories, each one with at most 20 steps. We fix $\gamma = 0.5$ for the *value iteration* RL algorithm (basically, values close from 1 would result in a better learning, reducing the number of iterations required to optimize sub-optimal policies; but it would also result in a much higher convergence time). For the *IRL-MaxEnt* algorithm, we set the number of training iterations to 10000. This simulation runs on CPU using a server machine equipped with an Intel Xeon Gold 6152/2.1 GHz, and 384G DDR4 RAM.

Recommendation Component. We set $\delta = 0.5$ for $\mathcal{C}_e$, and $\lambda = 0.1$ for our algorithm. We consider a system of $M = 1000$ users. For each one, we simulate 100 online interactive sessions to train their expert-based recommendation agent. Then, we test the performance of their learned recommendation policy by simulating 1000 online interaction session under ρ_{π}^* (each with length $l \leq 20$). The results are averaged and presented per baseline and evaluation metric in the next section. We run this simulation on a desktop computer equipped with an Intel i7-8550U CPU, GTX 720ti, and 8G DDR4 RAM.

6   Experimental Results

In this section, we evaluate our framework, and compare it to the baseline approaches introduced in Sect. 5.4.

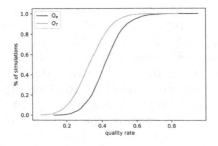
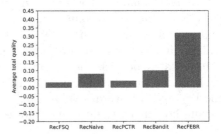

Fig. 2. Cumulative distribution of Q_T and Q_e for 1000 simulated sessions using our approach *RecFEBR*.

Fig. 3. Comparison of the average total quality Q_T of baseline approaches and *RecFEBR*.

First, Fig. 2 shows that FEBR efficiently leads to positive quality consumption (Q_e) when following the optimal user recommendation policy learned by

Algorithm 1. Therefore, this confirms that the constructed Q-Learning algorithm, based on the optimal expert policy π_e^* and the proposed user-expert state similarity classifier, can effectively optimize a high-quality (long-term) user policy, which recommends beneficial evaluated content. However, greedy action-value optimizations (that happens in lines [11–14] of Algorithm 1 when $\alpha(s_t) = 0$) can result in low-quality content recommendations that decrease the value of Q_T (because Q_r may take negative values, while Q_e is still stable at these states). This could happen due to some detrimental explorations at the user recommendation stage, when users discover new videos that are neither well scored by the system nor evaluated by experts. This situations may results in sub-optimal demonstrations (noisy states), affecting the performance of the learned user policy that is optimized by our algorithm. In this analysis, we excluded the impact of a weak near-expert policy π_e^* learned at the stage of AL/IRL training: indeed, given the results of Fig. 2, we claim that π_e^* is overall performing well, since Q_e always results in increasing positive values.

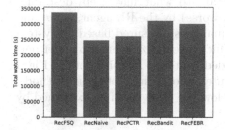

Fig. 4. Comparison of the total watch time W_T of baseline approaches and *RecFEBR*.

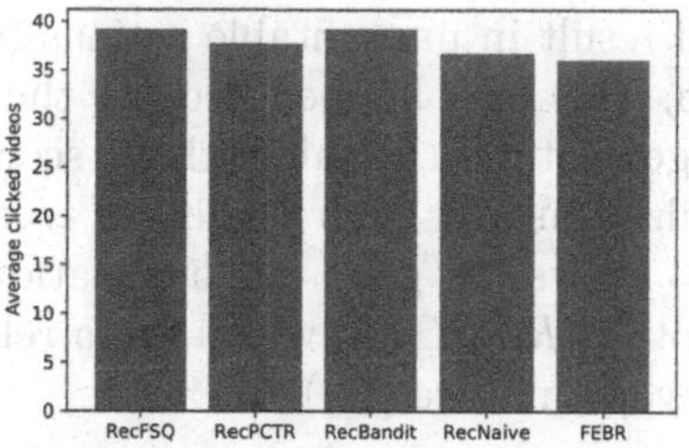

Fig. 5. Comparison of the average clicked videos C_T of baseline approaches and *RecFEBR*.

Second, based on Fig. 3, Fig. 4 and Fig. 5, we can confirm the three following points:

1. FEBR can effectively guide users through positive quality content by proposing relevant and beneficial recommendations, while maintaining almost the same total watch time and video clicks rate as other approaches. Thus, we can conclude that this simulation instance proves the efficiency of our approach in adapting IRL to capture expert behavior (despite the complexity and the ambiguity it involves) and inject high-quality content, ensuring a significant (positive) impact on Q_T with our proposed algorithm. In our approach, personalization is mainly achieved through the classification model based on state user-expert similarity comparisons. Moreover, we highlight that this performance is highly dependent on the choice of the similarity metric used by the classification model, as well as the similarity threshold. That is, an accurate model trained on large state datasets (built by a large number of experts and containing a high number of states) could be more efficient, and significantly improve performances. However, even with high expert contributions, this implies to reasonably adjust the similarity threshold (δ) to allow for more explorations, which could be useful to maintain the diversity of the recommended content and a high user engagement with the recommendation platform.

2. *RecNaive* will often fail (or likely take a long time) to learn a policy capable of delivering high-quality and personalized content. Then, this naive exploitation of the set of evaluated videos (where the agent is continuously exploring, due to random actions) will often recommend irrelevant contents. Thus, regardless of the higher quality that these recommendations can ensure in some successful scenarios, users will often skip many slates of recommended videos and interrupt watching, as shown by the value of W_T in Fig. 4. We note that a higher number of clicks does not mean higher watching time: it just ensures that the recommended slate produced positive user response by selecting a video, which will then generate a certain level of watching engagement.

3. As we can see in Fig. 5, *RecFSQ*, *RecPCTR* and *RecBandit* cannot ensure a sufficient exposure to content of high quality. The low values of Q_T (compared to W_T and C_T) achieved by these RL methods is due to the fact that they only follow user objectives. This behavior (contrary to what may seem desirable) could result in unprofitable actions (or even worse) by the RL agent, again and again. This may happen because the state quality is measured based on system engagement metrics (algorithmic scoring), which incentivize agents to prefer personalization over high quality of recommended contents. In this context, Fig. 4 and 3 shows the good personalization and interaction results of these methods, except for *RecPCTR*, which has a relatively low W_T (this could be explained by its myopic nature [11]).

7 Conclusion

In this paper, we proposed FEBR, a configurable AL/IRL-based framework for quality content recommendations leveraging expert evaluations. We developed a MDP environment that exploits the experts' knowledge and their personal preferences to derive an optimal policy that maximizes an unknown reward function, using the MaxEnt IRL model. We then used this policy to build our recommender agent based on a Q-learning algorithm, which optimizes a user recommendation policy using a classifier to match similar user-expert states. Experiments on video recommendations (using a simulated RL-based RS) show that expert-driven recommendations using our approach could be an efficient solution to control the quality of the recommended content, while keeping a high user engagement rate.

For future works, an important challenge would be to generalize this approach to systems of large dimension. Besides, one could extend this work to study the case of unreliable experts, who tend to manipulate the system for malicious or personal purposes. It is also interesting to mitigate the effects of the cold start problem in the end-user recommendation process, which indirectly affects recommendations in case of poor state matching by the classifier (which may result in beneficial but non-personalized recommendations). It may also be interesting to develop a decentralized version of the framework using deep neural networks to better learn the expert's policy (with less constraints on the reward function), thus enabling a better scalability for systems of high dimension. It may also bring more insights for running similar experiments in real-life conditions.

References

1. Shah, K., Salunke, A., Dongare, S., Antala, K.: Recommender systems: an overview of different approaches to recommendations. In: ICIIECS 2017, pp. 1–4 (2017)
2. Ziebart, B., Maas, A., Bagnell, J., Dey, A.: Maximum entropy inverse reinforcement learning. In: Proceedings of AAAI, pp. 1433–1438 (2008)
3. Ng, A., Russell, S.: Algorithms for inverse reinforcement learning. In: Proceedings of the 17th International Conference on Machine Learning, pp. 663–670 (2000)
4. Abbeel, P., Ng, A.: Apprenticeship learning via inverse reinforcement learning. In: ICML 69 (2004)
5. Sutton, R., Barto, A.: Reinforcement Learning: An Introduction. A Bradford Book (2018)
6. Ie, E., et al.: RecSim: a configurable simulation platform for recommender systems (2019). https://arxiv.org/abs/1909.04847
7. Adomavicius, G., Tuzhilin, A.: Toward the next generation of recommender systems: a survey of the state-of-the-art and possible extensions. IEEE Trans. Knowl. Data Eng. **17**, 734–749 (2005)
8. Lee, M., et al.: WeBuildAI: participatory framework for algorithmic governance. Proc. ACM Hum. Comput. Interact. **3**, 1–35 (2019)
9. Hussein, A., Gaber, M., Elyan, E., Jayne, C.: Imitation learning: a survey of learning methods. ACM Comput. Surv. **50**, 1–35 (2017)
10. Massimo, D., Ricci, F.: Harnessing a generalised user behaviour model for next-POI recommendation. In: Proceedings of the 12th ACM Conference on Recommender Systems, pp. 402–406 (2018)
11. Ie, E., et al.: SlateQ: a tractable decomposition for reinforcement learning with recommendation sets. In: IJCAI 2019, pp. 2592–2599, July 2019
12. Sunehag, P., Evans, R., Dulac-Arnold, G., Zwols, Y., Visentin, D., Coppin, B.: Deep reinforcement learning with attention for slate Markov decision processes with high-dimensional states and actions. CoRR. abs/1512.01124 (2015). arxiv.org/abs/1512.01124
13. Christakopoulou, K., Radlinski, F., Hofmann, K.: Towards conversational recommender systems. In: ACM SIGKDD 2022, pp. 815–824 (2016)
14. Youtube Blog: The Four Rs of Responsibility, Part 2: Raising authoritative content and reducing borderline content and harmful misinformation (2019). https://blog. youtube/inside-youtube/the-four-rs-of-responsibility-raise-and-reduce. Accessed 15 Aug 2021
15. Hariri, N., Mobasher, B., Burke, R.: Context adaptation in interactive recommender systems. In: Proceedings of the 8th ACM Conference on Recommender Systems, pp. 41–48 (2014)
16. Amatriain, X., Lathia, N., Pujol, J., Kwak, H., Oliver, N.: The wisdom of the few: a collaborative filtering approach based on expert opinions from the web. Association for Computing Machinery (2009)
17. Cho, J., Kwon, K., Park, Y.: Collaborative filtering using dual information sources. IEEE Intell. Syst. **22**, 30–38 (2007)

18. Mahmood, T., Ricci, F.: Learning and adaptivity in interactive recommender systems. In: Proceedings of the Ninth International Conference on Electronic Commerce, pp. 75–84 (2007). https://doi.org/10.1145/1282100.1282114
19. Bohnenberger, T., Jameson, A.: When policies are better than plans: decision-theoretic planning of recommendation sequences. Association for Computing Machinery (2001). https://doi.org/10.1145/359784.359829
20. Fotopoulou, E., Zafeiropoulos, A., Feidakis, M., Metafas, D., Papavassiliou, S.: An interactive recommender system based on reinforcement learning for improving emotional competences in educational groups. In: Kumar, V., Troussas, C. (eds.) ITS 2020. LNCS, vol. 12149, pp. 248–258. Springer, Cham (2020). https://doi.org/10.1007/978-3-030-49663-0_29
21. Auer, P., Cesa-Bianchi, N., Fischer, P.: Finite-time analysis of the multiarmed bandit problem. Mach. Learn. **47**, 235–256 (2002). https://doi.org/10.1023/A:1013689704352
22. Lin, C., Xie, R., Guan, X., Li, L., Li, T.: Personalized news recommendation via implicit social experts. Inf. Sci. **254**, 1–18 (2014). www.sciencedirect.com/science/article/pii/S002002551300594X
23. Davoodi, E., Kianmehr, K., Afsharchi, M.: A semantic social network-based expert recommender system. Appl. Intell. **39**, 1–13 (2013). https://doi.org/10.1007/s10489-012-0389-1
24. Anand, S., Griffiths, N.: A market-based approach to address the new item problem. In: Proceedings of the Fifth ACM Conference on Recommender Systems, pp. 205–212 (2011). https://doi.org/10.1145/2043932.2043970
25. Ge, H., Caverlee, J., Lu, H.: TAPER: a contextual tensor-based approach for personalized expert recommendation. In: Proceedings of the 10th ACM Conference on Recommender Systems, pp. 261–268 (2016). https://doi.org/10.1145/2959100.2959151
26. Bok, K., Jeon, I., Lim, J., Yoo, J.: Expert finding considering dynamic profiles and trust in social networks. Electronics **8**(10), 1165 (2019)
27. Kumar, A., Fu, J., Tucker, G., Levine, S.: Stabilizing off-policy Q-learning via bootstrapping error reduction. In: Proceedings of the 33rd International Conference on Neural Information Processing Systems (2019). arxiv.org/abs/2112.11022
28. Lesnikowski, A., Souza Pereira Moreira, G., Rabhi, S., Byleen-Higley, K.: Synthetic data and simulators for recommendation systems: current state and future directions. ArXiv, SimuRec 2021, ACM RecSys 2021, abs/2112.11022 (2021)
29. Zhao, X., Xia, L., Ding, Z., Yin, D., Tang, J.: Toward simulating environments in reinforcement learning based recommendations. CoRR.abs/1906.11462 (2019). arxiv.org/abs/1906.11462
30. Huang, J., Oosterhuis, H., Rijke, M., Hoof, H.: Keeping dataset biases out of the simulation: a debiased simulator for reinforcement learning based recommender systems. In: Fourteenth ACM Conference on Recommender Systems, pp. 190–199 (2020). https://doi.org/10.1145/3383313.3412252

Bird@Edge: Bird Species Recognition at the Edge

Jonas Höchst[1(✉)] , Hicham Bellafkir[1], Patrick Lampe[1],
Markus Vogelbacher[1], Markus Mühling[1], Daniel Schneider[1], Kim Lindner[2],
Sascha Rösner[2], Dana G. Schabo[2], Nina Farwig[2], and Bernd Freisleben[1]

[1] Department of Mathematics and Computer Science, University of Marburg,
Marburg, Germany
{hoechst,bellafkir,lampep,vogelbacher,muehling,schneider,
freisleb}@informatik.uni-marburg.de
[2] Department of Biology, University of Marburg, Marburg, Germany
{kim.lindner,sascha.roesner,dana.schabo,
nina.farwig}@biologie.uni-marburg.de

Abstract. We present Bird@Edge, an *Edge AI* system for recognizing
bird species in audio recordings to support real-time biodiversity monitoring. Bird@Edge is based on embedded edge devices operating in a
distributed system to enable efficient, continuous evaluation of soundscapes recorded in forests. Multiple ESP32-based microphones (called
Bird@Edge Mics) stream audio to a local Bird@Edge Station, on which
bird species recognition is performed. The results of several Bird@Edge
Stations are transmitted to a backend cloud for further analysis, e.g.,
by biodiversity researchers. To recognize bird species in soundscapes, a
deep neural network based on the EfficientNet-B3 architecture is trained
and optimized for execution on embedded edge devices and deployed on
a NVIDIA Jetson Nano board using the DeepStream SDK. Our experiments show that our deep neural network outperforms the state-of-the-
art BirdNET neural network on several data sets and achieves a recognition quality of up to 95.2% mean average precision on soundscape recordings in the Marburg Open Forest, a research and teaching forest of the
University of Marburg, Germany. Measurements of the power consumption of the Bird@Edge components highlight the real-world applicability
of the approach. All software and firmware components of Bird@Edge
are available under open source licenses.

Keywords: Bird species recognition · Edge computing · Passive
acoustic monitoring · Biodiversity

J. Höchst and H. Bellafkir—These authors contributed equally.

1   Introduction

The continuous loss of biodiversity is particularly evident from the sharp decline of bird populations in recent decades. Birds are important for many ecosystems, since they interconnect habitats, resources, and biological processes, and thus serve as important early warning bioindicators of an ecosystem's health. Thus, changes in bird species in time and space should be detected as early as possible.

Traditionally, this is achieved by human experts who walk around a natural habitat to look at birds and listen to bird sounds, identify bird species present in the sounds, and take notes of their occurrence. In recent years, this is often supported by placing microphones in the natural habitats of birds and recording their sounds. The audio data recorded in this way is then evaluated either manually by human experts or by means of automatic analysis methods to recognize bird species in soundscapes. The disadvantages of this approach are: (a) there is a potentially large amount of recorded audio data that can usually only be evaluated after the end of the recording time, and (b) there is an inherent time delay between recording the audio data and delivering the recognition results.

In this paper, we combine Edge Computing and Artificial Intelligence (AI) to present Bird@Edge, an *Edge AI* system for recognizing bird species in audio recordings to support real-time biodiversity monitoring. Bird@Edge is based on embedded edge devices operating in a distributed system to enable efficient, continuous evaluation of soundscapes recorded in forests. Multiple microphones based on ESP32 microcontroller units (called Bird@Edge Mics) stream audio to a local Bird@Edge Station, on which bird species recognition is performed. The recognition results of different Bird@Edge Stations are transmitted to a backend cloud for further analysis, e.g., by biodiversity researchers.

To recognize bird species in soundscapes, a deep neural network based on the EfficientNet-B3 architecture is trained and optimized for execution on embedded edge devices and deployed on a NVIDIA Jetson Nano board using the Deep-Stream SDK. Our experimental results show that our deep neural network model outperforms the state-of-the-art BirdNET neural network on several data sets and achieves a recognition quality of up to 95.2% mean average precision on soundscape recordings in the Marburg Open Forest, a research and teaching forest of the University of Marburg, Germany. Measurements of the power consumption of a Bird@Edge Station and the Bird@Edge Mics highlight the real-world applicability of the approach. All software and firmware components of Bird@Edge are available under open source licenses[1]. Our contributions are:

- We present a novel Edge AI approach for recognizing bird species in audio recordings; it supports efficient live data transmission and provides high-quality recognition results.
- We propose a deep neural network based on the EfficientNet-B3 architecture optimized for execution on embedded edge devices to identify bird species in soundscapes.

---

[1] https://github.com/umr-ds/BirdEdge.

– We evaluate our Edge AI approach in terms of recognition quality, runtime performance, and power consumption.

The paper is organized as follows. Section 2 discusses related work. In Sect. 3, the design and implementation of Bird@Edge are presented. Section 4 describes our deep neural network for bird species recognition. Section 5 discusses experimental results in terms of recognition quality, runtimes, and power consumption. Section 6 concludes the paper and outlines areas of future work.

2 Related Work

In this section, we discuss related work with respect to current machine learning approaches for bird species recognition in audio recordings and edge AI approaches for biodiversity monitoring.

2.1 Bird Species Recognition

For many years, bird populations were monitored manually by ornithologists who identified birds visually and acoustically on site. The introduction of autonomous recording units (ARU) opened new possibilities. Although such passively recorded data does not provide any visual information, the resulting bird surveys conducted by humans from sound recordings are comparable to traditional monitoring approaches in the field [2].

Furthermore, machine learning methods, such as Convolutional Neural Networks (CNN), are increasingly being used for automatically recognizing bird species in soundscapes. For example, BirdNET is a task-specific CNN architecture trained on a large audio data set using extensive data pre-processing, augmentation, and mixup that achieves state-of-the-art performance [14]. The audio spectrograms are generated using a Fast Fourier Transform (FFT) with a high temporal resolution. BirdNet is based on a ResNet [7] architecture and is capable of identifying 984 North American and European bird species.

More recently, BirdNET-Lite[2] has been released. This neural network is optimized for mobile and edge devices and can recognize more than 6,000 bird species. It takes raw audio as its input and generates spectrograms on-the-fly. Mühling et al. [19] proposed a task-specific neural network created by neural architecture search [24]. It won the BirdCLEF 2020 challenge [12]. It also operates on raw audio data and contains multiple auxiliary heads and recurrent layers.

Recently, Vision Transformers (ViT) achieved great improvements in computer vision tasks [4] and audio event classification [6]. Puget [20] adopted a ViT architecture for bird song recognition and achieved results comparable to CNNs. However, the annual birdcall identification challenge (BirdCLEF [13]) is currently dominated by approaches based on CNNs. The top approaches typically use ensembles of CNNs and heavy parameter tuning. The winning approach

---

[2] https://github.com/kahst/BirdNET-Lite.

at BirdCLEF 2021, for example, uses Mel spectrograms, network architectures based on ResNet-50 [7], and gradient boosting to refine the results using metadata. The runners-up Henkel et al. [8] presented an ensemble of nine CNNs. During training, they used 30 s Mel spectrograms to mitigate the effect of the weakly labeled training data and applied a novel mixup scheme within and across training samples for extensive data augmentation. Furthermore, a binary bird call/no bird call classifier contributed to the final result. However, combining several machine learning models leads to a considerably increased computational effort.

2.2   Edge AI for Biodiversity Monitoring

Executing machine learning algorithms on edge devices leads to a quantitative increase of data through continuous observation, where previously only individual data points could be collected with manual effort, often including a bias of individual experiences depending on, e.g., habitat or bird species. Merenda et al. [18] survey several approaches based on the execution of machine learning methods on hardware with limited resources. Gallacher et al. [5] deployed 15 sensors in a large urban park to process recorded audio data of bats locally, which allowed monitoring their activities for several months. Given that the system has only been operated in an urban environment, the limitations of this approach are that network connectivity must be available via WiFi, and that a fixed power supply must be present. Novel deep learning approaches presented by Disabato et al. [3] further improved bird song recognition at the edge. These approaches provide high accuracy while reducing computational and memory requirements, with limited battery lifetimes of up to 12.4 days on an STM32H743ZI microcontroller. Likewise, Zualkernan et al. [25] compare different edge computing platforms based on neural networks using bat species classification as an example. While the NVIDIA Jetson Nano is the only device capable of executing a TensorRT model on its GPU, both the Raspberry Pi 3B+ and the Google Coral showed good results when executing a reduced TensorFlow-Lite model.

3   Bird@Edge

Bird@Edge is designed as an *Edge AI* system based on distributed embedded edge devices to enable efficient, continuous evaluation of soundscapes recorded in forests. Multiple Bird@Edge Mics stream audio wirelessly to a local Bird@Edge Station, on which bird species recognition is performed. The recognition results of different Bird@Edge Stations are transmitted to a backend for further analysis. The results are stored in a time series database and can be visualized, as shown in Fig. 1. Using hidden microphones also supports recognizing very elusive species that are hard to detect while ecologists are present in field to conduct a census.

A Bird@Edge Station consumes significantly more power than a microphone node, but can run a neural network for bird species recognition for more than one audio stream. We can feed 1 to 10 audio streams into the neural network and

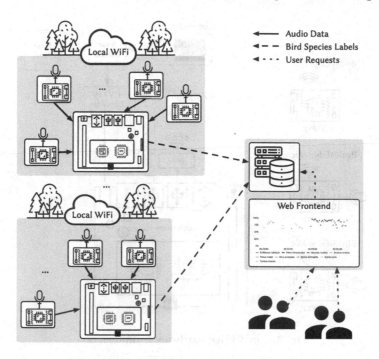

Fig. 1. Overview over the Bird@Edge system

thus operate a variable number of Bird@Edge Mics at one Bird@Edge Station. Different numbers of Bird@Edge Mics may be present when a new microphone node appears (e.g., by switching it on) or leaves (e.g., due to battery shortage).

To generate a list of bird species at a Bird@Edge Station, chunks of an incoming audio stream are passed to the neural network, which may return multiple results, since we process mixtures of recorded bird songs, i.e., soundscapes. These potentially multiple results per audio segment are then collected and aggregated into larger intervals in the time series database in the backend cloud. The size of the interval can be dynamically changed and visualized in near real-time. In addition, the status of the microphone nodes and potential problems can be detected much faster than collecting data only every few days.

3.1 Bird@Edge Hardware

The hardware used for Bird@Edge consists of (a) Bird@Edge Mics, which are in charge of recording and transmitting audio at the deployed location; (b) Bird@Edge Stations, which receive audio streams from multiple Bird@Edge Mics and execute the Bird@Edge processing pipeline. Figure 2 provides an overview of the hardware components used in Bird@Edge.

A Bird@Edge Mic consists of an Espressif ESP32 microcontroller that has a dual-core CPU running at 80 MHz, Bluetooth and WiFi connectivity, as well as

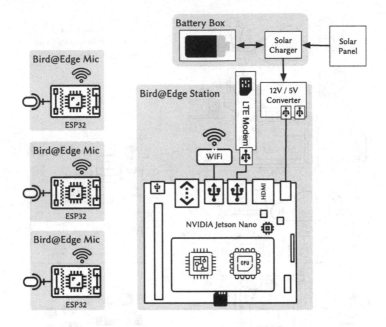

Fig. 2. Bird@Edge hardware components

multiple input and output options, including an I2S (Inter-IC Sound) bus. Connected to it is a Knowles SPH0645LM4H microphone capable of recording audio in the range 50 Hz and 15 kHz[3]. A Bird@Edge Mic can be powered either using single 18650 Li-ion cells or using one of the widely available USB power banks. The price of a Bird@Edge mic of 22€ to 50€ is composed of the ESP32, depending on the offer and model 5€ to 15€, the I2S microphone 7–12€ and a battery for 10€–20€. All components can be placed in a small case of $10 \times 10 \times 5$ cm, which does not exceed the weight of 500 g.

At the heart of a Bird@Edge Station is a NVIDIA Jetson Nano. It allows the efficient execution of machine learning models in a low power environment. A Realtek RTL8812BU-based USB WiFi is used to enable wireless networking with the board and allow connection to the Bird@Edge Mics. In addition, a Huawei E3372H LTE modem is installed to connect to the Internet in rural areas. The station is powered by 12 V solar battery system connected to the Jetson Board via a 12 V/5 V step down converter. The hardware of a Bird@Edge Station costs about 110€, with 50€ for the Jetson Nano, 20€ for the USB WiFi adapter, and 40€ for the LTE modem. The components of an Bird@Edge Station, including a solar charge controller, can be fitted into an industrial enclosure measuring $25 \times 18 \times 12$ cm, weighing less than 1.5 kg in total.

---

[3] https://www.knowles.com/docs/default-source/default-document-library/sph0645lm4h-1-datasheet.pdf.

3.2   Bird@Edge Software

Bird@Edge consists of a variety of software components that enable its smooth configuration and operation. Figure 3 shows these software components, as well as the data flows and interaction possibilities of the users with the system.

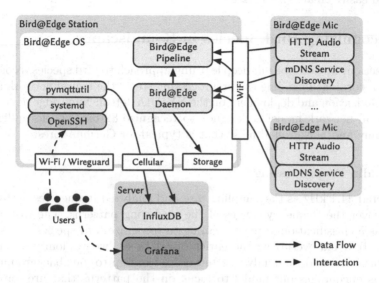

Fig. 3. Bird@Edge software components

The software for the Bird@Edge Mics is built using components of the Espressif Development Framework (ESP-IDF), i.e., HTTP Server, Multicast DNS Implementation, and I2S drivers. When booting up, the Bird@Edge Mic connects to the WiFi network (SSID: BirdEdge) with the best signal strength and reports its own accessibility via the service identifier mDNS. Then, the HTTP server is started, which provides the audio stream of the microphone for the Bird@Edge station. To detect connection interruptions, the WiFi connection is also checked at intervals of one second with the aid of ICMP and, if necessary, the WiFi connection is re-established. The Bird@Edge Mic software is available online[4].

The software running on a Bird@Edge Station is based on the NVIDIA Jetson Nano Development Kit Operating System, which in turn is based on Ubuntu Linux. The central component responsible for detecting the Bird@Edge Mics, executing the processing pipeline and transmitting the results is called birdedged (Bird@Edge Daemon). It continuously searches for newly connected Bird@Edge devices and restarts the processing pipeline accordingly when devices are found or dropped. Bird species recognition results from the processing pipeline are captured and transmitted to the InfluxDB server system. The server system

---

[4] https://github.com/umr-ds/BirdEdge/tree/main/BirdEdge-Client.

that collects data from potentially multiple Bird@Edge implementations runs Grafana, a dashboard visualization WebUI designed specifically for stream data[5].

The operating system running on Bird@Edge Stations is built using pimod [10] and is available online[6]. NVIDIA's licenses do not allow to redistribute complete operating system images, however pimod allows to reduce the necessary steps and easily create the images.

4   Recognizing Bird Species in Soundscapes

In this section, we describe our deep learning approach to bird species recognition in audio recordings including the preprocessing steps, the neural network as well as its optimization and deployment on the NVIDIA Jetson Nano edge device. The deep neural network model is designed to recognize 82 bird species indigenous in Germany and background noise that is typical for German forests.

4.1   Audio Preprocessing

We selected 44.1 kHz as the sampling rate and analyzed frequencies up to 22.05 kHz to cover the frequency ranges of the bird song patterns. The task is considered as a classification problem, aiming to recognize bird species in 5-s audio snippets. To avoid overfitting and enrich our data set, we randomly select these 5-s snippets and add randomly selected noise from up to four background samples. This encourages our model to focus on the patterns that are important for species recognition. The recognition is based on visual representations of the frequency spectrum as it changes over time, called spectrograms. In our case, we use Mel spectrograms that are generated using 128 Mel bands and an FFT window size of 1,024.

4.2   Neural Network Architecture

Our approach to recognize bird species relies on an EfficientNet-B3 [22] architecture pre-trained on ImageNet [21]. The model is fine-tuned in two phases to target domain using the Adam [15] optimizer. In the first phase, we only train the last, randomly initialized layer for 40 epochs with an initial learning rate of 0.004, while the remaining layers with pre-trained weights are frozen. In the second phase, we train all layers of the model until convergence, while reducing the initial learning rate by a factor of 10. Furthermore, a binary cross-entropy loss combined with modulation factors motivated by the success of focal loss [16] in the field of object detection are used to emphasize difficult samples during the training process. Since the underlying data set is only weakly labeled, we use positive training samples for one species as negative samples for the others. Furthermore, samples labeled negative from expert feedback are defined as hard negatives in the following. Our loss function is defined as follows:

---

[5] https://grafana.com.

[6] https://github.com/umr-ds/BirdAtEdge-OS.

$$L = \sum_{k=1}^{K} l(y_k, p_k),$$

$$l(y, p) = \begin{cases} -\alpha_{pos}(1-p)^{\gamma} \log(p) & \text{if } y \text{ is positive} \\ -\alpha_n p^{\gamma} \log(1-p) & \text{if } y \text{ is negative} \\ -\alpha_{hn} p^{\gamma} \log(1-p) & \text{if } y \text{ is hard negative} \end{cases}$$

where K is the number of bird classes, p_k is the predicted probability for the k-th class, y_k is the k-th ground truth label, α_{pos} is the weighting factor for positive labels, α_n for negative or undefined labels, α_{hn} for hard negative labels and γ is the focusing parameter.

We implemented our approach using the TensorFlow deep learning framework [1]. For audio processing and especially spectrogram generation, we use the librosa library [17].

4.3 Optimizing the Neural Network for Edge Devices

To speed up inference, we optimized our model using the TensorRT[7] library. This library includes an inference optimizer for CUDA-capable target devices that applies various operations, such as quantization and memory optimization, to reduce the inference time. In particular, the floating point precision is reduced by quantizing to FP16 or INT8, while maintaining high accuracy. We optimized our model by using FP16 quantization in addition to the original FP32 weights, since the NVIDIA Jetson Nano does not support INT8 computations natively. Furthermore, we applied target-specific auto-tuning to select the best algorithms and quantization for each layer.

4.4 Inference

We use the DeepStream SDK[8] to deploy our optimized model on the NVIDIA Jetson Nano board with high throughput rates. DeepStream is based on the GStreamer framework and provides a pipeline that takes an input stream and performs hardware accelerated inference on it. An overview of our pipeline composed with DeepStream is presented in Fig. 4. First, the N HTTP streams are read and parsed from the WiFi signal. Since the microphone we used (see Sect. 3 for details) induces noise in the lowest frequency bands, we apply a highpass filter that attenuates all frequencies 120 Hz to each stream. These frequencies are irrelevant for bird species recognition and can therefore be neglected. We prefer the Chebyshev highpass filter over the windowed sinc filter, because it is much faster. Next, we use DeepStream's stream muxer to bundle our streams into one batch and forward the data to the NvInferAudio plugin. This plugin provides

---

[7] https://developer.nvidia.com/tensorrt.
[8] https://developer.nvidia.com/deepstream-sdk.

inference for audio streams and automatically generates the respective Mel spectrograms. Finally, the spectrograms are passed to our model with a batch size of N, and the obtained predictions are retrieved. To be able to process the streams in real-time with a high temporal resolution, we take 5 s snippets with a stride of one second.

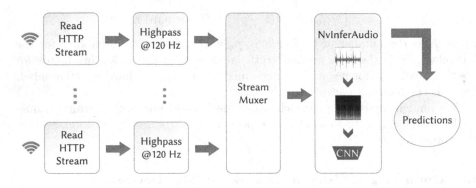

Fig. 4. Overview of the Bird@Edge processing pipeline

5   Experimental Evaluation

In this section, we present experimental results in terms of (a) bird species recognition quality and execution speed, (b) visualization of bird recognition results, as well as (c) power consumption measurements of a Bird@Edge Station and a Bird@Edge Mic.

5.1   Bird Species Recognition Quality and Execution Speed

Data Sets. Our neural network models were evaluated and compared to Bird-NET [14] and BirdNET-Lite (see footnote 2) on data sets collected from three sources. We recorded a first data set with AudioMoth devices [9] in the Marburg Open Forest (MOF). The recordings were labeled on a 5 s basis by human experts. In total, 33 species occur in the MOF data set. Since the amount of labeled data in the MOF data set is not sufficient to train a deep learning model, we acquired further data sets by crawling data from the online bird song collections Xeno-Canto [23] and iNaturalist [11]. The assets included in these data sets have often higher quality and contain less background noise. In our evaluation, we took up to 10% of the files of each class. To make sure that we do not feed snippets without bird calls, we first applied the heuristic used by Kahl et al. [14] and selected up to three 5 s snippets containing a bird call for each test file. Table 1 shows an overview of the training and test data.

Table 1. Overview of the training and test data.

Data set	MOF	Xeno-Canto	iNaturalist
Training	4,294	104,989	30,631
Test	913	2,144	1,365

Quality Metrics. To evaluate the performance of our bird species recognition approach, we use average precision (AP) as our quality metric. The AP score is the most commonly used quality measure for retrieval results and approximates the area under the recall-precision curve. The task of bird call recognition can be considered as a retrieval problem for each species where the annotated audio samples represent the relevant documents. Then, the AP score is calculated from the list of ranked documents as follows:

$$AP(\rho) = \frac{1}{|R \cap \rho^N|} \sum_{k=1}^{N} \frac{|R \cap \rho^k|}{k} \psi(i_k),$$

$$\text{with} \quad \psi(i_k) = \begin{cases} 1 & \text{if } i_k \in R \\ 0 & \text{otherwise} \end{cases}$$

where N is the length of the ranked document list (total number of analyzed audio snippets), $\rho^k = \{i_1, i_2, \ldots, i_k\}$ is the ranked document list up to rank k, R is the set of relevant documents (audio snippets containing a bird call), $|R \cap \rho^k|$ is the number of relevant documents in the top-k of ρ and $\psi(i_k)$ is the relevance function. Generally speaking, AP is the average of the precision values at each relevant document. To evaluate the overall performance, the mean AP score is calculated by taking the mean value of the AP scores from each species.

Table 2. Results (mAP).

Method	MOF	XC	iNat
BirdNET [14]	0.833	0.725	0.725
BirdNET-Lite (see footnote 2)	0.859	0.737	0.714
EfficientNet-B3	0.952	0.820	0.811
Bird@Edge	0.952	0.816	0.819

Results. First, we evaluated the recognition quality of our models, namely the original trained model (EfficientNet-B3) as well as the optimized model (Bird@Edge) and compare the results to BirdNET and BirdNET-Lite. While EfficientNet-B3 is evaluated with TensorFlow on a workstation, the Bird@Edge model is run on the NVIDIA Jetson Nano for inference.

Table 3. Model inference runtimes.

Model	Device	Inference time (ms)
BirdNET-Lite (see footnote 2)	Raspberry Pi-4B	279
Bird@Edge (FP32)	Jetson Nano	64
Bird@Edge	Jetson Nano	54

BirdNET and BirdNET-Lite take the recording location as additional meta-data along with the corresponding audio input. As longitude and latitude, we take the coordinates of the Marburg Open Forest for all data sets, since we only use bird species resident in this specific forest for evaluation. Since the length of the audio input of the BirdNET models differs from our approach, the 5 s samples are split into two 3 s snippets with an overlap of 1 s and the results are averaged for the final prediction.

Table 2 summarizes the experimental bird species recognition results. Our original model (EfficientNet-B3) outperforms BirdNET-Lite as well as BirdNET by roughly 10% in terms of mAP on all data sets considered. While keeping the recognition quality, the optimized Bird@Edge model achieves an inference runtime of 64 ms per spectrogram, as shown in Table 3. Adding model quantization with 16-bit floating point precision where appropriate effectively reduces the inference runtime on the NVIDIA Jetson Nano board by 10 ms. We also compared the runtimes of our models to BirdNET-Lite. Similar to BirdNET-Pi[9], we ran BirdNET-Lite on a Raspberry Pi-4B with 4 CPU threads in parallel. Table 3 reveals that our setting is more than four times faster.

5.2 Visualization of Bird Species Recognition Results

Figure 5 shows a Grafana screenshot of an automatically generated graph of the recognized bird species of a Bird@Edge station. To generate the figure, the publicly available soundscape audio file XC706150 from Xeno-Canto[10] of the target area was played back and captured by the Bird@Edge Mic. The clock time is shown on the x-axis. The confidence of the recognition is plotted on the y-axis. The data is grouped according to the recognized bird species labels, distinguished by color. For every Bird@Edge Mic, a separate figure is generated, and its parameters, e.g., plotted time frame or selection of species, can be configured.

Some observations can be derived from this simple visualization. First, there are several recognized occurrences of *Coccothraustes coccothraustes* (hawfinch) in two clusters. *Picus canus* (grey-headed woodpecker) is detected multiple times over the duration of 12 s, and *Sitta europaea* (Eurasian nuthatch) is detected in two clusters each at the beginning and end of the observation period. All three observations indicate that individuals were heard on the recordings and were

---

[9] https://github.com/mcguirepr89/BirdNET-Pi.
[10] https://xeno-canto.org/706150.

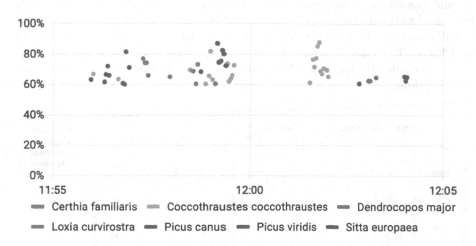

Fig. 5. Grafana panel (x-axis: clock time; y-axis: recognition confidence) showing recognized bird species of a certain Bird@Edge Mic, based on Xeno-Canto file XC706150, recorded by user *brickegickel* (Color figure online)

in the area at these times. For *Loxia curvirostra* (red crossbill) and *Dendrocopos major* (great spotted woodpecker), only 4 and 2 observations were made, respectively; these were probably heard only in the background. More sophisticated analyses can be performed based on researchers' requirements, such as heat maps of the occurrence of species based on their geo-positions, or time-based plots. This can include both short-term considerations, such as the time of day at which certain species are active, or long-term aspects, such as during which period a particular species is particularly active.

5.3 Power Consumption

An important aspect for the applicability of Bird@Edge in real applications is its power consumption. Therefore, we measured the power consumption of a Bird@Edge Station and a Bird@Edge Mic.

To measure the power consumption of a Bird@Edge Station, we used the internal power monitors of the NVIDIA Jetson Nano, since these enable the differentiation between CPU, GPU, and total power consumption. The power measurements were performed in different profiles: a) the 10 W maximum performance profile (default), b) the 5 W low power profile from NVIDIA, and c) a custom low power profile created for Bird@Edge. In this custom power profile, only 2 of the 4 CPU cores were used, running at a maximum frequency of 614 MHz, and the GPU was limited to a maximum of 230 MHz. As a baseline, the power consumption is measured with 5 connected Bird@Edge mics, and only the measured values while the pipeline is running are averaged. In this setup, the maximum performance mode requires 4.86 W, the low power profile 4.19 W and the custom low power mode only requires 3.16 W, i.e., roughly 35% compared to the maximum performance mode with no performance degradation observable. Our observations during the execution of the experiments suggest that the GPU's dynamic frequency scaling algorithm tends to be too conservative to permanently lower the clock and thus prevents the possible lower power consumption.

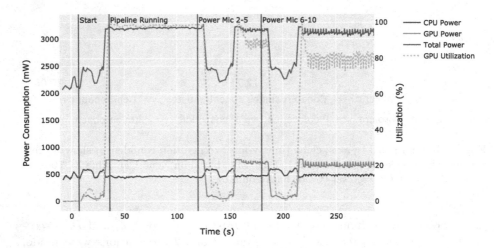

Fig. 6. Power consumption of a Bird@Edge Station in a dynamic scenario.

Figure 6 shows the power consumption of a Bird@Edge station in a short scenario with a changing number of connected Bird@Edge Mics. At the beginning, the system is switched on, but the neural network for bird species is not running; the system needs 2.1 W in this state. At t = 0, the neural network is started with a Bird@Edge Mic already connected to the station. The neural network model is loaded into memory from t = 6, for which the CPU requires up to 0.59 W. From time t = 36, i.e., 30 s after the start of the pipeline, the neural network model runs and forwards results to the backend. In this phase, the Bird@Edge station requires an average of 3.18 W. At t = 120 and t = 180, 4 and 5 additional Bird@Edge Mics are switched on, which first connect to the Bird@Edge Station via WiFi, then are discovered via mDNS, which results in the reconfiguration of the processing pipeline and its restart. In both cases, the reboot took about 35 s, with 5 s for WiFi connection and discovery, and 30 s for pipeline reboot. With 5 and 10 Bird@Edge Mics connected, the Bird@Edge Station requires 3.16 W and 3.13 W, respectively. Particularly noteworthy is the station's lower power consumption when a larger number of Bird@Edge Mics are connected. Figure 6 indicates that GPU utilization is lower with many Bird@Edge Mics connected, compared to smaller numbers of Bird@Edge Mics (98% with 1 client, 88% with

5 clients, 80% with 10 clients). This is probably due to internals of the Deep-Stream SDK and may be influenced by the implementation, e.g., with respect to the handling of unused streams.

The magnitude of the Bird@Edge Station's power consumption necessitates the use of an LFP, VRLA or AGM battery, which at 12 V typically have a capacity of 50 to 200 Ah. The available 60 to 2400 Wh allow the operation of a Bird@Edge Station from 7 up to 31 days. In combination with a solar panel between 50 and 100 W, a continuous operation is also possible during periods of weak sunlight.

To measure the power consumption of a Bird@Edge Mic, we used a Monsoon High Voltage Power Monitor[11] and connected the ESP32 using the 3.3 V input. The measurements of a Bird@Edge Mic show a power usage of 665 mW whenever the stream is activated and data is sent to the station. The power measurements were performed with three different off-the-shelf ESP32 boards, since the additional electronics present on the boards can have an additional impact on power consumption. The three boards differed only slightly in terms of power consumption: 0.452 W was needed by the *Adafruit HUZZAH32*, 0.452 W by the *Joy-IT NodeMCU ESP32*, and 0.421 W by the *SparkFun ESP32 Thing Plus*. The latter[12] is the board of choice for our application, due to the lowest power consumption, a direct LiPo battery connector, and an external WiFi antenna.

To get a realistic estimation of the battery life of a Bird@Edge Mic, further measurements were performed with 3.7 Volt via the corresponding connectors for LiPo batteries. The SparkFun board required 0.468 W or 126.6 mA in operation, whereas the Adafruit board required 132.9 mA, or 0.492 W. LiPo batteries are available in a wide range of capacities, from 100 mAh to over 30000 mAh. Typical capacities, as they are found in smartphones and can be purchased cheaply, are around 3500 mAh, which allow a runtime of 27.6 h. In combination with a small solar panel of around 10 W, continuous operation is thus easily feasible.

6 Conclusion

We presented Bird@Edge, an *Edge AI* system for recognizing bird species in audio recordings to support real-time biodiversity monitoring. Bird@Edge is composed of embedded edge devices, such as ESP32-based microphones and NVIDIA Jetson Nano boards, operating in a distributed system to enable efficient, continuous evaluation of soundscapes recorded in forests. We presented a deep neural network based on the EfficientNet-B3 architecture and optimized for execution on a NVIDIA Jetson Nano board to recognize bird species in soundscapes. It outperforms the state-of-the-art BirdNET neural network on several data sets and achieves a recognition quality of up to 95.2% mean average precision on soundscape recordings in the Marburg Open Forest, a research and teaching forest of the University of Marburg, Germany. Measurements of the

---

[11] https://www.msoon.com/high-voltage-power-monitor.
[12] https://www.sparkfun.com/products/15663.

power consumption of Bird@Edge Station and Bird@Edge Mics show that the system has an acceptable demand of 3.18 W plus 0.492 W for each Bird@Edge Mic, which can be covered by reasonably sized batteries and solar panels, highlighting the real-world applicability of the approach. All software and firmware components of Bird@Edge are available under open source licenses[13].

There are several areas for future research. For example, self-supervised learning could be used to leverage the vast amount of unlabeled data and to improve the recognition quality on the target domain. Furthermore, continual and federated learning of machine learning models at the edge are interesting future research topics. Finally, a real-world test of several Bird@Edge deployments should be performed to identify potential problems in harsh environments.

Acknowledgments. This work is funded by the Hessian State Ministry for Higher Education, Research and the Arts (HMWK) (LOEWE Natur 4.0, LOEWE emergenCITY, and hessian.AI Connectom AI4Birds), the German Academic Exchange Service (DAAD) (Transformation Partnership Program; Project OLIVIA), and the German Research Foundation (DFG, Project 210487104 - Collaborative Research Center SFB 1053 MAKI).

References

1. Abadi, M., et al.: TensorFlow: large-scale machine learning on heterogeneous systems (2015). https://www.tensorflow.org/
2. Darras, K., et al.: Comparing the sampling performance of sound recorders versus point counts in bird surveys: a meta-analysis. J. Appl. Ecol. **55**(6), 2575–2586 (2018). https://doi.org/10.1111/1365-2664.13229
3. Disabato, S., Canonaco, G., Flikkema, P.G., Roveri, M., Alippi, C.: Birdsong detection at the edge with deep learning. In: 2021 IEEE International Conference on Smart Computing (SMARTCOMP), pp. 9–16. IEEE (2021)
4. Dosovitskiy, A., et al.: An image is worth 16x16 words: transformers for image recognition at scale. In: 9th International Conference on Learning Representations, ICLR 2021, Austria (2021)
5. Gallacher, S., et al.: Shazam for bats: internet of things for continuous real-time biodiversity monitoring. IET Smart Cities **3**(3), 171–183 (2021)
6. Gong, Y., Chung, Y., Glass, J.R.: AST: audio spectrogram transformer. In: Interspeech 2021, pp. 571–575 (2021). https://doi.org/10.21437/Interspeech
7. He, K., Zhang, X., Ren, S., Sun, J.: Deep residual learning for image recognition. In: 2016 IEEE Conference on Computer Vision and Pattern Recognition (CVPR) (2016). https://doi.org/10.1109/CVPR.2016.90
8. Henkel, C., Pfeiffer, P., Singer, P.: Recognizing bird species in diverse soundscapes under weak supervision. In: Faggioli, G., Ferro, N., Joly, A., Maistro, M., Piroi, F. (eds.) Working Notes of CLEF 2021 - Conference and Labs of the Evaluation Forum, Bucharest, Romania, 21–24 September 2021. CEUR Workshop Proceedings, vol. 2936, pp. 1579–1586. CEUR-WS.org (2021). http://ceur-ws.org/Vol-2936/paper-134.pdf

---

[13] https://github.com/umr-ds/BirdEdge.

9. Hill, A.P., Prince, P., Snaddon, J.L., Doncaster, C.P., Rogers, A.: Audiomoth: a low-cost acoustic device for monitoring biodiversity and the environment. HardwareX **6**, e00073 (2019). https://doi.org/10.1016/j.ohx.2019.e00073

10. Höchst, J., Penning, A., Lampe, P., Freisleben, B.: PIMOD: a tool for configuring single-board computer operating system images. In: 2020 IEEE Global Humanitarian Technology Conference (GHTC 2020), Seattle, USA, pp. 1–8, October 2020. https://doi.org/10.1109/GHTC46280.2020.9342928

11. iNaturalist: A community for naturalists. https://www.inaturalist.org/

12. Kahl, S., et al.: Overview of BirdCLEF 2020: bird sound recognition in complex acoustic environments. In: Cappellato, L., Eickhoff, C., Ferro, N., Névéol, A. (eds.) Working Notes of CLEF 2020 - Conference and Labs of the Evaluation Forum, Thessaloniki, Greece, 22–25 September 2020. CEUR Workshop Proceedings, vol. 2696. CEUR-WS.org (2020). http://ceur-ws.org/Vol-2696/paper_262.pdf

13. Kahl, S., et al.: Overview of BirdCLEF 2021: bird call identification in soundscape recordings. In: Faggioli, G., Ferro, N., Joly, A., Maistro, M., Piroi, F. (eds.) Working Notes of CLEF 2021 - Conference and Labs of the Evaluation Forum, Bucharest, Romania, 21–24 September 2021. CEUR Workshop Proceedings, vol. 2936, pp. 1437–1450. CEUR-WS.org (2021). http://ceur-ws.org/Vol-2936/paper-123.pdf

14. Kahl, S., Wood, C.M., Eibl, M., Klinck, H.: BirdNET: a deep learning solution for avian diversity monitoring. Eco. Inform. **61**, 101236 (2021). https://doi.org/10.1016/j.ecoinf.2021.101236

15. Kingma, D.P., Ba, J.: Adam: a method for stochastic optimization. In: Bengio, Y., LeCun, Y. (eds.) 3rd International Conference on Learning Representations, ICLR 2015, San Diego, CA, USA, 7–9 May 2015, Conference Track Proceedings (2015). https://arxiv.org/abs/1412.6980

16. Lin, T.Y., Goyal, P., Girshick, R., He, K., Dollar, P.: Focal loss for dense object detection. In: 2017 IEEE International Conference on Computer Vision (ICCV), October 2017

17. McFee, B., et al.: librosa: audio and music signal analysis in python. In: Proceedings of the 14th Python in Science Conference, vol. 8 (2015)

18. Merenda, M., Porcaro, C., Iero, D.: Edge machine learning for AI-enabled IoT devices: a review. Sensors **20**(9), 2533 (2020)

19. Mühling, M., Franz, J., Korfhage, N., Freisleben, B.: Bird species recognition via neural architecture search. In: Cappellato, L., Eickhoff, C., Ferro, N., Névéol, A. (eds.) Working Notes of CLEF 2020 - Conference and Labs of the Evaluation Forum, Thessaloniki, Greece, 22–25 September 2020. CEUR Workshop Proceedings, vol. 2696. CEUR-WS.org (2020). http://ceur-ws.org/Vol-2696/paper_188.pdf

20. Puget, J.F.: STFT transformers for bird song recognition. In: Working Notes of CLEF 2021 - Conference and Labs of the Evaluation Forum, Bucharest, Romania, 21–24 September 2021. CEUR Workshop Proceedings, vol. 2936. CEUR-WS.org (2021). http://ceur-ws.org/Vol-2936/paper-137.pdf

21. Russakovsky, O., et al.: ImageNet large scale visual recognition challenge. Int. J. Comput. Vision **115**(3), 211–252 (2015)

22. Tan, M., Le, Q.V.: Efficientnet: rethinking model scaling for convolutional neural networks. In: Chaudhuri, K., Salakhutdinov, R. (eds.) Proceedings of the 36th International Conference on Machine Learning, ICML 2019, 9–15 June 2019, Long Beach, California, USA. Proceedings of Machine Learning Research, vol. 97, pp. 6105–6114. PMLR (2019)

23. Xeno-canto: Sharing bird sounds from around the world. https://www.xeno-canto.org/

24. Zoph, B., Le, Q.V.: Neural architecture search with reinforcement learning. In: 5th International Conference on Learning Representations, ICLR 2017, Toulon, France, 24–26 April 2017, Conference Track Proceedings (2017)
25. Zualkernan, I., Judas, J., Mahbub, T., Bhagwagar, A., Chand, P.: An AIoT system for bat species classification. In: 2020 IEEE International Conference on Internet of Things and Intelligence System (IoTaIS), pp. 155–160 (2021). https://doi.org/ 10.1109/IoTaIS50849.2021.9359704

Solvability of Byzantine Fault-Tolerant Causal Ordering Problems

Anshuman Misra and Ajay D. Kshemkalyani(✉)

University of Illinois at Chicago, Chicago, IL 60607, USA
{amisra7,ajay}@uic.edu

Abstract. Causal ordering in an asynchronous setting is a fundamental paradigm for collaborative software systems. Previous work in the area concentrates on ordering messages in a faultless setting and on ordering broadcasts under various fault models. To the best of our knowledge, Byzantine fault-tolerant causal ordering has not been studied for unicasts and multicasts in an asynchronous setting. In this paper we first show that protocols presented in previous work fail for unicasts and multicasts under Byzantine faults in an asynchronous setting. Then we analyze, propose, and prove results on the solvability of the related problems of causal unicasts, multicasts, and broadcasts in an asynchronous system with one or more Byzantine failures.

Keywords: Byzantine fault-tolerance · Causal order · Broadcast · Causality · Asynchronous · Message-passing

1 Introduction

Causality is an important tool in reasoning about distributed systems [15]. Theoretically causality is defined by the *happens before* [16] relation on the set of events. In practice, logical clocks [17] are used to timestamp events (messages as well) in order to capture causality. If message $m1$ causally precedes $m2$ and both are sent to p_i, then $m1$ must be delivered before $m2$ at p_i to enforce causal order [2]. Causal ordering ensures that causally related updates to data occur in a valid manner respecting that causal relation. Applications of causal ordering include distributed data stores, fair resource allocation, and collaborative applications such as social networks, multiplayer online gaming, group editing of documents, event notification systems, and distributed virtual environments.

The only work on causal ordering under the Byzantine failure model is the recent result by Auvolat et al. [1] which considered Byzantine-tolerant causal broadcasts, and the work in [11,12,25] which relied on broadcasts. To our knowledge, there has been no work on Byzantine-tolerant causal ordering of unicasts and multicasts. It is important to solve this problem under the Byzantine failure model as opposed to a failure-free setting because it mirrors the real world.

© The Author(s), under exclusive license to Springer Nature Switzerland AG 2022
M.-A. Koulali and M. Mezini (Eds.): NETYS 2022, LNCS 13464, pp. 87–103, 2022.
https://doi.org/10.1007/978-3-031-17436-0_7

Table 1. Solvability of Byzantine causal unicast, broadcast, and multicast in a fully asynchronous setting. Results for multicasts are the same as for unicasts, see Sect. 7. FIP = Full-Information Protocol.

Problem	Model	Liveness + Weak safety	Weak safety − Liveness	Strong safety + Liveness	Strong safety − Liveness
Unicast Sect. 5	No signatures	(1) no Theorem 1	(2) yes Theorem 2	(3) no Theorem 3	(4) no Theorem 4
	w/ signatures	(5) no[a] Theorem 5	(6) yes implied by Theorem 2	(7) no Theorem 6	(8) no Theorem 7
	FIP	(9) yes Sect. 8	(10) yes implied by Theorem 2	(11) no Sect. 8	(12) no Sect. 8
Broadcast Sect. 6	No signatures	(13) yes algorithm in [1]	(14) yes algorithm in [1]	(15) no Theorem 8	(16) no Theorem 9
	w/signatures	(17) yes implied by (13)	(18) yes implied by (14)	(19) no Theorem 10	(20) no Theorem 11
	FIP	(21) yes implied by (13)	(22) yes implied by (14)	(23) no Sect. 8	(24) no Sect. 8

[a] This is "yes" if the Byzantine processes are rational, see Sect. 8.

The main contributions of this paper are as follows:

1. The RST algorithm [23] provides an abstraction of causal ordering of point-to-point and multicast messages, and all other (more efficient) algorithms can be cast in terms of this algorithm. We describe an attack on liveness, that we call the artificial boosting attack, that can force all communication to stop when running the RST algorithm.
2. We prove that causal ordering of unicasts and multicasts in an asynchronous system with even one Byzantine node is impossible because liveness cannot be guaranteed. We define weak safety and strong safety and prove that if liveness is to be guaranteed, then weak safety cannot be guaranteed. Further, we prove that strong safety cannot be guaranteed. We also prove these results assuming digital signatures are allowed.
3. We prove that for causal ordering of broadcasts under Byzantine faults, if liveness is to be guaranteed, then weak safety can be guaranteed. Further, we prove that strong safety cannot be guaranteed. We also prove these results assuming digital signatures are allowed.
4. We show that for unicasts, multicasts, and broadcasts, a Full-Information Protocol (FIP) [2,9] can provide liveness + weak safety, but no strong safety. We also show that for rational processes, which act Byzantine only if they cannot be detected/suspected, the unsolvability results remain except for liveness + weak safety for unicasts and multicasts, with digital signatures.

Table 1 summarizes the main results about the solvability of the related problems of unicast, broadcast, and multicast in an asynchronous system with Byzantine faults.

2   Previous Work

Algorithms for causal ordering of point-to-point messages under a fault-free model have been described in [23,24]. These point-to-point causal ordering algorithms extend to implement causal multicasts in a failure-free setting [6,7,13,14,22]. The RST algorithm [23] is a canonical algorithm for causal ordering.

There has been some work on causal broadcasts under various failure models. Causal ordering of broadcast messages under crash failures in asynchronous systems was introduced in [2]. This algorithm required each message to carry the entire set of messages in its causal past as control information. The algorithm in [21] implements crash fault-tolerant causal broadcast in asynchronous systems with a focus on optimizing the amount of control information piggybacked on each message. An algorithm for causally ordering broadcast messages in an asynchronous system with Byzantine failures is proposed in [1]. There has been recent interest in applying the Byzantine fault model to implement causal consistency in distributed shared memory and replicated databases [11,12,25]. These rely on broadcasts, e.g., on Byzantine reliable broadcast [3] in [12] and on PBFT (total order broadcast) [5] in [11]. To the best of our knowledge, no paper has examined the feasibility of or solved causal ordering of unicasts and multicasts in an asynchronous system with Byzantine failures.

3   System Model

The distributed system is modelled as an undirected graph $G = (P,C)$. Here P is the set of processes communicating asynchronously over a geographically dispersed network. Let $|P| = n$. C is the set of communication channels over which processes communicate by message passing. The channels are assumed to be FIFO. G is a complete graph. For a message send event at time t_1, the corresponding receive event occurs at time $t_2 \in [t_1, \infty)$. A correct process behaves exactly as specified by the algorithm whereas a Byzantine process may exhibit arbitrary behaviour including crashing at any point during the execution. A Byzantine process cannot impersonate another process or spawn new processes. Besides authenticated channels and use of signatures, we do not consider the use of other cryptographic primitives.

Let e_i^x, where $x \geq 0$, denote the x-th event executed by process p_i. In order to deliver messages in causal order, we require a framework that captures causality as a partial order on a distributed execution. The *happens before* [16] relation, denoted $\rightarrow$, is an irreflexive, asymmetric, and transitive partial order defined over events in a distributed execution that captures causality.

Definition 1. *The happens before relation on events consists of the following rules:*

1. **Program Order:** *For the sequence of events $\langle e_i^1, e_i^2, \ldots \rangle$ executed by process p_i, $\forall\, k, j$ such that $k < j$ we have $e_i^k \rightarrow e_i^j$.*
2. **Message Order:** *If event e_i^x is a message send event executed at process p_i and e_j^y is the corresponding message receive event at process p_j, then $e_i^x \rightarrow e_j^y$.*
3. **Transitive Order:** *Given events e and e'' in execution trace α, if $\exists\, e' \in \alpha$ such that $e \rightarrow e' \wedge e' \rightarrow e''$ then $e \rightarrow e''$.*

Next, we define the happens before relation $\rightarrow$ on the set of all application-level messages R.

Definition 2. *The happens before relation on messages consists of the following rules:*

1. *The set of messages delivered from any $p_i \in P$ by a process is totally ordered by $\rightarrow$.*
2. *If p_i sent or delivered message m before sending message m', then $m \rightarrow m'$.*
3. *If $m \rightarrow m' \wedge m' \rightarrow m''$ then $m \rightarrow m''$.*

Definition 3. *The causal past of message m is denoted as $CP(m)$ and defined as the set of messages in R that causally precede message m under $\rightarrow$.*

We require an extension of the happens before relation on messages to accommodate the possibility of Byzantine behaviour. We present a partial order on messages called *Byzantine happens before*, denoted as $\xrightarrow{B}$, defined on S, the set of all application-level messages that are both sent by and delivered at correct processes in P.

Definition 4. *The Byzantine happens before relation consists of the following rules:*

1. *The set of messages delivered from any correct process $p_i \in P$ by any correct process is totally ordered by $\xrightarrow{B}$.*
2. *If p_i is a correct process and p_i sent or delivered message m (to/from another correct process) before sending message m', then $m \xrightarrow{B} m'$.*
3. *If $m \xrightarrow{B} m' \wedge m' \xrightarrow{B} m''$ then $m \xrightarrow{B} m''$.*

The Byzantine causal past of a message is defined as follows:

Definition 5. *The Byzantine causal past of message m, denoted as $BCP(m)$, is defined as the set of messages in S that causally precede message m under $\xrightarrow{B}$.*

The correctness of a Byzantine causal order unicast/multicast/broadcast is specified on $(R, \rightarrow)$ and $(S, \xrightarrow{B})$. We now define the correctness criteria that a causal ordering algorithm must satisfy. Ideally, strong safety and liveness should be satisfied because, as we show for application semantics, strong safety is desirable over weak safety.

Definition 6. **Weak Safety:** $\forall m' \in BCP(m)$ such that m' and m are sent to the same correct process(es), no correct process delivers m before m'.

Definition 7. **Strong Safety:** $\forall m' \in CP(m)$ such that m' and m are sent to the same correct process(es), no correct process delivers m before m'.

Definition 8. **Liveness:** Each message sent by a correct process to another correct process will eventually be delivered.

When $m \xrightarrow{B} m'$, then all processes that sent messages along the causal chain from m to m' are correct processes. This definition is different from $m \rightarrow_M m'$ [1], where M was defined as the set of all application-level messages delivered at correct processes, and $MCP(m')$ could be defined as the set of messages in M that causally precede m'. When $m \rightarrow_M m'$, then all processes, *except the first*, that sent messages along the causal chain from m to m' are correct processes. Our definition of $\xrightarrow{B}$ (Definition 4) allows for the purest notion of safety – weak safety (Definition 6) – which we show as result (2) in Table 1 that can be guaranteed to hold under unicasts and multicasts. The equivalent safety definition, that could be defined on MCP instead of BCP, would not be guaranteed under unicasts and multicasts, but is satisfied under broadcasts [1]. Our definition of $\xrightarrow{B}$ and $\rightarrow_M$ [1] both make the assumption that from the second to the last process that send messages along the causal chain from m to m', are correct processes.

4 Attacks Due to Byzantine Behaviour

All existing algorithms for implementing causal order for point-to-point messages in asynchronous systems use some form of *logical timestamps*. This principle is abstracted by the RST algorithm [23]. Each message m sent to p_i is accompanied by a *logical timestamp* in the form of a matrix clock providing information about send events in the causal past of m. This is to ensure that all messages $m' \in CP(m)$ whose destination is p_i are delivered at p_i before m. The implementation is as follows:

1. Each process p_i maintains (a) a vector $Delivered_i$ of size n with $Delivered_i[j]$ storing a count of messages sent by p_j and delivered by p_i, and (b) a matrix M_i of size $n \times n$, where $M_i[j,k]$ stores the count of the number of messages sent by p_j to p_k as known to p_i.
2. When p_i sends message m to p_j, m has a piggybacked matrix timestamp M^m, which is the value of M_i before the send event. Then $M_i[i,j] = M_i[i,j] + 1$.
3. When message m is received by p_i, it is not delivered until the following *delivery condition* is met: $\forall k, M^m[k,i] \leq Delivered_i[k]$.
4. After delivering a message m, p_i merges the logical timestamp associated with m with its own matrix clock, as $\forall j, k, M_i[j,k] = \max(M_i[j,k], M^m[j,k])$.

A Byzantine process may fabricate values in the matrix timestamp in order to disrupt the causal ordering of messages in an asynchronous execution. The attacks are described in the following subsections.

4.1 Artificial Boosting Attack

A Byzantine process p_j may increase values of $M_j[x, *]$ beyond the number of messages actually sent by process x to one or more processes. When p_j sends a message with such a Byzantine timestamp to any correct process p_k, it will result in p_k recording Byzantine values in its M_k matrix. These Byzantine values will get propagated across correct processes upon further message passing. This will finally result in correct processes no longer delivering messages from other correct processes because they will be waiting for messages to arrive that have never been sent.

As an example, consider a single malicious process p_j. p_j forges values in its M_j matrix as follows: if p_j knows that p_i (where i may be j) has sent x messages to p_l, it can set $M_j[i, l] = (x + d)$, $d > 0$. When p_k delivers a message from p_j, it sets $M_k[i, l] = (x + d)$. Finally, when p_k sends a message m to p_l, p_l will wait for messages to arrive from p_i (messages that p_i has never sent) before delivering m. This is because $(Delivered_l[i] \leq x) \wedge (M^m[i, l] = x + d)$ $\implies (Delivered_l[i] < M^m[i, l])$. Therefore, p_l will never be able to deliver m. A single Byzantine process p_j has effectively blocked all communication from p_k to p_l. This attack can be replicated for all pairs of processes by p_j. Thus, a single Byzantine process can block all communication (including between each pair of correct processes), thus mounting a liveness attack.

4.2 Safety Violation Attack

A Byzantine process p_j may decrease values of $M^m[*, k]$ to smaller values than the true causal past of message m and send it to a correct process p_k. This may cause m to get delivered out of order at p_k resulting in a causal violation. Furthermore, if p_j decreases the values of $M^m[*, *]$ to smaller values than the true causal past of message m then, once m is delivered to p_k and p_k sends a message m' to correct process p_l, there may be a further causal violation due to a lack of transitive causal data transfer from m to p_k prior to sending m'. These potential causal violations are a result of the possibility of a message getting delivered before messages in its causal past sent to a common destination.

As an example, consider a single malicious process p_j. p_j forges values in the M^m matrix as follows: if p_j knows that p_i has sent x messages to p_k, p_j can set $M^m[i, k] = x - 1$ and send m to p_k. If m is received at p_k before the xth message m' from p_i is delivered, m may get delivered before m' resulting in a causal violation of strong safety at p_i. In another attack, if p_j knows that p_i has sent y messages to p_l, it can reduce $M^m[i, l] = y - 1$ and send m to p_k. Assume p_k delivers m and sends m' to p_l. If m' arrives at p_l before m'', the yth message from p_i to p_l, arrives at p_l, m' may get delivered before m'' resulting in a causal violation of strong safety at p_l. In this way, a malicious process may cause violations of strong safety (but not weak safety) at multiple correct processes by sending a single message with incorrect causal control information.

5   Results for Unicasts

Causal order of messages can be enforced by either: (a) performing appropriate actions at the receiver's end, or (b) performing appropriate actions at the sender's end.

To enforce causal ordering at the receiver's end, one needs to track causality, and some form of a logical clock is required to order messages (or events) by utilizing timestamps at the receiving process. Traditionally, logical clocks use transitively collected control information attached to each incoming message for this purpose. The RST abstraction [23] (refer Sect. 4) is used. However, in case there is a single Byzantine node p_j in an asynchronous system, it can change the values of M_j at the time of sending m to p_i. This may result in safety or liveness violations when p_i communicates with a third process p_k as explained in Sect. 4. Lemma 1 proves that transitively collected control information by a receiver can lead to liveness attacks in asynchronous systems with Byzantine nodes.

As it is not possible to ensure causal delivery of messages by actions at the receiver's end, therefore, constraints on when the sending process can send messages need to be enforced to maintain causal delivery of messages. Each sender process would need to wait to get an acknowledgement from the receiver before sending the next message. Messages would get delivered in FIFO order at the receiver. While waiting for an acknowledgment, each process would continue to receive and deliver messages. This is important to maintain concurrency and avoid deadlocks. This can be implemented by using non-blocking synchronous sends, with the added constraint that all send events are *atomic* with respect to each other. However, Lemma 2 proves that even this approach would fail in the presence of one or more Byzantine nodes. Theorem 1 puts these results together and proves that it is impossible to causally order unicast messages in an asynchronous system with one or more Byzantine nodes.

Lemma 1. *A single Byzantine process can execute a liveness attack when control information for causality tracking is transitively propagated and used by a receiving process for enforcing causal order under weak safety of unicasts.*

Proof. Transitively propagated control information for causality tracking, whether by explicitly maintaining the counts of the number of messages sent between each process pair, or by maintaining causal barriers, or by encoding the dependency information optimally or by any other mechanism, can be abstracted by the causal ordering abstraction [23], described in Sect. 4. Each message m sent to p_k is accompanied with a *logical timestamp* in the form of a matrix clock providing an encoding of $CP(m)$. The encoding of $CP(m)$ effectively maintains an entry to count the number of messages sent by p_i to p_j, $\forall p_i, p_j \in P$. Such an encoding will consist of a total of n^2 entries, n entries per process. Therefore, in order to ensure that all messages $m' \in CP(m)$ whose destination is p_k are delivered at p_k before m, the matrix clock M whose definition and operation was reviewed in Sect. 4 is used to encode $CP(m)$.

Let $m' \xrightarrow{B} m$, where m' and m are sent by p_i and p_j, respectively, to common destination p_k. The value $M_i[i, k]$ after sending m' propagates transitively along the causal chain of messages to p_j and then to p_k. But before p_j sends m to p_k, it has received a message m'' (transitively) from a Byzantine process p_x in which $M^{m''}[y, k]$ is artificially inflated (for a liveness attack using $M^{m''}[y, k]$). This inflated value propagates on m from p_j to p_k as $M^m[y, k]$. To enforce weak safety between m' and m, p_k implements the delivery condition in rule 3 of the RST abstraction (Sect. 4), and will not be able to deliver m because of p_x's liveness attack wherein $M^m[y, k] \nleq Delivered_k[y]$. p_k uniformly waits for messages from any process(es) that prevent the delivery condition from being satisfied and thus waits for $M^m[y, k] - Delivered_k[y]$ messages from p_y, which may never arrive if they were not sent. (If p_k is not to keep waiting for delivery of the arrived m, it might try to flush the channel from p_y to p_k by sending a *probe* to p_y and waiting for the *ack* from p_y. This approach can be seen to violate liveness, e.g., when p_x attacks p_k via p_i on $M^{m'}[j, k]$ and via p_j on $M^m[i, k]$. Morever, p_y may never reply with the *ack* if it is Byzantine, and p_k has no means of differentiating between a slow channel to/from a correct p_y and a Byzantine p_y that may never reply. So p_k waits indefinitely.) Therefore, the system is open to liveness attacks in the presence of a single Byzantine node.   □

Lemma 2. *A single Byzantine process can execute a liveness attack even if a sending process sends a message only when the receiving process is guaranteed not to be subject to a weak safety attack, i.e., only when it is safe to send the message and hence its delivery at the receiver will not violate weak safety, on causal order of unicasts.*

Proof. The only way that a sending process p_i can ensure weak safety of a message m it sends to p_j is to enforce that all messages m' such that $m \xrightarrow{B} m'$ and m' is sent to p_j will reach the (common) destination p_j after m reaches p_j. Assuming FIFO delivery at a process based on the order of arrival, m will be delivered before m'.

The only way the sender p_i can enforce that m' will arrive after m at p_j is not to send another message to any process p_k after sending m until p_i knows that m has arrived at p_j. p_i can know m has arrived at p_j only when p_j replies with an *ack* to p_i and p_i receives this *ack*. However, p_i cannot differentiate between a malicious p_j that never replies with the *ack* and a slow channel to/from a correct process p_j. Thus, p_i will wait indefinitely for the *ack* and not send any other message to any other process. This is a liveness attack by a Byzantine process p_j.   □

Theorem 1. *It is impossible to guarantee liveness and weak safety while causally ordering point-to-point messages in an asynchronous message passing system with one or more Byzantine processes.*

Proof. From Lemmas 1 and 2, no actions at a sender or at a receiver can prevent a liveness attack (while maintaining weak safety). The theorem follows.   □

Theorem 2. *It is possible to guarantee weak safety without a liveness guarantee while causally ordering point-to-point messages in an asynchronous message passing system with one or more Byzantine processes.*

Proof. The theorem that weak safety can be maintained without liveness guarantees was indirectly proved in the proofs of Lemma 1 and Lemma 2.   □

Theorem 3. *It is impossible to guarantee strong safety (while guaranteeing liveness) while causally ordering point-to-point messages in an asynchronous message passing system with one or more Byzantine processes.*

Proof. Consider $m' \in CP(m)$ sent to common destination p_r, where m' and m are sent by p_i and p_k, respectively. If p_i sends the next messages after m' only when it is safe to do so (as described in the proof of Lemma 2), an attack on strong safety can be mounted because a Byzantine p_i may not follow the above rule; it may send a subsequent message before getting an ack for message m', and message m along the causal chain beginning with a subsequent message may be delivered to the common destination p_r before m' is delivered. Thus, this option cannot be used to guarantee strong safety while guaranteeing liveness.

The only other way for safe delivery of m is for p_r to rely on transitively propagated control information about $CP(m)$. There exists a chain of messages ordered by $\rightarrow$ from m' to m and sent by processes along this path H. We use the RST abstraction for the transmission of control information about $CP(m)$. Let $M_i[i,r]$ be x when m' is sent. A Byzantine process along H, that sends m'', can set $M^{m''}[i,r]$ to a lower value x' than x and thereby propagate x' instead of x along H. $M_k[i,r]$ that is piggybacked on m as $M^m[i,r]$ will be less than x. Hence, a strong safety attack can be mounted at p_r.

Thus, no action at the sender or at the receiver can prevent a strong safety attack.   □

Theorem 4. *It is impossible[1] to guarantee strong safety (even without guaranteeing liveness) while causally ordering point-to-point messages in an asynchronous message passing system with one or more Byzantine processes.*

Proof. The proof of Theorem 3 showed strong safety can never be satisfied. This result was independent of liveness attacks. The same result holds even if liveness attacks can be mounted, and Theorem 1 showed liveness attacks could be mounted on weak safety requirements, which implies they can also be mounted on strong safety requirements.   □

5.1 Results for Unicasts Allowing Digital Signatures

Theorem 5. *It is impossible to guarantee liveness while satisfying weak safety using digital signatures while causally ordering point-to-point messages in an asynchronous message passing system with one or more Byzantine processes.*

Proof. Lemma 2 (sending a message only when a receiver is guaranteed not to have a weak safety attack) can be seen to hold even with the use of digital

---

[1] Here in Theorems 4, 7, 9, and 11, we rule out the trivial solution of not delivering any messages to guarantee strong safety.

signatures. So the only remaining option to guarantee liveness (while satisfying weak safety) is to try to use transitively received control information.

In the RST abstraction, a sending process p_i will sign its row of M^m whereas row s ($\forall s \in P$) is signed by p_s. This allows the receiver process p_j to do the max of its row $M_j[s, *]$ and $M^m[s, *]$ ($\forall s \in P$), both of which were signed by P_s, and update its M_j matrix.

The same liveness attack (while satisfying weak safety), as shown in the proof and scenario in Lemma 1, can be mounted when $y = x$ (i.e., using $M^{m''}[y = x, k]$ in that proof), even with the use of digital signatures. This is because a Byzantine process p_x can always sign its inflated row x entries of M_x. Although this allows the receiver to be reassured that entries in the xth row of M^m were not forged by anyone, it does not help in avoiding the indefinite wait of the liveness attack mounted by p_x.

Thus, liveness cannot be guaranteed while satisfying weak safety despite using digital signatures. □

Theorem 6. *It is impossible to guarantee strong safety while satisfying liveness using digital signatures while causally ordering point-to-point messages in an asynchronous message passing system with one or more Byzantine processes.*

Proof. Consider $m' \in CP(m)$ sent to common destination p_r, where m' and m are sent by p_i and p_k, respectively. If p_i relies on sending the next messages after m' only when it is safe to do so (as described in the proof of Lemma 2), a Byzantine p_i can cause strong safety to be violated by not following the above rule, as shown in the proof of Theorem 3. Thus, this option cannot be used.

The only other way for safe delivery of m while satisfying liveness is for p_r to rely on transitively propagated control information about $CP(m)$; for this we assume the RST abstraction. Consider the following sequence: correct process p_i sends a message m' to p_r, then sends a (signed) message m'' (containing the rows of M_i as $M^{m''}$, where row s is signed by p_s) to p_j. p_j, a Byzantine process, delivers message m'', acts on the message, and then sends a message m_1 to p_k. However, on receiving the message m'' from p_i, p_j does not update $M_j[i, *]$ with the most recently signed row $M^{m''}[i, *]$ received but uses an older row, also signed (earlier) by p_i, pretending as though p_i's message m'' had never been delivered and processed. p_k uses this (older) row of $M_j[i, *]$ received on m_1 as $M^{m_1}[i, *]$ and sets $M_k[i, *]$ to this older value which does not get replaced by p_i's signed row that was piggybacked on m''. p_k now forwards this older row, signed by p_i, as part of M^m it piggybacks on m it sends to p_r. p_r can deliver m even if m' from p_i has not been received. Here, p_i, p_k, and p_r are all correct processes and m' (sent by p_i to p_r) $\rightarrow m$ (sent by p_k to p_r), yet p_r may deliver m before m', thus violating strong safety. The use of digital signatures does not help in preventing such a violation. Hence, a strong safety attack can be mounted at p_r. □

Theorem 7. *It is impossible (see footnote 1) to guarantee strong safety (even without guaranteeing liveness) using digital signatures while causally ordering* *point-to-point messages in an asynchronous message passing system with one or more Byzantine processes.*

Proof. The proof of Theorem 6 showed strong safety can never be satisfied even using digital signatures. This result was independent of liveness attacks. This same result holds even if liveness attacks can be mounted, and Theorem 5 showed liveness attacks could be mounted on weak safety requirements, which implies they can also be mounted on strong safety requirements. □

6   Results for Broadcasts

Byzantine Reliable Broadcast (BRB) has traditionally been defined based on Bracha's Byzantine Reliable Broadcast (BRB) [3,4]. For this algorithm to work, it is assumed that less then $n/3$ processes are Byzantine. When a process does a broadcast, it invokes br_broadcast() and when it is to deliver such a message, it executes br_deliver(). In the discussion below, it is implicitly assumed that a message is uniquely identified by a (sender ID, sequence number) tuple. BRB satisfies the following properties.

- Validity: If a correct process br_delivers a message m from a correct process p_s, then p_s must have executed br_broadcast(m).
- Integrity: For any message m, a correct process executes br_deliver at most once.
- Self-delivery: If a correct process executes br_broadcast(m), then it eventually executes br_deliver(m).
- Reliability (or Termination): If a correct process executes br_deliver(m), then every other correct process also (eventually) executes br_deliver(m).

As causal broadcast is an application layer property, it runs on top of the BRB layer. Byzantine Causal Broadcast (BCB) is invoked as BC_broadcast(m) which in turn invokes br_broadcast(m') to the BRB layer. Here, m' is m plus some control information appended by the BCB layer. A br_deliver(m') from the BRB layer is given to the BCB layer which delivers the message m to the application via BC_deliver(m) after the processing in the BCB layer. The control information is abstracted by the *causal barrier* [1,10] which tracks the immediate or direct dependencies and is bounded by $O(n)$. In addition to the BCB-layer counterparts of the properties satisfied by BRB, BCB must satisfy safety and liveness. Liveness and weak safety can be satisfied as given by the protocol in [1]. Next, we analyze the possibility of strong safety and liveness, and all four combinations (refer Table 1) if digital signatures can be used.

Theorem 8. *It is impossible to guarantee strong safety and liveness while causally ordering broadcast messages in an asynchronous message passing system with one or more Byzantine process.*

Proof. Strong safety (along with liveness) cannot be ensured by requiring the sender to wait for acknowledgements $ack1$ to its broadcast that the message has been BC_delivered, and for receivers to wait for an ack $ack2$ from the sender that the message has been BC_delivered to all recipients, before broadcasting further messages. This is because a Byzantine process p_x may read a message m before it is br_delivered, and broadcast m_1 without waiting for $ack2$. A third correct process p_y may then br_deliver and BC_deliver m_1 before m. So no action at the sender can enforce strong safety.

The only option left is for the receiver to use transitively propagated information. So we assume the causal barrier abstraction for tracking (transitive) dependencies for broadcasts. Consider a Byzantine process p_j that reads message m broadcast from a correct process p_i while it is being processed by the BRB layer before br_delivery at p_j, takes action based on it and broadcasts m_1 (thus, $m \rightarrow m_1$ semantically) but excludes m from the causal barrier of m_1. A correct process p_k may BC_deliver m_1 before m. It then broadcasts m' which may be BC_delivered by a correct process p_l before m, thus violating strong safety.

Effectively, by p_j dropping m from the causal barrier of m_1, the relation $m \rightarrow m_1$ (and hence $m \rightarrow m'$) was changed to $m \nrightarrow m_1$ (and $m \nrightarrow m'$). As this action of logically swapping the order of the semantic "BC_deliver(m)" and BC_broadcast(m_1) was solely under the local control of a Byzantine process, no protocol can exist to counter this action.   □

Examples of strong safety violations in real-world applications:

1. Social Media Posts: Correct processes may see $post\_b$ by a Byzantine process, whose contents depend on $post\_a$, before they see $post\_a$.
2. Multiplayer Gaming: A Byzantine process can cause strong safety violations to get an advantage over correct processes in winning the game.

Theorem 9. *It is impossible (see Footnote 1) to guarantee strong safety even without liveness guarantees while causally ordering broadcast messages in an asynchronous message passing system with one of more Byzantine process.*

Proof. The proof of Theorem 8 showed strong safety can never be satisfied. This result was independent of liveness attacks. So even if liveness attacks cannot be mounted on broadcasts (refer algorithm in [1]), strong safety cannot be guaranteed.   □

Theorem 10. *It is impossible to guarantee strong safety (while satisfying liveness) using digital signatures while causally ordering broadcast messages in an asynchronous message passing system with even one Byzantine processes.*

Proof. The same proof of Theorem 8 applies because the action by a Byzantine process that causes the strong safety attack is local to that process and signing messages and/or causal barriers will not help because it only authenticates the messages and/or causal barriers.   □

Theorem 11. *It is impossible (see Footnote 1) to guarantee strong safety (even without satisfying liveness) using digital signatures while causally ordering broadcast messages in an asynchronous message passing system with even one Byzantine processes.*

Proof. The proof of Theorem 10 showed strong safety can never be satisfied even using digital signatures. This result was independent of liveness attacks. So even if liveness attacks cannot be mounted on broadcasts, strong safety cannot be guaranteed.   □

7 Byzantine Causal Multicast (BCM)

In a multicast, a send event sends a message to multiple destinations that form a subset of the process set P. Different send events by the same process can be addressed to different subsets of P. This models dynamically changing multicast groups and membership in multiple multicast groups. There can exist overlapping multicast groups. In the general case, there are $2^{|P|} - 1$ groups. Although there are several algorithms for causal ordering of multicasts under dynamic groups, such as [6,7,13,14,22], none consider the Byzantine failure model.

Byzantine Reliable Multicast (BRM) [18,19] has traditionally been defined based on Bracha's Byzantine Reliable Broadcast (BRB) [3,4]. For these algorithms to work, it is assumed that in every multicast group G, less then $|G|/3$ processes are Byzantine. When a process does a multicast, it invokes br_multicast() and when it is to deliver such a message, it executes br_deliver(). In the discussion below, it is assumed that a message is uniquely identified by a (sender ID, sequence number) tuple. BRM satisfies the following properties.

- Validity: If a correct process br_delivers a message m from a correct process p_s, then p_s must have executed br_multicast(m).
- Integrity: For any message m, a correct process executes br_deliver at most once.
- Self-delivery: If a correct process executes br_multicast(m), then it eventually executes br_deliver(m).
- Reliability (or Termination): If a correct process executes br_deliver(m), then every other correct process in the multicast group G also (eventually) executes br_deliver(m).

As causal multicast is an application layer property, it runs on top of the BRM layer. Byzantine Causal Multicast (BCM) is invoked as BC_multicast(m) which in turn invokes br_multicast(m') to the BRM layer. Here, m' is m plus some control information appended by the BCM layer. A br_deliver(m') from the BRM layer is given to the BCM layer which delivers the message m to the application via BC_deliver(m) after the processing in the BCM layer. In addition to the BCM-layer counterparts of the properties satisfied by BRM, BCM must satisfy safety and liveness (Sect. 3).

All the existing algorithms for causal multicast use transitively collected control information about causal dependencies in the past – they vary in the size of the control information, whether in the form of causal barriers as in [10,22] or in the optimal encoding of the theoretically minimal control information as in [6,7,13,14]. The RST algorithm still serves as a canonical algorithm for the causal ordering of multicasts in the BCM layer, and it can be seen that the same liveness attack described in Sect. 4 can be mounted on the causal multicast algorithms. Furthermore, all the results and proofs given in Sect. 5 for unicasts, and summarized in Table 1, apply to multicasts with straightforward adaptations. The intuitive reason is given below.

A liveness attack is possible in the point-to-point model because a "future" message m from p_i to p_j can be advertised by a Byzantine process p_x, i.e., the dependency can be transitively propagated by p_x via $p_{x_1} \dots p_{x_y}$ to p_j, without that message m actually having been sent (created). When the advertisement reaches p_j it waits indefinitely for m. Had a copy of m also been transitively propagated along with its advertisement, this liveness attack would not have been possible. But in point-to-point communication, m must be kept private to p_i and p_j and cannot be (transitively) propagated along with its advertisement. The same logic holds for multicasts – p_i can withold a multicast m to group G_x but advertise it on a later multicast m' to group G_y, even if using Byzantine Reliable Multicast (BRM) which guarantees all-or-none delivery to members of G_y. When a member of G_y receives m', it also receives the advertisement "m sent to $p_j (\in G_x)$", which may get transitively propagated to p_j which will wait indefinitely. Therefore, results for unicasts also hold for multicasts.

In contrast, in Byzantine causal broadcast [1], the underlying Bracha's Byzantine Reliable Broadcast (BRB) layer which guarantees that a message is delivered to all or none of the (correct) processes ensures that the message m is not selectively withheld. This m propagates from p_i to p_j (directly, as well as indirectly/transitively in the form of (possibly a predecessor of) entries in the causal barriers) while simultaneously guaranteeing that m is actually eventually delivered from p_i to p_j by the BRB layer. Thus a liveness attack is averted in the broadcast model.

8   Discussion

On Broadcast vs. Unicast. Byzantine causal broadcast is solvable [1]. Then why is Byzantine fault-tolerant causal order for point-to-point communication impossible? The problem is that a single Byzantine adversary can launch a liveness attack by artificial boosting. In Byzantine causal broadcast, all messages are sent to every process in the system and the underlying Byzantine reliable broadcast layer [3] ensures that every correct process receives the exact same set of messages. Upon receiving m, the receiving process simply waits for its logical clock to catch up with m's timestamp (each broadcast delivered will increment one entry in the logical clock) and deliver m once it is safe to do so. After delivering message m, the receiving processes' logical clock is greater than or equal to m's timestamp. This means that a receiving process does not need to merge message m's timestamp into its own logical clock upon delivering m. Hence no amount of artificial boosting can result in a liveness attack in Byzantine causal broadcast. In case of causal ordering for unicasts and multicasts, every process receives a different set of messages. When a process p_i delivers message m, it means that

p_i has delivered all messages addressed to it in the causal past of m. However, it requires the timestamp attached to m to ascertain the messages in the causal past of m that are not addressed to p_i. Therefore, the receiving process needs to merge the timestamp of the delivered message into its own logical clock so that subsequent messages sent by it can be timestamped with their causal past.

Full-Information Protocols (FIP). The system model rules out full-information protocols (FIP) [9] where the entire transitively collected message history is used as control information – because (i) a message from p_i to p_j or to G needs to be kept private to those two processes or to G, and (ii) a FIP obviates the need for causal ordering. Encrypting messages from p_i to p_j or to G, on which is superimposed the FIP, can provide (liveness + weak safety), but not strong safety, for unicasts and multicasts – however, the cost of a FIP is prohibitively high and as noted in (ii), a FIP obviates the need for causal ordering which rules out this approach. Note, liveness (+ weak safety) can be provided because a Byzantine process must send the messages contained in any inflated message advertisement, in the message history. Also, strong safety cannot be provided because attacks analogous to those in Theorems 3, 6 and 4, 7 proofs can be mounted, wherein a Byzantine process selectively suppresses the message history. A FIP can neither provide strong safety for broadcasts – using reasoning similar to Theorems 8, 10 and 9, 11 proofs, it is seen that a Byzantine process has local control over selectively suppressing message history.

Strong Safety vs. Weak Safety. It is impossible to guarantee strong safety for broadcasts (and unicasts). The Byzantine causal broadcast algorithm in [1] provides only weak safety but this is not always useful in practice because it requires $\xrightarrow{B}$ to hold but correct processes cannot identify whether $\xrightarrow{B}$ or just $\rightarrow$ holds when processing an arrived message. In the absence of strong safety, the examples given after Theorem 8 demonstrate that a Byzantine causal broadcast algorithm is not useful to users of certain applications. (Weak safety suffices to prevent double-spending in the money-transfer algorithm [1] using BC_broadcast, because actually Byzantine causal order is not required for this application; source order is sufficient [8] and weak safety does not violate source order.)

Rational vs. Irrational Byzantine Agents. A *rational* Byzantine agent will mount an attack only if it is not detected/suspected. It can be seen that all impossibility results for strong safety (cases in Table 1) hold even for rational agents because deleting entries, whether signed or in a FIP or neither, from the causal past is entirely local to the Byzantine agent and undetectable by others. Only Theorem 5 for liveness + weak safety under signed messages will not hold for rational agents because in the proof of Lemma 1 on which it depends, the attacker p_x that inflates $M^{m''}[y, k]$ can do so only for $y = x$ – as it cannot sign for p_y and can sign only for $p_y = p_x$. The attack victim p_k can suspect p_x when p_k continues waiting for the delivery condition to be satisfied (or does not receive the *ack* soon enough). Note, in the proof of Lemma 1 (for Theorem 1), if p_k does not get the messages (or the *ack* to *probe*) from p_y in reasonable time, p_k can suspect p_y (as p_y may be Byzantine) and stop waiting for it, although Byzantine p_x mounted the attack and goes unsuspected. Further, in the proof of Lemma 2 on which Theorems 1 and 5 depend, if the sender p_i does not get an *ack* from receiver p_j in a reasonable amount of time, p_i can suspect p_j as being Byzantine; however, Lemma 2 is essentially using some elements of synchronous communication and so it cannot be said that a possibility result holds for rational agents in a truly asynchronous system.

In view of the impossibility result of Theorem 1, algorithms for liveness + weak safety in a stronger asynchrony model are given in [20].

References

1. Auvolat, A., Frey, D., Raynal, M., Taïani, F.: Byzantine-tolerant causal broadcast. Theoret. Comput. Sci. **885**, 55–68 (2021)
2. Birman, K.P., Joseph, T.A.: Reliable communication in the presence of failures. ACM Trans. Comput. Syst. (TOCS) **5**(1), 47–76 (1987)
3. Bracha, G.: Asynchronous byzantine agreement protocols. Inf. Comput. **75**(2), 130–143 (1987). https://doi.org/10.1016/0890-5401(87)90054-X
4. Bracha, G., Toueg, S.: Asynchronous consensus and broadcast protocols. J. ACM **32**(4), 824–840 (1985). https://doi.org/10.1145/4221.214134
5. Castro, M., Liskov, B.: Practical byzantine fault tolerance. In: Seltzer, M.I., Leach, P.J. (eds.) Proceedings of the Third USENIX Symposium on Operating Systems Design and Implementation (OSDI), pp. 173–186 (1999)
6. Chandra, P., Gambhire, P., Kshemkalyani, A.D.: Performance of the optimal causal multicast algorithm: a statistical analysis. IEEE Trans. Parallel Distrib. Syst. **15**(1), 40–52 (2004). https://doi.org/10.1109/TPDS.2004.1264784
7. Chandra, P., Kshemkalyani, A.D.: Causal multicast in mobile networks. In: 12th International Workshop on Modeling, Analysis, and Simulation of Computer and Telecommunication Systems (MASCOTS), pp. 213–220 (2004). https://doi.org/10.1109/MASCOT.2004.1348235
8. Collins, D., et al.: Online payments by merely broadcasting messages. In: 50th Annual IEEE/IFIP International Conference on Dependable Systems and Networks, DSN 2020, pp. 26–38 (2020)
9. Fagin, R., Halpern, J.Y., Moses, Y., Vardi, M.Y.: Reasoning About Knowledge. MIT Press, Cambridge (1995). https://doi.org/10.7551/mitpress/5803.001.0001
10. Hadzilacos, V., Toueg, S.: A modular approach to fault-tolerant broadcasts and related problems. Technical report, 94-1425, Cornell University, p. 83 pages (1994)
11. Huang, K., Wei, H., Huang, Y., Li, H., Pan, A.: Byz-GentleRain: an efficient byzantine-tolerant causal consistency protocol. arXiv preprint arXiv:2109.14189 (2021)
12. Kleppmann, M., Howard, H.: Byzantine eventual consistency and the fundamental limits of peer-to-peer databases. arXiv preprint arXiv:2012.00472 (2020)
13. Kshemkalyani, A.D., Singhal, M.: An optimal algorithm for generalized causal message ordering (abstract). In: Proceedings of the Fifteenth Annual ACM Symposium on Principles of Distributed Computing, p. 87. ACM (1996). https://doi.org/10.1145/248052.248064
14. Kshemkalyani, A.D., Singhal, M.: Necessary and sufficient conditions on information for causal message ordering and their optimal implementation. Distrib. Comput. **11**(2), 91–111 (1998). https://doi.org/10.1007/s004460050044

15. Kshemkalyani, A.D., Singhal, M.: Distributed Computing: Principles, Algorithms, and Systems. Cambridge University Press, Cambridge (2011). https://doi.org/10.1017/CBO9780511805318
16. Lamport, L.: Time, clocks, and the ordering of events in a distributed system. Commun. ACM **21**(7), 558–565 (1978)
17. Liskov, B., Ladin, R.: Highly available distributed services and fault-tolerant distributed garbage collection. In: Proceedings of the Fifth Annual ACM Symposium on Principles of Distributed Computing, pp. 29–39 (1986)
18. Malkhi, D., Merritt, M., Rodeh, O.: Secure reliable multicast protocols in a WAN. In: Proceedings of the 17th International Conference on Distributed Computing Systems, pp. 87–94 (1997). https://doi.org/10.1109/ICDCS.1997.597857
19. Malkhi, D., Reiter, M.K.: A high-throughput secure reliable multicast protocol. J. Comput. Secur. **5**(2), 113–128 (1997). https://doi.org/10.3233/JCS-1997-5203
20. Misra, A., Kshemkalyani, A.D.: Byzantine fault tolerant causal ordering. CoRR abs/2112.11337 (2021). https://arxiv.org/abs/2112.11337
21. Mostefaoui, A., Perrin, M., Raynal, M., Cao, J.: Crash-tolerant causal broadcast in o (n) messages. Inf. Process. Lett. **151**, 105837 (2019)
22. Prakash, R., Raynal, M., Singhal, M.: An adaptive causal ordering algorithm suited to mobile computing environments. J. Parallel Distrib. Comput. **41**(2), 190–204 (1997)
23. Raynal, M., Schiper, A., Toueg, S.: The causal ordering abstraction and a simple way to implement it. Inf. Process. Lett. **39**(6), 343–350 (1991)
24. Schiper, A., Eggli, J., Sandoz, A.: A new algorithm to implement causal ordering. In: Bermond, J.-C., Raynal, M. (eds.) WDAG 1989. LNCS, vol. 392, pp. 219–232. Springer, Heidelberg (1989). https://doi.org/10.1007/3-540-51687-5_45
25. Tseng, L., Wang, Z., Zhao, Y., Pan, H.: Distributed causal memory in the presence of byzantine servers. In: 2019 IEEE 18th International Symposium on Network Computing and Applications (NCA), pp. 1–8 (2019)

Relaxed Reliable Broadcast
for Decentralized Trust

João Paulo Bezerra[1], Petr Kuznetsov[1(✉)], and Alice Koroleva[2]

[1] LTCI, Télécom Paris, Institut Polytechnique de Paris, Palaiseau, France
petr.kuznetsov@telecom-paris.fr
[2] ITMO University, Saint Petersburg, Russia

Abstract. Reliable broadcast is a fundamental primitive, widely used as a building block for data replication in distributed systems. Informally, it ensures that system members deliver the same values, even in the presence of equivocating Byzantine participants. Classical broadcast protocols are based on centralized (globally known) *trust assumptions* defined via sets of participants (*quorums*) that are likely not to fail in system executions. In this paper, we consider the reliable broadcast abstraction in *decentralized trust* settings, where every system participant chooses its quorums locally. We introduce a class of relaxed reliable broadcast abstractions that perfectly match these settings. We then describe a broadcast protocol that achieves *optimal consistency*, measured as the maximal number of different values from the same source that the system members may deliver. In particular, we establish how this optimal consistency is related to parameters of a *graph representation* of decentralized trust assumptions.

Keywords: Reliable broadcast · Quorum systems · Decentralized trust · Consistency measure

1 Introduction

Reliable broadcast is widely used for replicating data in countless applications: storage systems, state-machine replication, cryptocurrencies, etc. Intuitively, a reliable broadcast protocol allows a system member (the *source*) to broadcast a value, and ensures that correct system members agree on the value they deliver, despite arbitrary (*Byzantine* [21]) behavior of some of them (including the source) and asynchrony of the underlying network. More precisely, the primitive ensures the following properties:

- (Validity) If the source broadcasts m, then every correct process eventually delivers m.
- (Consistency) If correct processes p and q deliver, respectively, m and m', then $m = m'$.

Supported by TrustShare Innovation Chair.

M.-A. Koulali and M. Mezini (Eds.): NETYS 2022, LNCS 13464, pp. 104–118, 2022.
https://doi.org/10.1007/978-3-031-17436-0_8

- (Integrity) Every correct process delivers at most one value, and, if the source is correct, only if it previously broadcast it.
- (Totality) If a correct process delivers a value, then every correct process eventually delivers a value.

Classical reliable broadcast algorithms, starting from Bracha's broadcast [4], assume that "enough" system members remain correct. In the *uniform* fault model, where processes fail with equal probabilities, independently of each other, this assumption implies that only less than one third of processes can fail [5].

More general fault models can be captured via *quorum systems* [23]. Formally, a quorum system is a collection of member subsets (*quorums*). Every two quorums must have at least one correct process in common, and in every system run, at least one quorum must only contain correct processes.

Intuitively, quorums encapsulate *trust* the system members express to each other. Every quorum can act on behalf of the whole system: before delivering a value from a potentially Byzantine source, one should make sure that a quorum of system members have *acknowledged* the value. Conventionally, these trust assumptions are centralized: all participants share the same quorum system.

In a large-scale distributed system, it might be, however, difficult to expect that all participants come to the same trust assumptions. It could be more realistic to resort to *decentralized trust* assumptions by allowing each participant to individually choose its quorum system.

Damgård et al. [12] appear to be the first to consider the decentralized trust setting. They focused on solving broadcast, verifiable secret sharing and multiparty computation, assuming *synchronous* communication. Recently, the approach has found promising applications in the field of cryptocurrencies, with the advent of Ripple [28] and Stellar [25] that were conceived as *open* payment systems, alternatives to *proof-of-work*-based protocols [27,31]. In particular, Stellar and its followups [14,15] determine necessary and sufficient conditions on the individual quorum systems, so that a well-defined subset of participants can solve the problems of consensus and reliable broadcast.

In this paper, we propose to take a more general, and arguably more realistic, perspective on decentralized trust. Instead of determining the weakest model in which a given problem can be solved, we rather focus on determining the strongest problem that can be solved in a given model. Indeed, we might have to accept that individual trust assumptions are chosen by the users independently and may turn out to be poorly justified. Furthermore, as in the real world, where a national economy typically exhibits strong internal trust but may distrust other national economies, the system may have multiple mutually distrusting "trust clusters". Therefore it is important to characterize the class of problems that can be solved, given specific decentralized trust assumptions.

To this purpose, we introduce a class of *relaxed* broadcast abstractions, k-*consistent reliable broadcast* (k-CRB), $k \in \mathbb{N}$, that appear to match systems with decentralized trust. If the source of the broadcast value is correct, then k-CRB ensures the safety properties of reliable broadcast (Consistency and Integrity). However, if the source is Byzantine, then Consistency is relaxed so that correct participants are allowed to deliver *up to k* distinct values. Moreover, we also refine the Totality property: if a correct process delivers a value, then every *live* correct process eventually delivers a value *or* produces an irrefutable evidence that the source is Byzantine (a process is live in a given execution if at least one of its quorums consists of correct processes only)[1]. In other words, we introduce the *accountability* feature to the broadcast abstraction: either the live correct processes agree on the values broadcast by the source or detect its misbehavior.

The question now is how to determine the smallest k such that k-CRB can be implemented given specific decentralized trust assumptions. We show that the trust assumptions induce a collection of *trust graphs*. It turns out that the optimal k is then precisely the size of the largest *maximum independent set* over this collection of graphs.

Reliable broadcast is a principal building block for higher-order abstractions, such as state-machine replication [8] and asset transfer [11,16]. We see this work as the first step towards determining the strongest relaxed variants of these abstractions that can be implemented in decentralized-trust settings.

The rest of the paper is organized as follows. In Sect. 2, we present our system model. In Sect. 3, we recall definitions of classical broadcast primitives and introduce a relaxed variant adjusted for decentralized trust settings—*k-consistent broadcast* (*k*-CB). Section 4 introduces a graph representation of trust assumptions, which is used to establish a lower bound on parameter the k. In Sect. 5, we introduce a stronger primitive, k-consistent reliable broadcast (k-CRB) and describe its implementation. Finally, we discuss related work in Sect. 6, and we draw our conclusions in Sect. 7.

2   System Model

2.1   Processes

A distributed system is composed of a set of *processes* $\Pi = \{p_1, ..., p_n\}$. Every process is assigned an *algorithm* (we also say *protocol*), an automaton defined as a set of possible *states* (including the *initial state*), a set of *events* it can produce and a transition function that maps each state to a corresponding new state. An event is either an *input* (a call operation from the application or a message received from another process) or an *output* (a response to an application call or a message sent to another process); *send* and *receive* denote events involving communication between processes.

2.2   Executions and Failures

A *configuration* C is the collection of states of all processes. In addition, C^0 is used to denote a special configuration where processes are in their initial states. An *execution* (or a *run*) Σ is a sequence of events, where every event is associated

---

[1] Intuitively, we may not be able to guarantee liveness to the processes that, though correct, do not "trust the right people".

with a distinct process and every *receive*(m) event has a preceding matching *send*(m) event. A process *misbehaves* in a run (we also call it *Byzantine*) if it produces an event that is not prescribed by the assigned protocol, given the preceding sequence of events, starting from the initial configuration C^0. If a process does not misbehave, we call it *benign*. In an infinite run, a process *crashes* if it prematurely stops producing events required by the protocol; if a process is benign and never crashes we call it *correct*, and it is *faulty* otherwise. Let $part(\Sigma)$ denote the set of processes that produce events in an execution Σ.

2.3   Channels and Digital Signatures

Every pair of processes communicate over a *reliable channel*: in every infinite run, if a correct process p sends a message m to a correct process q, m eventually arrives, and q receives a message from p only if p sent it. We impose *no synchrony assumptions*. In particular, we assume no bounds on the time required to convey a message from one correct process to another. In the following, we assume that all messages sent with a protocol execution are *signed*, and the signatures can be *verified* by a third party. In particular, each time a process p receives a protocol message m from process q, p only accepts m if it is properly signed by q. We assume a computationally bound *adversary*: no process can forge the signature of a benign process.

2.4   Decentralized Trust

We now formally define our decentralized trust assumptions. A *quorum map* $Q : \Pi \to 2^{2^{\Pi}}$ provides every process with a set of process subsets: for every process p, $Q(p)$ is the set of *quorums of* p. We assume that p includes itself in each of its quorums: $\forall Q \in Q(p) : p \in Q$. Intuitively, $Q(p)$ describes what process p *expects* from the system. We implicitly assume that, from p's perspective, for every quorum $Q \in Q(p)$, there is an execution in which Q is precisely the set of correct processes. However, these expectations may be violated by the environment. We therefore introduce a *fault model* $\mathcal{F} \subseteq 2^{\Pi}$ (sometimes also called an *adversary structure*) stipulating which process subsets can be faulty. In this paper, we assume *inclusion-closed* fault models that do not force processes to fail: $\forall F \in \mathcal{F}, F' \subseteq F : F' \in \mathcal{F}$. An execution Σ *complies with* $\mathcal{F}$ if the set of faulty processes in Σ is an element of $\mathcal{F}$.

Given a faulty set $F \in \mathcal{F}$, a process p is called *live in* F if it has a *live quorum in* F, i.e., $\exists Q \in Q(p) : Q \cap F = \emptyset$. Intuitively, if p is live in every $F \in \mathcal{F}$, such that $p \notin F$, then its trust assumptions are justified by the environment.

For example, let the uniform f-*resilient* fault model: $\mathcal{F} = \{F \subseteq \Pi : |F| \le f\}$. If $Q(p)$ includes all sets of $n - f$ processes, then p is guaranteed to have at least one live quorum in every execution. On the other hand, if $Q(p)$ expects that a selected process q is always correct ($q \in \cap_{Q \in Q(p)} Q$), then p is not live in any execution with a faulty set such that $q \in F$. In the rest of the paper, we assume that the model is provided with *trust assumptions* $(Q, \mathcal{F})$, where Q is a quorum map and $\mathcal{F}$ is a fault model.

3   The Broadcast Primitive

The broadcast abstraction exports input events *broadcast(m)* and output events *deliver(m)*, for value m in a *value set* $\mathcal{M}$. Without loss of generality, we assume that each broadcast instance has a dedicated *source*, i.e., the process invoking the *broadcast* operation.[2] Below we recall the classical abstractions of consistent and reliable broadcast [6]. The *consistent broadcast* abstraction satisfies:

- (Validity) If the source is correct and broadcasts m, then every correct process eventually delivers m.
- (Consistency) If correct processes p and q deliver m and m' respectively, then $m = m'$.
- (Integrity) Every correct process delivers at most one value and, if the source p is correct, only if p previously broadcast it.

A reliable broadcast protocol satisfies the properties above, plus:

- (Totality) If a correct process delivers a value, then every correct process eventually delivers a value.

For our lower bound, we introduce a relaxed version of consistent broadcast. A *k-consistent broadcast protocol* (*k*-CB) ensures that in every execution Σ (where $F \in \mathcal{F}$ is its faulty set), the following properties are satisfied:

- (Validity) If the source is correct and broadcasts m, then every *live* correct process eventually delivers m.
- (*k*-Consistency) Let M be the set of values delivered by the correct processes, then $|M| \leq k$.
- (Integrity) A correct process delivers at most one value and, if the source p is correct, only if p previously broadcast it.

In this paper, we restrict our attention to *quorum-based* protocols [22]. Intuitively, in a quorum-based protocol, every process p is expected to make progress if the members of one of its quorums $Q \in \mathcal{Q}(p)$ appear correct to p. This should hold even if the actual set of correct processes in this execution is different from Q. The property has been originally introduced in the context of consensus protocols [22]. Here we extend it to broadcast. Formally, we introduce the following property that completes the specification of *k*-CB:

- (Local Progress) For all $p \in \Pi$ and $Q \in \mathcal{Q}(p)$, there is an execution in which only the source and processes in Q take steps, p is correct, and p delivers a value.

---

[2] One can easily turn this (one-shot) abstraction into a *long-lived* one, in which every process can broadcast arbitrarily many distinct values by equipping each broadcast value with a source identifier, a unique *sequence number* and its signature.

The key differences of k-CB over a classical consistent broadcast lies in the Validity and the k-Consistency properties. Our Validity property only ensures progress to *live* correct processes (based on their local quorums). Also, since some processes may trust the "wrong people", it might happen that a faulty source convinces the correct processes to deliver distinct values. However, given a fault model $\mathcal{F}$, the k-Consistency property establishes an upper bound k in values that can be delivered. In the classical consistent broadcast, no conflict is allowed in values delivered for a given $\mathcal{F}$, the bound k on such primitive is then equal to 1 (which clearly also holds for reliable broadcast).

4 Bounds for k-Consistent Broadcast Protocol

4.1 A Graph Representation of Executions

We use our trust assumptions $(\mathcal{Q}, \mathcal{F})$ to build a graph representation of the execution, in order to investigate the cases in which disagreement may occur in the network, that is, when two or more correct processes deliver distinct values. Let $S : \Pi \to 2^{\Pi}$ be a map providing each process with one of its quorums, that is, $S(p) \in \mathcal{Q}(p)$. Let $\mathcal{Z}$ be the family of all possible such maps S.

Given $F \in \mathcal{F}$ and $S \in \mathcal{Z}$, we build a undirected graph $G_{F,S}$ as follows: the nodes in $G_{F,S}$ are correct processes and the edges are drawn between a pair of nodes if their quorums intersect in at least one correct process. Formally, $G_{F,S}$ is a pair $(\Pi_F, E_{F,S})$ in which:

- $\Pi_F = \Pi - F$
- $(p, q) \in E_{F,S} \Leftrightarrow S(p) \cap S(q) \nsubseteq F$

Example 1. Consider a system with $\Pi = \{p_1, p_2, p_3, p_4\}$, a faulty set $F = \{p_3\}$ and quorum systems:

$$\mathcal{Q}(p_1) = \{\{p_1, p_2, p_3\}, \{p_1, p_3, p_4\}\} \quad \mathcal{Q}(p_2) = \{\{p_1, p_2, p_3\}, \{p_2, p_3, p_4\}\}$$

$$\mathcal{Q}(p_3) = \{\{p_1, p_2, p_4\}, \{p_2, p_3, p_4\}\} \quad \mathcal{Q}(p_4) = \{\{p_1, p_3, p_4\}, \{p_2, p_4\}, \{p_3, p_4\}\}$$

Considering only the correct processes (p_1, p_2 and p_4), there are 12 different combinations of quorums $S \in \mathcal{Z}$ for these trust assumptions. Let $S_1 \in \mathcal{Z}$ such that: $S_1(p_1) = \{p_1, p_2, p_3\}$, $S_1(p_2) = \{p_2, p_3, p_4\}$ and $S_1(p_4) = \{p_2, p_4\}$. And let $S_2 \in \mathcal{Z}$ such that: $S_2(p_1) = \{p_1, p_2, p_3\}$, $S_2(p_2) = \{p_2, p_3, p_4\}$ and $S_2(p_4) = \{p_3, p_4\}$. Figure 1 shows the graphs G_{F,S_1} and G_{F,S_2}, observe that every pair of quorums used to generate G_{F,S_1} intersects in a correct process, thus resulting in a fully connected graph. On the other hand, since $S_2(p_1) \cap S_2(p_4) \subseteq F$, G_{F,S_2} is not fully connected.

We recall the following definitions from *graph theory*:

Definition 1 (Independent Set). *A set of nodes I is an* independent set *of a graph $G_{F,S}$ if no pair of nodes in I is adjacent, i.e., $\forall p, q \in I : (p, q) \notin E_{F,S}$.*

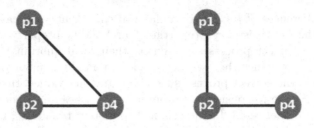

Fig. 1. Graph structures of Example 1: G_{F,S_1} and G_{F,S_2} respectively.

Definition 2 (Independence Number). *The* independence number *of a graph $G_{F,S}$ is the size of its largest independent set.*

Within an independent set of $G_{F,S}$, the quorums of each pair of nodes do not intersect in a correct process. The independence number of $G_{F,S}$ helps us in understanding the level of disagreement that might occur in an execution, as we show in the following for any protocol implementing k-CB.

Theorem 1. *Let $G_{F,S}$ be the graph generated over a fixed $F \in \mathcal{F}$ and $S \in \mathcal{Z}$. Let $G_{F,S}$ have an independent set of size k. Then there exists an execution in which up to k distinct values can be delivered by correct processes.*

Proof. Let r be the source. If $I = \{p_1, ..., p_k\}$ is an independent set of $G_{F,S}$ of size k, then $\forall p_i, p_j \in I : S(p_i) \cap S(p_j) \subseteq F$. By the definition of Local Progress, it exists an execution Σ_i such that $part(\Sigma_i) = \{r\} \cup S(p_i)$ and p_i delivers a value m_i. It then suffices for r and other faulty processes in $S(p_i)$ to behave exactly as they do within Σ_i in order to produce the same result. Since the system is asynchronous, it is possible that p_i delivers a value before any correct process in $part(\Sigma_i)$ receives a message from any $p' \notin part(\Sigma_i)$. In other words, the network behaves as if it was temporarily partitioned. Now for each $p_i \in I$, let Σ_i be an execution as described above, we can build Σ such that all executions Σ_i are subsequences of Σ, in which no correct process receives any information of conflicting values before $p_1, ..., p_k$ deliver $m_1, ..., m_k$, respectively.

Example 2. Coming back to Example 1, we see that the nodes in G_{F,S_1} are fully connected (form a clique), thus resulting in G_{F,S_1} having independence number 1. On the other hand, the biggest independent set in G_{F,S_2} is $\{p_1, p_4\}$, which means G_{F,S_2} has independence number 2. In an execution where F is the faulty set and processes first hear from quorums in S_2 to deliver a value, then there is an unavoidable possibility that p_1 and p_4 deliver distinct values if p_3 is the source.

4.2   Lower Bound on k

Given the pair $(\mathcal{Q}, \mathcal{F})$, we define the family of graphs $\mathcal{G}_{\mathcal{Q},\mathcal{F}}$ that includes all possible $G_{F,S}$, where $F \in \mathcal{F}$ and $S \in \mathcal{Z}$. Recall that every such $S \in \mathcal{Z}$ associates each process to one of its quorums.

Definition 3 (Inconsistency Number). *Let $\mu : \mathcal{G}_{Q,\mathcal{F}} \to N$ map each $G_{F,S} \in \mathcal{G}_{Q,\mathcal{F}}$ to its independence number. The* inconsistency number *of $(Q, \mathcal{F})$ is then $k_{max} = max(\{\mu(G_{F,S}) | G_{F,S} \in \mathcal{G}_{Q,\mathcal{F}}\})$.*

Theorem 2. *No algorithm can implement k-CB with $k < k_{max}$.*

Proof. For a particular $G_{F,S} \in \mathcal{G}_{Q,\mathcal{F}}$, Theorem 1 implies that within an independent set $I : |I| = k$, up to k distinct values can be delivered by the correct processes. As the independence number is the size of the maximum independent set(s) of a graph, by taking the highest independence number in $\mathcal{G}_{Q,\mathcal{F}}$ we get the worst case scenario. It is always possible to build an execution where k_{max} processes deliver k_{max} distinct values before any correct process is able to identify the misbehavior.

Example 3. Coming back to Example 1 again, if we take S_3 such that $S_3(p_1) = S_3(p_2) = \{p_1, p_2, p_3\}$ and $S_3(p_4) = \{p_3, p_4\}$, we have both $(p_1, p_4) \notin E_{F,S_3}$ and $(p_2, p_4) \notin E_{F,S_3}$, while $(p_1, p_2) \in E_{F,S_3}$. The independence number of G_{F,S_3} is 2, which means that despite G_{F,S_2} having more edges then G_{F,S_3}, the same number of distinct values can be delivered by correct processes. For $\mathcal{F} = \{\{p_3\}\}$, since the quorums of p_1 and p_2 always intersect in a correct process, no graph has independence number higher then G_{F,S_3}, thus, considering Q from Example 1 and $\mathcal{F}$, the optimal k for an algorithm implementing k-CB would be 2.

5   Accountable Algorithm for Relaxed Broadcast

In the specification of k-CB, we inherently assume the possibility of correct processes disagreeing in the delivered value in the presence of a faulty source, but the maximal number of distinct delivered values is determined by $(Q, \mathcal{F})$.

In practice, one may need some form of Totality, as in reliable broadcast. We might want the (live) correct processes to reach some form of agreement on the set of values they deliver.

In our setting, we have to define the Totality property, taking into account the possibility of them delivering different values, in case the source is misbehaving. Therefore we strengthen the protocol by adding an accountability feature: once a correct process detects misbehavior of the source, i.e., it finds out that the source signed two different values, it can use the two signatures as a *proof of misbehavior*. The proof can be then independently verified by a third party. We model the accusation as an additional output *accuse(mb)*, where *mb* is a proof that the source misbehaved (e.g. a set of signatures from the source for distinct values). When a process p produces *accuse(mb)*, we say that p *accuses the source* (of misbehavior with proof *mb*). Now, in addition to the properties of k-CB, the *k-consistent reliable broadcast* (k-CRB) abstraction satisfies:

- (Weak Totality) If a correct process delivers a value, then every *live* correct process eventually delivers a value or accuses the source.
- (Accuracy) A correct process p accuses the source only if the source is faulty.

- (Certitude) If a correct process accuses the source, every correct process eventually does so.

We present our k-CRB implementation in Algorithm 1. Each process maintains local variables *sentecho, delivered, accused* and *echoes*. Boolean variables *sentecho, delivered* and *accused* indicate whether p_i has already sent *ECHO*, delivered a value and accused the source, resp., in the broadcast instance. Array *echoes* keeps track of *ECHO* messages received from other processes.

The source broadcasts m by sending a *SEND* message to every process in the system. If a process p_i receives either *[SEND,m]* or *[ECHO,m]* for the first time, p_i sends *[ECHO,m]* to every other process. If a received *ECHO* contains a value m_2 that conflicts with a previously received value m_1, p_i sends the *ACC* message to every process with the tuple (m_1, m_2) as a proof of misbehavior. Once p_i receives echoes with m from at least one of its quorums, it delivers m. Once p_i receives an *ACC* message containing a proof of misbehavior, even though p_i has already delivered a value, it also sends *ACC* to every process before notifying the application. Note that a correct process only sends *ECHO* for a single value, and delivers a value or accuses the source once.

If process p_i delivers a value m after receiving *ECHO* from every process in $Q_i \in \mathcal{Q}(p_i)$, we say that p_i *uses* Q_i. In our correctness arguments, we fix an execution of Algorithm 1 with a faulty set $F \in \mathcal{F}$, and assume that the processes use quorums defined by a fixed map $S \in \mathcal{Z}$.

Lemma 1. *Let $G_{F,S}$ be the graph generated over F and S with $(p,q) \in E_{F,S}$, if p delivers m_1 and q delivers m_2, then $m_1 = m_2$.*

Proof. Since p delivers m_1 using $S(p)$, every process in $S(p)$ sent *[ECHO,m_1]* to p. Similarly, all processes in $S(q)$ sent *[ECHO,m_2]* to q. Assume that $m_1 \neq m_2$, since $(p,q) \in E_{F,S} \Leftrightarrow S(p) \cap S(q) \not\subseteq F$, some correct process sent *ECHO* with m_1 to p and m_2 to q, which is not allowed by the protocol.

As a consequence of Lemma 1, p and q might deliver distinct values only if $(p,q) \notin E_{F,S}$.

Theorem 3. *Let k be the independence number of $G_{F,S}$, then k is an upper bound in the number of distinct values that can be delivered by correct processes.*

Proof. Lemma 1 states that if the quorums of correct processes intersect in a correct process, they cannot deliver conflicting values using those quorums. Let I be an independent set in $G_{F,S}$ of size k and assume that more than k distinct values are delivered, then for some $q \notin I, \exists p \in I : (p,q) \in E_{F,S}$, in which p and q deliver distinct values, a contradiction.

Theorem 4. *Consider a distributed system with trust assumptions $(\mathcal{Q}, \mathcal{F})$. Let k_{max} be the inconsistency number of $(\mathcal{Q}, \mathcal{F})$. Then Algorithm 1 implements k_{max}-consistent reliable broadcast.*

Algorithm 1: 1-Phase Broadcast Algorithm: code for process p_i

---

Local Variables:

$sentecho \leftarrow FALSE;$ \\Indicate if p_i has sent $ECHO$

$delivered \leftarrow FALSE;$ \\Indicate if p_i has delivered a value

$accused \leftarrow FALSE;$ \\Indicate if p_i has accused the source

$echoes \leftarrow [\bot]^N;$ \\Array of received $ECHO$ messages from others processes

upon invoking broadcast(m): { If p_i is the source }

  $send\ message\ [SEND,m]\ to\ all\ p_j \in \Pi;$

upon receiving a message [$SEND$,m] from p_j:

  $if(\neg sentecho)$:

    $sentecho \leftarrow TRUE;$

    $send\ message\ [ECHO,m]\ to\ all\ p_j \in \Pi;$

upon receiving a message [$ECHO$,m] from p_j:

  $echoes[j] \leftarrow m;$

  $if(there\ exists\ echoes[k] \neq \bot\ such\ that\ echoes[k] \neq echoes[j])$:

    $m1 \leftarrow echoes[j];$

    $m2 \leftarrow echoes[k];$

    $send\ message\ [ACC,(m1,m2)]\ to\ all\ p_j \in \Pi;$

    $accuse\ (m1, m2);$ \\ Notify the accusation to the application

  $if(\neg sentecho)$:

    $sentecho \leftarrow TRUE;$

    $send\ message\ [ECHO,m]\ to\ all\ p_j \in \Pi;$

upon receiving a message [ACC,$(m1,m2)$] from p_j:

  $if(\neg accused)$

    $accused \leftarrow TRUE;$

    $send\ message\ [ACC,(m1,m2)]\ to\ all\ p_j \in \Pi;$

    $accuse\ (m1, m2);$ \\ Notify the accusation to the application

upon receiving $ECHO$ for m from every $q \in Q_i, Q_i \in \mathcal{Q}(p_i)$:

  $if(\neg delivered)$

    $delivered \leftarrow TRUE;$

    $deliver\ m;$ \\ Notify the delivery of m to the application

---

Proof. (Integrity) Immediate from the algorithm: a correct process only delivers a value once, and if the source is correct and broadcasts m, no process can deliver a value different from m.

(Accuracy) A correct process accuses the source after receiving echoes with distinct values or an accusation from another process. In both cases, the signature of the source is verified. Correct processes do not broadcast distinct values, and since a faulty process cannot forge signatures of a correct one, it follows that distinct values can only come from a faulty source.

(Certitude) In both situations in which a correct process accuses misbehavior, it previously sends an ACC message to every process in the network containing a pair of distinct values. The message is then eventually received by every correct process in the network, which accuses the source as well.

(Validity) When a correct process broadcasts m, it sends $[SEND,m]$ to every process in the network. Every correct process eventually receives the message and echoes it to every process. If a correct process has a live quorum Q, it will eventually receive $ECHO$ with m from all the processes in Q and deliver the value.

(Weak Totality) A correct process p sends an $ECHO$ message to every process after receiving it if p has not previously echoed a value. Consequently, if some correct process receives an $ECHO$ message, every correct process eventually does so. If p delivers a value, it must have received at least one $ECHO$ message, in which case, every correct process eventually receives and echoes a value. If a correct process q has a live quorum Q, it eventually receives $ECHO$ from all processes in Q. Two cases are then possible. If all of the $ECHO$ messages received by q contains the same value, then q delivers it. Otherwise, q accuses misbehavior.

(k_{max}-Consistency) Let $G'_{F,S}$ be the graph whose independence number is k_{max}. By Theorem 3, the number of distinct values that can be delivered by correct processes in a given execution is bounded by k_{max}. As, by definition, k_{max} is the higher independence number of graphs in $\mathcal{G}_{Q,\mathcal{F}}$, k_{max}-*consistency* is ensured.

An algorithm implementing k-CRB satisfies the required properties of k-CB, thus, it also implements k-CB. From Theorem 2, no algorithm can implement k-CB with $k < k_{max}$, therefore, Theorem 4 implies that Algorithm 1 implements k-CB, and consequently k-CRB, with optimal k.

Computing Inconsistency Parameters. A straightforward approach to find the inconsistency number of $(\mathcal{Q}, \mathcal{F})$ consists in computing the independence number of all graphs $G_{F,S} \in \mathcal{G}_{Q,\mathcal{F}}$. The problem of finding the largest independent set in a graph (called *maximum independent set*), and consequently its independence number, is the *maximum independent set problem* [30], known to be *NP-complete* [26]. Also, the number of graphs in $\mathcal{G}_{Q,\mathcal{F}}$ may exponentially grow with the number of processes. However, as the graphs might have similar structures (for example, the same quorums for some processes may appear in multiple graphs), in many practical scenarios, we should be able to avoid redundant calculations and reduce the overall computational costs.

6   Related Work

Assuming synchronous communication, Damgård et al. [12] described protocols implementing broadcast, verifiable secret sharing and multiparty computation in the decentralized trust setting. They introduce the notion of *aggregate adversary structure* $\mathcal{A}$: each node is assigned a collection of subsets of nodes that the adversary might corrupt at once.

Ripple [28] is arguably the first practical partially synchronous system based on decentralized trust assumptions. In the Ripple protocol, each participant express its trust assumptions in the form of an *unique node list* (UNL), a subset of nodes of the network. In order to accept transactions, a node needs to "hear" from at least 80% of its UNL, and according to the original white paper [28], assuming that up to 20% of the nodes in an UNL might be Byzantine, the overlap between every pair of UNL's needed to prevent forks was believed to be ≥20%. The original protocol description appeared to be sketchy and informal, and later works detailed the functioning of the protocol and helped to clarify under which conditions its *safety* and *liveness* properties hold [2,3,9,24]. In particular, it has been spotted [3] that its safety properties can be violated (a *fork* can happen) with as little as 20% of UNLs overlap, even if there are no Byzantine nodes. It then establishes an overlap bound of >40% to guarantee consistency without Byzantine faults. In a further analysis, assuming that at most 20% of nodes in the UNLs are Byzantine, [9] suggests an overlap of >90% in order to prevent forks, but also provide an example in which the liveness of the protocol is violated even with 99% of overlap. Recently, a formalization of the algorithm was presented in [2], and a better analysis of the correctness of the protocol in the light of an *atomic broadcast* abstraction was given by Amores-Cesar et al. [2].

The Stellar consensus protocol [25] introduces the *Federated Byzantine Quorum System* (FBQS). A quorum Q in the FQBS is a set that includes a *quorum slice* (a trusted subset of nodes) for every node in Q. Correctness of Stellar depends on the individual trust assumptions and are only guaranteed for nodes in the so called *intact set*, which is, informally, a set of nodes trusting the "right people". García-Pérez and Gotsman [14] formally argue about Stellar consensus, by relating it to Bracha's Broadcast Protocol [4], build on top of a FBQS. The analysis has been later extended [15] to a variant of state-machine replication protocol that allows *forks*, where disjoint intact sets may maintain different copies of the system state.

Cachin and Tackmann [7] defined the notion of *Asymmetric Quorum Systems*, based on individual adversary structures. They introduced a variant of broadcast whose correctness is restricted to a *guild*, a subset of nodes that, similarly to the intact nodes in the Stellar protocol, have the "right" trust assumptions. Executions with a guild also ensure consistency (correct processes do not deliver distinct values). In our approach, we relax the consistency property, allowing for more flexible trust assumptions, while using accountability to ensure correctness for every live correct process.

In the similar vein, Losa et al. [22], define the quorum system used by Stellar using the notion of a *Personal Byzantine Quorum System* (PBQS), where every process chooses its quorums with the restriction that if Q is a quorum for a process p, then Q includes a quorum for every process $q' \in Q$. They show that for any quorum-based algorithm (close to what we call an algorithm satisfying the Local Progress property), consensus is not achievable in partially synchronous systems where two processes have quorums not intersecting on a correct process. The paper also determines the conditions under which a subset of processes can locally maintain safety and liveness, even though the system might not be globally consistent. We use a similar approach in the context of broadcast, and in addition to a relaxed consistency guarantee, we also parameterize the level of disagreement in the network using the individual trust assumptions.

Albouy et al. [1] gives a relaxed reliable broadcast for a model where the adversary also has (limited) control over communication links, and can therefore suppress messages sent to correct processes. This model captures the *silent churn* phenomenon, in which participants may leave the system without notifying other peers. They implement a relaxed reliable broadcast primitive for a system with $n > 3f + 2d$ processes, where f is the number of Byzantine members and d the number of correct processes that may not receive a message (suppressed by the adversary). Their protocol ensures safety (no conflicting value is delivered by correct processes) while the *Totality* property is relaxed: up to d correct processes might be prevented from delivering a value.

In the context of distributed systems, accountability has been proposed as a mechanism to detect "observable" deviations of system nodes from the algorithms they are assigned with [17–19]. Recent proposals [10,13,29] focus on *application-specific* accountability that only heads for detecting misbehavior that affects correctness of the problem to be solved, e.g., consensus [10,29] or lattice agreement [13]. Our k-CRB algorithm generally follows this approach, except that it implements a *relaxed* form of broadcast, but detects violations that affect correctness of the stronger, conventional reliable broadcast [6].

7   Concluding Remarks

In this paper, we address a realistic scenario in which correct processes choose their trust assumptions in a purely decentralized way. The resulting structure of their trust relations may cause inevitable violations of consistency properties of conventional broadcast definitions. Our goal is to precisely quantify this inconsistency by considering relaxed broadcast definitions: k-consistent broadcast and k-consistent reliable broadcast.

In case the broadcast source is Byzantine, the abstractions allow correct processes to deliver up to k different values. We show that k, the optimal "measure of inconsistency", is the highest independence number over all graphs $G_{F,S}$ in a family $\mathcal{G}_{\mathcal{Q},\mathcal{F}}$ determined by the given trust assumptions $(\mathcal{Q}, \mathcal{F})$. We show that this optimal k can be achieved by a *k-consistent reliable broadcast* protocol that, in addition to k-consistency also provides a form of accountability: if a correct process delivers a value, then every live correct process either delivers some value or detects the source to be Byzantine.

A natural question for the future work is to quantify inconsistency in higher-level abstractions, such as distributed storage or asset-transfer systems [11,16] that can be built atop the relaxed broadcast abstractions. Another interesting direction would be in self-reconfigurable systems [13]: since we expect the system to admit disagreement, once a Byzantine process is detected, other participants may want to update their trust assumptions. It is also extremely appealing to generalize the very notion of a quorum system to *weighted* quorums, where the contribution of a quorum member is proportional to its *stake* in an asset transfer system [20]. This opens a way towards *permissionless* asset transfer systems with relaxed guarantees.

References

1. Albouy, T., Frey, D., Raynal, M., Taïani, F.: Byzantine-tolerant reliable broadcast in the presence of silent churn. In: Johnen, C., Schiller, E.M., Schmid, S. (eds.) SSS 2021. LNCS, vol. 13046, pp. 21–33. Springer, Cham (2021). https://doi.org/10.1007/978-3-030-91081-5_2
2. Amores-Sesar, I., Cachin, C., Mićić, J.: Security analysis of ripple consensus. arXiv preprint arXiv:2011.14816 (2020)
3. Armknecht, F., Karame, G.O., Mandal, A., Youssef, F., Zenner, E.: Ripple: overview and outlook. In: Conti, M., Schunter, M., Askoxylakis, I. (eds.) Trust 2015. LNCS, vol. 9229, pp. 163–180. Springer, Cham (2015). https://doi.org/10.1007/978-3-319-22846-4_10
4. Bracha, G.: Asynchronous byzantine agreement protocols. Inf. Comput. **75**(2), 130–143 (1987)
5. Bracha, G., Toueg, S.: Asynchronous consensus and broadcast protocols. J. ACM (JACM) **32**(4), 824–840 (1985)
6. Cachin, C., Guerraoui, R., Rodrigues, L.: Introduction to Reliable and Secure Distributed Programming. Springer, Heidelberg (2011). https://doi.org/10.1007/978-3-642-15260-3
7. Cachin, C., Tackmann, B.: Asymmetric distributed trust. In: OPODIS, vol. 153, pp. 7:1–7:16 (2019)
8. Castro, M., Liskov, B.: Practical byzantine fault tolerance. In OSDI: Symposium on Operating Systems Design and Implementation. USENIX Association, Co-sponsored by IEEE TCOS and ACM SIGOPS, February 1999
9. Chase, B., MacBrough, E.: Analysis of the XRP ledger consensus protocol. arXiv preprint arXiv:1802.07242 (2018)
10. Civit, P., Gilbert, S., Gramoli, V.: Polygraph: accountable byzantine agreement. IACR Cryptology ePrint Archive 2019/587 (2019)
11. Collins, D., et al.: Online payments by merely broadcasting messages. In: 50th Annual IEEE/IFIP International Conference on Dependable Systems and Networks, DSN 2020, Valencia, Spain, 29 June–2 July 2020, pp. 26–38. IEEE (2020)
12. Damgård, I., Desmedt, Y., Fitzi, M., Nielsen, J.B.: Secure protocols with asymmetric trust. In: Kurosawa, K. (ed.) ASIACRYPT 2007. LNCS, vol. 4833, pp. 357–375. Springer, Heidelberg (2007). https://doi.org/10.1007/978-3-540-76900-2_22
13. de Souza, L.F., Kuznetsov, P., Rieutord, T., Tucci Piergiovanni, S.: Accountability and reconfiguration: self-healing lattice agreement. CoRR, abs/2105.04909 (2021)
14. García-Pérez, Á., Gotsman, A.: Federated byzantine quorum systems (extended version). arXiv preprint arXiv:1811.03642 (2018)
15. García-Pérez, Á., Schett, M.A.: Deconstructing stellar consensus (extended version). arXiv preprint arXiv:1911.05145 (2019)
16. Guerraoui, R., Kuznetsov, P., Monti, M., Pavlovic, M., Seredinschi, D.: The consensus number of a cryptocurrency. In: Robinson, P., Ellen, F. (eds.) PODC, pp. 307–316. ACM (2019)
17. Haeberlen, A., Kuznetsov, P.: The fault detection problem. In: Proceedings of the 13th International Conference on Principles of Distributed Systems (OPODIS 2009), December 2009

18. Haeberlen, A., Kuznetsov, P., Druschel, P.: The case for byzantine fault detection. In: Proceedings of the Second Workshop on Hot Topics in System Dependability (HotDep 2006), November 2006
19. Haeberlen, A., Kuznetsov, P., Druschel, P.: PeerReview: practical accountability for distributed systems. In: Proceedings of the 21st ACM Symposium on Operating Systems Principles (SOSP 2007), October 2007
20. Kuznetsov, P., Pignolet, Y., Ponomarev, P., Tonkikh, A.: Permissionless and asynchronous asset transfer [technical report]. CoRR, abs/2105.04966 (2021). To appear at DISC 2021
21. Lamport, L., Shostak, R., Pease, M.: The Byzantine generals problem. ACM Trans. Program. Lang. Syst. **4**(3), 382–401 (1982)
22. Losa, G., Gafni, E., Mazières, D.: Stellar consensus by instantiation. In: 33rd International Symposium on Distributed Computing (DISC 2019). Schloss Dagstuhl-Leibniz-Zentrum fuer Informatik (2019)
23. Malkhi, D., Reiter, M.: Byzantine quorum systems. Distrib. Comput. **11**(4), 203–213 (1998)
24. Mauri, L., Cimato, S., Damiani, E.: A formal approach for the analysis of the XRP ledger consensus protocol. In: ICISSP, pp. 52–63 (2020)
25. Mazieres, D.: The stellar consensus protocol: a federated model for internet-level consensus. Stellar Dev. Found. **32**, 1–45 (2015)
26. Miller, R.: Complexity of Computer Computations: Proceedings of a Symposium on the Complexity of Computer Computations, held March 2022, 1972, at the IBM Thomas J. Watson Research Center, Yorktown Heights, New York, and sponsored by the Office of Naval Research, Mathematics Program, IBM World Trade Corporation, and the IBM Research Mathematical Sciences Department. Springer, New York (2013). https://doi.org/10.1007/978-1-4684-2001-2
27. Nakamoto, S.: Bitcoin: a peer-to-peer electronic cash system. Decentralized Bus. Rev. 21260 (2008)
28. Schwartz, D., Youngs, N., Britto, A., et al.: The ripple protocol consensus algorithm. Ripple Labs Inc White Paper **5**(8), 151 (2014)
29. Shaer, A., Dolev, S., Bonomi, S., Raynal, M., Baldoni, R.: BEE'S STRATEGY AGAINST BYZANTINES replacing byzantine participants. In: Izumi, T., Kuznetsov, P. (eds.) SSS 2018. LNCS, vol. 11201, pp. 139–153. Springer, Cham (2018). https://doi.org/10.1007/978-3-030-03232-6_10
30. Tarjan, R.E., Trojanowski, A.E.: Finding a maximum independent set. SIAM J. Comput. **6**(3), 537–546 (1977)
31. Wood, G.: Ethereum: a secure decentralized generalized transaction ledger. White Paper (2015)

A Self-stabilizing Minimum Average Stretch Spanning Tree Construction

Sinchan Sengupta[✉], Sathya Peri, and Parwat Singh Anjana

Department of Computer Science and Engineering, Indian Institute of Technology,
Hyderabad, India
{cs17resch11002,cs17resch11004}@iith.ac.in, sathya_p@cse.iith.ac.in

Abstract. Stretch is a metric in the construction of spanning trees that measures the deviation in the distance between a pair of nodes in the tree compared to its shortest distance in the underlying graph. This paper proposes a silent self-stabilizing low stretch spanning tree construction protocol *BuildTree*, that is based on a Low Diameter Decomposition (LDD) technique. The *LDD* involves steps wherein the graph is decomposed into a small number of connected blocks or clusters, each having a low diameter value. The proposed *BuildTree* algorithm generates a spanning tree with an average stretch of $n^{\mathcal{O}(1)}$ and converges to a correct configuration in $\mathcal{O}(n + \Delta \cdot \eta)$ rounds, where n, Δ and η is the number of nodes in the graph, the maximum size of a cluster and the number of clusters, respectively. To the best of our knowledge, this is the first known work of using self-stabilization in order to make low stretch tree constructions fault-tolerant.

Keywords: Stretch · Spanning tree · Self-stabilization · Fault tolerance

1 Introduction and Related Work

Let $G = (V, E)$ be an undirected, unweighted and connected graph, where V is the set of nodes, E is the set of edges, with $|V| = n$ and $|E| = m$. Let $T = (V, E')$ be a spanning tree on G, with $E' \subseteq E$. We define distance $d_G(x, y)$ as the number of edges on the shortest path from x to y in G, the subscript denoting the induced subgraph on which distance is calculated.

Stretch (σ) between a pair of nodes x and y is defined as:

$$\sigma(x, y) = \frac{d_T(x, y)}{d_G(x, y)}$$

It is intuitive that $d_T(x, y)$ is lower bounded by $d_G(x, y)$, and hence $\sigma(x, y) \geq 1$ for any $x, y \in G$.

The average stretch factor of spanning tree T can be defined as:

$$\lambda(T) = \frac{1}{m} \sum_{(u,v) \in E} \sigma(u, v) \qquad (1)$$

© The Author(s), under exclusive license to Springer Nature Switzerland AG 2022
M.-A. Koulali and M. Mezini (Eds.): NETYS 2022, LNCS 13464, pp. 119–135, 2022.
https://doi.org/10.1007/978-3-031-17436-0_9

Table 1. Related Work. Here, D denotes the diameter of the graph.

	Average stretch value	# Rounds	Self-stabilization
Alon et al. [2]	$2^{\mathcal{O}(\sqrt{\log n \cdot \log \log n})}$	-	No
Ghaffari et al. [19]	$n^{o(1)}$	$(D + \sqrt{n}).n^{o(1)}$	No
Becker et al. [6]	$\log^3 n$	$\mathcal{O}(D)$	No
This work	$\mathbf{n}^{\mathcal{O}(1)}$	$\mathcal{O}(\mathbf{n} + \mathbf{\Delta} \cdot \eta)$	**Yes**

It can be noted that $n - 1$ is a trivial upper bound on the value of stretch in a spanning tree for an unweighted graph but providing such a bound for the *average* stretch is not straightforward. An alternate definition for average stretch can be defined in terms of the distance between all the $\binom{n}{2}$ pairs of nodes. However, we will focus on the definition of stretch expressed in terms of the edges as shown in Eq. (1).

The problem of finding T that minimizes the average stretch (λ) is known as the *Minimum Average Stretch spanning Tree (MAST)* [5,7] problem. MAST is known to be NP-Hard, proved via reduction from another well-known NP-Hard problem known as Minimum Fundamental Cycle Basis [12]. The seminal solution to MAST proposed by Alon et al. [2] is a centralized solution. A distributed version of the same is proposed Ghaffari et al. in [19]. Another recently distributed solution to MAST can be found in [6]. Note that all these techniques stem from the LDD technique in graphs.

In this paper, we aim to provide a *fault-tolerant* distributed algorithm that constructs a MAST in the wake of network failures. We focus on transient faults that can cause the network topology to change at certain sporadic time instances. An effective way to deal with any such finite transient failures is through *Self-stabilization*, introduced by Dijkstra in [15]. It is a technique for restoring a system to a lawful state in a finite number of steps, independent of the initial state of the system. We use self-stabilization as a fault tolerance technique to make our designed algorithm resilient to transient faults.

The MAST construction given by the same authors in Gurjar et al. [21] terminates in $\mathcal{O}(n)$ rounds of the CONGEST model, however, the worst case average stretch was not analyzed. They also offer a weak form of fault-tolerance where faulty edges are replaced using the *All Best Swap Edges* problem [21]. Also related to our work, a synchronous self-stabilizing graph clustering construction known as the (k, r)-Clustering problem [9,26], primarily focus on decomposing the graph into clusters. These clusters have a predefined radius and maintains a certain number of cluster heads for each cluster. This is similar to the k-dominating set problem [27]. Self-stabilizing shortest-path trees have been studied in [3,24] and BFS tree constructions in [10,23]. The comparison of the proposed approach with state-of-the-art is given in Table 1.

The proposed MAST construction is based on LDD of graphs as found in [4, 22]. Our self-stabilizing technique is similar in the way general shortest-path trees are maintained in [13,25]. Additionally, we maintain cluster information in the low stretch tree.

The following significant contributions are claimed in this paper:

- We propose *BuildTree: a silent self-stabilizing minimum average stretch spanning tree* construction algorithm (see Sect. 4). To the best of our knowledge, this is the first work that presents an approach to construct a low average stretch tree resilient to transient failures using non-masking fault-tolerance techniques like self-stabilization.
- The proposed *BuildTree* construction technique is loosely based on the LDD of graphs on which the non-self-stabilizing versions of [2] and [19] works.
- We show that the average stretch of $n^{\mathcal{O}(1)}$ as analyzed for the non-self-stabilizing algorithm in [19] also holds in our case with self-stabilization (Sect. 4.5, Theorem 1). The proposed algorithm terminates in $\mathcal{O}(n + \Delta \cdot \eta)$ rounds and correctly generates a low average stretch tree (Sect. 4.5, Theorem 3).

The rest of the paper is organized as follows; Sect. 2 illustrates the system model. The distributed cluster tree used to design the proposed protocol is discussed in Sect. 3. The analysis of the BuildTree algorithm is given in Sect. 4.5. We then conclude with some future research directions in Sect. 5.

2   Preliminaries and Model

Self-stabilization is usually defined in a setting where nodes and edges in a graph can recover and crash arbitrarily. Since its inception in [15], self-stabilization has been used by distributed systems to recover from arbitrary (transient or fleeting) faults. A system is said to be self-stabilizing if starting from any arbitrary initial state (or configuration), it can converge to a legal (or legitimate) state, within finite time. The time required for this convergence to a legal state is known as the stabilization time (or recovery period). By *configuration* of a system we mean the union of the local state (values of their variables) of all the processes in the system. For readability, please note that the terms *valid* and *legal* are used interchangeably.

The system is said to be *stable* if the time between recovery of the system and the next encountered fault is sufficiently large. We assume in accordance with the traditional model of Dijkstra, that there are no faults during the recovery period of our algorithm. Any algorithm to become self-stabilizing must satisfy the following two properties [20]:

1. **Closure**: If the system is in a legal configuration, it continues to remain so with every valid move of the algorithm, until an error or failure occurs.
2. **Convergence**: Irrespective of starting state, the system eventually returns to a legal state.

It is worthy to note that our proposed protocol is *semi-uniform*, where the nodes in a system are aware of a privileged process called the *Root*. A self-stabilizing algorithm generally consists of a set of *rules*, where we have a *guard* followed by an *action*. The guard is a Boolean predicate defined on some local parameters (variables). When this predicate is satisfied for a node x, we say that x is *activated* or *enabled*, and x is permitted to execute its action. After executing its action, x is said to be *neutralized*.

A configuration X_i of the system proceeds to X_{i+1} (i.e., $X_i \to X_{i+1}$) if a non-empty subset of nodes in X are enabled and they execute their action in a single instance. A *terminal* configuration is one in which none of the nodes in a configuration are enabled. An *execution* is termed as a maximal sequence of configurations $\langle X_0, X_1, ..., X_{i-1}, X_i, ...\rangle$ (can be both finite or infinite), such that $X_{i-1} \to X_i$. We focus on silent self-stabilization, in which the (finite) execution of our algorithm ends with a configuration X_k, where X_k is terminal.

In the above setting, a *scheduler* (or *daemon*) is responsible for choosing at least one of the enabled processes to execute. We assume that our algorithm works under the most general *distributed unfair daemon*. The daemon is *unfair* in the sense that it is free to choose any enabled process, any arbitrary number of times over and over again for execution, possibly ignoring other enabled nodes. A particular enabled process is guaranteed to be chosen by such a scheduler only when it is the *only* enabled process in the system. An algorithm that works under this stringent model is assumed to work under any other weaker model, for example, the *weakly fair daemon*. The asynchronicity of our algorithm comes from such an assumption. A related concept in stabilization is *silence*. A *silent self-stabilizing* algorithm Σ is defined with respect to set of specifications $\prod$, where the following properties hold true [14,18]:

- **Termination**: All valid executions of Σ are finite.
- **Partial Correctness**: All terminal configurations of the system produced by the algorithm Σ satisfy the properties in $\prod$.

Self-stabilizing algorithms are generally assumed to run infinitely in the system [17]. However, *silence* is a special property in a self-stabilizing system that enables it to terminate. An execution (under the assumed daemon) for such a silent system is always finite and all terminal configurations are valid under the specifications of the system. The stabilization time of a silent self-stabilizing system is analogously defined as the maximum number of rounds the daemon takes to arrive at a terminal configuration. When a node becomes silent, the values in its variables and registers do not change. Silence is a much stronger and desirable property in a fault-tolerant setting that makes the system design simpler and elegant [14].

2.1   Model

We assume the *distance-1 model* [16] in this paper. It is also called the *locally shared memory model* or the *state model*, which allows a node to read the states (variables and registers) of all its neighbors but not modify (update) them. However, a node can modify its own local variables.

For evaluating the time complexity of our algorithm, the notion of *round* is used [8]. Let $E \in \zeta$ be an execution, where ζ is the set of all possible executions for the algorithm. Further, let us decompose E as $E = e_1 e_2 e_3 \dots$. The *first round* of E is the minimal prefix of E (say, e_1) that contains the execution of any one action of the protocol or where all the processes are neutralized. The second round for E is the first round in $e_2 e_3 e_4 \dots$. A recursive definition follows for each subsequent rounds. The number of rounds required for a distributed algorithm to terminate (i.e., when all nodes become silent) is used to determine its time complexity.

We also assume that the nodes *apriori* have a knowledge of the value of n, i.e. the size of the network. This can be achieved by executing a pair of broadcast and converegcast. This knowledge of n is needed since it determines the bound on the inter-cluster edges used in our protocol. Lastly, each node $u \in V$ has a unique identifier, denoted as id_u, that can be expressed in $\mathcal{O}(\log n)$ bits.

3   Distributed Cluster Tree

To construct a low average stretch spanning tree, at the heart of our designed protocol, we use a Distributed Cluster Tree (DCT). This DCT is a modified spanning tree induced by the clusters of the original underlay graph. Historically, all low diameter decomposition schemes for constructing low average stretch spanning trees, as explored in [2,6,19], uses similar clustering techniques. The computation of the final spanning tree in our proposed algorithm is expected to mimic the DCT as illustrated below. The definition used here finds its roots in [19].

Definition 1. *Let $G = (V, E)$ be an undirected and unweighted graph, where $|V| = n$. The corresponding $N-$node distributed cluster tree T can be represented as $T = (V', E', H, \Psi)$, where $V' = \{C_1, C_2, ..., C_N\}$ is the set of clusters that partition V; $E' \subseteq E$; H is the set comprising of cluster leaders and Ψ maps E' to E. The cluster tree T satisfies the following:*

1. *The induced clusters $V' = \{C_1, C_2, ..., C_N\}$ partition the entire graph such that $\bigcup_{i=1}^{N} C_i = V$ and for $C_i, C_j \in V'$, $C_i \cap C_j = \phi$.*
2. *There is a single cluster leader in each induced cluster of V', that is, $\forall 1 \leq i \leq N, |H \cap C_i| = 1$, and $|H| = N$.*
3. *Each cluster C_i induces an intra-cluster tree T_i on the vertices of the subgraph $G[C_i]$. Each such T_i is a spanning tree rooted at H_i, which is the cluster leader of C_i.*
4. *Ψ gives a mapping from E' to E, where each inter-cluster edge $(C_i, C_j) \in E'$ is mapped to an edge $(v_i, v_j) \in E$. Here, $v_i \in C_i$ and $v_j \in C_j$ and the edge (v_i, v_j) connects clusters C_i, C_j.*

It is intuitive to understand that the distributed cluster tree, as defined above, will be connected since the induced subgraph $G[C_i]$ is connected for every cluster C_i and each C_i is connected to some other cluster C_j by condition 4.

4   The Self-stabilizing Construction

This section illustrates how to develop a self-stabilizing solution to the MAST problem using our BuildTree algorithm. In Sect. 4.1, we present a high-level overview of the proposed approach, including a discussion of various notations and variables. In Sect. 4.3, we discuss how to construct the actual silent self-stabilizing MAST.

4.1   Proposed Approach Overview

The MAST construction by Alon et al. in [2] proceeds iteratively, with the $k'th$ iteration as follows:

1. Partition the edges of the graph into sets $E_1, E_2, ..., E_k$ such that the cluster sets $\{C_i\}$ have a diameter $D \in 2^{\mathcal{O}(\sqrt{6 \cdot \log n \cdot \log \log n})}$.
2. Find a BFS tree for each C_i
3. Contract each C_i into a single super-vertex and pass this graph structure to iteration $k + 1$. Continue until a single vertex remains in the graph.

The solution provided by Ghaffari et al. in [19] is a refinement of the above algorithm, where the BFS tree of Step 2 is constructed in a more sophisticated manner. They use a randomized protocol that outputs a carefully chosen BFS tree that reduces the stretch further.

Our solution is loosely based on the approach proposed by Alon et al. [2]. The probabilistic treatment in [19] is not straightforward to be translated into a self-stabilizing solution. Nonetheless, the main challenge is to reproduce the distributed edge partitioning and super-vertex contraction as given in [2] in our own construction. To circumvent solving these problems individually, we use a DCT. It helps partition the graph into clusters, each cluster having a low diameter. Every node $x \in V$ has access to a variable cl_x which gives the set of nodes which constitutes its own cluster. This abstraction solves the super-vertex contraction. We also create and maintain two trees given by the variables $Parent_x$ and $ClusterParent_x$, where each node x can identify two trees: first, the intra-cluster spanning tree (rooted at the cluster leader of each cluster) encompassing all the nodes in an individual cluster; and second, the tree consisting of the clusters as super-vertices. Whenever the topology deviates, a node can detect an error locally and executes one of the rules as given in Algorithm 2 to rectify itself. This execution sets off a chain of (possible) further rectifications amongst the other nodes. The self-stabilizing algorithm kicks off when the an arbitrary node detects an anomaly and the algorithm terminates when none of the nodes are enabled in the system. This signifies the restoration of the system to a legal configuration. By maintaining the intra-cluster trees and the inter-cluster edges simultaneously, we solve the edge partitioning problem and obtain the MAST (low average stretch DCT) as our required output.

4.2   Notations and Variables

Let the node with the lowest *id* in the graph G be R (which will be the root of the final MAST). Further, let R_{cl} be the cluster containing the root R. The variables used in the algorithm (rooted at node x) are as follows:

- $dist_x$: Hop distance of x from the CL in the cluster of x.
- cl_x: The set of nodes in the cluster of x.
- $ClusterID_x$: The contracted node representing the cluster of x. The *id* of the CL in the cluster of x is set as the *id* of the entire cluster.
- $Parent_x$: The parent in the intra-cluster BFS tree rooted at CL.
- $ClusterParent_x$: Parent of $clusterID_x$ in the inter-cluster tree.
- $ClusterDist_x$: The distance of $clusterID_x$ from the root cluster R_{cl}.
- $\Gamma(x)$: Neighbours of x in G.
- Neigh(x): The cluster(s) neighbour(s) of cl_x.
- D: Upper bound on the diameter of each cluster.
- $status_x \in \{-1, 1, \perp\}$: Value of $\perp$ denotes a node is correct. Values of -1 and 1 are used during broadcast and convergecast actions of the algorithm.

Definition 2 (Cluster (C)). *A subset of nodes of the graph, where $Diam(C) \leq D$ and the number of inter-cluster edges incident to each cluster $\leq \frac{8 \cdot \log n}{D}$.*

The optimum value of the cluster diameter D is determined by the user, as explained in the following sub-section.

Definition 3 (Cluster Leader (CL)). *A node with the lowest id in the cluster. i.e., $CL = argmin_{\forall x \in cl_x}\{id_x\}$ and $CL\_ID = min_{\forall x \in cl_x}\{id_x\}$.*

The CL is the root node from where the BFS tree is explored in a particular cluster. As new nodes are added into a cluster to grow its size, the new node has a smaller *id* than the current leader. The cluster leader also changes accordingly.

Definition 4 (Boundary Node (BN)). *A node at the gateway to a different cluster, i.e., a node which has a neighbour in the underlay that belongs to a different cluster.*

$$BN = \{x \mid \exists\, v \in \Gamma(x) \wedge ClusterID_x \neq ClusterID_v\} \tag{2}$$

The boundary nodes are the ones that contribute towards expanding the cluster size and the addition of the inter-cluster edges.

Definition 5 (Invalid Node). *We say that a node u is invalid, if it satisfies any of the following:*

1. $ClusterID_u = id_x \wedge CL\_ID \neq id_x$
2. $ClusterID_u \neq id_x \wedge CL\_ID = id_x$
3. u is not a boundary node $\wedge\ (\exists\ v \in \Gamma(u),\ ClusterID_u \neq ClusterID_v \wedge ClusterParent_u = ClusterID_v)$
4. $dist_u \neq dist_{Parent_u} + 1$

The first two conditions check that if a node has the same *id* as the entire cluster, it must be the CL. The third condition ensures that a node can have a parent outside the cluster only if it is a boundary node that lies at the gateway of a cluster. The last condition checks if the BFS tree constructed inside each cluster, rooted at the CL, is consistent. These conditions are verified using various *rules* given in Algorithm 2.

Definition 6 (Invalid Cluster). *A cluster C is said to be invalid if any of the following hold:*

1. $\exists u \in C$, *such that u is an* Invalid node.
2. $dist_C \neq dist_{ClusterParent_C} + 1$
3. $\exists u, v \in C, checkDiam(u, v) = false$

A cluster is invalidated if any node inside that cluster is invalid or if the cluster super-vertex violates the parent-child distance relationship of the DCT. Also, if a particular pair of nodes do not comply with the diameter criteria, the cluster is rejected. Figure 1 illustrate the first phase of the construction.

The remainder of the section is dedicated to the actual construction procedure of the required MAST.

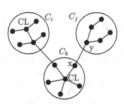

Fig. 1. Three clusters are shown here. The Cluster Leader (CL) of Cluster C_k is shown as the central node. An intra-cluster BFS tree rooted at the CL is constructed at each cluster. Gateway nodes x and y are connected by an inter-cluster edge. Each cluster has a size limited by the value given in [22]. The entire structure is comprising of intra-cluster BFS trees in each cluster, and the inter-cluster edges between possible gateway nodes give the final DCT (low-stretch spanning tree).

4.3   Building a Self-stabilizing Low Stretch Tree

Identifying low diameter clusters is the first stage in building a low stretch tree. Inside each cluster, the cluster nodes are connected in a BFS tree form, rooted at CL. This BFS tree is a tree within a cluster. The clusters (abstracted as super-vertices) are then minimally connected among themselves. For the first step, we use ideas from the work of Ghaffari et al. [19]. They showed that setting the diameter value of each cluster to a predefined quantity D (as a function of n) reduces the average stretch in each cluster. The details on how to calculate the optimal cluster diameter D from G can be found in [19]. A simpler analysis for setting an optimal value of D can also be found in [22]. They further limit the number of inter-cluster edges incident to each cluster to be upper bounded by $\frac{4 \cdot \log m}{D} \approx \frac{8 \cdot \log n}{D}$ (since $m \leq n^2$) to decreases average stretch in the final DCT. We adopt their technique and design our algorithm based on this.

BuildTree is divided into a few components: the actual rules for tree construction are given in Algorithm 2. The supporting predicates used by the algorithm are given in Table 2; and the declarations are given in Algorithm 1. Let us first discuss the various functions used in BuildTree.

- `InsideClusterPath(u)`: This sets up the *correct* parent and distance relationship in the intra-cluster tree. After rectification, the status is set to $\perp$, which indicates that u is now locally consistent wrt the intra-cluster tree.
- `OutsideClusterPath(u)`: This sets up the *correct* parent and distance relationship in the inter-cluster tree. The cluster parent is chosen in such a way that the number of inter-cluster edges is minimized.
- `Propagate(u,newclDist,newOCPar)`: Here, the new cluster distance and new cluster parent are recursively set for all the elements in a cluster. It is invoked when there needs to be an update of cluster information.
- `SetCluster(u,v)`: All the nodes in the cluster of node u and nodes in the cluster of v are merged here. The updated merged cluster is stored in the cluster of u, and the new cluster leader is set. The new BFS intra-cluster tree is also created.

Table 2. Predicates executed at node u

Label	Predicate
$R_1(u)$	$status_u = 1 \wedge IncorrTreeRoot(u)$
$R_2(u)$	$status_u = 1 \wedge IncorrClustRoot(u)$
$incorrTreeRoot(u)$	$(status_u \neq status_{Parent_u}) \vee (Parent_u \notin Neigh(u)) \vee (dist_u < dist_{Parent_u} + 1)$
$incorrClustRoot(u)$	$(ClusterID_u = ClusterID_{ClusterParent_u}) \vee (ClusterParent_u \notin Neigh(u)) \vee (ClusterDist_u < ClusterDist_{Parent_u} + 1)$
$ICCorr(u)$	$(\exists v \in Neigh(u) | ClusterID_u = ClusterID_v \wedge dist_v + 1 < dist_u)$
$OCCorr(u)$	$(\exists v \in Neigh(u) | ClusterID_u \neq ClusterID_v \wedge ClusterDist_v + 1 < ClusterDist_u)$
$checkDiam(u,v)$	$max_{x,y \in cl_v \cup \{u\}} dist_{cl_u}(x,y) \leq Diam$
$checkICEdge(u,v)$	$|\{y : y \in Neigh(x) \wedge ClusterID_y \neq ClusterID_x, \text{ where } x \in cl_v \cup \{u\}\}| \leq \frac{8 \cdot \log n}{D}$
$validCluster(u)$	$\forall v \in cl_u : status_u = \perp$

Algorithm 1: BuildTree: Function Declarations

1 **InsideClusterPath(u)**
3      $Parent_u = argmin_{(v \in \Gamma(u) \wedge status_u = \perp) \wedge (ClusterID_v = ClusterID_u)}(dist_v + 1)$
4      $dist_u = dist_{Parent_u} + 1$
5      $status_u = \perp$
6 **OutsideClusterPath(u)**
8      $ClusterParent_u =$
        $argmin_{(v \in (ClusterID_u) \wedge ClusterID_v \neq ClusterID_u)}|Neigh(u)| + |Neigh(v)|$
9      $ClusterDist_u = ClusterDist_{ClusterParent_u} + 1$
10     $Propagate(v, ClusterDist_u, ClusterParent_u)$ for every $v \in Neigh(u)$, where
        $ClusterID_u = ClusterID_v$
11 **Propagate(u,newclDist,newOCPar)**
13     $ClusterDist_u = newclDist, ClusterParent_u = newOCPar$
14   Call $Propagate(v, newclDist, newOCPar)$, for each
        $v \in Neigh(u) \wedge (ClusterID_u = ClusterID_v)$
15 **SetCluster(u,v)**
17     $cl_u \leftarrow cl_u \cup cl_v$
18   Set $CL \leftarrow argmin_{x \in cl_u} ID_x$
19     $\forall x \in cl_u : ClusterID_x \leftarrow CL$
20     $Neigh(ClusterID_u) \leftarrow \{y : y \in Neigh(x) \wedge ClusterID_y \neq ClusterID_x$, where $x \in cl_u\}$
21   Set $Parent_{CL} \leftarrow null$ and $dist_{CL} = 0$
22     $\forall x \in cl_u \setminus \{CL\}$: Invoke $InsideClusterPath(x)$

Algorithm 2: Rules of BuildTree (executed at node u)

1. $status_u = \perp \wedge \neg ICCorr(u) \wedge (incorrTreeRoot(u) \vee status_{Par_u} = -1) \rightarrow status_u = -1$
2. $status_u = \perp \wedge \neg OCCorr(u) \wedge (incorrClustRoot(u) \vee status_{OCPar_u} = -1) \rightarrow status_u = -1$
3. $status_u = -1 \wedge (\forall v \in Child(u)|status_v = 1) \rightarrow status_u = 1$
4. $R_1(u) \wedge (\exists v \in \Gamma(u)|status_v = \perp) \rightarrow InsideClusterPath(u)$
5. $R_2(u) \wedge (\exists v \in \Gamma(u)|clustid_v \neq clustid_u \wedge status_v = \perp) \rightarrow OutsideClusterPath(u)$
6. $status_u \neq \perp \rightarrow InsideClusterPath(u)$
                $OutsideClusterPath(u)$
7. $\exists v \in \Gamma(u) \wedge clustid_v \neq clustid_u : checkDiam(u, v) \wedge checkICEdge(u, v) \wedge validCluster(v) \rightarrow$
    $SetCluster(u, v)$
8. $OCCorr(u) \rightarrow OutsideClusterPath(u)$

We now discuss the predicates used.

- `incorrTreeRoot(u)`: Indicates that the node u is inconsistent either wrt its parent in the intra-cluster tree or has incorrect distance values.
- `incorrClustRoot(u)`: Indicates that the node u is inconsistent either wrt its parent in the inter-cluster tree or has incorrect distance values in the inter-cluster super-vertex tree.
- `ICCorr(u)`: This indicates that there exists a neighbour of u that can give a better distance value in the BFS tree compared to its current intra-cluster tree parent.
- `OCCorr(u)`: Same as above. Here, distance is calculated wrt the inter-cluster tree parent.
- `CheckDiam(u,v)`: Checks whether node u can be merged into the cluster of v, by investigating the diameter of the supposedly increased cluster.
- `checkICEdge(u)`: Checks whether the merged cluster of u and v will have the number of incident inter-cluster edges less than the bound of $\frac{8 \cdot \log n}{D}$.
- `validCluster(u)`: Checks if every node inside a cluster has a valid status.

Note that functions $InsideClusterPath(u)$ and $OutsideClusterPath(u)$ work in tandem for correcting the intra and inter-cluster trees. Similarly, the predicate pairs $incorrTreeRoot$ and $incorrClustRoot$, $ICCorr$ and $OCCorr$ complement each other for detecting the faulty parent-child relationships in them. Since any change in the intra-cluster BFS alignment can disrupt the whole DCT, these pairs appear together in order to rectify it iteratively.

4.4   Working

Starting from any initial configuration, the enabled nodes (that detect a local error, i.e. Invalid Node) are free to execute the rules as given in Algorithm 2, with a lower numbered rule given more preference than a higher numbered one. The execution continues until all the nodes become silent.

Each node is potentially a single, independent cluster. To expand the cluster size, a BN probes its neighbouring nodes that are in a different cluster if the adjoining cluster can be merged or not. The probing cluster checks the diameter constraint and the number of inter-cluster edges according to Rule 7 of Algorithm 2 in case of a possible merge. The update diameter after the possible joining of clusters is verified by the checkDiam() predicate, whereas the number of inter-cluster edges is verified by checkICEdge(). If these rules are satisfied, the merging is completed. The updated list of nodes in the new merged cluster is calculated and disseminated to the remaining nodes of the cluster by the Propagate() function present inside OutsideClusterPath(). The new CL and the BFS trees are recomputed in the updated cluster, every time a merging is successfully performed. This is done by invoking the InsideClusterPath() function of Rule 7.

Recovery from Faults: Nodes having *status* variable set to $\perp$ to indicate that its error-free. A status value of -1 and 1 on the other hand, indicate that the node and the subtree rooted at that node is corrupted respectively. These values are used in a manner known as *information and propagation feedback* [11,13]. The nodes having status values of 1 and -1 are said to be *frozen* [13], and they cannot be added to any part of the spanning tree being constructed. In short, no node addition rule like Rule 1, 2, 4, 5, 7, or 8 can work on these nodes.

A node decides if it is faulty by inspecting predicates 3−6. They are just an extension of the conditions stated earlier for detecting an Invalid Node (Definition 5) and an Invalid Cluster (Definition 6). The predicates ICCorr() and OCCorr() help in deciding whether the correction needs to be done in the intra-cluster or the inter-cluster tree. Note that Rule 2 and Rule 8 are used each time when the DCT parent-child consistency is checked. They also check if the nodes ensure the cycle-free property by checking that every node has a single parent in the final tree (except the *Root*).

Note that during the cluster formation phase, a node can join a cluster only if it satisfies the diameter constraint. Suppose we have a cluster of size $Diam - 1$. Two nodes are far apart and decide to add their neighbors. If both are allowed atomically, then the total diameter would be $Diam + 1$. Even if such a situation arises, checkDiam() predicate would be invalidated and Rule 7 would be invoked to rearrange the clusters.

4.5   Analysis

Let x and y be two vertices in clusters C_x and C_y respectively. Let B be the final DCT obtained after *BuildTree* terminates. Let B' be the modified BFS tree version of B where each cluster in B is represented as a super-vertex in B', and inter-cluster tree edges in B remaining the same. Also, let λ be the average stretch for B'. Assume τ to be a path between x and y in B.

Lemma 1. *The expected length of τ is at most $3 \cdot \lambda \cdot D$.*

Proof. τ consists of both inter-cluster and intra-cluster edges since nodes x and y lie in different clusters (in C_x and C_y respectively). Again, by the definition of average stretch of a tree, λ gives the mean of the number of edges in B'. Hence, we have: $\lambda = $ *Number of clusters in B'* $+ 1$. Now,
Expected number of edges in τ = *Number of inter-cluster edges in B'* + (*Number of clusters in B'*)·(*Maximum Diameter of a cluster*).
= *Average stretch of B'* + (*Average stretch of B'* + 1)·$(2 \cdot D)$
= $\lambda + (\lambda + 1) \cdot (2 \cdot D)$
$\leq 3 \cdot \lambda \cdot D$.   □

We conclude by stating the main result of this section, where we give a bound on the worst case average stretch of the constructed tree.

Theorem 1. *It is always possible to construct a low stretch spanning tree B from G, such that the average stretch of B is $n^{\mathcal{O}(1)}$.*

Proof. Let `Stretch(m)` be the maximum possible average stretch of a spanning tree defined on G. Let B be this tree that corresponds to the maximum stretch. Now, maximum number of edges possible in G' is $\frac{4 \cdot \log m}{D} \cdot m$ edges.

`Stretch(m)` can now be defined as:

$$\text{Stretch(m)} \leq \text{(Fraction of inter-cluster edges)}$$
$$\cdot \text{(Expected no. of edges in } \tau) \tag{3}$$
$$\leq \frac{4 \cdot \log m}{D} \cdot 3 \cdot \text{Stretch}(\frac{4 \cdot \log m}{D} \cdot m) \cdot D$$

Let $D = (4 \cdot \log m) \cdot m^{\frac{k}{2}} \leq m^k$, i.e., $\frac{4 \cdot \log m}{D} = m^{\frac{-k}{2}}$, for a constant $k > 1$. We now show by induction that $\text{Stretch(m)} \leq 2 \cdot m^{2k}$.

$$\text{Stretch(m)} \leq m^{\frac{-k}{2}} \cdot \text{Stretch}(m^{1-\frac{k}{2}}) \cdot 3 \cdot m^k$$
$$= 3 \cdot m^{\frac{k}{2}} \cdot \text{Stretch}(m^{1-\frac{k}{2}})$$
$$\leq 6 \cdot m^{\frac{k}{2}} \cdot m^{2k-k^2} = 6 \cdot m^{\frac{5k}{2}-k^2}$$
$$\leq m^{\mathcal{O}(1)} + 6 \cdot m^{\frac{5k}{2}-k^2} \leq 2 \cdot m^{2k}.$$

It is known that for any graph, $m \leq n^2$.

$$\therefore \text{Stretch(m)} \leq 2 \cdot n^{4k} \approx n^{\mathcal{O}(1)}.$$

Hence, B has an average stretch of $n^{\mathcal{O}(1)}$.   □

4.6   Partial Correctness

Let us now define the valid state of the system. We say that a configuration X is *valid*, if each node $u(\neq Root) \in X$ satisfies the following safety predicate:

$$
\begin{aligned}
(status_u = \perp) \wedge ((Parent_u \in \Gamma(u) \wedge (dist_u = dist_{Parent_u} + 1)) \\
\wedge (ClusterDist_u = ClusterDist_{ClusterParent_u} + 1) \\
\wedge checkDiam(u, u) \\
\wedge checkICEdge(u, u)
\end{aligned}
\tag{4}
$$

The safety predicate above incorporates the correct distance value wrt the intra-cluster and inter-cluster trees, the permissible diameter value of a cluster and the inter-cluster edges of the cluster. The predicates used here are described in the *BuildTree* algorithm.

We now argue the correctness of the *BuildTree* algorithm with the help of the following result.

Lemma 2. *A configuration X is valid iff X is terminal.*

Proof. Let us look into the reverse direction first. We want to show that a terminal configuration X will always be valid. Recall that X will be terminal if none of the nodes are activated, i.e. *guard* condition in none of the Rules are satisfied. Let us assume for contradiction that $u(\neq Root) \in X$ be a process which is not legal. Hence, $dist_u \neq dist_{Parent_u} + 1$ (this implies that $ClusterDist_u \neq ClusterDist_{ClusterParent_u} + 1$ may also be true). Now, since $status_u = \perp$, u will execute Rule 1 and invoke the subtree freezing mechanism, until all nodes in T_u have status set to 1. After that, u executes Rule 4 and 5 to restore the correct state. Other nodes in T_u also execute Rules 4 and 5, and set their state to $\perp$. Hence, all nodes turn valid and none have their *guard* enabled, generating a terminal configuration. Also note that, in a terminal configuration, predicates *checkDiam* and *checkICEdge* is always *true*, since a cluster merge request by some other node will never be executed in the first place if the diameter or inter-cluster edge count is violated. Since this checking is performed before merging, the predicates are always *true*.

The forward direction is straightforward. If all nodes in a configuration X are valid, none of the processes are enabled. Hence, the system is in a terminal state. $\square$

4.7   Termination

We discuss the termination guarantee and the *round* complexity in the remainder of this section.

We now look at the following result regarding the number of rounds taken for rectifying the error and bringing the system to a legal state. Recall that we measure the time taken for stabilization in terms of the number of rounds between the activation of error and restoring the system to a correct configuration, assuming no other faults occur in between.

Lemma 3. *If u be a faulty node and T_u be the intra-cluster subtree rooted at u then the BuildTree protocol needs $3 \cdot |T_u|$ rounds to restore the correct distance values (namely, d) for the low stretch tree B.*

Proof. After node u detects that it is faulty with the help of Predicate $incorrTreeRoot$, Rule 1 is enabled in u and the rectification process begins. The freezing mechanism makes three distinct passes in the subtree T_u of the faulty node. In the first pass, it sets $status_v = -1$ for each $v \in T_u$, in a level wise top-down manner, starting from u and ending at the leaves of T_u. In the second pass, all the leaf nodes of T_u have their guards enabled and the convergecast wave starts in a bottom-up fashion as per Rule 3. Each node from the bottom have their status set to 1 and this pass terminates at u with $status_u = 1$. In the third and final pass, u executes Rule 4. Due to this action, u is restored as a legal node and a top-down wave begins from u and every node in T_u executes Rule 4. This enables the entire subtree to be legalized and no other node can reduce the distance variable in T_u.

Since we made three passes over T_u to correct the fault of a single node u, we conclude that the *BuildTree* protocol needs $3 \cdot |T_u|$ rounds to fix the incorrect distance values and neutralize every node in B. □

Lemma 4. *Let the number of clusters in B be η and the maximum cluster size be Δ, then the additional number of rounds taken by the BuildTree algorithm for restoring the inter-cluster distance (ClusterDist) values of each node in T_u of a faulty node u, is upper bounded by $\eta \cdot \Delta$.*

Proof. Imagine a worst-case scenario where the *Root* of B has only one child u and u is faulty. The freezing mechanism discussed earlier restores the correct $dist$ values w.r.t. B. However, while this rectification process was underway, the inter-cluster distances as captured by *ClusterDist* gets altered. To correct this, each enabled node also executes Rule 4 and Rule 7. As a result, the predicate `OutsideClusterPath()` is invoked by each time Rule 7 is executed, and the `Propagate()` method is called once by each node in each cluster. `Propagate()` terminates when all the nodes in a cluster with incorrect *ClusterDist* are rectified.

Since each node in a cluster executes `Propagate()` once during the last pass of the freezing method, we incur an additional number of rounds equal to $\eta \cdot \Delta$. This bound holds in any order of execution of nodes under the distributed unfair daemon. □

The following result illustrates the round complexity of the *BuildTree* algorithm.

Lemma 5. *The cluster joining request of a node u takes $\mathcal{O}(n)$ rounds. to execute.*

Proof. Let v be the neighbour of u, with $ClusterID_u \neq ClusterID_v$ and u makes a request to join cl_v. Further, assume that $|V| = n \leq Diam$ and $|cl_v| = n - 1$. In such a case, the predicate $checkDiam$ iterates over the entire vertex set. Existing algorithms [28] for checking the diameter terminate in $\mathcal{O}(n)$ rounds. Hence, the result follows. □

Theorem 2. *The* BuildTree *algorithm takes* $\mathcal{O}(n + \eta \cdot \Delta)$ *rounds to terminate and converge to a legal configuration.*[1]

Proof. This follows directly from the previous results. The rectification of tree distances $dist$ takes $3 \cdot |T_u|$ rounds, whereas, the $ClusterDist$ values are restored in at most $\eta \cdot \Delta$ rounds. Cluster joining requests can take a maximum of $\mathcal{O}(n)$ rounds. So, it takes a total of at most $3 \cdot |T_x| + \eta \cdot \Delta + n$ rounds for *BuildTree* to terminate. Now, note that $|T_u| \leq n$. Hence the result follows.   □

We conclude this section with the main result of this paper.

Theorem 3. *The BuildTree protocol is a silent self-stabilizing algorithm that terminates in* $\mathcal{O}(n + \Delta \cdot \eta)$ *asynchronous rounds in the worst case and converges to a valid configuration.*

Proof. BuildTree is a *silent* self-stabilizing algorithm since it satisfies both *Termination* and *Correctness* conditions, as shown in Theorem 2 and Lemma 2 respectively. The round complexity is analyzed keeping in mind the distributed unfair daemon, that is inherently asynchronous.

It is clearly evident that the bound for average stretch hold for the self-stabilizing construction as well. Hence, the low stretch tree B obtained by the BuildTree protocol also has a worst case average stretch of $n^{\mathcal{O}(1)}$.   □

5   Conclusion and Future Work

In this work, we have given a novel deterministic self-stabilizing construction of a low average stretch spanning tree. The construction of this tree was done using efficient graph partitioning techniques. The average stretch factor of $n^{\mathcal{O}(1)}$ for this tree however is not optimal. The current lower bound for this problem is due to Abraham et al. in [1] that gives an expected stretch of $\mathcal{O}(\log n \log \log n)$ for a pair of nodes, via petal decomposition. This lower bound however, has not yet been extended to distributed solutions. But it still remains an open question whether we can have deterministic algorithms to match this bound or obtain the optimal $\Omega(1)$ average stretch. It would also be interesting to see if self-stabilizing solutions can be given for the MAST construction in [6], which gives the best average stretch of $\log^3 n$ in the distributed domain.

BuildTree is the first known silent self-stabilizing protocol for constructing a low average stretch spanning tree. Here, our aim was to preserve both the distance and the cluster information in the wake of transient faults. The round complexity of the proposed protocol was found to be $\mathcal{O}(n + \Delta \cdot \eta)$. However, it would have been nice if a worst case upper bound on $\eta \cdot \Delta$ was known as a function of n, diameter, maximum degree, or any other standard parameters of the graph. Intuitively, an amortized analysis gives us a trivial bound of $\Delta \cdot \eta \leq n$, but a worst case value of this product would be more useful.

---

[1] It is clear that *BuildTree* protocol takes $\mathcal{O}(n \cdot \log n)$ bits of space at each node for its execution.

Estimation of the stabilization time in steps for BuildTree protocol is left as future work. It was observed that designing a potential function for proving the correctness was difficult in our algorithm. We were unable to find a suitable candidate function that could capture the global minimization of the average stretch value since MAST is not yet known to admit a polynomial time solution.

References

1. Abraham, I., Neiman, O.: Using petal-decompositions to build a low stretch spanning tree. In: Proceedings of the Forty-Fourth Annual ACM Symposium on Theory of Computing, pp. 395–406 (2012)
2. Alon, N., Karp, R.M., Peleg, D., West, D.: A graph-theoretic game and its application to the k-server problem. SIAM J. Comput. **24**(1), 78–100 (1995)
3. Arora, A., Gouda, M., Herman, T.: Composite routing protocols. In: Proceedings of the Second IEEE Symposium on Parallel and Distributed Processing 1990, pp. 70–78. IEEE (1990)
4. Awerbuch, B.: Complexity of network synchronization. J. ACM (JACM) **32**(4), 804–823 (1985)
5. Bartal, Y.: Probabilistic approximation of metric spaces and its algorithmic applications. In: Proceedings of 37th Conference on Foundations of Computer Science, pp. 184–193. IEEE (1996)
6. Becker, R., Emek, Y., Ghaffari, M., Lenzen, C.: Distributed algorithms for low stretch spanning trees. In: 33rd International Symposium on Distributed Computing (DISC 2019), vol. 146, p. 4 (2019)
7. Borradaile, G., Chambers, E.W., Eppstein, D., Maxwell, W., Nayyeri, A.: Low-stretch spanning trees of graphs with bounded width. arXiv preprint arXiv:2004.08375 (2020)
8. Bui, A., Datta, A.K., Petit, F., Villain, V.: Snap-stabilization and PIF in tree networks. Distrib. Comput. **20**(1), 3–19 (2007)
9. Caron, E., Datta, A.K., Depardon, B., Larmore, L.L.: A self-stabilizing K-clustering algorithm using an arbitrary metric. In: Sips, H., Epema, D., Lin, H.-X. (eds.) Euro-Par 2009. LNCS, vol. 5704, pp. 602–614. Springer, Heidelberg (2009). https://doi.org/10.1007/978-3-642-03869-3_57
10. Chen, N.S., Yu, H.P., Huang, S.T.: A self-stabilizing algorithm for constructing spanning trees. Inf. Process. Lett. **39**(3), 147–151 (1991)
11. Cournier, A.: A new polynomial silent stabilizing spanning-tree construction algorithm. In: Kutten, S., Žerovnik, J. (eds.) SIROCCO 2009. LNCS, vol. 5869, pp. 141–153. Springer, Heidelberg (2010). https://doi.org/10.1007/978-3-642-11476-2_12
12. Deo, N., Prabhu, G., Krishnamoorthy, M.S.: Algorithms for generating fundamental cycles in a graph. ACM Trans. Math. Softw. (TOMS) **8**(1), 26–42 (1982)
13. Devismes, S., Ilcinkas, D., Johnen, C.: Self-stabilizing disconnected components detection and rooted shortest-path tree maintenance in polynomial steps. arXiv preprint arXiv:1703.03315 (2017)
14. Devismes, S., Johnen, C.: Silent self-stabilizing BFS tree algorithms revisited. J. Parallel Distrib. Comput. **97**, 11–23 (2016)
15. Dijkstra, E.W.: Self-stabilization in spite of distributed control. In: Dijkstra, E.W. (ed.) Selected Writings on Computing: A Personal Perspective, pp. 41–46. Springer, New York (1982). https://doi.org/10.1007/978-1-4612-5695-3_7

16. Ding, Y.: Fault tolerance in distributed systems using self-stabilization (2014)
17. Dolev, S.: Self-stabilization, March 2000 (2000)
18. Dolev, S., Gouda, M.G., Schneider, M.: Memory requirements for silent stabilization. Acta Informatica **36**(6), 447–462 (1999)
19. Ghaffari, M., Karrenbauer, A., Kuhn, F., Lenzen, C., Patt-Shamir, B.: Near-optimal distributed maximum flow. In: Proceedings of the 2015 ACM Symposium on Principles of Distributed Computing, pp. 81–90 (2015)
20. Ghosh, S.: Distributed Systems: An Algorithmic Approach. Chapman and Hall/CRC, Boca Raton (2014)
21. Gurjar, A., Peri, S., Sengupta, S.: Distributed and fault-tolerant construction of low stretch spanning tree. In: 2020 19th International Symposium on Parallel and Distributed Computing (ISPDC), pp. 142–149. IEEE (2020)
22. Harvey, N.: Low-stretch trees. https://www.cs.ubc.ca/~nickhar/Cargese1.pdf. Accessed 19 Feb 2022
23. Huang, S.T., Chen, N.S.: A self-stabilizing algorithm for constructing breadth-first trees. Inf. Process. Lett. **41**(2), 109–117 (1992)
24. Johnen, C., Tixeuil, S.: Route preserving stabilization. In: Huang, S.-T., Herman, T. (eds.) SSS 2003. LNCS, vol. 2704, pp. 184–198. Springer, Heidelberg (2003). https://doi.org/10.1007/3-540-45032-7_14
25. Kosowski, A., Kuszner, L.: A self-stabilizing algorithm for finding a spanning tree in a polynomial number of moves. In: Wyrzykowski, R., Dongarra, J., Meyer, N., Waśniewski, J. (eds.) PPAM 2005. LNCS, vol. 3911, pp. 75–82. Springer, Heidelberg (2006). https://doi.org/10.1007/11752578_10
26. Larsson, A., Tsigas, P.: Self-stabilizing (k,r)-clustering in wireless ad-hoc networks with multiple paths. In: Lu, C., Masuzawa, T., Mosbah, M. (eds.) OPODIS 2010. LNCS, vol. 6490, pp. 79–82. Springer, Heidelberg (2010). https://doi.org/10.1007/978-3-642-17653-1_6
27. Nguyen, M.H., Hà, M.H., Nguyen, D.N., et al.: Solving the k-dominating set problem on very large-scale networks. Comput. Soc. Netw. **7**(1), 1–15 (2020)
28. Peleg, D., Roditty, L., Tal, E.: Distributed algorithms for network diameter and girth. In: Czumaj, A., Mehlhorn, K., Pitts, A., Wattenhofer, R. (eds.) ICALP 2012. LNCS, vol. 7392, pp. 660–672. Springer, Heidelberg (2012). https://doi.org/10.1007/978-3-642-31585-5_58

Analysis of Interactions Among Infrastructure Provider Fronting Content Provider

Hamid Garmani[(✉)], Mohamed El Amrani, Driss Ait Omar,
Mohamed Ouaskou, and Mohamed Baslam

Information Processing and Decision Support Laboratory, Faculty of Sciences and
Technics, Sultan Moulay Slimane University, Beni Mellal, Morocco
garmani.hamid@gmail.com

Abstract. In conventional architecture the Content Providers (CPs) are need of topology information, it is hard for them to establish a pricing plan. To solve these problems, we propose a novel architecture based on Software Defined Networks. In this architecture, the Infrastructure Provider (IP) hosts the cache servers and decides the content pricing. We develop game-theoretic models to study the interaction between IP and CP. We use a generalized Zipf distribution to model content popularity. We analyzed the interactions between the IPs as a non-cooperative game. We use a Stackelberg game to capture the interactions between the CP and IPs. Across the mathematical study, we demonstrate the uniqueness of the Nash equilibrium. An iterative and distributed algorithm based on best response dynamics is proposed to achieve the equilibrium point.

Keywords: CDN · CP · IP · Non-cooperative game · Nash equilibrium

1 Introduction

With the rapid growth of global data traffic, which achieved 2.5 exabytes per month in 2014 and exceed 24.3% exabytes per month by 2022. According to Cisco, video traffic will account for 71% of total IP traffic by 2022 [2]. As more users watch more videos on their devices, content providers (CPs), e.g., Hulu or amazon prime video, should offer good content delivery services.

In Content Delivery Networks (CDNs) the CPs host several cache servers, when a user requests content from each CP, the CP responds to the request by using the suitable cache server. This is a technique to improve the Quality of Services of the users, but, it is not the best solution as it has the following weaknesses: 1) CPs do not have information on the topology, which is hosted by the IP, therefore it is hard for the CPs to take the best decision; 2) it is hard to guess which cache server is the best one that must respond to the user's request; 3) for some CPs, it is expensive for them to manage their individual cache servers, which limits the application of CDNs.

M.-A. Koulali and M. Mezini (Eds.): NETYS 2022, LNCS 13464, pp. 136–146, 2022.
https://doi.org/10.1007/978-3-031-17436-0_10

The authors in [19] investigated the potential gains of reconfiguration flexibilities. The authors make CDN-IP infrastructure demand aware, that is, to re-optimize it towards the changing users' demands over time. They presented an optimization framework and conduct an extensive evaluation using data from a large European IP. In [16,17] the authors investigated neutrality of Internet and its consequence on the content distribution chain. They studied the system with a single CDN actor who seeks to maximize his income that model mathematically according to parameters such as service, transport and storage prices. The authors in [12] investigated the impact of a CDN on some other major actors, namely, the users, the IP and the CP, by comparing the outcome with that of reasonable behavior. In [1] the authors analyzed the interactions between the main providers in the Internet content distribution chain. This analysis led us to design two non-cooperative games, one between the CPs and the other between the Internet content distribution network providers. In [18] The authors have modeled the economic interactions between the different actors of the content distribution chain, using the framework of game theory. They show the uniqueness of the Nash equilibrium. The authors in [13] proposed a pricing model to establish an economic incentive mechanism for caching and sharing content in Information-Centric Networks that consists of an IP, and a CP.

Software-Defined Networks (SDN) are expected to enhance the functionality of the network. The IP can record the content request on the network by using the SDN protocol. In addition, it has complete information on the topology. Motivated by this point, we suggest a novel architecture, in which the IP hosts all the cache servers behind the Digital Subscriber Line Access Multiplexer [14], which are applied to cache the contents for the users.

The main contributions of this work can, therefore, be summarized as follows:

- We developed an analytical framework for the distribution of popular content on the Internet, which comprises multiple IPs, single CPs, and a set of users.
- We investigate the interplay between IPs as a function of one market parameter: network access price.
- We study a game between IPs as a non-cooperative game. The analyzed economic interaction in our model is not involved by the existing works.
- We use the Stackelberg game to analyze the interaction between IPs and CP.
- We analytically prove the existence of an equilibrium between IPs, and then we applied the best response algorithm for learning Nash equilibrium.
- Numerical analysis reveals the impact of system parameters on providers'(CP and IPs) strategies.

The remaining part of this letter is organized as follows. In Sect. 2 we introduce the system model. In Sect. 3 we formulate the Stackelberg game. In Sect. 4 we analyze the pricing game. We show numerical simulation in Sect. 5. In Sect. 6, we conclude this letter.

2   Problem Modeling

We consider a network with several users, M IPs, and one CP. Each IP can decide to either cache the entire or portion of the L items. The caching strategy adopted by each IP is denoted by y_l that takes value 1 if the IP_j decides to cache item l and takes value 0 if the IP_j decides to not cache item l. Each IP_j choose a price ρ_j and CP choose cashing price c. users' behavior is a function of IPs prices, see (1). Figure 1 shows the monetary flow among different entities with various prices. A detailed summary of notations is presented in Table 1.

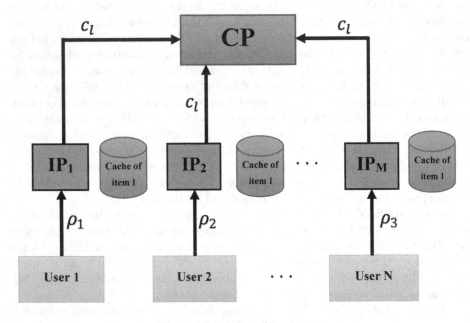

Fig. 1. Network architecture.

The users' demands of item l are affected by one market parameter service price [4,8–10]. The linear demand of item l is

$$\Delta_{jl} = \sigma_{jl} - \gamma_{jl}^{jl}\rho_{jl} + \sum_{m=1,m\neq j}^{M} \gamma_{jl}^{ml}\rho_{ml} \tag{1}$$

σ_{jl} is the potential demand of users to item l at IP_j. γ_{jl}^{ml} is the responsiveness of Δ_{jl} to price ρ_{ml} of item l of IP_m. The demand Δ_{jl} of item l decreases in the price it charges, ρ_{jl}, and increases in the price charged by its opponent ρ_{jm}.

Assumption 1. *The sensitivity γ verifies:*

$$\gamma_{jl}^{jl} \geq \sum_{m=1,m\neq j}^{M} \gamma_{jl}^{ml}, \quad \forall\, j = 1,...,M.$$

Assumption 1 is used to ensure the uniqueness of the Nash equilibrium.

Table 1. Summary of notation.

Notation	Description
M	Number of IPs
L	The library size
σ_{jl}	The potential demand of users
γ_{jl}^{ml}	The responsiveness of Δ_{jl} to price ρ_{ml} of item l of IP_m
Δ_{jl}	The users demands of item l
Γ_j	The utility function of IP_j
ρ_{jl}	The price of the item l fixed by IP_l
c_l	The caching price of item l fixed by CP
$y_l = 1$	A variable to indicate if item l is cached
$\Phi_l \Delta_{jl}$	The demand of item l of IP_j
Φ_l	Zipf popularity distribution
l^η	The rank of item l
η	The skewness of the popularity distribution

The utility function Γ_j of the IP_j is the difference between the obtained payoff and the costs:

$$\Gamma_j = \sum_{l=1}^{L} \rho_{jl}\Phi_l\Delta_{jl} - \sum_{l=1}^{L} c_l y_l \Phi_l \Delta_{jl} - \sum_{l=1}^{L} c_l(1 - y_l)\Phi_l\Delta_{jl} \qquad (2)$$

where ρ_{jl} is the price of the item l fixed by IP_l. c_l is the caching price of item l fixed by CP. $y_l = 1$ is a variable to indicate if item l is cached. $\Phi_l\Delta_{jl}$ is the demand of item l of IP_j. The first term $\sum_{l=1}^{L} \rho_{jl}\Phi_l\Delta_{jl}$ is all the revenue that the IP_j can get from the users, the other terms $\sum_{l=1}^{L} c_l y_l \Phi_l \Delta_{jl}$ and $\sum_{l=1}^{L} c_l(1 - y_l)\Phi_l\Delta_{jl}$ are how much the IP should pay for the content that it requests from the CP. Each user requests an item, which is selected independently according to a discrete distribution ϕ_l, where $1 \leq l \leq L$, and L is the library size. We assume that the item l is requested by their popularity, characterized by Zipf popularity distribution ϕ_l [5,11]. The Zipf popularity distribution of item l is defined by $\phi_l = A^{-1}l^{-\eta}$, where $A = \sum_{l=1}^{L} h^{-\eta}$, l^η is the rank of item l, and η is the skewness of the popularity distribution.

The utility function of the CPs is

$$\varXi = \sum_{j=1}^{M} \left(\sum_{l=1}^{L} c_l y_l \Phi_l \Delta_{jl} + \sum_{l=1}^{L} c_l(1 - y_l)\Phi_l\Delta_{ij} \right) \qquad (3)$$

3   Stackelberg Game Modelling

The Stackelberg game is a game between two sets of players leaders and followers [7]. The leaders act first while the followers act according to the leaders decisions.

At the first stage of the Stackelberg game, the CP fixed caching price c. At the second stage, given the caching price c, the IPs fixed the price ρ (Fig. 2).

Stackelberg game

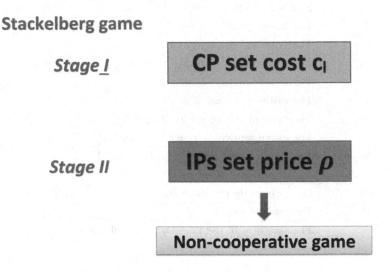

Fig. 2. Stackelberg game modeling.

We formulate a two-stage Stackelberg game among IPs and CP as follows:

- **Players**: IPs and CP.
- **Strategy**: The strategies are the price ρ and the caching price c.
- **Payoff**: The utility function are given in (3) and (2).

Firstly, we solve the first stage of the Stackelberg game, where the CP chooses caching price c to maximize his utility.

The optimization problem of the CP is formulated as follows

$$\max_{c} \Xi = \sum_{j=1}^{M} \left(\sum_{l=1}^{L} c_l y_l \Phi_l \Delta_{jl} + \sum_{l=1}^{L} c_l (1 - y_l) \Phi_l \Delta_{ij} \right) \tag{4}$$

$$s.t. \qquad 0 \leq c_l \leq c_l^{max}$$

where c_l^{max} denotes the maximum caching price of the CP.

Theorem 1. *The optimal solution for Problem* (4) *takes values of either 0 or* c_l^{max}.

Proof. The solution of a maximization (minimization) problem with an objective function that has a linear relationship with the variable is the boundary point of the feasible interval. Therefore, since the relationship between utility function Ξ and c_l is linear, to maximize the utility functions, they just take on the boundary values. Since $c_l \in [0, c_l^{max}]$, therefore, they can be either 0 or c_l^{max}.

We investigate the impact of c_l on the policies of the IPs through numeric analysis in Sect. 4.

Secondly, we consider the second stage game. Given the caching price c_l, we investigate the game between IPs as a non-cooperative game. The non-cooperative game is analyzed in the next section.

4   Price Game

4.1   Game Formulation

Let $\Theta_l = [\mathcal{M}, \{\Omega_{jl}\}, \{\Gamma_j(.)\}]$ denote the non-cooperative price game (NPG), where $\mathcal{M} = \{1, ..., M\}$ is the set of IPs, Ω_{jl} is the strategy set of price and Γ_j is the utility function of IP_j. We assume that the strategy spaces Ω_{jl} is compact and convex sets with maximum and minimum constraints. Thus, for each IP_j we consider as strategy spaces the closed intervals: $\Omega_{jl} = \left[\underline{\rho}_{jl}, \overline{\rho}_{jl}\right]$. Let, the price vector $\rho_l = (\rho_{1l}, ..., \rho_{Ml})^T \in \Omega_l^F = \Omega_{1l} \times \Omega_{2l} \times ... \times \Omega_{Ml}$.

4.2   Game Analysis

Definition 1. *A price vector* $\rho_l^* = (\rho_{1l}^*, ..., \rho_{Ml}^*)$ *is a Nash equilibrium of the NPG* Θ_l *if*

$$\forall (j, \rho_{jl}) \in (\mathcal{M}, \Omega_{jl}), \quad \Gamma_j(\rho_{jl}^*, \rho_{-jl}^*) \geq \Gamma_j(\rho_{jl}, \rho_{-jl}^*)$$

Theorem 2. *The NPG* Θ_l *admits a unique Nash equilibrium.*

Proof. The second derivative of the utility function Γ of IP_j is

$$\frac{\partial^2 \Gamma_j}{\partial \rho_{jl}^2} = -2 \sum_{l=1}^{L} \gamma_{jl}^{jl} \Phi_l \leq 0 \tag{5}$$

The second derivative of the utility function is negative, then the utility function is concave, which ensures existence of a Nash equilibrium in the NPG Θ_l.

We use the following proposition that holds for a concave game [15]: If a concave game satisfies the dominance solvability condition:

$$-\frac{\partial^2 \Gamma_j}{\partial \rho_{jl}^2} - \sum_{m=1, m \neq j}^{M} \left| \frac{\partial^2 \Gamma_j}{\partial \rho_{jl} \partial \rho_{ml}} \right| \geq 0 \tag{6}$$

then, the NPG Θ_l admits a unique Nash equilibrium.

The mixed partial is written as:

$$\frac{\partial^2 \Gamma_j}{\partial \rho_{jl} \partial \rho_{ml}} = \sum_{l=1}^{L} \gamma_{jl}^{ml} \Phi_l \geq 0 \tag{7}$$

Then,

$$-\frac{\partial^2 \Gamma_j}{\partial \rho_{jl}^2} - \sum_{m=1,m\neq j}^{M} \left| \frac{\partial^2 \Gamma_j}{\partial \rho_{jl} \partial \rho_{ml}} \right| = \sum_{l=1}^{L} \Phi_l \left(2\gamma_{jl}^{jl} - \sum_{m=1,m\neq j}^{M} \gamma_{jl}^{jm} \right) \qquad (8)$$

Thus, the NPG Θ_l admits a unique Nash equilibrium.

4.3 Learning Nash Equilibrium

The best response algorithm [3,6] is composed of a sequence of rounds, in each round after the first, every IP observes the prices chosen by its opponents in previous rounds and input them in its decision process to update its price. Algorithm 1 summarizes the best response learning steps that every IP has to perform to find Nash equilibrium.

Algorithm 1. Best response Algorithm

1: Initialize vectors $\rho_l(0) = [\rho_{1l}(0), ..., \rho_{Ml}(0)]$ randomly;
2: **For each** IP_j and item l at time instant t computes:

  – $\rho_{jl}(t+1) = \underset{\rho_{jl} \in \Omega_{jl}}{\operatorname{argmax}} \left(\Gamma_j(\rho_l(t)) \right).$

3: **If** $\forall j \in \mathscr{M}$, $|\rho_{jl}(t+1) - \rho_{jl}(t)| < \epsilon$, then STOP.
4: **Else**, $t \leftarrow t+1$ and go to step (2).

---

5 Numerical Investigation

In this section, we perform the simulation results to illustrate the competitive interactions between providers (CP and IP). We will present the convergence of the best response algorithm to the Nash equilibrium and the impact of the system parameters on the provider prices. To simplify the analysis, we consider a scenario that includes four IPs, one item, and one CPs.

Figure 3 shows, the curves of the convergence to the Nash Equilibrium price. The best response algorithm converges to the unique Nash equilibrium price. In addition, the speed of convergence is relatively high. Figure 3 demonstrates the uniqueness of the Nash equilibrium point at which no IP can profitably deviate given the strategies of other adversaries, which ensures the uniqueness of the equilibrium for keeping the economy stable and achieving economic growth.

Figure 4 shows the impact of caching price c on the Nash equilibrium price of the four IPs. When c increases, the Nash equilibrium price increases. It comes from the fact that when the caching price is cheaper, the IPs lower their prices for attracting more users. On the other hand, when caching price is expensive, IPs need to increase their price to compensate for the increase in the caching price.

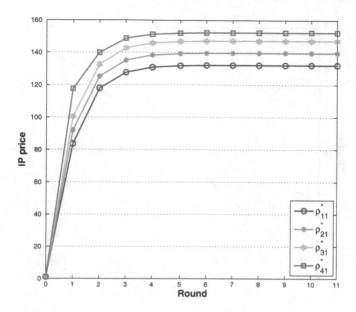

Fig. 3. Convergence to the Nash equilibrium price.

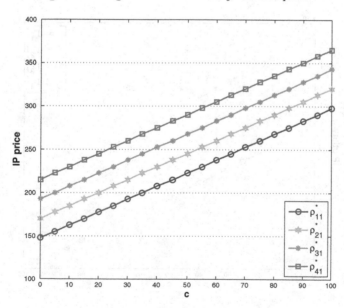

Fig. 4. Nash equilibrium price as a function of caching price c.

We plot the utility function of CP as a function of caching price c in Fig. 5. Utility function increase with respect to the caching price. When the caching

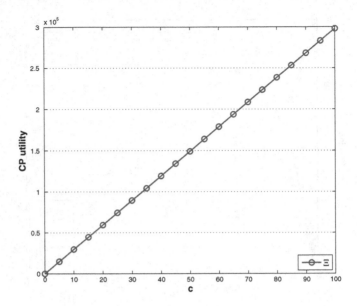

Fig. 5. Utility function of CP as a function of caching price c.

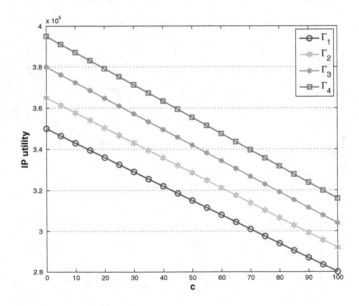

Fig. 6. Utility function of IP as a function of caching price c.

price increases, the revenue from caching increases. In fact, the revenue of CP increases. Caching increases CP revenue.

Figure 6 shows the utility function of the four IPs with respect to caching cost c. Low caching cost tends to yield higher utility compared to the expensive caching cost, this is because when the caching cost increases the IP increases its price to compensate caching cost.

6 Conclusion

This paper proposed a novel architecture, different from conventional architecture, in which the IP deploys cache servers. In this way, we can offer the highest QoS to the users. In addition, the IP decides the content pricing. The competition among IPs is investigated by using the non-cooperative game. Additionally, we have used a Stackelberg game to study the interaction between CP and IP. We consider that the popularity of content follows a generalized Zipf distribution. We demonstrated the uniqueness of the Nash equilibrium. The simulation results show the impact of system parameters on IP and CP policies.

References

1. Ait Omar, D., El Amrani, M., Baslam, M., Fakir, M.: A game-theoretic approach for the internet content distribution chain. In: Podelski, A., Taïani, F. (eds.) NETYS 2018. LNCS, vol. 11028, pp. 270–285. Springer, Cham (2019). https://doi.org/10.1007/978-3-030-05529-5_18
2. Cisco, I.: Cisco visual networking index: forecast and methodology, 2016–2021. In: CISCO White Paper 518 (2017)
3. El Amrani, M., Garmani, H., Ait Omar, D., Baslam, M., Minaoui, B.: Analyzing the dynamic data sponsoring in the case of competing internet service providers and content providers. Mob. Inf. Syst. **2021**, 6629020 (2021)
4. Garmani, H., Ait Omar, D., El Amrani, M., Baslam, M., Jourhmane, M.: Analysis of a dynamics duopoly game with two content providers. Chaos Solitons Fractals. **131**, 109466 (2019)
5. Garmani, H., Ait Omar, D., El Amrani, M., Baslam, M., Jourhmane, M.: The effect of caching on CP and ISP policies in information-centric networks. Mob. Inf. Syst. **2020**, 8895271 (2020)
6. Garmani, H., Ait Omar, D., El Amrani, M., Baslam, M., Jourhmane, M.: Joint beacon power and beacon rate control based on game theoretic approach in vehicular ad hoc networks. Infocommun. J. **13**(1), 58–67 (2021)
7. Garmani, H., El Amrani, M., Baslam, M., El Ayachi, R., Jourhmane, M.: A Stackelberg game-based approach for interactions among Internet service providers and content providers. NETNOMICS: Econ. Res. Electron. Netw. **20**(2–3), 101–128 (2019)
8. Garmani, H., Omar, D.A., Amrani, M.E., Baslam, M., Jourhmane, M.: A game theory approach for UAV-based flying access networks. Int. J. Netw. Virtual Organ. **24**(1), 84–105 (2020)
9. Garmani, H., Omar, D.A., Amrani, M.E., Baslam, M., Jourhmane, M.: Nash bargaining and policy impact in emerging ISP-CP relationships. Int. J. Ad Hoc Ubiquit. Comput. **35**(3), 117–135 (2020)
10. Garmani, H., Omar, D.A., Amrani, M.E., Baslam, M., Jourhmane, M.: A non-cooperative game-theoretic framework for sponsoring content in the internet market. J. Commun. Softw. Syst. **16**(4), 8 (2020)

11. Garmani, H., Outanoute, M., Baslam, M., Jourhmane, M.: New competition-based approach for caching popular content in ICN. In: Podelski, A., Taïani, F. (eds.) NETYS 2018. LNCS, vol. 11028, pp. 286–300. Springer, Cham (2019). https://doi. org/10.1007/978-3-030-05529-5_19
12. Gourdin, E., Maillé, P., Simon, G., Tuffin, B.: The economics of CDNs and their impact on service fairness. IEEE Trans. Netw. Serv. Manag. **14**(1), 22–33 (2017)
13. Hajimirsadeghi, M., Mandayam, N.B., Reznik, A.: Joint caching and pricing strategies for popular content in information centric networks. IEEE J. Sel. Areas Commun. **35**(3), 654–667 (2017)
14. Kerpez, K.J., Cioffi, J.M., Ginis, G., Goldburg, M., Galli, S., Silverman, P.: Software-defined access networks. IEEE Commun. Mag. **52**(9), 152–159 (2014)
15. Lasaulce, S., Debbah, M., Altman, E.: Methodologies for analyzing equilibria in wireless games. IEEE Signal Process. Mag. **26**(5), 41–52 (2009)
16. Maillé, P., Simon, G., Tuffin, B.: Toward a net neutrality debate that conforms to the 2010s. IEEE Commun. Mag. **54**(3), 94–99 (2016)
17. Maillé, P., Tuffin, B.: How do content delivery networks affect the economy of the internet and the network neutrality debate? In: Altmann, J., Vanmechelen, K., Rana, O.F. (eds.) GECON 2014. LNCS, vol. 8914, pp. 222–230. Springer, Cham (2014). https://doi.org/10.1007/978-3-319-14609-6_15
18. Pham, T.M., Fdida, S., Antoniadis, P.: Pricing in information-centric network interconnection. In: IFIP Networking Conference, 2013. pp. 1–9. IEEE (2013). http://ieeexplore.ieee.org/abstract/document/6663526/
19. Zerwas, J., Poese, I., Schmid, S., Blenk, A.: On the benefits of joint optimization of reconfigurable CDN-ISP infrastructure. IEEE Trans. Netw. Serv. Manag. **19**, 158–173 (2021)

Networking

An Eventually Perfect Failure Detector on ADD Channels Using Clustering

Laine Rumreich$^{(\boxtimes)}$ and Paolo A. G. Sivilotti

The Ohio State University, Columbus, OH, USA
rumreich.1@osu.edu, paolo@cse.ohio-state.edu

Abstract. We present an implementation of an eventually perfect failure detector, $\Diamond$P, in a partitionable network with arbitrary topology. This network is built on weak assumptions using ADD channels, which are defined as requiring the existence of constants K and D, not known to the processes, such that for every K consecutive messages sent, at least one is delivered within time D. The best previous implementation of $\Diamond$P on ADD channels uses a heartbeat-based approach with time-to-live values for messages. The message size complexity of this existing implementation is O($En \log n$) for the entire network for any given heartbeat. In contrast, the solution presented in this paper organizes the network into clusters, each with a single leader, to reduce the message size complexity to O(En). The algorithm is structured as a series of superpositioned layers and a proof of correctness is given for the $\Diamond$P oracle based on these layers. We compare the performance of the cluster-based failure detector with that of the best previous solution on various topologies using simulation.

Keywords: Failure detector · ADD channel · Superpositioning · Clustering

1 Introduction

1.1 Context

A failure detector is a distributed oracle that can be queried for information about crashed processes. Failure detectors are a type of consensus problem in that all nodes in a network must agree on the status of all other nodes. However, consensus problems cannot be solved deterministically in an asynchronous system with failures [5,7]. This is known as the impossibility result. Chandra et al. [3] proposed using unreliable failure detectors as an alternative to circumvent this impossibility result. Unreliable oracles make mistakes by incorrectly suspecting correct processes or failing to suspect crashed processes. Although these oracles are allowed to make mistakes, this paper concerns an eventually perfect failure detector, meaning the oracle is only allowed to make these mistakes for a finite amount of time.

© The Author(s), under exclusive license to Springer Nature Switzerland AG 2022
M.-A. Koulali and M. Mezini (Eds.): NETYS 2022, LNCS 13464, pp. 149–166, 2022.
https://doi.org/10.1007/978-3-031-17436-0_11

The eventually perfect failure detector class, $\Diamond$P, was defined by Chandra and Tough [3] and is characterized by the properties of *strong completeness* and *eventual strong accuracy*. These properties are defined as the following:

1. Strong completeness: every crashed process is eventually permanently suspected by every process
2. Eventual strong accuracy: Every correct process is eventually not suspected by every correct process.

Many previous implementations of $\Diamond$P assume models of partial synchrony with bounded message delay or reliable communication [6,14]. Sastry and Pike [15] proposed an algorithm using much weaker assumptions for the communication channel. This communication channel is known as an Average Delayed/Dropped (ADD) channel. This channel promises a certain number of messages are received in a given amount of time. Both the number of dropped messages and the amount of time are unknown to the process, however.

The failure detector defined in this paper is built on top of an ADD channel because it is the weakest communication channel used in previous implementations of $\Diamond$P. Kumar and Welch [10] built upon the initial failure detector result on ADD channels by allowing an arbitrary connected network. This implementation also concerns a $\Diamond$P algorithm on a network of arbitrary topology. Finally, Vargas, Rajsbaum, and Reynaldo constructed an eventually perfect failure detector on ADD channels for an arbitrarily connected network with an improved message size complexity [17]. This improvement was based on the addition of a time-to-live value and heartbeat-based approach, both of which are common techniques in networking.

1.2   Motivation

The result from Vargas, Rajsbaum, and Reynaldo using time-to-live values with a heartbeat-based algorithm has a message complexity size of $O(n\log n)$ per node per heartbeat, which is equivalent to $O(En\log n)$ per heartbeat. This complexity is improved to $O(En)$ in this implementation using a hierarchy of clusters in the network. This hierarchy of clusters can be constructed dynamically from an arbitrary network.

1.3   Contribution

The central contribution of this work is in the reduction in complexity size of the previous best implementation of an eventually perfect failure detector built on ADD channels. This reduction in size complexity requires the additional logical complexity of clustering, a hierarchy of nodes, and the use of superpositioning techniques to organize and structure the algorithm. A proof of correctness for this algorithm is constructed based on the correctness of the underlying algorithm and the addition of an overlay network of nodes to transmit information between leaders. An additional contribution of this work is the addition of a simulation of the algorithm to show convergence for the failure detector comparing the cluster-based algorithm discussed in this work to the original implementation. This simulation compares a variety of topologies and shows that networks with a topology optimized for clusters have improved convergence performance.

2 Background

2.1 Eventually Perfect Failure Detectors

$\Diamond P$ can give unreliable information about process crashes for only a finite prefix. Eventually, it must provide *only* correct information about crashed processes. The oracle $\Diamond P$ is of interest because it is both powerful and implementable. $\Diamond P$ is sufficiently powerful to solve many fundamental problems such as consensus [3]. Unlike Perfect (P) [3], Strong (S) [3], and Marabout detectors [8], $\Diamond P$ is the only oracle implementable in partially synchronous systems [12].

2.2 ADD Channels

The communication channel this work is built on is known as an Average Delayed/Dropped (ADD) channel [15]. An ADD channel from nodes p to q, given unknown constants K and D, satisfies the following two properties:

- The channel does not create or duplicate messages
- For every K consecutive messages sent by p to q, at least one is delivered to q within D time

In addition, processes on ADD channels can fail only by crashing, pairs of processes are connected via two reciprocal ADD channels, and each process has access to a local clock that generates ticks at a constant rate.

2.3 Heartbeat and Time-to-Live

Both heartbeats and time-to-live (TEL) values are used in this work based on the logic from the Vargas et al. [17] version of the algorithm for a failure detector on ADD channels. In that algorithm, heartbeats are used to keep track of the distance of a message across the network. This heartbeat will eventually fade out when a process fails. TEL values are then used to track the intensity level of a message such that as messages travel through the network, the intensity decreases. TELs are commonly used in networking to limit the lifetime of message packets [11].

2.4 Group Membership and Clustering

Group Membership is a similar but separate problem from Consensus. The value that must be agreed upon, group membership, is allowed to change due to asynchronous failures, and non faulty processes may be removed when they are erroneously suspected to have crashed. Techniques used to circumvent the impossibility of Consensus can also be applied to solve the Group Membership Problem [2]. Group membership can be used to generate clusters based on various properties. An unreliable failure detector can be used to generate these groups. Many algorithms can be used to form clusters statically [9].

2.5   Superpositioning

Superpositioning is a general technique for structuring complex algorithms by decomposing these algorithms into distinct layers [1]. In the context of action systems, as used in this paper, each layer augments the layers below with new features (actions and variables) while preserving the functional properties of those lower layers [4]. In order for this preservation of functional correctness to hold, however, the superpositioning of actions and variables must be done in a disciplined way. In particular, while actions introduced in higher layers can *use* (read) the values of variables from lower layers, they must not *modify* (write) these variables. Any variables introduced in a layer, on the other hand, can be both read and written by actions within that layer. This approach allows for a separation of concerns. Each layer can make use of the services provided by lower layers in order to implement some new functionality. That functionality, in turn, is available to higher layers that respect the discipline of superpositioning.

3   Algorithm

3.1   Overview

The following algorithm solves $\Diamond P$ using a two-level hierarchical version of the Vargas et al. [17] $\Diamond P$ algorithm. In this new hierarchical version of the algorithm, the network is categorized into mutually exclusive clusters that form the first level of the hierarchy. Each cluster has a single leader and the set of leaders form the top level of the hierarchy. Each cluster in the network can then be conceptualized as a single node, and $\Diamond P$ is solved between this collection of nodes. Additionally, $\Diamond P$ is solved locally within clusters.

The clusters described for this algorithm must be constructed deliberately for the algorithm to work. The construction of these clusters is described here but not implemented in the pseudocode. The clusters must have the following characteristics: (1) Each cluster has a single leader (2) Each node is either a leader or a cluster node that is assigned to a single leader (3) The entire cluster must be connected using nodes only in the current cluster- that is, it remains connected if all other nodes are removed.

3.2   Description

Cluster nodes communicate information to other nodes in their cluster using a variable called *cluster_HB_bag*, which contains heartbeat and TEL information for their cluster only. These cluster nodes also *forward* information across an overlay network to and from their leader and their neighbors. Leader nodes participate in both the cluster-level and network-level failure detection. They consolidate failure information from their cluster and pass along heartbeat information about other clusters to the leaders. They also update their cluster on the rest of the network through the overlay network messages. In addition to the algorithms for failure detection, a *leader election* algorithm occurs when a leader node has been suspected of failing by one of the nodes in its cluster. The leader election algorithm determines a new leader for a particular cluster. If a cluster has been partitioned, the leader election algorithm will result in one additional leader. The new leader information must also be propagated to all other nodes in the network.

3.3   Layers of Superpositioning

The algorithm presented in this section is constructed in layers rather than as one large algorithm. Some of these layers run on the same nodes, but they are presented in this way to organize the tasks for the heartbeat algorithm separated for the overlay network and clustering requirements. To prove that these layers do not negatively interfere with each other, superpositioning is used. To guarantee the safety properties of the lower levels, lower levels cannot read variables that are written at a higher level. Variables in lower levels of the algorithm also guard higher levels against performing tasks and can trigger actions to occur. For example, a cluster node that becomes separated from its assigned leader will trigger the leader election layer to run. Figure 1 illustrates the five layers of the algorithm including where the shared variables originate and are used in higher layers.

Layer Name	Variables Defined	Variables Accessed
1. Heartbeat - Leader		cluster, cluster_suspect, leaders, leader_clusters
2. Forwarding Overlay		cluster, leader_clusters
3. Leader Notification	leaders, leader_clusters	cluster, leader
4. Leader Election	leader	cluster, cluster_suspect
5. Heartbeat - cluster	cluster, cluster_suspect	

Fig. 1. Algorithm layering and shared variables

3.4   Layer 1: Heartbeat - Leader

The top layer of this algorithm, the heartbeat running on leaders, is the primary method of achieving $\Diamond P$. The overlay network running on the layer below allows this layer to be abstracted as running on leaders that are directly connected without cluster nodes in between. Information is sent and received by leaders using messages that are composed of sets of three-tuples. A single three-tuple includes heartbeat information about the leader plus a simple suspect list composed of only **true** and **false** values comprising the information about that leader's cluster. The set of three-tuples relays heartbeat information about the entire network. This algorithm updates the suspect list for leader nodes, which stores the status of every other node in the network and is thus the primary data structure in the proof of $\Diamond P$ for leader nodes. Algorithm 1 contains the pseudocode for this layer.

Algorithm 1. Heartbeat - Leader **Leader Node** p

Constants:

1: $T, n, neighbors$

Variables:

2: $leader\_clusters, leaders$
3: $leader\_bag, cluster\_suspect, cluster$
4: $clock() \leftarrow 1$
5: **for each** i in Π **do**
6: $\quad suspect[i] \leftarrow false$
7: **end for**
8: **for each** i in $leaders$ **do**
9: $\quad leader\_lastHB[i] = 0$
10: $\quad leader\_timeout[i] = T$
11: $\quad leader\_TTL[i] \leftarrow 1$
12: **end for**

Information Send

13: **every** T units of time of $clock()$
14: **begin:**
15: $\quad leader\_bag \quad \leftarrow \quad \{(p, |leaders| - 1, cluster\_suspect)\}$
16: $\quad$ **for each** $i \in leaders \setminus \{p\}$ **do**
17: $\quad\quad$ **if** $leader\_TTL[i] > 1$ **then**
18: $\quad\quad\quad external\_cluster\_suspect \leftarrow GET\_CLUSTER\_SUSPECT(i, leader\_clusters)$
19: $\quad\quad\quad leader\_bag \leftarrow leader\_bag \cup \{(i, leader\_TTL[i] - 1, external\_cluster\_suspect)\}$
20: $\quad\quad$ **end if**
21: $\quad$ **end for**

22: $\quad$ **for each** $q \in neighbors \setminus cluster$ **do** $\triangleright$ send to non-cluster neighbors
23: $\quad\quad$ **send**($< leader\_bag >$) to q
24: $\quad$ **end for**

25: $\quad$ **for each** $q \in neighbors \cap cluster$ **do** $\triangleright$ send to cluster neighbors
26: $\quad\quad is\_outgoing \leftarrow true$
27: $\quad\quad TLL \leftarrow |cluster| - 1$
28: $\quad\quad$ **send**($< leader\_bag, TTL, is\_outgoing >$) to q
29: $\quad$ **end for**
30: **end**

Information Receive

31: **upon** receiving $< lead\_bag, TTL, is\_outgoing >$ from $q \in cluster$

32: **begin:**
33: $\quad$ **if** not($is\_outgoing$) **then**
34: $\quad\quad$ **for each** $(r, m, array) \in lead\_bag$ such that $r \notin neighbors \setminus \{q\}$ **do**
35: $\quad\quad\quad$ **if** $leader\_TTL[r] \leq m$ **then**
36: $\quad\quad\quad\quad leader\_TTL[r] \leftarrow m$
37: $\quad\quad\quad\quad$ **for each** $node \in leader\_clusters.get(r)$ **do**
38: $\quad\quad\quad\quad\quad suspect[node] \leftarrow array[node]$
39: $\quad\quad\quad\quad$ **end for**
40: $\quad\quad\quad\quad$ **if** $suspect[r] = true$ **then**
41: $\quad\quad\quad\quad\quad suspect[r] \leftarrow false$
42: $\quad\quad\quad\quad\quad ESTIMATE\_TIMEOUT(r)$
43: $\quad\quad\quad\quad$ **end if**
44: $\quad\quad\quad\quad leader\_lastHB[r] \leftarrow clock()$
45: $\quad\quad\quad$ **end if**
46: $\quad\quad$ **end for**
47: $\quad$ **end if**
48: **end**

49: **upon** receiving $< lead\_bag >$ from $q \notin cluster$
50: **begin:**
51: $\quad$ $\triangleright$ Begin from line 34
52: **end**

53: **procedure** ESTIMATE_TIMEOUT(r)
54: $\quad$ **if** $r \in leaders$ **then**
55: $\quad\quad leader\_timeout[r] \leftarrow 2 \cdot leader\_timeout[r]$
56: $\quad$ **end if**
57: **end procedure**

58: **procedure** GET_CLUSTER_SUSPECT($r, leader\_clusters$)
59: $\quad current\_cluster \leftarrow leader\_clusters.get(r)$
60: $\quad j \leftarrow 0$
61: $\quad$ **for each** $i \in current\_cluster$ **do**
62: $\quad\quad array[j] \leftarrow suspect[i]$
63: $\quad\quad j \leftarrow j + 1$
64: $\quad$ **end for**
65: $\quad$ **return** $array$
66: **end procedure**

Leader Timeout

66: **when** $leader\_timeout[q] = clock() - leader\_lastHB[q]$
67: **begin:**
68: $\quad suspect[q] \leftarrow true$
69: **end**

3.5   Layer 2: Overlay Network Message Forwarding

The next layer of this algorithm is the overlay network layer, which transfers information between leader nodes through the cluster nodes. This layer runs only on cluster nodes. The basic structure of the overlay network is to forward messages by broadcasting information to neighbors each heartbeat. Neighbors within the current node's cluster also receive information about whether the current message is *incoming* or *outgoing*. Outgoing messages are those that originated from the current node's leader and will thus be ignored by the leader. Cluster nodes will also update their local suspect list using information from outgoing messages if they are more recent than the current information. For cluster nodes, this suspect list is used to store the status information of every other node in the network and is thus the primary data structure in the proof of $\Diamond P$ for cluster nodes. The detailed pseudocode for this algorithm is included in the Appendix.

Algorithm 2. Forwarding Overlay **Cluster Node** p

Constants:
1: $T, n, neighbors$
Variables:
2: $clock() \leftarrow 1$
3: $leader\_clusters, cluster$
4: **for** each i in Π **do**
5:      $suspect[i] \leftarrow false$ ▷ suspect list for entire network
6: **end for**
7: $FORWARD\_MESSAGES(leader\_clusters, cluster)$

3.6   Layer 3: Leader Notification

A cluster may become partitioned due to failures in the network. When this occurs, a new leader will be elected for one of the halves of the partitioned cluster. When a new leader is elected due to a partitioned cluster, this algorithm spreads that information to existing leader nodes. This allows the leader heartbeat algorithm to accurately update the information from leaders about their clusters. The detailed pseudocode for this algorithm is included in the Appendix.

Algorithm 3. Leader Notification **Cluster Node** p

Variables:
1: $clock() \leftarrow 1$
2: $leaders, leader\_clusters, cluster, leader$
3: **if** leader changes **then**
4:      $leaders, leader\_clusters \leftarrow ALERT(cluster, leader)$
5: **end if**

3.7   Layer 4: Leader Election

The leader election layer of the algorithm performs a basic leader election for a single cluster when the leader fails or the cluster is partitioned. Both of these actions require the addition of a new leader in the algorithm. The pseudocode for the leader election algorithm on ADD channels has been constructed previously [16] and is not included here. The triggering of a new leader election action is guarded by information from the layer below.

Algorithm 4. Leader Election **Node** p

Constants:

1: $T, n, neighbors$

Variables:

2: $clock() \leftarrow 1$

3: $leader, cluster, cluster\_suspect$

3: **if** $cluster\_suspect[leader]$ **then**

4:    $leader \leftarrow \Omega(cluster)$

5: **end if**

3.8   Layer 5: Heartbeat - Cluster

The bottom layer of this algorithm is the heartbeat $\Diamond$P algorithm within clusters. It is running on every node and updates cluster-level suspect information. The logic of this layer is separated based on if the current node is a leader or not. Information from other clusters is not transferred in this layer. Cluster-level information that is transferred by leaders is updated in this level. Cluster-level suspect information is used to inform the shared **cluster** variable.

Algorithm 5. Heartbeat - Cluster: **Cluster Node** p

Constants:

1: $T, n, neighbors$

Variables:

2: $clock() \leftarrow 1$, $cluster, cluster\_bag$

3: **for each** i in $cluster$ **do**

4:    $cluster\_lastHB[i] = 0$

5:    $cluster\_suspect[i] \leftarrow false$

6:    $cluster\_timeout[i] = T$

7:    $cluster\_TTL[i] \leftarrow 1$

8: **end for**

Cluster Send

9: **every** T units of time of $clock()$

10: **begin:**

11:    $cluster\_bag \leftarrow \{(p, |cluster| - 1)\}$

12:    **for each** $i \in cluster \setminus \{p\}$ **do**

13:       **if** $cluster\_suspect[i] = false$ and $cluster\_TTL[i] > 1$ **then**

14:          $cluster\_bag \leftarrow cluster\_bag \cup \{(i, cluster\_TTL[i] - 1)\}$

15:       **end if**

16:    **end for**

17:    **for each** $q \in neighbors \cap cluster$ **do**

18:       **send**($< cluster\_bag >$) to q

19:    **end for**

20: **end**

Cluster Receive

21: **upon** receiving $< gr\_bag >$ from $q \in$ *cluster*

22: **begin:**

23:   **for each** $(r, m) \subseteq gr\_bag$ such that $r \notin neighbors \setminus \{q\}$ **do**

24:     **if** $cluster\_TTL[r] \leq m$ **then**

25:       $cluster\_TTL[r] \leftarrow m$

26:       **if** $cluster\_suspect[r] = true$ **then**

27:         $cluster\_suspect[r] \leftarrow false$

28:         $ESTIMATE\_TIMEOUT[r]$

29:       **end if**

30:       $cluster\_lastHB[r] \leftarrow clock()$

31:     **end if**

32:   **end for**

33: **end**

34: **procedure** ESTIMATE_TIMEOUT(r)

35:   $cluster\_timeout[r] \leftarrow 2 \cdot cluster\_timeout[r]$

36: **end procedure**

Timeout

36: **when** $cluster\_timeout[q] = clock() - cluster\_lastHB[q]$

37: **begin:**

38:   $cluster\_suspect[q] \leftarrow true$

39: **end**

Algorithm 6. Heartbeat - Cluster: **Leader Node** p

Constants:

1: $T, n, neighbors$

Variables:

2: $clock() \leftarrow 1$

3: $cluster, cluster\_bag$

4: **for each** i in $cluster$ **do**

5:   $cluster\_lastHB[i] = 0$

6:   $cluster\_suspect[i] \leftarrow false$ ▷ suspect list for cluster only

7:   $cluster\_timeout[i] = T$

8:   $cluster\_TTL[i] \leftarrow 1$

9: **end for**

Cluster Send

10: **every** T units of time of $clock()$

11: **begin:**

12:   $cluster\_bag \leftarrow \{(p, |cluster| - 1)\}$

13:   **for each** $i \in cluster \setminus \{p\}$ **do** ▷ only include the cluster members

14:     **if** $cluster\_suspect[i] = false$ and $TTL[i] > 1$ **then**

15:       $cluster\_bag \leftarrow cluster\_bag \cup \{(i, TTL[i] - 1)\}$

16:     **end if**

17:   **end for**

18:   **for each** $q \in neighbors \cap cluster$ **do** ▷ only send to neighbors in cluster

19:     send($< cluster\_bag >$) to q

20:   **end for**

21: **end**

Cluster Receive

22: **upon** receiving $< gr\_bag >$ from $q \in$
    $cluster$

23: **begin:**   ▷ receive from a cluster
    member

24:   **for** each $(r, m) \in gr\_bag$ such that
      $r \notin neighbors \setminus \{q\}$ **do**

25:     **if** $TTL[r] \leq m$ **then**

26:       $TTL[r] \leftarrow m$

27:       **if** $cluster\_suspect[r] = true$
      then

28:         $cluster\_suspect[r] \leftarrow false$

29:         $ESTIMATE\_TIMEOUT[r]$

30:       **end if**

31:       $cluster\_lastHB[r] \leftarrow clock()$

32:     **end if**

33:   **end for**

34: **end**

35: **procedure** ESTIMATE_TIMEOUT(r)

36:   **if** $r \in cluster$ **then**

37:     $cluster\_timeout[r] \leftarrow 2 \cdot$
      $cluster\_timeout[r]$

38:   **end if**

39: **end procedure**

Timeout

66: **when** $cluster\_timeout[q] = clock() -$
    $cluster\_lastHB[q]$

67: **begin:**

68:   $cluster\_suspect[q] \leftarrow true$

69: **end**

4   Overlay Network

4.1   The Network Graph $G(t^\epsilon)$

The proof of $\Diamond P$ will be constructed on the arbitrary network graph G after some point in time after all failures have occurred. Graph G at some time t is defined as $G(t) = (correct(\alpha, t), E')$ with $E' = \{(u, v) | (u, v) \in E \text{ and } u, v \in correct(\alpha, t)\}$. Now define t^f to be the earliest time when all the failures in α have occurred. We must now show that after time t^f the graph G will no longer change, and all messages from failed processes cease to circulate.

Lemma 1. *The graph G has the following properties.*

1. $G(t) = G(t')$ for all $t, t' \geq t^f$
2. *There is a time $t^\epsilon \geq t^f$ after which the last message from the set of crashed processes is delivered to a correct process.*

Proof. Let Π be the set of all nodes in the network.

Part One: By construction, at time t^f all failures have occurred. Now it must be the case that $crashed(\alpha, t) = crashed(\alpha, t')$ for all $t, t' \geq t^f$. Since $correct(\alpha, t) = \Pi \setminus crashed(\alpha, t)$, then by the definition of $G(t)$ it is true that $G(t) = G(t')$ for all $t, t' \geq t^f$.

Part Two: The algorithm described in this work has two separate node types: leader nodes and cluster nodes. Every faulty leader clearly sends a finite number of heartbeat messages before crashing. Then, by the properties of the ADD channel, these messages are lost, delivered or experience arbitrary delays. Thus there exists a time $t^\epsilon \geq t^f$ after which the last message sent by the set of faulty leader processes is delivered. Cluster nodes also send a finite number of heartbeat messages and the proof applies by the same argument. Cluster nodes also forward messages to and from other nodes. Each of these messages are bounded by a timeout value by construction and thus will stop being forwarded in some finite amount of time. Now it is clear that for both leader and cluster nodes, there exists a time $t^\epsilon \geq t^f$ after which the last message sent by the set of faulty leader processes is delivered.

From this point we will assume that we have reached time t^ϵ such that all failures have occurred and all messages from failed nodes have finished circulating through the network. Similarly, all references to graph G from this point on refer to some time after t^ϵ. https://www.overleaf.com/project/61dde39fc5e336dabd0727fe.

The Overlay Network. G' In this section we will now define a graph G'. In particular, we will show that G is an implementation of the model G'.

To define G', consider the model for a network defined by Vargas et al. [17] defining a set of processes $\Pi = \{1, 2, ..., n\}$ connected by ADD channels in both directions and represented an undirected graph $G' = (V, E)$ where $V = \Pi$. This network consists of *channels* and *processes*.

Channels. The channels in this model are ADD channels, meaning they satisfy the definition from [15].

Processes. Processes may fail only by crashing. Given an execution α, a process p is said to crash at time t if p does not perform any event in α after time t and crashed(α, t) is the set of all processes that have crashed by time t. A process p is correct at time t if p has not crashed by time t and $correct(\alpha, t) = \Pi \setminus crashed(\alpha, t)$.

We will define a relation from the overlay network in the algorithm to the underlying network. The following section will demonstrate how the overlay network can be viewed as an implementation of the underlying network.

4.2   Overlay Network Relation

Consider the topology of the network defined in the $\Diamond$P with clusters algorithm in this paper. We will show that this graph topology can be considered an implementation of the underlying network defined using ADD channels.

Recall that the network is partitioned into distinct, connected clusters, each with a single leader. Consider each cluster as a single node with the same connections to other clusters as the original topology, but as a single connection. A representation of the connection from the network to the abstract view of the network is shown in Fig. 2 and Fig. 3. The following sections will prove that this abstraction results in a network with ADD channel properties.

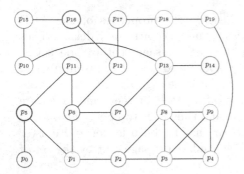

Fig. 2. Network Topology Overlay, G

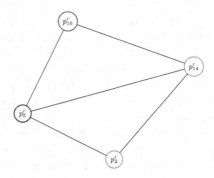

Fig. 3. Network Topology, G′

5   Proof of ◇P

5.1   Proof Outline

The proof of ◇P for this algorithm is based on two parts:

1. A proof that this algorithm is an implementation of the abstraction constructed by Vargas et al. [17], represented by the graph G'
2. The proof of ◇P by Vargas et al. [17] on graph G'

The rest of this section concerns part one only. The proof of ◇P follows from part one and Vargas et al. [17].

5.2   Proof of Overlay Network Model

This section concerns G', which is a graph of edges and nodes. The proof that the overlay network forms an abstraction between the network of leaders and the underlying network requires proving two things: that the edges of G' still satisfy the properties of ADD channels and that the nodes of G' still operate and fail in the correct way. In particular, this proof concerns the graph G' after some time t^ϵ.

Edges - ADD Channel. An ADD channel from p to q has associated constants K, D, such that the following properties are satisfied:

1. The channel does not create, modify, or duplicate messages
2. For every K consecutive messages sent by p to q, at least one is delivered to q within time D

Property 1. The first property of the overlay network that the implementation must satisfy is that the channel does not create, modify, or duplicate messages. The channels in the network topology will be modeled to not modify or duplicate messages, even though the underlying implementation does not fit these requirements. The overlay network modifies incoming messages by adding a TEL, but this value is removed when the message is relayed to the cluster leader, so we can model the network as one that does not modify the messages. The overlay network also allows duplicate messages because any new incoming message from outside or within the cluster will be broadcast to every neighbor in the cluster. However, these messages are labeled with a unique identifier, so if duplicates arrive at the leader, they can be ignored, and the model preserves the no-duplicates property.

Property 2. We must also show that for every K consecutive messages sent by p to q, at least one is delivered to q within time D. Without loss of generality, we will consider messages from leader 1, ℓ_1, to leader 2, ℓ_2. Let the path from ℓ_1 to ℓ_2 be $\ell_1, p_1, p_2, ..., p_n, \ell_2$. Now, each p is a node in an overlay network or is a cluster, which can be abstracted as a single leader node. Since each channel along this path is an ADD channel, there exists some K_i, D_i for each i along the path from ℓ_1 to ℓ_2. Now, a message from ℓ_1 is guaranteed to be received by ℓ_2 by the $K^t h$ consecutive message where K is: $K = \Pi_{i=0}^{n} K_i$. Similarly, this message will be delivered within time D where D is: $D = \Pi_{i=0}^{n} D_i$.

Nodes - Cluster Model. To match the underlying network, each cluster must be modeled by a single node. Clusters are running both a $\Diamond$P algorithm and a transmission network to transfer information. The overlay network must correctly transfer information from the edge of the cluster to the leader and back. The path must also be limited to cluster members only. The TEL of these messages guarantees that they will not survive past the length of the longest path of unique nodes in the cluster. Messages are broadcasted to and from nodes, so they are guaranteed to reach the leader and then back to the edge nodes. Incoming and outgoing messages are separated so that information coming from outside the cluster does not leave the cluster without modification. The primary requirement to show is that leaders have correct information that can then be sent through the overlay network to other leaders. The proof of correctness for the underlying $\Diamond$P algorithm applies directly to within-cluster communication. Finally, failures that cause clusters to no longer be connected or no longer have a functioning leader result in the construction of new clusters. These new clusters must be connected and have a leader, thus the model of the overlay network always remains consistent with the underlying network.

5.3   ◇ P

The Vargas et al. [17] proof of correctness for ◇P now applies to the network G' at time t^ϵ after all failures have occurred. Now, since G is an implementation of the G' abstract model, the proof of ◇P for the arbitrary network running the algorithm is complete.

6   Complexity

The size complexity of this algorithm is calculated based on the size and number of messages sent in the network for a single heartbeat. The following equation represents that value, where E represents the number of edges in the graph, E' is the number of edges within clusters, n is the number of nodes, and ℓ is the number of leaders:

$$O(E' \cdot \frac{n}{\ell} \log n) + O(E(n + \ell \cdot \log n)) \tag{1}$$

These two terms are separated based on the complexity at both hierarchy levels. The first term is the complexity of the heartbeat algorithm within clusters. The second term is the complexity of the leader-level heartbeat algorithm including the overlay network.

1. Cluster Heartbeat: The sum over each cluster node of the degree of the node times the (worst case) size of its HB_bag. The size of this variable is a $(\log n)$ encoding times the size of the cluster, sent to every neighbor.
2. Leader Heartbeat and Forwarding: A message including the HB_lead_bag (size number of leaders times $\log n$) plus an array of size n with the status (1 or 0) of every node in the network, sent across every edge in the network two times.

In order to minimize the complexity, the leader size must be chosen. At the extremes, which includes having each node as a leader and having no leaders, the complexity of the algorithm with clusters does not improve from $O(E \cdot n \log n)$. The complexity of the algorithm with clusters is reduced to $O(En)$ when the number of leaders is chosen to be $\log n$, $\sqrt{n}$ or any number of other values.

6.1   Leader Election Complexity

An additional aspect of the complexity of this algorithm is the leader election that occurs upon the failure of a leader node. The complexity of this algorithm would be a maximum of $O(E \cdot \log n)$ [13]. Thus this additional cost does not impact the overall message size complexity of this algorithm.

7 Experimental Results

In order to measure the expected-case behavior of our cluster-based $\Diamond P$ algorithm, a simulation was conducted over a variety of network topologies and failure modes [18]. Since the message space complexity can be calculated analytically (see previous section), this simulation focussed on the relative delay in convergence to an accurate suspect list in $\Diamond P$. The links between nodes are assumed to be ADD channels with identical delay and drop characteristics, so the convergence time is reported in number of heartbeats. Topologies considered range from a single chain at one extreme to a fully connected graph on the other.

Table 1 compares the convergence times for the original and cluster-based algorithms on a variety of topologies. Each topology has 100 nodes. Three different scenarios were tested with each topology: one node suspecting one other node, every node suspecting one node, and every node suspecting every other node.

Table 1. Heartbeats until convergence

Network	Leaders	Average Degree	Original Algorithm 1-1/M-1/M-M	Cluster Algorithm 1-1/M-1/M-M
Chain	5	.99	223/223/295	98/98/122
Chain	10	.99	223/223/295	50/50/62
Chain	15	.99	223/223/295	38/38/44
Chain Conn. Clusters	5	3.09	1/4/4	3/8/8
Chain Conn. Clusters	10	1.54	1/4/4	3/8/8
Chain Conn. Clusters	15	1.27	1/4/4	3/8/8
Fully Conn. Clusters	5	42	4/4/4	6/6/6
Fully Conn. Clusters	10	9.5	4/4/4	6/6/6
Fully Conn. Clusters	15	8.5	4/4/4	6/6/6
Fully Conn. Leaders	5	4.5	1/4/4	3/5/14
Fully Conn. Leaders	10	3.25	1/4/4	3/17/29
Fully Conn. Leaders	15	3.07	1/4/4	3/5/44
Average Connectedness	5	3.2	1/4/4	3/5/14
Average Connectedness	10	3.1	1/4/4	3/17/29
Average Connectedness	15	3.07	1/4/4	3/5/44
Fully Connected	5	49.5	1/1/3	3/5/5
Fully Connected	10	49.5	1/1/3	3/5/5
Fully Connected	15	49.5	1/1/3	3/5/5

The time to convergence is similar for both algorithms. The cluster-based algorithm performs better for sparsely connected graphs with large diameter. For densely connected graphs, the original algorithm's advantage diminishes with the number of erroneous suspicions.

8   Conclusion

This paper demonstrates a modification and improvement upon a previous implementation of an eventually perfect failure detector on ADD channels based on a hierarchical, cluster-based overlay network and superpositioning. This algorithm demonstrates a reduction in the message size complexity of the best previous implementation of $\Diamond$ P of complexity $O(E \cdot n \log n)$ down to complexity $O(En)$. Additionally, a simulation demonstrates a similar time to convergence for the cluster-based algorithm compared to the previous implementation. This convergence time was tested using a variety of network topologies. Future work could be done to expand the hierarchy of this algorithm to more than two levels to further improve the message complexity size.

Appendix

Algorithm 7. Transmit Leader Information **Node** p

1: **procedure** ALERT
2:    **every** T units of time of $clock()$
3:    **begin:**
4:         ▷ Where ADD_Transmit is the link level reliable transmission of information
5:       $ADD\_TRANSMIT(cluster, leader)$
6:    **end**
7: **end procedure**

Algorithm 8. Transmit Messages **Cluster Node** p

1: **procedure** FORWARD_MESSAGES
2:   **upon** receiving $<$ *leader_bag*, *TTL*, *is_outgoing* $>$ from $q \in cluster$
3:   **begin:**
4:     *local_leader_bag* $\leftarrow$ *leader_bag*
5:     $UPDATE\_SUSPECT(leader\_bag)$
6:   **end**

7:   **every** T units of time of *clock*()
8:   **begin:**
9:     ▷ Send to other clusters
10:    **if** *is_outgoing* **then** ▷ send outgoing information to non-cluster neighbors
11:      **for each** $q \in neighbors \setminus cluster$ **do**
12:        send($< local\_leader\_bag >$) to q
13:      **end for**
14:    **end if**
15: **end**

16: ▷ Within-cluster Send/Receive
17: **every** T units of time of *clock*()
18: **begin:**
19:    **if** $TTL > 1$ **then** ▷ Transfer incoming and outgoing information to other cluster members
20:      **for each** $q \in neighbors \cap cluster$ **do** ▷ only send to neighbors in cluster

21:        send($< leader\_bag, TTL - 1, is\_outgoing >$) to q
22:      **end for**
23:    **end if**
24: **end**

25: ▷ Receive from other clusters
26: **upon** receiving $< leader\_bag >$ from $q \notin cluster$
27: **begin:**
28:    **for each** $q \in neighbors \cap cluster$ **do**
29:      *is_outgoing* $\leftarrow$ *false*
30:      $TTL \leftarrow |cluster| - 1$
31:      *message* $\leftarrow$ *leader_bag*, *TTL*, *is_outgoing*
32:    **end for**
33: **end**

34: **every** T units of time of *clock*()
35: **begin:**
36:    **for each** $q \in neighbors \cap cluster$ **do**
37:      send($< message >$) to q
38:    **end for**
39: **end**
40: **end procedure**

41: ▷ Create local copy of suspect list
42: **procedure** UPDATE_SUSPECT(*leader_bag*)
43:   **for each** $(r, m, array) \in leader\_bag$ **do**
44:     **if** $leader\_TTL[r] \leq m$ **then**
45:       $leader\_TTL[r] \leftarrow m$
46:       **for each** $node \in leader\_clusters.get(r)$ **do**
47:         $suspect[node] \leftarrow array[node]$
48:       **end for**
49:       **if** $suspect[r] = true$ **then**
50:         $suspect[r] \leftarrow false$
51:         $ESTIMATE\_TIMEOUT(r)$
52:       **end if**
53:       $leader\_lastHB[r] \leftarrow clock()$
54:     **end if**
55:   **end for**
56: **end procedure**

References

1. Back, R.J., Sere, K.: Superposition refinement of parallel algorithms. In: FORTE (1991)
2. Chandra, T.D., Hadzilacos, V., Toueg, S.: The weakest failure detector for solving consensus. J. ACM **43**(4), 685–722 (1996). https://doi.org/10.1145/234533.234549
3. Chandra, T.D., Toueg, S.: Unreliable failure detectors for reliable distributed systems. J. ACM **43**(2), 225–267 (1996). https://doi.org/10.1145/226643.226647
4. Chandy, K.M., Misra, J.: Parallel Program Design: A Foundation. Addison-Wesley Publishing Company, Reading (1988)
5. Dolev, D., Dwork, C., Stockmeyer, L.: On the minimal synchronism needed for distributed consensus. J. ACM **34**(1), 77–97 (1987). https://doi.org/10.1145/7531.7533
6. Fetzer, C., Schmid, U., Susskraut, M.: On the possibility of consensus in asynchronous systems with finite average response times. In: 25th IEEE International Conference on Distributed Computing Systems (ICDCS 2005), pp. 271–280 (2005). https://doi.org/10.1109/ICDCS.2005.57
7. Fischer, M.J., Lynch, N.A., Paterson, M.S.: Impossibility of distributed consensus with one faulty process. J. ACM **32**(2), 374–382 (1985). https://doi.org/10.1145/3149.214121
8. Guerraoui, R.: On the hardness of failure-sensitive agreement problems. Inf. Process. Lett. **79**(2), 99–104 (2001)
9. Jain, A.K., Dubes, R.C.: Algorithms for Clustering Data. Prentice-Hall Inc, Hoboken (1988)
10. Kumar, S., Welch, J.: Implementing $\lozenge P$ with bounded messages on a network of add channels. Parallel Process. Lett. **29** (2017). https://doi.org/10.1142/S0129626419500026
11. Kurose, J.F., Ross, K.W.: Computer Networking: A Top-Down Approach, 7th edn. Pearson, Boston (2016)
12. Larrea, M., Fernandez, A., Arevalo, S.: On the implementation of unreliable failure detectors in partially synchronous systems. IEEE Trans. Comput. **53**(7), 815–828 (2004). https://doi.org/10.1109/TC.2004.33
13. Rajsbaum, S., Raynal, M., Vargas, K.: Brief announcement: leader election in the add communication model. In: Stabilization, Safety, and Security of Distributed Systems: 22nd International Symposium, pp. 229–234 (2020). https://doi.org/10.1007/978-3-030-64348-5_18
14. Raynal, M., Mourgaya, E., Mostefaoui, A.: Asynchronous implementation of failure detectors. In: 2013 43rd Annual IEEE/IFIP International Conference on Dependable Systems and Networks (DSN), p. 351. IEEE Computer Society, Los Alamitos, CA, USA, June 2003. https://doi.org/10.1109/DSN.2003.1209946
15. Sastry, S., Pike, S.: Eventually perfect failure detectors using add channels. In: ISPA, pp. 483–496, August 2007
16. Sergio Rajsbaum, M.R., Godoy, K.V.: Leader election in arbitrarily connected networks with process crashes and weak channel reliability. In: 22nd International Symposium on Stabilization, Safety, and Security of Distributed Systems (2020)
17. Vargas, K., Rajsbaum, S., Raynal, M.: An eventually perfect failure detector for networks of arbitrary topology connected with add channels using time-to-live values. Parallel Process. Lett. **30**(02), 2050006 (2020). https://doi.org/10.1142/S0129626420500061
18. Zirger, K., Rumreich, L., Sivilotti, P.: Failure Detector with Clusters Simulation (2022). https://github.com/osu-rsrg

Making CSMA Collision-Free and Stable Using Collaborative Indexing

J. J. Garcia-Luna-Aceves[✉] and Dylan Cirimelli-Low

Computer Science and Engineering Department, University of California,
Santa Cruz, CA 96064, USA
jj@soe.ucsc.edu, dcirimel@ucsc.edu

Abstract. CSMA with collaborative indexing (CSMA/CI) is introduced, in which nodes collaborate with one another using carrier sensing and short signaling packets to establish collision-free schedules without the need for time slotting or the definition of transmission frames as in TDMA. The throughput of CSMA/CI is compared with the throughput of TDMA with a fixed transmission schedule, ALOHA, CSMA, and CSMA/CA analytically and with simulation experiments.

Keywords: Channel access · Transmission scheduling · CSMA

1 Introduction

A striking aspect of channel-access in wireless networks today is that, while enormous progress has been attained in making the physical-layer of wireless nodes much more powerful and efficient, the same amount of progress has not been attained in the methods used at the medium-access control layer. Carrier-sense multiple access (CSMA) [16] and CSMA with collision avoidance (CSMA/CA) are widely used channel-access methods for the sharing of common radio channels in ad-hoc networks today. In fact, they are integral parts of the IEEE 802.11 protocol standard. While carrier sensing provides a major improvement over ALOHA [1], in which nodes access a common channel without any coordination, CSMA and CSMA/CA, experience substantial performance degradation as traffic load increases; furthermore, these methods cannot provide channel-access delay guarantees. As Sect. 2 summarizes, many approaches have been developed over the years to limit or eliminate the negative effects of multiple-access interference (MAI) that result from multiple nodes offering packets to a common channel. These approaches [4,15] can be characterized into contention-based and contention-free methods. Contention-based methods like ALOHA are relatively simple to implement but result in poor channel utilization at high loads and cannot provide channel-access delay guarantees. Contention-free methods result in high channel utilization and channel-access delay guarantees; however, most require fixed schedules, clock synchronization or complex signaling.

Our focus in this paper is on augmenting the way in which CSMA operates over a single channel by taking advantage of the fact that the data-storage

M.-A. Koulali and M. Mezini (Eds.): NETYS 2022, LNCS 13464, pp. 167–183, 2022.
https://doi.org/10.1007/978-3-031-17436-0_12

capacity available today in wireless-network nodes, even in simple nodes that are part of IoT deployments, is many orders of magnitude larger and cheaper than it was 40 or 50 years ago when ALOHA and CSMA were first introduced. For simplicity we focus on fully-connected wireless networks; however, our results can be augmented with collision avoidance techniques and integrated with the signaling of IEEE 802.11 DCF.

Section 3 introduces *CSMA with Collaborative Indexing* (**CSMA/CI**). The simple premise in the design of CSMA/CI is to use carrier sensing and a shared index of the nodes sharing the channel to establish a collision-free transmission schedule in a distributed and autonomic manner. Nodes collaborate with one another using CSMA and short signaling packets similar to those used in CSMA/CA to create and maintain a shared index. The shared index is used to define the order in which nodes should be allowed to transmit data packets without MAI from other transmissions. Signaling packets are sent very often initially when there is large demand for nodes to be added to the shared index, and are sent sporadically once nodes have spent enough time growing the size of the index and most nodes are part of the collision-free schedule. No central controller, time slotting or transmission frames requiring clock synchronization are needed for CSMA/CI to establish collision-free transmission schedules with channel-access delay guarantees.

Section 4 computes the throughput attained with CSMA/CI and the average delays incurred to attain steady-state operation during which signaling overhead is minimum. Section 5 compares the throughput of CSMA/CI with the throughput of TDMA, CSMA, CSMA/CA and ALOHA using numerical results from the analytical model, and using discrete-event simulations in ns-3 [18]. The results show that CSMA/CI renders efficient and stable collision-free channel access taking advantage of carrier sensing, data-storage capacity, and very simple signaling. In addition, simulation results show that CSMA/CI established stable transmission schedules remarkably fast. Section 6 presents our conclusions and outlines directions for future work.

2   Related Work

Channel-access methods can be viewed as contention-based and contention-free [4]. ALOHA [1] is the simplest example of contention-based methods, and most of them have used physical-layer mechanisms like time slotting, carrier sensing, successive interference cancellation, directional antennas, multiple antennas, code-division multiple access, and multiple channels to improve on the performance of ALOHA. Another approach used to improve channel utilization is the use of short handshake signaling packets between senders and receivers to limit multiple access interference (MAI). Starting with the early work by Capetanakis [5], many approaches have been proposed based on distributed algorithms intended to resolve packet collisions over multiple rounds of retransmissions of the packets that encounter MAI. More recent approaches include the use of machine-learning techniques (e.g., [6,24]) or shared information regarding the state of the channel (e.g., [10]) in the selection of time slots or the amount of back-off applied after packet collisions.

Many contention-free methods have been proposed, and most of them require transmission frames consisting of a fixed number of time slots or a time-slotted channel, and use different algorithms to establish transmission schedules [4, 20] unless a static time-slot allocation is used. The mechanisms that have been used for scheduling include distributed elections of time slots for broadcast or unicast transmissions (e.g., [2, 3, 19]), and the reservation of time slots based on voting or node-to-node handshakes (e.g., [21–23, 26]).

A number of prior methods eliminate the need of fixed-length transmission frames by using lexicographic ordering of the identifiers of transmitting nodes, geographical or virtual coordinates related to the connectivity of nodes [7], or a common tree of periodic schedules of variable periods [14]. However, all these approaches must use time slotting supported at the physical layer.

Starting with the Distributed Queue Random Access Protocol (DQRAP) [25], several methods have used the notion of a distributed transmission queue to control access to the channel and avoid MAI. They differ on how the distributed transmission queue is maintained, and the approaches use time slotting and mini-slots (e.g., [25]), control handshakes between senders and intended receivers (e.g., SITA [13]), or a predefined target value for the queue size [11, 12, 17]. A salient feature of these approaches compared to the approach we present in this paper is that the transmission schedule adopted by nodes is not a direct consequence of nodes storing a list of the active nodes using the shared channel.

3   CSMA with Collaborative Indexing (CSMA/CI)

3.1   Information Stored and Maintained

Each node executing CSMA/CI stores a copy of the shared index listing the order in which nodes are allowed to transmit once an index of at least two node entries exists. Each node also stores and maintains an index-cycle counter (IC) stating how many additional index cycles must take place before the system is in steady state. The local copy of the index is initialized to be empty and IC is set to N_c, which is a configuration parameter intended to allow many join-index turns during the first index cycles following initialization.

Nodes exchange four types of packets to update and use the shared index, namely: Request-to-Initialize (RTI), Connect-to-Index (CTI), data, and Deletion-to-Index (DTI) packets. The RTI-CTI exchanges described below constitute an admission control mechanism used to initialize the shared index at each active node sharing the channel with the schedule of data transmissions free of MAI and organized into index cycles. By contrast, CSMA/CA only resolves channel access for a single data packet. Nodes can determine when the shared index has been initialized in a distributed manner, and at that point CTI's can be sent by new nodes only after they hear data packets with a specific flag set. Carrier sensing is used by nodes to skip an empty transmission turn in an index cycle, and nodes send DTI's when they wish to leave the shared index for long time periods.

Request-to-Initialize (RTI) Packet: An RTI is used to initialize the index and specifies the packet type, the identifier of the sender, a channel-reservation time, and error checking. The channel-reservation time is the length of time that the channel is reserved for other nodes to submit requests to be added to the index. An RTI is similar to a Request-To-Send (RTS) packet in CSMA/CA. However, an RTS is intended for a specific receiver while an RTI is intended for all other nodes and provides multiple opportunities for the transmission of requests by any of them in response to the RTI.

Each join-index can last at most one turn-around time, the transmission time for a CTI, and a maximum propagation delay. Accordingly, the number of join-index turns A intended by the sender of an RTI is implied by the channel-reservation time stated in the RTI packet.

Connect-to-Index (CTI) Packet: A node sends a CTI in response to an RTI to request being added to the index. A CTI specifies the packet type, the identifier of the sender, the identifier of the sender of the last packet received correctly, and error checking.

A CTI is different from a Clear-To-Send (CTS) in CSMA/CA, which is intended for the sender of an RTS to immediately send a data packet. By contrast, a CTI has a dual purpose: it allows all other nodes to add the identifier of the sending node to the shared index, and it provides an acknowledgment to the last packet transmitted successfully.

Data Packet: A node sends a data packet to transmit application data, acknowledge a prior packet, and manage the allocation of join-index turns once the shared index has been initialized. Accordingly, a data packet specifies the packet type, the identifier of its sender, the identifier of the sender of the last packet received correctly, an index-cycle counter (IC), a request flag (RF), the identifier of the intended receiver of the payload, the payload length, the data payload, and error checking.

Including the identifiers of the sender of the last successful packet in the header of a data packet eliminates the need for a separate acknowledgment packet that would consume more channel time because of framing requirements. The index-cycle counter indicates whether the index must be allowed to grow rapidly $(IC > 0)$ or is in steady state $(IC = 0)$. An RTI is allowed to follow a data packet only when $RF = 1$.

Deletion-to-Index (DTI) Packet: A node sends a DTI to stop its participation in the index and states: the packet type, the identifier of its sender, the identifier of the sender of the last packet received successfully, and error checking. A node transmits a DTI during its own transmission turn.

In the rest of this paper we assume that nodes that join the index remain in it until they fail and hence do not use DTI's. A node in a typical wireless network would simply remain transmitting packets as needed containing application data or control signaling needed at higher layers of the protocol stack.

3.2 Initializing the Shared Index

Before nodes can start transmitting data packets, they must establish a shared index that defines the schedule with which nodes listed in the index transmit data packets without MAI.

Figure 1 illustrates the transmission of RTI's for the case in which RTI's are unsuccessful. In the example shown in the figure, the RTI's from nodes a, b, and c are transmitted within the vulnerability period of packet transmissions according to CSMA. This time period is at most equal to the maximum propagation delay needed for the packet signal to reach a node sensing carrier (τ_m) plus the time needed for the node to start detecting carrier (η).

Once a node transmits an RTI, it schedules its retransmission at a time equal to the channel reservation time needed to allow A join-index turns for nodes to send CTI's in response to the RTI, plus an additional random retransmission time T_r seconds with $0 \leq T_r \leq T_m$. The time allocated to each of the A join-index turns must be long enough to include the time needed for the sender of a CTI to transition from listening to transmit mode (ω), the transmission time of a CTI (α), the maximum propagation delay (τ_m) for the CTI to reach all other nodes, and an additional τ_m seconds to account for the maximum length of time between the first and the last CTI sent during the same join-index turn. Accordingly, each of the A join-index turns lasts at most $\ell = \omega + \alpha + 2\tau$, and a node retransmits an RTI after $(A)(\ell) + T_r$ seconds.

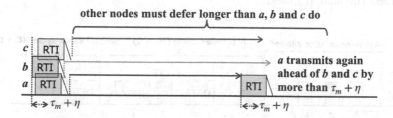

Fig. 1. Failed RTI transmissions leading to first RTI success

A node that has an RTI to transmit and detects carrier must wait for a backoff time $T_b > (A)(\ell) + T_m$, so that those nodes whose RTI's collided have another chance to succeed. A node that backs off transmits its RTI after T_b seconds if no RTI from another node is received or carrier is detected.

The value of A is a configuration parameter intended to allow many join-index turns during the initialization of the index. Given that index initialization takes place when the wireless network is first started and having more than a few hundred of nodes in a wireless LAN is highly unlikely, making $A = 2^8$ or 2^9 is reasonable for networks of up to a few hundred nodes. Having many successful

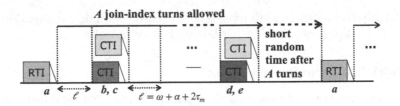

Fig. 2. Failed attempt to initialize index after RTI success

CTI's during initialization reduces contention among CTI's in the index cycles following initialization.

In the example shown in Fig. 1, the carrier of the RTI retransmission by node a is detected by nodes b and c before their retransmission timers expire, which allows the RTI from node a to succeed. Once the first RTI is sent without MAI, all other nodes know that the shared index has been started with the sender of the RTI as the *head of the index*.

Figure 2 shows an example in which node a sends an RTI successfully and hence all other nodes learn that node a is the head of the index. However, none of the CTI's sent in response of the RTI from a succeed. The join-index turns are either not used or occupied by more than one CTI. Accordingly, as the figure illustrates, node a retransmits its RTI after $(A)(\ell) + T_r$ seconds, and no other node is allowed to transmit an RTI.

Figure 3 shows an example in which at least one CTI succeeds after an RTI is sent without MAI and hence the head of the index (node a in the example) can start *index cycles* consisting of data-packet transmissions by the nodes that have joined the shared index.

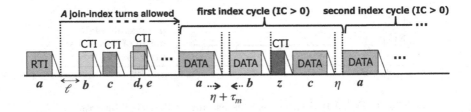

Fig. 3. Successful attempt to initialize the shared index

In the example of Fig. 3, the CTI from node b acknowledges the RTI from node a, which then knows that it is the head of the index. The CTI from node c acknowledges the CTI from node b, and no other CTI succeeds during the channel-reservation time of the RTI. Node a initiates the first index cycle with a data packet that acknowledges the CTI from node c. Nodes b and c also send data packets during the first index cycle, node z sends a CTI successfully following the data packet from node b, and no other CTI succeeds in the same cycle. Accordingly, node z is added to the shared index and the sequence of data packet transmissions in the next cycle is $a \rightarrow b \rightarrow z \rightarrow c$.

We assume that CTI's sent in response to an RTI are sent using A join-index turns following the RTI. A node with a CTI to be sent randomly selects only one of the A RTI's. If the node does not receive a packet that acknowledges its CTI, it backs off randomly and attempts to transmit its CTI during a future index cycle if the index is initialized, or after a subsequent transmission of an RTI otherwise.

3.3   Providing Join-Index Turns in Index Cycles

A node that needs to join the shared index once the index has been initialized can transmit a CTI only at the beginning of a join-index turn following a data packet that has $RF = 1$. The first few index cycles following the shared index initialization are such that a join-index turn is allowed after each data packet transmission in order to allow more nodes to quickly join the shared index.

The number of join-index turns allowed in each index cycle is controlled by means of the index-cycle counter (IC) included in each data packet. The head of the index sets $IC = N_c$ in its first data-packet transmission. The rest of the nodes that listen to that transmission use the same value for their first data-packet transmissions, and each node in the shared index decrements the value of IC by one after each data-packet transmission, and eventually $IC = 0$.

As long as $IC > 0$, nodes set $RF = 1$, which results in an index-join turn following each data packet for the first N_c index cycles after the index is initialized, and provides many opportunities for CTI's to succeed in order to grow the shared index quickly when many nodes need to be added to the index.

Once $IC = 0$, only the head of the index sets $RF = 1$ in its data packets, and the rest of the nodes set $RF = 0$. This results in a single join-index turn following the data packet from the head of the index in each index cycle. At most one new node can be added to the index in a given cycle, and its position follows the position of the head of the index.

A node with a CTI to send waits for the start of the next join-index turn and then transmits. This simple transmission strategy adapts to the three channel-access phases of CSMA/CI. If a node does not receive a packet that acknowledges its own CTI, the node backs off immediately and tries to send a CTI at a future random time that is larger than the length of the current index cycle.

If only one CTI is transmitted during a join-index turn, its duration consists of the time needed for the sender of the CTI to turn from listening to transmit mode (ω), the time needed to transmit the CTI (α), and the propagation delay for the CTI to reach the next node in the index (τ). If multiple nodes transmit CTI's concurrently during a join-index turn, the time duration of that turn also includes the time difference ϵ between the transmission of the first and the last CTI sent concurrently during the turn, with $\epsilon \leq \tau_m$ being the result of different propagation delays from the transmitter of a data packet and the nodes sending CTI's following that.

If no CTI is sent during a join-index turn, the node in the next index position takes only η seconds to detect carrier; however, the node must wait for an additional maximum propagation delay τ_m to ensure that differences in propagation delays do not cause MAI. An example of MAI avoidance based on this time padding is when the next node in the index is very close to the previous node in the index while a node that could send a CTI is far away from both nodes. In this case, without the added waiting time the next node $x + 1$ in the index could assume that no CTI is being sent simply because it is very close to the previous node x in the index and the carrier from the CTI from a far-away node does not reach node $x + 1$ within η seconds after node $x + 1$ receives the transmission from node x. In the example of Fig. 3, $IC = N_c > 2$, which makes all nodes set $RF = 1$ in their data packets. Accordingly, a join-index turn follows each data-packet transmission in the two index cycles shown. The value of N_c is not critical, and we assume $N_c = 10$ in our simulations.

3.4   Sending Data Packets in Index Cycles

Channel access in CSMA/CI after the first N_c index cycles occur consists of a sequence of index cycles with a single join-index turn per cycle. The order of transmissions by nodes in the shared index is determined by the position of the join-index turn during which the nodes transmitted their CTI's successfully. Figure 4 illustrates the transmission of data packets in CSMA/CI with the head of the index being node a.

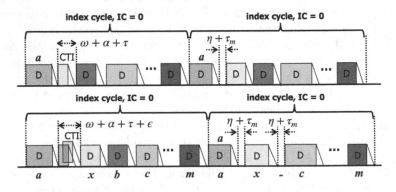

Fig. 4. Steady-state channel access with CSMA/CI once $IC = 0$

The first index cycle shown in the example results in a successful CTI transmission, the second and fourth cycles shown have empty join-index turns, and the third cycle has a collision of two CTI's sent concurrently. The fourth index cycle in the figure has node b being silent, and node c transmitting as soon as it determines that there is no packet from node b.

The duration of a packet-transmission turn consists of the turn-around time needed for the sender of the data packet to start transmitting, the transmission time of the data packet, and the propagation delay incurred by the data packet to reach nodes that may need to send CTI's to join the index. A data packet can last at most one *maximum channel access turn* (MCAT), so that no node can keep using the channel indefinitely.

A node that has joined the shared index and does not have user data to send when its transmission turn occurs remains silent. A node n that follows a silent node s in the shared index uses carrier sensing to determine when it can start transmitting after receiving the transmission from node p preceding node s in the index. To account for differences in propagation delays from p to s and from p to n, node n waits for $\eta + \tau_m$ seconds after the transmission from node p to decide that it can start transmitting. If the head of the index is silent, a node with a CTI to be sent waits for $\eta + \tau_m$ to determine that the node is silent before transmitting.

3.5   Handling Errors, Node Failures, and Nodes Leaving and Joining the Network

The ACK to the last packet received correctly included in each CTI and data packet allows transmitting nodes to learn about the occurrence of transmission errors in their CTI's due to MAI or channel effects, and the occurrence of errors in data packets due to channel effects.

A node that leaves the shared index intentionally sends a DTI during its last cycle and the rest of the nodes update the index accordingly. However, nodes must handle the failure of nodes that have joined the shared index, and steps must be taken to allow new nodes to join the shared index without disrupting the transmission turns assigned to the nodes that have already joined the index.

As we have described in Sect. 3.3, nodes that want to join the shared index can only do so only after they receive a data packet stating $RF = 1$. The steps described in the previous section allow new nodes to join the shared index by simply inserting their identifiers in the ordered list of identifiers maintained by each node that belongs to the shared index, without causing any transmission disruptions in the current index cycle or future index cycles.

A node that has already joined the index and whose turn follows the turn assigned to a failed node waits to detect carrier from the data packet by the previous node in the index just as in the case when the previous node in the index is just silent during its turn. Multiple consecutive empty data-packet turns may occur if a sequence of silent and failed node occurs in the index, and each empty turn lasts $\eta + \tau_m$.

A node is declared to have failed and is deleted from the index after a few index cycles take place without a transmission from the node. This applies to the head of the index as well, and the next node in the shared index becomes the new head of the index.

A node that is just initialized must wait for a *startup time* that is longer than a few index cycles to access the channel. A new node populates its copy of the shared index and the value to use for IC by listening to the channel for a few index cycles. Once the startup time has elapsed, a node waits for the next data packet with $RF = 1$ to send a CTI if the node has acquired a non-empty index. A node sends an RTI if it does not hear any packets after the startup time elapses.

4   Throughput of CSMA/CI

We assume the same traffic model used to analyze ALOHA [1], CSMA [16], and many other channel-access methods in the past. According to this model, a large number of stations form a Poisson source sending packets to the shared channel with an aggregate mean rate of λ packets per unit time. Data packets have a time duration equal to δ seconds, and RTI's and CTI's last α seconds. The only source of errors is MAI and multiple concurrent transmissions fail and must all be retransmitted, and every packet propagates to all nodes with the same propagation delay τ. A fixed turn-around time of ω seconds is assumed for transitions from receive-to-transmit or transmit-to-receive modes, and the time needed for a node to detect carrier is η. A node that backs off does so for a random amount of time such that packet transmissions for new arrivals and backlogged arrivals can be assumed to be independent of one another. The only physical-layer feedback is the decoding of packets received without MAI, and the system operates in steady state.

To simplify our analysis, we approximate the strategy used by a node with a CTI to be sent as follows: (a) The node sends its CTI at the start of the next available join-index turn if the CTI became available during the initialization period of the shared index or in an index cycle taking place during steady-state operation; and (b) the node sends its CTI at the start of the next join-index turn if the CTI became available during the current index turn of one of the first N_c index cycles following an RTI, else the node backs off randomly and attempts its transmission at a future time.

In steady state, the throughput of CSMA/CI is the percentage of time the channel is used for the transmission of data packets during each index cycle. The following theorem states this result assuming that a transmitted data packet has a non-empty payload with probability ν, the number of nodes in the shared index is N, and $IC = 0$ at every node in the shared index, so that a single join-index turn is allowed per index cycle.

Theorem 1. *The throughput of CSMA/CI in steady state when the size of the shared index is N equals*

$$S = \frac{\nu \delta N}{N(\eta + \tau + (\delta + \omega - \eta)\nu) + \omega + \alpha + \tau + (\eta - \omega - \alpha)e^{-\lambda \rho}} \tag{1}$$

where $\rho = N(\eta + \tau + (\delta + \omega - \eta)\nu)$

Proof. Any node for which a CTI is ready for transmission during the current index cycle waits and transmits its CTI at the start of the next join-index turn following the transmission by the head of the index. Based on the model assumptions, $\tau_m = \tau$ and the probability p_ε that the join-index turn of an index cycle

of length N has no CTI transmissions equals the probability that no CTI's are
ready for transmission during a period of time of length

$$\rho = N(\nu[\omega + \delta + \tau] + (1 - \nu)([\eta + \tau]) = N(\eta + \tau + (\delta + \omega - \eta)\nu) \quad (2)$$

Accordingly, $p_\varepsilon = e^{-\lambda\rho}$ and hence the average time consumed by the join-index
turn of a cycle is

$$T_j = (\eta + \tau)p_\varepsilon + (\omega + \alpha + \tau)(1 - p_\varepsilon) = \omega + \alpha + \tau + (\eta - \omega - \alpha)e^{-\lambda\rho} \quad (3)$$

The average time of a data-packet turn of an index cycle is

$$T_d = \nu(\omega + \delta + \tau) + (1 - \nu)(\eta + \tau) = \eta + \tau + \nu(\delta + \omega - \eta) \quad (4)$$

The average duration of an index cycle is then $T_j + NT_d$, and the average
time spent sending data packets with payloads is $U = N\nu\delta$. The result in Eq. (5)
follows by taking the ratio $U/(T_j + NT_d)$ and substituting Eqs. (3) and (4).

5   Performance Comparison

We compare the performance of CSMA/CI with the performance of CSMA with
ACK's, ALOHA with ACK's and CSMA/CA to emphasize the dramatic performance improvements attained with the use of a shared index maintained
collaboratively among nodes using signaling that is similar to the signaling used
in CSMA/CA. We compare CSMA/CI with TDMA with a fixed transmission
schedule because TDMA offers the best performance of traditional contention-
free methods, which helps us show that CSMA/CI attains better channel efficiency than all these methods without the need for complex hardware, careful
planning, or a pre-established infrastructure. We present numerical results from
our analytical model and simulations carried out using ns-3 [18].

5.1   Throughput Results from Analytical Model

Results are normalized to the length of a data packet by making $\delta = 1$ and using
$G = \lambda \times \delta$, where λ is the arrival rate of all packets. The normalized value of
other variables equals their ratios with δ.

We assume the following system parameters: The channel data rate is 10
Mbps, physical distances are 300 m, and data packet are 1500 bytes, which results
in a normalized $\tau = 8.3 \times 10^{-4}$. The turn-around time ω is assumed to be the
same as a propagation delay, and an ACK in ALOHA and CSMA consists of 40
bytes.

To compare CSMA/CI and TDMA with ALOHA, CSMA and CSMA/CA,
we make the simplifying assumption that a node in the TDMA schedule and a
node already in the shared index transmits a data packet during its time slot
or index turn whenever there is any packet arrival within δ seconds prior to the
start of its time slot or turn. Assuming that the arrival of packets is Poisson

with parameter λ, it follows that $\nu = 1 - e^{-\lambda\delta}$. With this assumption, the result in Theorem 1 can be restated as follows:

$$S_{csma/ci} = \frac{\delta N \left(1 - e^{-\lambda\delta}\right)}{N(\eta + \tau + (\delta + \omega - \eta)\left(1 - e^{-\lambda\delta}\right)) + W} \tag{5}$$

where

$$W = \omega + \alpha + \tau + (\eta - \omega - \alpha)e^{-\lambda\rho}$$
$$\rho = N \left(\eta + \tau + (\delta + \omega - \eta)\left(1 - e^{-\lambda\delta}\right)\right)$$

For the case of TDMA with a fixed schedule, the length of a time slot equals the length of a data packet, a turn-around time, and the propagation delay. Therefore, the throughput of TDMA is

$$S_{tdma} = \frac{\delta \left(1 - e^{-\lambda\delta}\right)}{\delta + \omega + \tau} \tag{6}$$

The throughput results for ALOHA and non-persistent CSMA with ACK's, and non-persistent CSMA/CA are given by the following equations [8,10] assuming that the length of an RTS and CTS equals the length of an ACK (α):

$$S_{aloha} = \frac{\lambda\delta e^{-2\lambda\delta}}{1 + \lambda e^{-\lambda\delta}\left(\tau + \lambda e^{-\lambda\delta}[\omega + \alpha + \tau]\right)} \tag{7}$$

$$S_{csma} = \frac{\delta}{\omega + \alpha + \tau + \frac{1}{\lambda} + e^{\lambda(\omega+\tau)}(\delta + 2\omega + 2\tau)} \tag{8}$$

$$S_{csma/ca} = \frac{\delta}{\delta + 2\alpha + 4\omega + 5\tau + \frac{1}{\lambda} + e^{\lambda(\omega+\tau)}(\alpha + 2\tau + \omega)} \tag{9}$$

Figure 5 shows throughput results from the analytical model. CSMA/CI is much more efficient than all the other methods at light to moderate loads and is as efficient as TDMA at high loads for any size of the shared index larger than 2.

5.2   Results from Simulation Experiments

We compare the average throughput of TDMA with a fixed schedule, CSMA/CI, ALOHA with ACK's, CSMA with ACK's, and CSMA/CA using the ns-3 simulator [18]. The simulation experiments were based on fully-connected networks of 10, 50 and 100 nodes placed randomly over a 212 m × 212 m grid resulting in propagation delays of at most 1 μs. No channel capture or channel errors occur, the data rate is 10 Mbps, and the transmission rate for the PLCP (Physical Layer Convergence Procedure) preamble and header of 24 bytes is 1 Mbps.

ALOHA, CSMA, and CSMA/CA use a binary exponential backoff scheme with a maximum backoff time of 1 s. ACK's in ALOHA, CSMA, and CSMA/CA are set to 14 bytes of IEEE 802.11 ACK's. The time slots in fixed-schedule TDMA accommodate the largest packet size. Data packets in CSMA/CI add 30 bytes, which suffices to carry the necessary signaling and support a payload length of up to 2048 bytes, which is sufficient to support Ethernet frames. When calculating the throughput of CSMA/CI, we consider the time spent successfully transmitting data packets, excluding the CSMA/CI header.

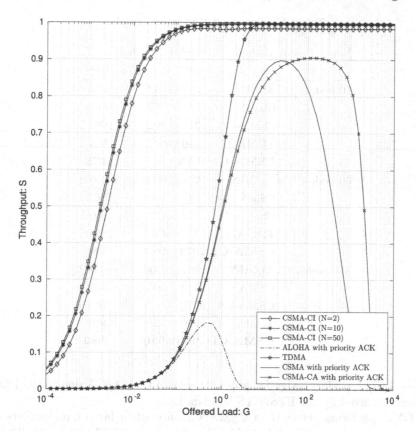

Fig. 5. Throughput of TDMA, ALOHA, CSMA, CSMA/CA, and CSMA/CI

Throughput Results. Table 1 shows the normalized throughput for TDMA, ALOHA, CSMA, CSMA/CA and CSMA/CI. We consider networks with 10 and 50 nodes and data payloads of 218 bytes, 1500 bytes, and an even combination of them. The table shows the mean of 10 trials for each experiment lasting 10 min. Standard deviations were negligible for all MAC protocols because of the long duration of each 10 min experiment. CSMA/CI attains far better throughput than ALOHA, CSMA, and CSMA/CA independently of the network size or payload type, with better than 94% throughput in all cases. The small throughput degradation with small payloads in CSMA/CI results from the relatively larger overhead of propagation delays and turn-around times in queue turns with short packets.

ALOHA performs much worse with large and mixed payloads because the average vulnerability period of a data packet is larger. In fact, as the network size increases, its throughput vanishes due to the amount of MAI. CSMA and CSMA/CA perform better with large payloads, because the overhead of priority ACK's and handshake packets is comparatively smaller than with small data

Table 1. Normalized throughput results

Network size	Method	Packet size (bytes)		
		218	50%/50%	1500
10 nodes	ALOHA	.271	.132	.096
	CSMA	.643	.805	.862
	CSMA-CA	.373	.462	.693
	TDMA	.260	.625	.991
	CSMA-CI	**.975**	**.977**	**.978**
50 nodes	ALOHA	.028	.003	<.001
	CSMA	.643	.805	.862
	CSMA-CA	.373	.447	.693
	TDMA	.260	.625	.991
	CSMA-CI	**.977**	**.980**	**.980**
100 nodes	ALOHA	.002	<.001	<.001
	CSMA	.643	.805	.862
	CSMA-CA	.373	.447	.693
	TDMA	.260	.625	.991
	CSMA-CI	**.980**	**.980**	**.980**

packets. CSMA performs significantly better than CSMA/CA due to the PLCP overhead incurred by the RTS/CTS handshake.

TDMA performs better than CSMA/CI only when large data packets are transmitted most of the time. In SMA/CI outperforms TDMA when small packets are transmitted, data traffic involves a heterogeneous mix of packet lengths, nodes do not send data payloads every time they are given a chance to transmit.

CSMA/CI eliminates an inherent problem in TDMA resulting from the need to use fixed-length transmission opportunities that may be either too short or too long, which results in packet fragmentation or decrease channel utilization.

Delay Results. Figure 6 shows the short delays incurred in adding *all* network nodes to the shared index starting from the time when the first RTI is successful. Results are shown for a system with 10, 25, 50 and 100 nodes. The simulation experiments use RTI's with values of A of 256 or 512. All nodes which receive an RTI choose at random from the A join-index turns to transmit in. The value of N_c used in the experiments is 10. For small values of n, the node join times are uniformly distributed within the A join slots with high probability. The results for $n = 100$ show that a higher value of A is desirable for large networks, because then fewer nodes need to join the index during index cycles.

The time within which all nodes join the shared index in CSMA/CI is remarkably short. As Fig. 6 shows, even in a large system of 100 nodes, the time needed for all nodes to be added to the shared index on a completely autonomic basis is shorter than 250 ms.

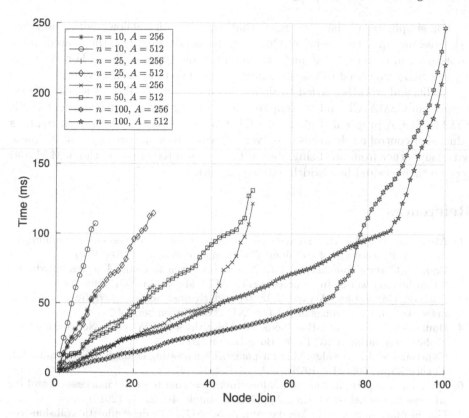

Fig. 6. Average delay for all nodes to join the shared index in CSMA-CI

6   Conclusions

We introduced CSMA/CI, a new channel-access method that quickly attains collision-free transmissions and provides maximum channel-access delay guarantees in fully-connected wireless networks taking advantage of carrier sensing, the data-storage capacity of communicating nodes, and simple signaling. The signaling overhead in CSMA/CI is very small once the system reaches steady state, but permits nodes to quickly join the system. The performance results show that CSMA/CI performs better than contention-based protocols as well as TDMA. The shared-index approach used in CSMA/CI also eliminates the need for a central node to orchestrate channel access to prevent MAI as it is done in IEEE 802.11 point coordination function (PCF) and IEEE 802.11e hybrid coordination function (HCF).

This paper focused on fully-connected wireless networks. However, similar approaches to those we have introduced for CSMA/CA [9] can be applied to CSMA/CI to address the negative effects of hidden terminals. Our future work focuses on augmenting the signaling of CSMA/CI to work efficiently in multi-hop wireless networks.

For simplicity, we have assumed that all nodes have flows with the same priorities and quality of service (QoS) requirements. However, the shared-index approach can certainly take into account multiple types of flows. For example, a given node may need to transmit more than once in an index cycle.

Additional work is needed to define priorities and quality of service (QoS) support in CSMA/CI, and to compare the resulting solution to the recent IEEE 802.11e EDCA proposal (Enhanced DCF Channel Access), which itself requires admission-control mechanisms to prevent flows of the same priority that compete with each other from not being able to have guarantee access without MAI and receive their desired bandwidth, latency, or jitter.

References

1. Abramson, N.: The ALOHA system-another alternative for computer communications. In: Proceedings of Fall Joint Computer Conference 1970 (1970)
2. Bao, L., Garcia-Luna-Aceves, J.J.: A new approach to channel access scheduling for ad hoc net-works. In: Proceedings of ACM MobiCom 2001, July 2001
3. Bao, L., Garcia-Luna-Aceves, J.J.: Hybrid channel access scheduling in ad hoc networks. In: Proceedings of IEEE ICNP 2002, November 2002
4. Boukersche, A., et al.: Handbook of Algorithms for Wireless Networking and Mobile Computing. CRC Press, Boca Raton (2005)
5. Capetanakis, J.: Tree algorithm for packet broadcasting channel. IEEE Trans. Inf. Theory 25(5), 505–515 (1979)
6. Chu, Y., et al.: Application of reinforcement learning to medium access control for wireless sensor networks. Eng. Appl. Artif. Intell. 46, 23–32 (2015)
7. Garcia-Luna-Aceves, J.J., Masilamani, A.N.: NOMAD: deterministic collision-free channel access with channel reuse in wireless networks. In: Proceedings of IEEE SECON 2011, June 2011
8. Garcia-Luna-Aceves, J.J.: Carrier-sense multiple access with collision avoidance and detection. In: Proceedings of ACM MSWiM 2017, November 2017
9. Garcia-Luna-Aceves, J.J.: Implementing correct and efficient collision avoidance in multi-hop ad-hoc networks. In: Proceedings IEEE IPCCC 2018, November 2018
10. Garcia-Luna-Aceves, J.J.: KALOHA: ike i ke ALOHA. In: Proceedings of IEEE MASS 2019, November 2019
11. Garcia-Luna-Aceves, J.J., Cirimelli-Low, D.: Queue-sharing multiple access. In: Proceedings of ACM MSWiM 2020, November 2020
12. Garces, R., Garcia-Luna-Aceves, J.J.: Collision avoidance and resolution multiple access with transmission groups. In: Proceedings of IEEE INFOCOM 1997, April 1997
13. Jakllari, G., Ramanathan, R.: A sync-less time-divided MAC protocol for mobile ad-hoc networks. In: IEEE MILCOM 2009, October 2009
14. Jakllari, G., Neufled, M., Ramanathan, R.: A framework for frameless TDMA using slot chains. In: Proceedings of IEEE MASS 2012, October 2012
15. Jurdak, R., et al.: A survey, classification and comparative analysis of medium access control protocols for ad hoc networks. IEEE Commun. Surv. Tutor. 6(1), 2–16 (2004)
16. Kleinrock, L., Tobagi, F.A.: Packet switching in radio channels: part I - carrier sense multiple-access modes and their throughput-delay characteristics. IEEE Trans. Commun. 23(12), 1400–1416 (1975)

17. Muir, A., Garcia-Luna-Aceves, J.J.: An efficient packet-sensing MAC protocol for wireless networks. Mob. Netw. Appl. **3**(2), 221–234 (1998)
18. NS3 Network Simulator. https://www.nsnam.org
19. Ramanathan, S., Lloyd, E.L.: Scheduling algorithms for multihop radio networks. IEEE/ACM Trans. Netw. **1**(2), 166–177 (1993)
20. Sgora, A., et al.: A survey of TDMA scheduling schemes in wireless multihop networks. ACM Comput. Surv. **47**(3), 1–39 (2015)
21. Tang, Z., Garcia-Luna-Aceves, J.J.: A protocol for topology-dependent transmission scheduling. In: Proceedings of IEEE WCNC 1999, September 1999
22. Tang, Z., Garcia-Luna-Aceves, J.J.: Hop reservation multiple access (HRMA) for ad-hoc networks. In: Proceedings of IEEE INFOCOM 1999 (1999)
23. Vergados, D.J., et al.: Local voting: optimal distributed node scheduling algorithm for multihop wireless networks. In: INFOCOM Workshop 2017 (2017)
24. Wang, S., et al.: Deep reinforcement learning for dynamic multichannel access in wireless networks. IEEE Trans. Cogn. Commun. Netw. **4**(2), 257–265 (2018)
25. Xu, W., Campbell, G.: A distributed queuing random access protocol for a broadcast channel. In: Proceedings of ACM SIGCOMM 1993, October 1993
26. Zhu, C., Corson, M.S.: A five phase reservation protocol (FPRP) for mobile ad hoc networks. In: Proceedings of IEEE INFOCOM 1998 (1998)

ProgDTN: Programmable Disruption-Tolerant Networking

Markus Sommer$^{(\boxtimes)}$ ⓘ, Jonas Höchst ⓘ, Artur Sterz ⓘ, Alvar Penning ⓘ, and Bernd Freisleben ⓘ

Department of Mathematics and Computer Science, University of Marburg, Marburg, Germany
{msommer,hoechst,sterz,penning,freisleb}@informatik.uni-marburg.de

Abstract. Existing routing algorithms for disruption-tolerant networking (DTN) have two main limitations: (a) a particular DTN routing algorithm is typically designed to achieve very good performance in a specific scenario, but has limited performance in other scenarios, and (b) DTN routing algorithms do not take advantage of network programmability to profit from its benefits. We present *ProgDTN*, a novel approach to support *programmable disruption-tolerant networking* by allowing network operators to implement and adapt routing algorithms without knowledge of a router's interior workings using the popular JavaScript language. To consider the specific properties of a particular application scenario, network operators can incorporate context information of DTN bundles and nodes in their routing algorithms. ProgDTN is based on DTN7, a flexible and efficient open-source, platform-independent implementation of the Bundle Protocol version 7. Our experimental evaluation demonstrates that using ProgDTN to tailor a routing algorithm to a particular scenario achieves excellent results of up to 99.9% delivery ratio while reducing unnecessary transmissions by 92.9%. ProgDTN's implementation, our tailored scenario-specific routing algorithm, and code/data fragments for our experiments are released under permissive open-source licenses.

1 Introduction

Originating from developments related to the exploration of outer space, *disruption-tolerant networking (DTN)* has found its way into numerous terrestrial applications, e.g., in scenarios where communication networks are destroyed or disrupted and cannot be repaired for days. Apart from natural disasters, it may be hard for people to communicate via mobile devices in remote areas without a deployed telecommunication infrastructure. When end-to-end connectivity is not available, DTN can be utilized to keep communications going without the need for traditional infrastructures. However, utilizing DTN for communication requires custom network protocols, since protocols of the widely used TCP/IP stack are not well suited for such challenging situations. Therefore, several routing algorithms were developed for DTNs. Some are targeted at general purpose

M.-A. Koulali and M. Mezini (Eds.): NETYS 2022, LNCS 13464, pp. 184–200, 2022.
https://doi.org/10.1007/978-3-031-17436-0_13

applications, i.e., they rely on the connectivity inside the network or are based on conventional routing schemes, such as link-state routing. Other DTN routing algorithms are constructed for specific scenarios, such as the movement of people during a workday or emergency situations. We argue that each DTN routing algorithm is designed for a specific scenario in which it achieves very good performance, but has limited performance in other scenarios.

Conventional network protocols of the TCP/IP stack suffer from the same limitations, which motivated the introduction of *programmable networks* in the literature. For example, Software-defined Networking (SDN) offers programmable means of configuring networks using customized algorithms for processing and routing. Typically, this leads to optimized performance in terms of latency, throughput, and/or resilience. We argue that DTN should also take advantage of network programmability to profit from its benefits like time and cost savings, reduction of human error, customization, and improved performance. However, the SDN approach cannot directly be transferred to DTN, because SDN, in general, requires a coordinating entity that deploys (programmable) rules to network nodes. In most cases, a coordinating entity is not present in DTNs.

In this paper, we present *ProgDTN*, a novel approach to support *programmable disruption-tolerant networking* by allowing network operators to program a node's routing behavior based on DTN bundle metadata, additional bundle context, and node context. Node and bundle context can be used to reflect the specifics of a particular scenario, e.g., the speed of a node in a mobile scenario, the battery level of nodes in a scenario without fixed power supply, or geographic information of the context of a bundle. ProgDTN consists of a programming interface that allows a network operator to program the routing algorithm without knowledge of the router's interior workings. ProgDTN's implementation is based on DTN7 [16], a flexible and efficient open-source, platform-independent implementation of the Bundle Protocol version 7 [6], and uses JavaScript as the programming language, because it is widely used and easy to understand. In our experimental evaluation, we compare ProgDTN to four existing routing algorithms. We demonstrate that a programmable DTN routing algorithm tailored to a specific scenario achieves excellent results in terms of up to 99.9% delivery ratio while reducing unnecessary transmissions by 92.9% compared to other state-of-the-art DTN routing algorithms in an emergency response scenario. We achieve a low delivery time of bundles (1–15 s) and a low overhead in terms of CPU utilization and routing decisions. Our contributions are:

- We present ProgDTN, a novel approach for programmable DTN routing.
- We show that using ProgDTN, network operators can tailor routing algorithms to their individual scenarios by incorporating context information.
- We present a comparative experimental evaluation of ProgDTN, achieving excellent results in terms of delivery ratio, delivery times, and overhead.

– We make ProgDTN's implementation, our scenario-specific routing algorithm,[1] and code/data fragments of our experimental evaluation[2,3] available under permissive open-source licenses.

The paper is organized as follows. In Sect. 2, an overview of related work in the field of delay-tolerant routing is given. Sections 3 and 4 cover ProgDTN's design and implementation. Section 5 discusses the results of our experiments. Finally, Sect. 6 concludes the work and outlines areas for future work.

2   Related Work

This section gives a brief overview of related work on context-aware routing in general and context-aware routing in DTN.

Context-Aware Routing. Apart from using information about the network topology, context-aware routing algorithms use additional information to make routing decisions. Here, we focus on context-aware routing protocols for wireless mobile ad hoc networks (MANETs).

The History-based Routing Protocol for Opportunistic Networks (HiBOp) uses social information, such as club memberships or home addresses to infer the likelihood of encounters and improve routing decisions [5]. Dynamic Social Grouping-based Routing (DSR) is a routing algorithm that harnesses social grouping for efficient routing in ad hoc networks [7]. The Inheritance Inspired Context-Aware Routing Protocol (IICAR) follows a biology-inspired approach to routing based on Mendel's laws of inheritance [3].

The protocol proposed by Biswas et al. [4] uses the properties of ad hoc wireless networks. It maintains static context, such as node and interface types and social information, and dynamic context, e.g., geolocation, channel quality, and encounter frequency. The information is used to calculate utility scores, combined using a routing metric to determine a delivery probability for each message. Messages are forwarded to a) the closest short-range neighbor and b) a long-range neighbor selected based on the delivery probability and the distance.

The algorithm proposed by Errouidi et al. [9] uses context information to improve resilience in MANETs. It employs a fuzzy logic system for three context metrics, a node's remaining energy storage, distance between peers, and node mobility, to judge its "stability". This allows it to improve routing decisions by avoiding unstable nodes, which improves network stability and delivery metrics.

Context-Aware Delay-Tolerant Routing. The Context-Aware Adaptive Routing (CAR) protocol harnesses context information for routing decisions

---

[1] https://github.com/umr-ds/dtn7-go/tree/progdtn.
[2] https://github.com/umr-ds/progdtn-evaluation.
[3] https://dshare.mathematik.uni-marburg.de/index.php/s/8k6XZgKJp9kTMPS.

DTN and combines synchronous and asynchronous transmission [14,15]. Messages are transmitted synchronously using a distance vector routing approach if the recipient is located in the same neighborhood. If no direct connection between sender and recipient exists, asynchronous (DTN) transfer is used, where a node computes delivery probabilities of the directly connected nodes based on its context information. It is up to the network provider to define concrete attributes, utility functions, and weights for the generic approach.

The Sensor Context-Aware Routing (SCAR) protocol for distributed sensor networks [13] is based on the CAR protocol, omitting the distinction between synchronous and asynchronous transmissions. The approach only handles a single specific use case and does not attempt to provide a general routing algorithm.

A further routing scheme that competes with CAR was proposed by Johari et al. as Context-Aware Community Based Routing (CACBR) [11]. Message forwarding is based on a combination of network and context parameters, such as communities a peer belongs to, message delivery and forwarding history, and available buffer space and battery level.

In general, schemes that attempt to harness social and community relations are relatively common; another example is the Socially-Aware Adaptive Delay Tolerant Network (DTN) routing protocol by Ullah and Qayyum [19]. It utilizes a metric called degree centrality to estimate how well a node is embedded in a community to drive forwarding decisions.

Beak et al. [2] propose a version of the PRoPHET routing algorithm, improved by using context information. While the authors show that their proposed protocol outperforms regular PRoPHET, it still relies significantly on the underlying protocol, and the use of context information is limited.

Another approach was proposed by Rosas et al. [17]. It is not focused on designing a routing algorithm that includes context information, but instead measures the performance of different algorithms under different context values and then uses future context information to choose the optimal one.

To the best of our knowledge, no attempt has been made in related work to create a general-purpose, context-aware, programmable DTN routing system.

3   ProgDTN Design

In this section, we present the design of ProgDTN, including DTN fundamentals, system requirements, context information, and ProgDTN's architecture.

3.1   DTN Fundamentals

The data transmission unit of the *bundle protocol* is a *bundle*, which consists of multiple *blocks*. Each bundle must contain a *primary block* containing basic metadata, such as the bundle's ID, sender and recipient IDs, and a *payload block* that carries the bundle's payload. A bundle can also include an arbitrary number of *extension blocks*. While the DTN standard specifies several extension block types, it allows implementations to specify additional types.

A node in DTN operates in a store-carry-forward manner, i.e., when a bundle is received, it is stored in local, long-term storage, from where it will be regularly forwarded. When forwarding, the network daemon invokes the configured routing algorithm to select a subset of currently connected peers to which the bundle should be forwarded. The actual peer-to-peer connection is abstracted in a so-called *convergence layer* (CL) that may use any lower-layer communication protocol to achieve data transmission. ProgDTN is designed to be entirely independent of any specific communication infrastructure and works with any standard-compliant convergence layer.

3.2   System Requirements

ProgDTN's goal is to allow network operators to develop scenario-specific routing algorithms without modifying the DTN software itself. Furthermore, changes to the routing algorithm should not require recompilation of the DTN software to reduce the complexity of deploying new or adjusted routing algorithms. Instead, the forwarding rules are loaded at startup from a provided script file and interpreted by the DTN software. In this way, algorithms may be swapped by restarting the DTN software and giving it a different file to load. To specify these forwarding rules, we use a general-purpose programming language and embed an interpreter into the DTN software. This allows maximum flexibility without having to learn a new domain-specific language.

3.3   Context Information

ProgDTN belongs to the class of context-aware routing algorithms, i.e., routing decisions may be based on additional information of the environment in which the network exists. *Context* refers to any information about the nodes, bundles they are transmitting, or any other information that the network operator may deem helpful. ProgDTN does not put any semantic restrictions on context information, except that each piece of information needs to be uniquely named. Instead, we provide network operators with a generic, powerful interface for generating and processing relevant context information.

Context Types. ProgDTN distinguishes between two classes of context information, *bundle context* and *node context*. Bundle context is any additional information attached to an otherwise normal bundle, e.g., the physical location of the bundle's recipient, information about the originator or the recipient, and really anything that the network operator might think of. On the other hand, node context is information about a specific node, such as the node's location, the node's battery status, and its connectivity status. This information is not usually attached to other bundles, but if it must be communicated to other nodes, the node broadcasts it using a special context bundle.

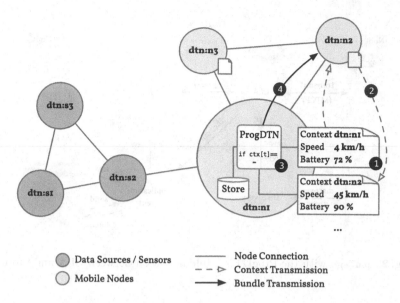

Fig. 1. Architectural overview of a DTN deployment utilizing ProgDTN

Context Generation. The naive approach for generating context information would be to have the DTN software itself generate the necessary information. This would, however, violate the ease of use goal, since it would require modification of the DTN software's code for each scenario. ProgDTN adopts an approach where context generation is left up to external programs. For this purpose, the DTN software exposes an interface through which context information can be injected. This interface should be based on a widely used communication protocol/architecture to ensure ease of use.

Context Transmission. Since context information needs to be attached to a bundle, and since it may be helpful for nodes to be able to exchange their contexts, we defined a custom extension block to carry context information. This extension block may either be attached to an existing bundle or be used to exchange context data with peers by sending a special *context bundle*. Extending a regular bundle with a context block allows nodes to use this information when making forwarding decisions.

3.4   ProgDTN Architecture

Figure 1 shows the architecture of a DTN deployment utilizing ProgDTN. The yellow circles depict mobile DTN nodes, whereas the violet circles show data sources in a hypothetical scenario. Each node is identified by the prefix dtn: followed by a name, such as n1, used as the address for bundle transmissions. The lines between the circles show connections between the particular nodes. Node dtn:n1 is used to visualize further concepts.

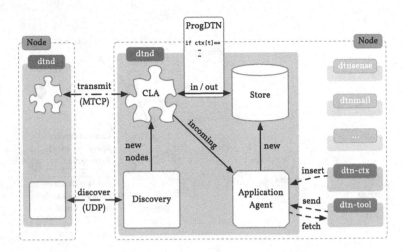

Fig. 2. dtn7-go with the ProgDTN implementation between CLA and Store

In general, when a bundle enters a DTN node, either by being created or received from a peer, it is placed into the node's local on-disk storage (store in Fig. 1). The bundle is then passed to the configured routing algorithm to select peers for forwarding. ProgDTN takes the position of the routing algorithm, which is visualized by the box entitled ProgDTN. It takes the particular bundle, which can itself have attached context information, and the context information for its node (shown as ❶ in Fig. 1), as well as the peer's context (❷). The context in this example is the speed and battery level of the transmitting node and for node dtn:n2. The interpreter (❸) then executes the routing script provided by the network operator, which must be aware of the available context data, and filters the list of connected peers to select the subset for forwarding. Once the routing program has returned the list of selected peers, the DTN software transmits the bundle to the selected peers (❹).

4   ProgDTN Implementation

ProgDTN's implementation is based on dtn7-go, a powerful DTN software suite developed in the DTN7 project[4]. dtn7-go implements the most recent draft of the bundle protocol (BP) version 7 [6] in the GO programming language [16].

Figure 2 shows the components of dtn7-go. The two dotted boxes indicate two DTN nodes, and the arrows between them show their interaction, data transmission (transmit), and peer discovery (discover). The arrows within the dtnd box visualize the data flow of bundles within a node. The right-hand side shows multiple tools that use an application agent (AA) to insert data to or retrieve data from dtn7-go. The AA then stores the received data in the node's local store. The bundle protocol abstracts peer-to-peer communication

---

[4] https://dtn7.github.io/.

using convergence layer adapters (CLAs), which can use a variety of protocols and technologies such as TCP, UDP, or even e-mail sent over Bluetooth. Each CLA exposes a defined API to the daemon, which can then transparently send & receive messages without having to bother with data serialization or transmission. To support connections in dynamic networks, dtn7-go uses a peer discovery mechanism that continuously broadcasts information on all of the node's CLAs and notifies the daemon about newly discovered peers. For forwarding decisions, dtn7-go includes an API that can be used to implement routing algorithms. Any *Go* datatype that satisfies this interface can be used as the router, and dtn7-go ships with various established routing algorithms. ProgDTN consists of an implementation of that interface and a set of extensions for receiving and storing bundle and node context.

4.1   Using JavaScript for Programmable Routing

We decided to use JavaScript as our general-purpose programming language for programmable DTN routing due to the following reasons: (a) JavaScript is very popular; according to a 2021 survey conducted by Stack Overflow[5], nearly 65% of developers work in JavaScript, giving it a roughly 17% lead over the second-placed general-purpose language Python at approximately 48%; and (b) JavaScript can be embedded into the GO programming language; there are several JavaScript interpreters written in GO, e.g., goja[6], which implements the ECMAScript standard version 5.1 with some additional features.

Thus, a routing algorithm is specified in a JavaScript file that gets loaded during startup of dtn7-go and compiled to bytecode representation for faster execution. Whenever a routing decision is made, the compiled JavaScript routing algorithm is invoked, which invokes a virtual machine (VM) able to interpret the JavaScript bytecode.

4.2   Programmable Routing Decisions

Any custom routing algorithm has to comply with the following API. First, the JavaScript code receives the bundle itself passed as a JavaScript object[7], as well as the bundle ID, represented as a string. Second, the ID of the bundle's source (as a string) and a list of strings representing the IDs of all currently available peers are passed to the routing algorithm. The final pieces of information are the bundle context, the node's context, and the context of all available peers. Whenever the algorithm receives context data, this data is encoded as JSON, a data serialization format that works well with JavaScript. The bundle's context can be updated using a callback function whenever this may be necessary.

---

[5] https://insights.stackoverflow.com/survey/2021.

[6] https://github.com/dop251/goja.

[7] The description of the bundle data structure is omitted for brevity. We refer to https://github.com/dtn7/dtn7-go/blob/d3b5e62a7f89994ececf98978bae499f32cc 920f/pkg/bpv7/bundle.go for further information.

If logging is required, it is possible to use the passed `loggingFunc` function to write an arbitrary string to the `dtn7-go`'s logs. The algorithm may then use any or all of this data to perform the actual forwarding decision. Any JavaScript code can be executed here, including third-party libraries. ProgDTN does not place any restrictions on the possible context data; it is up to the network operator to be aware of runtime requirements. Finally, the routing algorithm must return a list of node IDs to which the bundle should be forwarded. `dtn7-go` then takes care of forwarding the bundles to the chosen nodes using the corresponding CLAs.

4.3 Providing Context

To provide context information about the local node, we implemented a REST interface that receives information formatted in a key-value manner, where the value contains arbitrary data formatted as JSON. The context information is then saved in a global dictionary so that newer data for a given peer overwrites existing data. While the local node's context information is vital for routing decisions, so is its peers' context. Therefore, whenever two peers connect, they exchange their context information. Finally, for bundle context, the provided REST interface for bundle submission is extended to add context information to the bundle during its creation, again as arbitrary key-value pairs.

5 Experimental Evaluation

5.1 Emulation Environment

Network Emulation. To perform a large number of experiments, we used the *Common Open Research Emulator (CORE)* [1], an open-source network emulator[8]. CORE supports the execution of native binaries without re-implementing protocols, i.e., real-world code can be executed. Furthermore, we used the MACI experimental orchestration framework [10] to schedule a large number of experiments. All experiments were executed on an AMD EPYC 7742 server with 128 physical cores and 1 TB RAM, which executed up to 3 experiments in parallel.

Network Topology. We use a network topology that simulates a disaster scenario involving three parties, *civilians*, *responders*, and a *coordinator*. The scenario consists of 31 nodes arranged in a 2-circle topology, with the singular coordinator located in the center, five responders arranged in a circle around the coordinator, and 25 civilians arranged in the outer circle. Each responder is connected to 5 civilians, and the civilian clusters are connected on their edges. Each civilian sends bundles addressed to the coordinator, simulating information moving up the chain of command. The coordinator produces broadcast bundles that are supposed to be received by all civilians, which simulates announcements by the authorities to the population. The experiments simulate a network with a bandwidth of 54 MBit/s, 20 ms of delay, and a range of about 40 m.

---

[8] https://coreemu.github.io.

Table 1. Evaluation parameters

Parameter	Values
Bundles per node	10, 50, 100
Payload size	1 kB, 1 MB
Routing algorithm	Epidemic routing, Binary Spray & Wait, DTLSR, PRoPHET, ProgDTN epidemic, ProgDTN Binary Spray & Wait, ProgDTN

Experimental Parameters. All experiments are uniquely defined by a set of four parameters, summarized in Table 1 and discussed below. In total, 210 experiments were executed for one hour each. *Bundles per node* determine how many bundles each civilian and the coordinator send to the network. To avoid every node sending its data simultaneously, bundles are sent at (uniformly distributed) random times throughout the experiment. We used two different *payload sizes*, 1 kB and 1 MB, to mimic different use cases, with 1 kB serving as a stand-in for text messages and 1 MB being around the size of a small image. One of the two payload sizes was used for all nodes during every experiment. To maintain reproducibility and to reduce the chance of unfavorable initial conditions, each experiment was re-run five times with pre-determined PRNG-seeds.

Seven routing algorithms are used for comparison: *Epidemic Routing* [20] is the most widely used routing algorithm in DTN, sending bundles to all peers.

Binary Spray & Wait [18] is a modified version of Spray and Wait. A node holds n copies of a bundle, half of which are transferred to the first peer. The second peer then receives half of the remaining copies and so on. Each node that receives multiple copies of a bundle proceeds in the same way. A node will only forward the bundle to its intended recipient when only a single copy remains. Spyropoulos et al. [18] suggest a value of 10 as a reasonable initial multiplicity, which we adopted in our experiments.

PRoPHET [12] exploits the fact that in DTNs, nodes usually encounter each other more than once. Whenever two peers connect, they compute a probability of meeting again in the future. This probability declines over time if these particular nodes do not meet again. A node will forward a bundle to another node if the receiving node's probability of meeting the bundle's recipient is higher than the forwarding node's probability. We used the same parameters as the authors in their original paper for calculating delivery probabilities.

Delay-Tolerant Link-State Routing (DTLSR) [8] other than classical link-state routing once a link is lost, it is not immediately removed from routing considerations, but rather "tagged" with the time since the disconnection. When the routing table is computed, this time is interpreted as a link cost of Dijkstra's algorithm to find the shortest path between the current node and the destination.

ProgDTN Epidemic/Binary Spray & Wait are re-implementations of the respective algorithms in ProgDTN, which serve primarily to compare computational overheads. All parameters are the same as in the native implementations.

ProgDTN Emergency is a custom algorithm implemented using ProgDTN and tailored to the given scenario of our evaluation, where data only flows in two "directions": from civilians to the coordinator, or vice versa. Whether a node will forward a bundle to another node depends on three factors: (a) node type (coordinator, responder, civilian), provided at startup, (b) peer type, received by a node via a context bundle and (c) bundle type (unicast to coordinator, or broadcast to all civilians), carried by a bundle in a context block attached at bundle generation time. Unicasts (i.e., bundles from the civilians to the coordinator) are only forwarded along the inward direction, from civilians to responders to the coordinator, while civilians do not send their bundles to each other. The same applies to responders. Broadcasts flow outward, i.e., from the coordinator to the responders to the civilians; civilians distribute messages among each other. In both cases, responders do not forward bundles among other responders, but only serve as relays between civilians and the coordinator.

5.2   Results

We consider six metrics divided into two categories: network utilization and an overhead analysis. The network utilization metrics are the percentage of bundles successfully delivered, the duration of delivery, and the load generated in the network. Our overhead analysis considers the time to decide to whom a bundle should be forwarded, the percentage of bundles that do not carry a payload (metadata or context bundles), and how heavily a node's CPU is utilized.

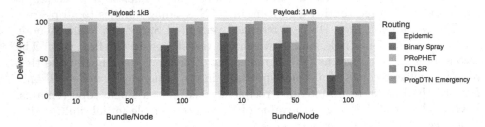

Fig. 3. Ratio of successfully delivered bundles for different parameters (Color figure online)

Delivery Ratios. Figure 3 shows the *delivery ratio*, i.e., the percentage of sent bundles that reach their destination. Each group on the x-axis represents a set of bundles per node, the y-axis shows the reached percentage of delivered bundles, the color denotes the routing algorithm, and each sub-figure shows the different payload sizes. For unicasts, successful delivery means that the coordinator receives the bundle, while for broadcasts, all potential recipients (i.e., the civilians) need to receive the bundle. The performance of ProgDTN Emergency is at least equal to all other routing algorithms. In many cases, it outperforms the other routing algorithms, with a delivery ratio of 99.9% in all scenarios. Not even Epidemic Routing (blue) achieves this level of success for high load scenarios, because it produces the highest load and can easily overload the network. Furthermore, PRoPHET (orange) is ill-suited for this scenario and achieves only mediocre results (depending on the experiment, between 43% and 70%). This does not mean that PRoPHET is a bad routing algorithm, but if a scenario does not conform to its assumptions, it will fail to achieve its intended result.

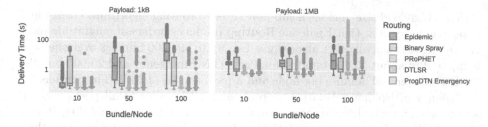

Fig. 4. Time to deliver a bundle to its destination for different parameters

Delivery Times. The next metric is *delivery time*, i.e., the time it takes for a bundle to reach its intended recipient. For broadcasts, we consider the delivery time to the first eligible recipient. The results are shown in Fig. 4; the x-axis shows bundles per node, the y-axis the delivery time on a logarithmic scale, the color denotes the routing algorithm, and each sub-figure shows the different payload sizes. ProgDTN Emergency shows results at least on-par with the other algorithms, with a median below 1 s, regardless of the scenario, and rare cases where the delivery time exceeds 15 s for high load scenarios. Epidemic Routing loses performance in higher-load scenarios due to excessive network load. In extreme cases, a bundle can take up to 15 min to reach its destination. However, the decrease in long-time outliers for the higher-payload scenario is because we only see initial, fast deliveries for this scenario, while once the system reaches congestion, bundles do not arrive at all and are thus absent from this graph. This observation is also consistent with the observation made for the delivery ratios. Under certain conditions, PRoPHET behaves quite erratic (one hour delivery time), because delivery probabilities are only updated for new connections, which leads to race conditions. This shows that PRoPHET it is not well suited for this scenario. However, all these variations of epidemic routing and PRoPHET are outliers, while the 75% quantile remains quite small, e.g., about 17 s for epidemic routing and 1 s for PRoPHET.

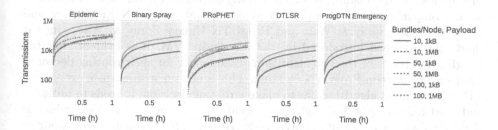

Fig. 5. Total number of bundle transmissions for different parameters

Network Load. Figure 5 shows the number of bundle transmissions throughout the experiment, where the x-axis shows the time and the y-axis the transmissions on a logarithmic scale. The color denotes the bundles per node, the line style and payload size, and each sub-plot shows a routing algorithm. From Fig. 5 it becomes apparent that Epidemic Routing produces orders of magnitude more transmissions than all other algorithms, i.e., up to 695,000 bundles over one hour compared to about 50,000 bundles for ProgDTN Emergency and 25,000 bundles for DTLSR for 100 bundles per node and a payload size of 1 kB. The cause is the inefficiency of Epidemic Routing; it replicates all bundles to all peers without any concern for whether a transmission increases the delivery probability. Binary Spray & Wait also produces a relatively high load level compared to algorithms other than Epidemic Routing, while the remaining algorithms have a somewhat similar load level. ProgDTN Emergency successfully avoids unnecessary transmissions and conserves network capacity. If this data is viewed in conjunction with Figs. 3 and 4, it is apparent that ProgDTN Emergency achieves high average delivery ratios of about 99.9% within 1 s, while other routing algorithms suffer in different quality metrics for various reasons.

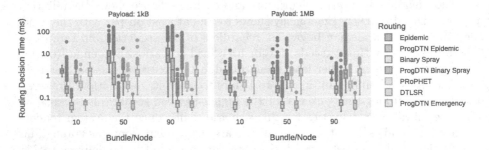

Fig. 6. Time to make a routing decision for different parameters

Routing Decisions. Figure 6 shows the time it takes to perform a routing decision for each algorithm. The x-axis groups different bundles per node, and the y-axis shows the time in ms it takes the routing algorithm to finish on a logarithmic scale. Each color represents a routing algorithm, while the two sub-plots show the results for different payload sizes. The focus of this metric is the comparison between Epidemic Routing and ProgDTN Emergency and between Binary Spray & Wait and ProgDTN Binary Spray & Wait, since it shows the overhead introduced by the JavaScript VM. It is evident that the ProgDTN variants of the two algorithms take longer for their routing decisions compared to the non-ProgDTN variants. This is not surprising, since every time a ProgDTN-based algorithm has to make a routing decision, it needs to initialize and start a JavaScript VM and then execute the actual routing code, which is interpreted rather than run as native code. However, the mean and 75% quantile is still well below 50 ms even in those cases. Furthermore, ProgDTN Emergency performs reasonably well with a median of about 1.5 ms and a 75% quantile of about 3 ms, regardless of the experiment. To summarize, the JavaScript VM introduces overhead that is compensated by the fact that ProgDTN can be used to implement a scenario-specific algorithm, reducing the average time to deliver a bundle.

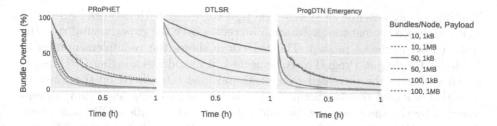

Fig. 7. Overhead in terms of percentage of bundles sent without a payload

Bundle Overhead. Since ProgDTN makes use of context bundles to let nodes exchange context information (see Sect. 3.3), the amount of additional traffic generated by these bundles needs to be quantified, since it may contradict the qualitative metrics of preserving network bandwidth. Figure 7 shows the overhead of all algorithms that transmit metadata bundles in terms of the percentage of sent bundles, where the x-axis denotes the experimental runtime, the y-axis the percentage of context bundles (in case of DTLSR so-called meta bundles). The color shows different bundles per node, and the line style represents the two payload sizes. Finally, each sub-figure shows a different routing algorithm. Note that only the three shown routing algorithms produce an overhead. Since each node sends a context or meta-bundle upon startup for all algorithms, they all start at 100% overhead; this percentage does, however, decrease rapidly as payload bundles start being transmitted. For both PRoPHET and ProgDTN Emergency, we see an exponential decrease with the overhead percentage converging to zero, but remember that PRoPHET does not achieve a satisfactory delivery ratio in this scenario. DTLSR, on the other hand, regularly broadcasts peer information to the whole network, so we see a higher overhead throughout the experiment.

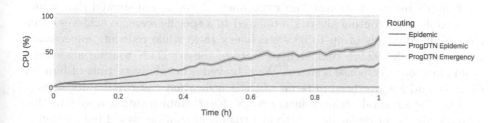

Fig. 8. CPU usage of three routing algorithms

CPU Usage. Figure 8 shows the overhead in terms of CPU usage. The x-axis denotes the experimental time. The y-axis shows the average CPU usage in percent of all nodes. The colors represent different routing algorithms. For this evaluation, we only consider Epidemic Routing, ProgDTN Epidemic, and ProgDTN Emergency to quantify the overhead of the CPU and the potential savings using a custom routing algorithm. The blue curve, representing Epidemic

Routing, gives a baseline for system load that correlates with network load shown in Fig. 5. Since the network saturation increases over the experimental run, the system load increases in step. The red curve shows the re-implementation of Epidemic Routing in ProgDTN. As expected, it introduces a higher CPU usage, which is due to the increased computational load introduced by the constant re-initialization of the JavaScript VM. The custom routing algorithm, as represented by the turquoise line, by contrast, shows the smallest CPU load, even though it also makes use of the same system as ProgDTN Epidemic. The reason is that if there are fewer bundles to transmit, the JavaScript VM is invoked less often, reducing the overall system load due to fewer transmissions. Thus, by reducing the number of transmissions, we can conserve computing power and therefore also electrical power in cases where a device might be battery-powered.

To summarize, ProgDTN Emergency achieves excellent results and outperforms all other routing algorithms in all metrics. The results of PRoPHET show that a routing algorithm not designed for a particular scenario does not achieve any satisfactory results. Epidemic Routing achieves good results for smaller payload sizes and a small numbers of bundles per node, but its delivery ratios decrease below 50% for high network load, while ProgDTN Emergency still achieves 99.9%. DTLSR also achieves excellent delivery ratios and delivery times, but its overhead in terms of meta-bundles is significant compared to ProgDTN Emergency. Finally, Binary Spray & Wait performs considerably well, but requires more transmissions to achieve comparable results to ProgDTN Emergency.

6   Conclusion

We presented *ProgDTN*, a novel approach to support *Programmable Disruption-tolerant Networking* by allowing network operators to program a node's routing behavior based on context information, without requiring knowledge of the router's interior workings. Our experimental evaluation showed that a programmable DTN routing algorithm tailored to a specific scenario achieves excellent results in terms of up to 99.9% delivery ratio while reducing unnecessary transmissions by 92.9% compared to state-of-the-art DTN routing algorithms in an emergency response scenario. We achieved a low delivery time of bundles (1–15 s), and low overhead in terms of CPU utilization and routing decisions.

There are several areas of future work. First, implementing a system that allows updating or replacing routing algorithms at runtime would reduce unnecessary downtimes and further reduce development and deployment hurdles. Second, allowing a centralized entity to reconfigure an entire DTN deployment would make the administration and monitoring of DTN nodes more flexible. Finally, although a network emulation gives valuable insights, evaluating ProgDTN on real hardware in a real mobile scenario would further solidify and confirm the applicability and feasibility of ProgDTN.

Acknowledgements. This work is funded by the Hessian State Ministry for Higher Education, Research and the Arts (HMWK) (LOEWE emergenCITY, LOEWE Natur

4.0), and the German Research Foundation (DFG, Project 210487104 - Collaborative Research Center SFB 1053 MAKI).

References

1. Ahrenholz, J.: Comparison of CORE network emulation platforms. In: MILCOM 2010 Military Communications Conference, pp. 166–171, October 2010. https://doi.org/10.1109/MILCOM.2010.5680218

2. Baek, K.M., Seo, D.Y., Chung, Y.W.: An improved opportunistic routing protocol based on context information of mobile nodes. Appl. Sci. **8**(8), 134 (2018). https://doi.org/10.3390/app8081344

3. Bansal, A., Gupta, A., Sharma, D.K., Gambhir, V.: IICAR-inheritance inspired context aware routing protocol for opportunistic networks. J. Ambient. Intell. Humaniz. Comput. **10**(6), 2235–2253 (2018). https://doi.org/10.1007/s12652-018-0815-2

4. Biswas, P.K., Mackey, S.J., Cansever, D.H., Patel, M.P., Panettieri, F.B.: Context-aware SmallWorld routing for wireless ad-hoc networks. IEEE Trans. Commun. **66**(9), 3943–3958 (2018). https://doi.org/10.1109/TCOMM.2018.2811486

5. Boldrini, C., Conti, M., Jacopini, J., Passarella, A.: HiBOp: a history based routing protocol for opportunistic networks. In: 2007 IEEE International Symposium on a World of Wireless, Mobile and Multimedia Networks, pp. 1–12, June 2007. https://doi.org/10.1109/WOWMOM.2007.4351716

6. Burleigh, S., Fall, K., Birrane, E.: Bundle Protocol Version 7. Internet draft, RFC Editor, March 2020. https://tools.ietf.org/html/draft-ietf-dtn-bpbis-24

7. Cabaniss, R., Madria, S., Rush, G., Trotta, A., Vulli, S.S.: Dynamic social grouping based routing in a mobile ad-hoc network. In: 2010 International Conference on High Performance Computing, pp. 1–8, December 2010. https://doi.org/10.1109/HIPC.2010.5713165

8. Demmer, M., Fall, K.: DTLSR: delay tolerant routing for developing regions. In: Proceedings of the 2007 Workshop on Networked Systems for Developing Regions, pp. 5:1–5:6. NSDR 2007, ACM, New York, NY, USA (2007). https://doi.org/10.1145/1326571.1326579

9. Er-rouidi, M., Moudni, H., Faouzi, H., Mouncif, H., Merbouha, A.: A fuzzy-based routing strategy to improve route stability in MANET based on AODV. In: El Abbadi, A., Garbinato, B. (eds.) NETYS 2017. LNCS, vol. 10299, pp. 40–48. Springer, Cham (2017). https://doi.org/10.1007/978-3-319-59647-1_4

10. Froemmgen, A., Stohr, D., Koldehofe, B., Rizk, A.: Don't repeat yourself: seamless execution and analysis of extensive network experiments. In: Proceedings of the 14th International Conference on emerging Networking EXperiments and Technologies (CoNEXT 2018) (2018). https://doi.org/10.1145/3281411.3281420

11. Johari, R., Gupta, N., Aneja, S.: CACBR: context aware community based routing for intermittently connected network. In: Proceedings of the 10th ACM Symposium on Performance Evaluation of Wireless Ad Hoc, Sensor, Ubiquitous Networks, pp. 137–140. PE-WASUN 2013, ACM, New York, NY, USA (2013). https://doi.org/10.1145/2507248.2507272

12. Lindgren, A., Doria, A., Schelén, O.: Probabilistic routing in intermittently connected networks. In: Dini, P., Lorenz, P., de Souza, J.N. (eds.) Service Assurance with Partial and Intermittent Resources, LNCS. vol. 3126, pp. 239–254. Springer, Heidelberg (2004). https://doi.org/10.1145/961268.961272

13. Mascolo, C., Musolesi, M.: SCAR: context-aware adaptive routing in delay tolerant mobile sensor networks. In: Proceedings of the 2006 International Conference on Wireless Communications and Mobile Computing, pp. 533–538. IWCMC 2006, ACM, New York, NY, USA (2006). https://doi.org/10.1145/1143549.1143656

14. Musolesi, M., Hailes, S., Mascolo, C.: Adaptive routing for intermittently connected mobile ad hoc networks. In: Sixth IEEE International Symposium on a World of Wireless Mobile and Multimedia Networks, pp. 183–189, June 2005. https://doi.org/10.1109/WOWMOM.2005.17

15. Musolesi, M., Mascolo, C.: CAR: Context-aware adaptive routing for delay-tolerant mobile networks. IEEE Trans. Mob. Comput. 8(2), 246–260 (2009). https://doi.org/10.1109/TMC.2008.107

16. Penning, A., Baumgärtner, L., Höchst, J., Sterz, A., Mezini, M., Freisleben, B.: DTN7: an open-source disruption-tolerant networking implementation of bundle protocol 7. In: Palattella, M.R., Scanzio, S., Coleri Ergen, S. (eds.) ADHOC-NOW 2019. LNCS, vol. 11803, pp. 196–209. Springer, Cham (2019). https://doi.org/10.1007/978-3-030-31831-4_14

17. Rosas, E., Garay, F., Hidalgo, N.: Context-aware self-adaptive routing for delay-tolerant networks in disaster scenarios. Ad Hoc Netw. 102, 102095 (2020). https://doi.org/10.1016/j.adhoc.2020.102095

18. Spyropoulos, T., Psounis, K., Raghavendra, C.S.: Spray and wait: an efficient routing scheme for intermittently connected mobile networks. In: Proceedings of the 2005 ACM SIGCOMM Workshop on Delay-tolerant Networking, pp. 252–259. WDTN 2005, ACM, New York, NY, USA (2005). https://doi.org/10.1145/1080139.1080143

19. Ullah, S., Qayyum, A.: Socially-aware adaptive delay-tolerant network (DTN) routing protocol. PLOS One. 17(1), 1–15 (2022). https://doi.org/10.1371/journal.pone.0262565

20. Vahdat, A., et al.: Epidemic Routing for Partially connected Ad Hoc Networks. Technical report. CS-200006, Duke University (2000)

Distributed Oracle for Estimating Global Network Delay with Known Error Bounds

Karla Vargas$^{(\boxtimes)}$ and Gregory Chockler

Computer Science Department, University of Surrey, Guildford, UK
`k.vargas@surrey.ac.uk`

Abstract. Partially synchronous models are often assumed for designing distributed protocols because they capture realistic timing assumptions, such as the asynchronous and synchronous periods that the system can experience. In some of these models, protocols need to estimate network delays. Some protocols fix the global message delay bound for all executions, which leads to sub-optimal solutions in terms of latency, because this bound must be chosen conservatively. And other protocols employ delay estimation mechanisms that only give an upper bound on the delay without quantifying the estimation error. The performance of these protocols depends on how close their estimations are in relation to the actual network delay. For instance, some Byzantine consensus protocols use timeouts based on this estimation. We formalize this problem as the *Global Delay Bound Estimation* (GDBE) and address it by introducing a distributed oracle that enriches partial synchronous models. This oracle produces estimates of the channel delays that allow processes to derive an efficient global bounded estimate. Oracles and global bounded estimates, provide a framework that facilitates the design of protocols for partially synchronous models and the analysis of their time complexity. We formalize the properties of the oracle and the proposed framework and show that it can be implemented in the presence of crash failures. In contrast, we prove that GDBE cannot be solved in the Byzantine failure model, and show how to circumvent this impossibility using an extra assumption. Finally, we show how to use our framework to implement a view synchronizer thus obtaining an efficient solution for Byzantine consensus.

Keywords: Oracle · Global delay · Timeout · Consensus · Crash failure · Byzantine failure · Channel delay · Synchronizer · Fixed delay · Partial synchrony · One-way delay

1 Introduction

Partial Synchrony. Partially synchronous models were proposed in [8] aiming to strike a balance between synchronous and asynchronous models to circumvent the FLP impossibility result [9] according to which there is no deterministic protocol for solving consensus in a crash-prone asynchronous system.

© The Author(s), under exclusive license to Springer Nature Switzerland AG 2022
M.-A. Koulali and M. Mezini (Eds.): NETYS 2022, LNCS 13464, pp. 201–221, 2022.
https://doi.org/10.1007/978-3-031-17436-0_14

Partially synchronous models capture real-life scenarios in which the network might experience unbounded delays but can behave timely as well. Thus, the various protocols designed for this model (e.g. [2,4,8,12,16]) must cope with unbounded delays during asynchronous periods while maintaining safety during the entire execution.

Delay Estimation. A common element shared by partial synchrony protocols with unknown delay bound Δ is a mechanism for estimating this delay. The quality of these delay estimates are important as they are used for setting various timeouts on which these protocols rely for correctness (e.g. [1,3]). Furthermore, the performance of these protocols critically depends on how close this estimates are to the actual delay bound Δ in a given execution.

In case every execution is guaranteed to be synchronous from the beginning implementing a mechanism for accurate estimation of the delay bound is straightforward. This problem becomes hard in the eventually synchronous model with unknown message delay. In this model, in every execution, the system behaves asynchronously until reaching a *Global Stabilization Time* (GST) after which the message delay is bounded by an a priori unknown constant Δ. Implementing an accurate delay estimation mechanism in this model would therefore require readjusting a potentially arbitrarily high estimate computed during the asynchronous period once GST is reached.

Contribution. In this paper, we propose a distributed oracle inspired by the *One-way delay estimation* problem [7] to enrich the GST model.

These oracles produce estimates for the delay bound of every channel. Each process takes the local channel delay estimates produced by the oracle, and eventually outputs a global delay estimation whose error is bounded by a known constant. We call this estimation algorithms Δ-*estimator*. The Δ-estimators provide a framework to facilitate the design of protocols in the GST model and derive precise bounds for the time complexity.

We propose a crash-fault tolerant implementation of a Δ-estimator in which eventually, all processes output the same estimate. We also proved that it is impossible to implement a Δ-estimator if at least one process can be Byzantine. This result shows that the existing delay estimation mechanisms for Byzantine settings can lead to delay estimates which are arbitrarily high after GST. We also propose a way to circumvent this impossibility and show how a Δ-estimator can be used to implement a view synchronizer thus obtaining a solution for Byzantine consensus [2].

The rest of this paper is organized as follows. In Sect. 2 we define formally what a channel delay oracle is and the properties their outputs must satisfy. We formalize the *Global Delay Bound Estimation* (GDBE) problem and define its properties in Sect. 3. In Sect. 4 we propose a crash-fault tolerant implementation of a Δ-estimator. In Sect. 5 we present an impossibility result for the Byzantine case and a way to circumvent it. We close this section by showing how Δ-estimator can be used for solving Byzantine consensus.

2   Model

2.1   Processes and Communication

We assume a system that consists of a set of n processes $\Pi = \{p_1, p_2, ..., p_n\}$ such that $n = f + c$, where $f > 0$ is the number of failures (crash or Byzantines) and $c > 0$ is the number of correct processes. Every pair of processes p_i and p_j is connected via a unidirectional communication channel $c_{i,j}$ that does not create or lose messages.

All processes have no synchronized clocks but the drift is bounded, i.e. each process can accurately measure the passage of real time. We assume the existence of an external real-time reference clock that cannot be queried by the processes. The range of the ticks of this clock is the set of natural numbers. We denote as correct(E) the set of processes that are correct in execution E and correct(E, t) is the set of processes that are correct at time t.

We consider a partial synchrony model [8] in which there exists a *Global Stabilization Time* (GST) unknown to processes, after which message transmission delays are bounded by some constant. Formally, for each channel $c_{i,j}$ connecting two processes p_i and p_j and for each execution E, there exists a $\delta_{i,j} > 0$ and a time GST $\leq t_{i,j}$ after which the delay of $c_{i,j}$ is bounded by $\delta_{i,j}$. Let us fix an execution E. We define

$$\Delta_E = max\{\delta_{i,j} | \delta_{i,j} \text{ is the bound delay of channel } c_{i,j} \text{ in execution } E \wedge p_i, p_j \in \Pi\}$$

as the *communication upper bound* in execution E. No process knows Δ_E in advance.

2.2   Channel Delay Oracle

Based on the One-Way Delay Estimation problem [7], which consists on deriving an efficient delay estimate of a channel in one direction, we enrich the system with an oracle that allows having a correct estimation of the delay of each channel individually.

Informally, algorithms that implement One-Way Delay Estimation, collect delay measurements of the channel and adjust their estimate depending on the data gathered through time. These algorithms do not require synchronized clocks[1]. Examples of One-Way Delay Estimation implementations can be found in [7, 10, 14, 15].

Each oracle outputs in each process p_i, an estimation of the upper bound of the delay of every output channel connecting p_i to every other process. We define the oracle for each process p_i as a function $\sigma_i : \Pi \times \mathbb{N} \to \mathbb{N}$ such that $\sigma_i(j, t)$ is the estimate of the delay of channel $c_{i,j}$ that goes from p_i to p_j at time t. We state two properties that a σ_i function must satisfy which are σ-completeness and σ-accuracy.

---

[1] If clocks are synchronized the problem is trivial because messages can be times-tamped.

Definition 1 (σ-Completeness). *For all executions E and for all processes $p_i, p_j \in \Pi$, if $p_i, p_j \in$ correct(E), then $\exists t' \geq t_{i,j} >$ GST such that*

> *Weak σ-completeness* $\forall t_0 \geq t'$. $\exists t \geq t_0$. $\delta_{i,j} \leq \sigma_i(j, t)$.
> *Strong σ-completeness* $\forall t \geq t'$. $\delta_{i,j} \leq \sigma_i(j, t)$.

Weak σ-completeness says that eventually, the function outputs *infinitely often* a value greater than $\delta_{i,j}$. Strong σ-completeness means that eventually, the function outputs *always* a value greater than $\delta_{i,j}$. We define the accuracy property that prevents the function to output unbounded values in the case in which the process on the other side of the channel is correct.

Definition 2 (σ-Accuracy). *There exists a constant $X_{i,j}$ such that for all executions E and for all processes $p_i, p_j \in \Pi$ where $p_i \in$ correct(E)*

> *If p_j is correct.* There $\exists t' \geq t_{i,j}$ such that $\forall t \geq t'$. $\sigma_i(j, t) \leq \delta_{i,j} \cdot X_{i,j}$.
> *If p_j is crashed.* Let t_f be the first time in which p_j crashes. There exists a constant $Q_{i,j}$ such that $\forall t \geq t_f + Q_{i,j} \cdot \sigma_{i,j}(t) = \infty$.

The behavior of the σ_i function in case when the other side of the channel is crashed is consistent with what the σ_i function is intended to do, output the delay of a point-to-point channel. We assume this since, at a very low level, the implementation of the σ_i function requires a response from the other process. Then, after the failure, the estimation grows until it eventually is ∞. The need of response from the other side of the channel is the reason the previous definitions do not include Byzantine failures. In that case, the output of the function does not necessarily satisfy any of these properties.

Note that this function can do mistakes before the GST and output ∞ even if the process is not crashed, and it does not output the liveness state of the process but the delay estimation, namely, σ_i function is not a failure detector.

Depending on the model or the problem specification, constant $X_{i,j}$ may or may not be known by the processes. We call GST$^+$ the time after which the σ functions of all processes are complete and accurate.

3   Problem Statement

We want to estimate the maximum channel delay Δ_E in an execution E. We call this problem *Global Delay Bound Estimation* (GDBE). Informally, we want each process p_i to have a variable Δ_i which contains the estimate of the current global message delay. Naturally, we need this output to eventually be as big as Δ_E, which as said before, can easily be done by increasing unboundedly the variable Δ_i but we ask the output to have a known upper bound. We define these properties more formally as follows.

Let $\Delta_i(E, t)$ be the global delay estimate of process p_i at time t in execution E.

Definition 3 (Δ-estimator). *An algorithm A is a Δ-estimator if its set $\mathcal{E}$ with all its executions satisfy the following properties:*

Completeness: $\forall E \in \mathcal{E}. \ \exists t'. \forall t \geq t'. \forall p_i \in \text{correct}(E, t)$

$$\Delta_E \leq \Delta_i(E, t) \tag{1}$$

Accuracy: *There exists a constant* $C \geq 1$ *such that* $\forall E \in \mathcal{E}. \ \exists t'. \forall t \geq t'. \forall p_i \in$ $\text{correct}(E, t)$

$$\Delta_i(E, t) \leq \Delta_E \cdot C \tag{2}$$

Definition 4 (Stabilization). *Let* A *be a* Δ-*estimator. Let* $\mathcal{E}$ *be the set of all executions of* A. *We say that* A *satisfies* **Stabilization** *if* $\forall E \in \mathcal{E}. \ \exists k. \ \exists t'. \forall t \geq$ $t'. \forall p_i \in \text{correct}(E, t)$

$$\Delta_i(E, t) = k \tag{3}$$

In other words, an algorithm that satisfies (1) must output an estimate which is at least as high as the maximum channel delay Δ_E in a given execution of A and, if it satisfies (2), no higher than $C \cdot \Delta_E$ for an a priori fixed constant C. The latter requirement rules out standard implementations that increase the delay estimate by an arbitrary amount every time its previous value is found to be too low [4]. In Sect. 4 we present an implementation of a *stable* Δ-estimator in the crash model were the σ-accuracy constant is known. In contrast, there are no Δ-estimators in the Byzantine model as we show in Sect. 5.

4 Solving **GDBE** for Crash Failures

In this section we propose an algorithm for the GDBE problem. We assume σ functions that satisfy strong σ-completeness and σ-accuracy. By using the σ-functions, it is straightforward to implement a Δ-estimator but making it stable requires more work.

To study the non-stable version of the algorithm, the reader may disregard all lines prefixed with $\star$. For the stable version, we assume that the constant of every σ function is know. We assume the same constant X for easier illustration but this algorithm works as well if we assume different constants for every process.

4.1 Algorithm

Every process p_i periodically executes lines 4–15. In line 7, process p_i queries its σ_i function for each process p_j. The result is stored into the array entry $currDelay_i[j]$. In case in which the output of the σ_i function is ∞, entry $\delta_i[j]$ is set to 0 (line 9) so when selecting a new estimate in lines 12 or 20, entry $\delta_i[j]$ is discarded since process p_j might have failed. For the stable version of the algorithm, if the output of the σ_i function is not ∞, the *stabilize*() function is called (line 11). In line 12, the maximum from array $currDelay_i$ is selected and stored into $\delta_i[i]$. Then, p_i sends a **ESTIMATE** message to every process (line 14) including $\delta_i[i]$. The message includes as well, an identifier for dealing with the asynchronous period before GST. In line 15, a new global estimate is calculated by selecting the maximum from the δ_i array.

Lines 16 to 20 deal with the reception of the ESTIMATE message. If the identifier contained in the message is lower than the current identifier, the message is discarded, otherwise, the recently received estimate from process p_j is stored on $\delta_i[j]$, and in line 20, a new global estimate is calculated again. By selecting the maximum from the δ_i array, it is selected the maximum from the received maximums and the local maximum which derives a value that satisfies completeness. Since all the values are the output of some σ function that satisfies accuracy, values are bounded, so the estimation satisfies accuracy as well.

Function *stabilize* on lines 22 to 27 eventually returns the same value once the outputs of the $\sigma_i(j)$ for some process p_j are on the interval $[\delta_{i,j}, \delta_{i,j} \cdot X]$ for some known constant X. This function helps to achieve stabilization.

Algorithm 1: Δ-estimator for a process p_i

---

1 $\star$ **CONSTANT** X;
2 currDelay$_i$[1..n] $\leftarrow\perp$, δ_i[1...n] $\leftarrow$ 0, $\Delta_i \leftarrow \infty$, msgId$_i$[1..n] $\leftarrow$ 0, ;
3 function σ_i;

4 **every** T units of time
5   **for** $j \neq i \in \{1, 2, ..., n\}$ **do**
6        $\star$ oldDelay$_i$ = currDelay$_i$[j];
7   currDelay$_i$[j] = σ_i(j);
8   **if** currDelay$_i$[j] = ∞ **then**
9           $\delta_i[j]$ = 0 ;
10        $\star$ **else**
11           $\star$ currDelay$_i$[j] $\leftarrow$ stabilize (oldDelay$_i$,currDelay$_i$[j]);
12     $\delta_i[i]$ = max{currDelay$_i$ $\neq \infty$};
13   msgId$_i$[i] $\leftarrow$ msgId$_i$[i] + 1;
14   **send** ESTIMATE($\delta_i[i]$,msgId$_i$[i]) to all;
15   Δ_i = max(δ_i);

16 **upon** receiving ESTIMATE(δ_j,msgId$_j$) from process p_j
    /* Condition for discarding old messages   */;
17   **if** msgId$_j$ > msgId$_i$[j] **then**
18   msgId$_i$[j] = msgId$_j$;
19        $\delta_i[j]$ = δ_j;
20   Δ_i = max(δ_i);

21 **function** stabilize(delay, currDelay$_i$[j]):
22   low = min(delay, currDelay$_i$[j]);
23   great = max(delay, currDelay$_i$[j]);
24   **if** low $\cdot$ X < great **then**
25   **return** delay
26   **else**
27   **return** great

Correctness Proof for Algorithm 1. Let E be an execution of Algorithm 1. Let Δ_E be the maximum delay in E. For every pair of processes $p_i, p_j \in$ correct(E) and the channel $c_{i,j}$ connecting process p_i to p_j, we call $t^{i,j} > $ GST the time after which all calls to $\sigma_i(j) \in I_{i,j} = [\delta_{i,j}, \delta_{i,j} \cdot X]$ for some known constant X. Let $\Sigma_j = \{a_\ell | a_\ell$ is the $\ell - th$ output of $\sigma_i(j)$ after time $t^{i,j}\}$ be the sequence of *correct* outputs of function $\sigma_i(j)$. Intuitively, a_ℓ is the output of the ℓ-th call of function $\sigma_i(j)$ starting from time $t^{i,j}$. Note that $\forall \ell, a_\ell \in I_{i,j}$.

Observation 1. *Let* $I = [\delta, \delta \cdot X]$ *be an interval with* $\delta, X \geq 0$. *For every* $i \leq j \in I$ *it holds that* $i \cdot X \geq j$.

Lemma 1. *For every process* $p_i, p_j \in$ correct(E), *if for some* $k \geq 1 \in \mathbb{Z}$, $b = currDelay_i[j] \in I_{i,j}$ *before calling* stabilize(a_k, b), *then* $\forall \ell \geq 0$

$$stabilize(a_{k+\ell}, currDelay_i[j]) = max\{a_k, a_{k+1}, ..., a_{k+\ell}, b\}$$

Proof. Proof by induction. Let $b \in I_{i,j}$ be the $currDelay_i[j]$ value before calling stabilize(a_k, b).

Base case: $l = 0$. When $a_{k+\ell} = a_k = b$ it is returned $great = a_k = b$.

Assume w.l.o.g $a_k < b$, then $low = a_k$ and $great = b$. Since $a_k, b \in I_{i,j}$, by Observation 1, condition in line 24 is not true and line 27 is executed instead, so $great = b$ is returned. And vice versa, if $b < a_k$, then a_k is returned. Therefore, stabilize(a_k, b) = $max\{a_k, b\}$.

Inductive hypothesis $l > 0$. By the end of the $k + \ell$-th call to stabilize, the value of $currDelay_i[j] = max\{a_k, a_{k+1}, ..., a_{k+\ell}, b\}$.

Inductive step: Let c be the value of $currDelay_i[j]$ before the $k+\ell+1$-th call to stabilize. By inductive hypothesis $c = max\{a_k, a_{k+1}, ..., a_{k+\ell}, b\}$, so $c \in I_{i,j}$.

Assume w.l.o.g $a_{k+\ell+1} < c$, then $low = a_{k+\ell+1}$ and $great = c$. Since $a_{k+\ell+1}, b \in I_{i,j}$, condition in line 24 is not true and line 27 is executed instead. Then $great = c$ is returned. And vice versa, if $c < a_{k+\ell+1}$, then $a_{k+\ell+1}$ is returned. Then,

$$stabilize(a_{k+\ell+1}, c) = max\{a_{k+\ell+1}, c\}$$
$$= max\{a_{k+\ell+1}, max\{a_k, a_{k+1}, ..., a_{k+\ell}, b\}\}$$
$$= max\{a_k, a_{k+1}, ..., a_{k+\ell}, a_{k+\ell+1}, b\}$$

Therefore, $\forall \ell \geq 0$ it holds that

$$stabilize(a_{k+\ell}, currDelay_i[j]) = max\{a_k, a_{k+1}, ..., a_{k+\ell}, b\} \qquad \square$$

Lemma 2. *For every* $p_i, p_j \in$ correct(E), *there exists* $v \in J_{i,j} = [\delta_{i,j}, \delta_{i,j} \cdot X^2]$ *and some* t' *such that* $\forall t \geq t' \geq t^{i,j}$ $currDelay_i[j] = v$.

Proof. Since the $\sigma_i(j)$ function is queried every T units of time and process p_j is correct, then for all $t > t_i, j$ $\sigma_i(j) \neq \infty$, so condition in line 8 is never true again and line 11 is executed instead. Let $\Sigma_j = \{a_1, a_2, ...\}$ be the set of correct outputs of $\sigma_i(j)$. Let $b = currDelay_i[j]$, before the call to $\texttt{stabilize}(a_1, b)$ and $a_m = max\{\Sigma_j\}$ such that m is the smallest index with which the maximum appears in Σ_j. Note that $I_{i,j} \subseteq J_{i,j}$.

Case 1: $\texttt{stabilize}(a_1, b) = a_1$

Let $y = currDelay_i[j]$ be the value before the call to $\texttt{stabilize}(a_m, y)$. By Lemma 1, $\texttt{stabilize}(a_m, y) = max\{a_1, ..., a_m\} = a_m$. Since for all $j > m$, $a_j \leq a_m$, by Lemma 1, $currDelay_i[j] = \texttt{stabilize}(a_j, a_m) = max\{a_j, a_m\} = a_m \in I_{i,j}$.

Case 2: $\texttt{stabilize}(a_1, b) = b$

The only case for this to happen is if $b \geq a_1$ and $a_1 \cdot X \geq b$. Observe that since $a_i \in I_{i,j} = [\delta_{i,j}, \delta_{i,j} \cdot X]$, then $b \in J_{i,j}$. We analyze the case in which $b \notin I_{i,j}$ since the other case is a particular case of Case 1.

Let $a_p = min\{\Sigma_j\}$ such that p is the smallest index with which the minimum appears in Σ_j. Note that the output of $\texttt{stabilize}(a_{p-1}, b) \in \{a_2, ..., a_{p-1}, b\}$.

- $currDelay_i[j] = a_k$ with $2 \leq k \leq p - 1$ before the p-th call to $\texttt{stabilize}$

  By Lemma 1, $\texttt{stabilize}(a_p, a_k) = max\{a_p, a_k\}$. Following the same argument as Case 1 we get that eventually,

  $$currDelay_i[j] = \texttt{stabilize}(a_\ell, a_k) = max\{a_k, a_p, ...a_\ell\} \in I_{i,j}. \; \forall p \leq \ell \in \mathbb{Z}$$

- $currDelay_i[j] = b$ before the p-th call to $\texttt{stabilize}$
  - If $a_p \cdot X < b$ then $\texttt{stabilize}(a_n, b) = a_n$. Following same argument as Case 1 we get that eventually

    $$currDelay_i[j] = \texttt{stabilize}(a_\ell, currDelay_i[j]) = max\{a_p, ..., a_\ell\} \in I_{i,j}$$

    $\forall \ell > p \in \mathbb{Z}$.
  - If $a_p \cdot X \geq b$ then $\texttt{stabilize}(a_p, b) = b$. Note that $\forall \ell > p \; a_\ell \geq a_p$ so condition $a_\ell \cdot X \geq b$ holds. Then, for every call of $\texttt{stabilize}(a_\ell, b)$ since condition in line 24 is false, line 27 is executed instead. Therefore,

    $$\texttt{stabilize}(a_\ell, b) = max\{b, a_p, ..., a_\ell\} \in J_{i,j}. \; \forall \ell > p \in \mathbb{Z} \qquad \square$$

Lemma 3. *For every $p_i \in \mathsf{correct}(E)$, there is a time t_f such that $\forall t \geq t_f$ $\delta_i[i] = currDelay_i[j]$ for some correct process p_j.*

Proof. By Lemma 2 there is a time after which every entry of $currDelay_i$ do not change. Let t^c be that time. Process p_i selects the maximum of the $currDelay_i$ array in line 12 stores it on $\delta_i[i]$. Note that the max returns the same value which is a $currDelay_i[j] \neq \infty$ for some correct process p_j. This line is executed every T units of time. Then, by time $t^c + T$ at most, $\delta_i[i] = currDelay_i[j]$ and by Lemma 2, since $currDelay_i[j]$ eventually do not change, $\forall t \geq t^c + T$. $\delta_i[i]$ do not change as well. $\square$

Lemma 4. *There is a time t_f such that $\forall t > t_f$ and for all $p_i, p_j \in \mathsf{correct}(E)$, $\delta_i[i] = \delta_j[i]$.*

Proof. By Lemma 3, eventually $\forall p_i \in \mathsf{correct}(E)$ $\delta_i[i] = v$ permanently. Since Δ_E holds eventually and process p_i sends a message every T units of time to every process, then every correct process p_j eventually receives a message from p_i containing $\delta_i[i]$. Those messages are received in line 19 so $\delta_j[i] = \delta_i[i]$.

Therefore, there exists t' such that $\forall t \geq t'$ entry $\delta_j[i] = \delta_i[i]$ for all $p_i, p_j \in \mathsf{correct}(E)$. $\qquad\square$

Lemma 5. *There is a time t_f such that $\forall t > t^f$ and for all $p_i, p_j \in \mathsf{correct}(E)$, $\Delta_i(t) = \Delta_j(t)$.*

Proof. By Lemma 4, all correct processes eventually have the same δ array. Therefore the $max\{\delta_i, \delta_j\}$ is the same in every correct process. $\qquad\square$

Corollary 1. *Algorithm 1 satisfies stabilization.*

Lemma 6. *Algorithm 1 satisfies completeness and accuracy with constant X^2.*

Proof. Fist we prove accuracy. By Lemmas 2 and 4, $\forall p_i \in \mathsf{correct}(E)$ eventually $\Delta_i \in [\delta_{j,k}, \delta_{j,k} \cdot X^2]$ permanently for some correct processes p_j and p_k. Let $\Delta_E = \delta_{\ell,m}$ be the maximum delay in execution E.

Case 1: $\delta_{j,k} = \delta_{\ell,m}$ then $\Delta_i \in [\Delta_E, \Delta_E \cdot X^2]$.
Case 2: $\delta_{j,k} \neq \delta_{\ell,m}$. Since $\delta_{j,k} \leq \delta_{\ell,m}$, then

$$\Delta_i \leq \delta_{j,k} \cdot X^2 \leq \delta_{\ell,m} \cdot X^2 \tag{1}$$

For the completeness, note that eventually, $\sigma_\ell(m) \geq \delta_{\ell,m} = \Delta_E$, then, by Lemma 2, eventually entry $currDelay_\ell[m] \geq \delta_{\ell,m}$. Then

$$\Delta_E = \delta_{\ell,m} \leq currDelay_\ell[m] \leq max\{currDelay_\ell\} \leq max\{\delta_\ell\} = \Delta_i \tag{2}$$

By (1) and (2) we conclude that $\Delta_E \leq \Delta_i \leq \Delta_E \cdot X^2$. $\qquad\square$

Note that there is a particular execution in which the estimate is actually $\Delta_E \times X^2$ and it is when some σ_i function from some process p_i outputs for some process $\Delta_E \cdot X$ for every call after GST^+.

5 Solving **GDBE** for Byzantine Failures

5.1 Lower Bound

Byzantine consensus protocols have been attracting a lot of attention these days due to the popularity of blockchains. Many of these protocols use timeouts on their consensus protocols for ensuring liveness, e.g. [1,3].

In this section, we show an impossibility result for systems with Byzantine failures. We show that it is not possible to implement a Δ-estimator in systems with at least one Byzantine process even if processes have access to a strong complete and accurate σ function.

For this proof, we assume that f is the number of Byzantine failures and the σ function of every process satisfies strong σ-completeness and σ-accuracy with constant X for all the channels.

Theorem 2. *There is no algorithm for the* GDBE *problem that satisfies completeness and accuracy if $f = 1$.*

Proof. Assume by contradiction that there exists a Δ-estimator A such that it satisfies completeness and accuracy with constant $C_A \geq 1$ for all executions E of A.

Consider an execution E_1 of A in Π in which all processes are correct, the maximum channel delay is Δ_{E_1} and it holds in $[1, \infty)$. Execution E_1 has as initial configuration C_0, where there are no messages in transit and all the buffers are empty. The message delays in E_1 are as follows.

Let us assume that there is a process p_b such that $\forall p_i \neq p_b$ the delay bound of channel $c_{b,i}$ in execution E_1 is $\delta_{b,i} = \Delta_{E_1} = \gamma \cdot C$ for some $\gamma > 0$ and $C > C_A$, and $\forall p_i \neq p_b, p_j$ the delay bound of channel $c_{i,j}$ is $\delta_{i,j} = \gamma$ (Fig. 1). Since A is complete and accurate, there exists a time t' such that

$$\forall t \geq t'. \; \forall p_i. \; \Delta_{E_1} \leq \Delta_i(E_1, t) \leq \Delta_{E_1} \cdot C_A \tag{3}$$

Consider execution E_2 that starts with configuration C_0 as in E_1, in which the channel delay $\forall p_i, p_j \neq p_b$ is $\delta_{i,j} = \gamma$, namely the same as in E_1, but the delay of the channels going from p_b to p_i is $\gamma \cdot C - \beta = \gamma$ for $\beta = \gamma \cdot (C-1)$. In this execution, process p_b is Byzantine and starting from time 0, it does not follow the algorithm specification by delaying the sending of its messages β units of time. This means that messages coming out from p_b will be delivered in execution E_2 at the same times as in execution E_1.

More formally, we describe how to modify execution E_1 to get execution E_2, i.e. all sending events performed by p_b are moved forward β units of time (Fig. 2). For every e_i sending event of message m_i to p_j performed by p_b, let t_i be the time at which it is performed in E_1. Move event e_i to be performed at time $t_i + \beta$ and replace any other event being performed by p_b. Since the delay of p_b in E_2 is $\gamma \cdot C - \beta$, message m_i it is delivered at time $t_i + \beta + \gamma \cdot C - \beta = t_i + \gamma \cdot C$ as in execution E_1. Then, the delivery event of message m_i performed by p_j in E_2 is at the same time as in E_1 but it is sent later in execution E_2.

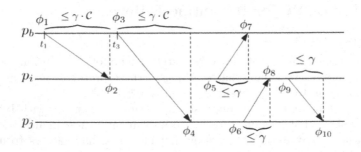

Fig. 1. Illustration of the message delay bounds of execution E_1

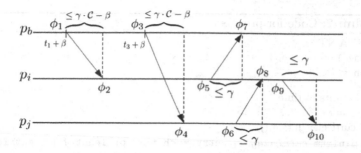

Fig. 2. Illustration of the result of moving forward β units of time events ϕ_1 and ϕ_3

Since p_b is Byzantine, there is no specification of the output of the channel delay function in every $p_i \neq p_b$, so it is correct to assume that the output of the channel delay function in execution E_2 is the same as in execution E_1 for every process p_i.

Then, all the events performed by every $p_i \neq p_b$ are the same in execution E_1 and E_2, thus executions E_1 and E_2 are indistinguishable $\forall p_i \neq p_b$, i.e. the set of received messages and operations performed by p_i are the same in E_1 and E_2, so it is true that the output

$$\Delta_i(E_1, t) = \Delta_i(E_2, t) \tag{4}$$

For all $t \geq t'$. Note that $\Delta_{E_2} = \gamma$ is the delay bound in execution E_2 and

$$\Delta_{E_2} = \gamma < \gamma \cdot C_A < \gamma \cdot C = \Delta_{E_1} \tag{5}$$

Since A is complete and accurate, there exists a time t'' such that

$$\forall t > t''. \ \forall p_i \neq p_b. \ \Delta_{E_2} \leq \Delta_i(E_2, t) \leq \Delta_{E_2} \cdot C_A \tag{6}$$

Let $t^f = \max \{t', t''\}$. By (3), (5) and (6)

$$\Delta_{E_2} \leq \Delta_i(E_2, t) \leq \Delta_{E_2} \cdot C_A < \Delta_{E_1} \leq \Delta_i(E_1, t) \leq \Delta_{E_1} \cdot C_A. \forall t \geq t^f$$

Which contradicts (4). Therefore, there is no algorithm that satisfies completeness and accuracy for the GDBE problem. □

5.2 Upper Bound

We showed that it is not possible to implement a Δ-estimator if there is at least one Byzantine process present. This is because it is not possible for processes to distinguish whether or not a Byzantine process is delaying the sending of messages, so it is impossible to derive complete global delay estimation even if the σ functions are complete and accurate for correct processes.

Algorithm 2: Code for process p_i

---

1 **CONSTANT** α, f;
2 currDelay$_i$[1..n] $\leftarrow \perp$, δ_i[1...n] $\leftarrow 0$, $\Delta_i \leftarrow \infty$;
3 function $\sigma(j)$;

4 **every** T units of time
5   **for** $j \neq i \in \{1, 2, ..., n\}$ **do**
6 | currDelay$_i$[j] = $\sigma_i(j)$;
      /* minimum $currDelay_i[k]$ entry such that at least $f+1$ entries
      from currDelay$_i$ are low equal than $currDelay_i[k]$ */;
7   sorted = sort(currDelay$_i$);
8   globalMin = sorted[f + 1] ;
9   Δ_i = globalMin + α;

Thus it is needed a global property known in advance that can help processes to output an estimate that satisfy completeness and accuracy, but that does not help to distinguish Byzantine processes. We assume that all messages are guaranteed to be received within a known interval but the minimum or maximum delay and which processes are Byzantine remain unknown to all processes. This model was first proposed in [11] as an ideal model of ethernet networks.

We assume a system with $n = 2f + 2$ processes where f is the number of Byzantine processes. Processes have access to function σ which satisfy weak σ-completeness and σ-accuracy. We assume that all messages are guaranteed to be received within a known interval α as specified in the following definition.

Definition 5 (The α assumption). *There $\exists \alpha, K > 0$, α known by processes such that $\forall p_i, p_j \in \text{correct}(E)$ $\delta_0 \leq \sigma_{i,j} \leq (\delta_0 + \alpha) \cdot K = \Delta_E \cdot K$ for some $\delta_0 > 0$.*

This means that the σ functions of all processes can return something lower than their actual delay but the discrepancy between outputs from correct processes is bounded and known.

5.3 Algorithm

Correctness Proof. Let E be an execution of Algorithm 2. Let Δ_E be the maximum communication delay in E. Recall that GST^+ is the time after which the σ functions of correct processes are complete and accurate, i.e. start to output something on interval $I = [\delta_0, (\delta_0 + \alpha) \cdot K]$.

Lemma 7. *Algorithm 2 satisfies completeness and accuracy.*

Proof. We need to show that $\forall p_i \in \text{correct}(E)$. $\forall t \geq \text{GST}^+ + T$. $\Delta_E \leq \Delta_i \leq \Delta_E \cdot \mathcal{C}$ for some constant $\mathcal{C}$.

Let $p_i \in \text{correct}(E)$. Since p_i is correct, it executes lines 5–9 every T units of time. Let $t \geq t^+$ be some time in which those lines are executed. In line 6 the σ function of every process is queried and in line 8 the $f + 1$-th value $v = currDelay_i[j]$ is selected from the sorted values from $currDelay_i$. Note that value v comes from function $\sigma_i(j)$, i.e. is the delay of the channel connecting p_i to p_j. We have to consider two cases.

Case 1: p_j is a correct process. Since $t \geq t^+$, function σ_i outputs values on interval I for correct processes. Thus $v \in I$. Then, by adding α to v on line 9 we get that $\Delta_E \leq \Delta_i = v + \alpha$.

As for the accuracy, since $v \leq (\delta_0 + \alpha) \cdot K = \Delta_E \cdot K$, by adding α to v on line 9 we get

$$v + \alpha \leq (\delta_0 + \alpha) \cdot K + \alpha \leq (\delta_0 + \alpha) \cdot (K + 1) \leq \Delta_E \cdot (K + 1)$$

Case 2: p_j is a Byzantine process. Since the $f + 1$-th value is selected, it means that there is a value $v' < v$ that comes from a correct process. Then, $\Delta_E \leq v' + \alpha \leq v + \alpha$. Therefore, completeness is satisfied.

For the accuracy, note that since there are $n = 2f + 2$ processes, by selecting the $f + 1$-th entry from *sorted*, there most be at least one value v' coming from a correct process such that $v' \geq v$. By Case 1, delays from a correct process are bounded by $v' \leq \Delta_E \cdot (K + 1)$, then $v \leq \Delta_E \cdot (K + 1)$.   □

5.4   Implementing Consensus with GDBE

In this section, we show how to use the Δ-estimator framework for solving Byzantine consensus. For this purpose, we rely on the *view synchronizer* interface proposed in [2]. A *synchronizer* produces notifications at each correct process to indicate when they must enter a new view (or round) v. Then, processes eventually converge to the same view for a long enough period to allow the consensus protocol to exchange messages leading to a decision.

Due to space constraints, we describe how to use the Δ-estimator on the synchronizer proposed in [2] and present the code of Algorithm 3 on the Appendix. Every time a process changes view, it is set a timer for the view duration. In the algorithm presented in [2], there is a function $F(v)$ which grows as the view number grows. Then, since the view number can only grow, the function $F(v)$ eventually reaches a value long enough for allowing processes to be on the same view and reach a decision. In this case, we replace the $F(v)$ with the result of the Δ-estimator. Here we only present the view synchronizer. The actual consensus protocol can be found on [2].

5.5   Correctness Proof

Note that a Δ-estimator outputs something on the interval $I = [\Delta, C \cdot \Delta]$ but it does not guarantee that the output in every process is the same. Then, we need to prove that the properties from the synchronizer specification remain the same after the use of the Δ-estimator.

We present the proofs involving the use of $F(v)$, some of the proofs need to be rewritten since the Δ-estimator does not guarantee that 1) the output in every process is the same and 2) the output in every view is non-decreasing. In some cases only part of the proof is needed and the rest can be found in [2]. Proofs can be found on the Appendix.

6 Related Work

To the best of our knowledge, there is no work devoted to formalizing the global bounded delay estimation problem, although this problem is indirectly studied in several works.

The partial synchrony model is introduced in [8]. They have presented different levels of partial synchrony by defining upper bounds either on the message delay or on the speed with which processes take a step or both. Lower bounds and upper bounds for the consensus are given for the different models presented.

In [4] the unreliable failure detectors were introduced as a distributed oracle for enriching asynchronous systems with a failure detector that outputs a list of processes that are suspected to be failed. An eventually perfect failure detector is proposed for a partially synchronous model and a timeout estimation technique is presented as well. Protocols for solving consensus using different failure detectors appear in this work too. Metrics for measuring the performance of failure detection and a new failure detection algorithm are introduced in [6]. This new algorithm does not estimate timeouts by measuring the delay as in previous implementations, but instead relies on the probabilistic behavior of the system for trying to predict when a new message arrives.

A view synchronizer is presented in [2] for partially synchronous systems. This work presents a precise specification of the view synchronizer and an implementation of an algorithm for view synchronization that can be used for solving the Byzantine consensus on leader-based rounds. Latency bounds for the synchronizer are given and some modern consensus protocols, such as [3,16], are modified for achieving one-shot consensus with the use of the view synchronizer.

A simple algorithm for estimating efficiently the one-way delay in a network is proposed in [7]. For this algorithm, it is assumed that processes do not have access to synchronized clocks but every process has a clock that allows it to measure time correctly and the delay on each direction is different. Using heuristics it derives the initial forward and reverse delays at the beginning of the protocol and then, using these parameters it sends a sequence of messages for adjusting the delays. We focused on this work since it illustrates more precisely the One-Way Delay estimation problem in theory and practice. A one-way delay estimation survey can be found in [5].

7   Conclusions

We introduced the *Global Delay Bound Estimation* problem that models the common task of estimating the global delay on the network. We defined a new distributed oracle that allows processes to derive the upper bound on the message delay Δ. Each process has access to an oracle that outputs the delays for the channels that connect the process with its neighbors. We defined Δ-estimators as algorithms that output an eventually bounded estimate of the global delay.

We proposed an algorithm for implementing a Δ-estimator on the crash model that satisfies an extra property: processes eventually agree on their output.

For the Byzantine case, we showed that it is not possible to derive a global estimation that satisfies completeness and accuracy even if there is just one Byzantine failure. Then, we propose a stronger model that allows implementing a Δ-estimator with $f = \frac{n-2}{2}$ failures. Finally, we showed how to use the Δ-estimator framework for implementing Byzantine consensus using a view synchronizer and proved its correctness.

Several interesting questions for this new model remain open. Consider the weak σ-completeness definition for the σ functions in which the output eventually satisfies being greater than the delay of the channel but infinitely often. Our conjecture is that it is not possible to implement a Δ-estimator on the GST model using σ functions that satisfy weak completeness if there are crash failures with no further knowledge about the delays.

In Sect. 5 we showed an implementation of a Δ-estimator assuming the existence of σ functions that satisfies weak σ-completeness but also the α-assumption which is the mechanism that allows coping with the previous lower bound. The question that remains open: is there a weaker model that would allow to implement a Δ-estimator on the Byzantine environment?

For the case of the crash model, we can implement consensus using an Ω failure detector that queries the Δ-estimator for setting the timeout and then uses a consensus protocol like the one in [13]. Eventual leader election does not require the use of a Δ-estimator because the output of the σ functions is sufficient for eventually electing a leader. Although using a Δ-estimator would allow a simpler way to analyze the time bounds for this problem.

Acknowledgement. We thank prof. Armando Castañeda (UNAM) for his useful insights during the writing of this paper.

A   Implementing Consensus with **GDBE**

A.1   Synchronizer

Algorithm 3: The fast FASTSYNC using the Δ-estimator

```
1  function start():
2  |   if view⁺ = 0 then
3  |   |   send WISH(1);

4  when timer_view expires
5  |   send WISH(max(view + 1, view⁺)) to all;

6  periodically
7  |   if timer_view is enabled then
8  |   |   send WISH(view⁺) to all;
9  |   else if max_views[i] > 0 then
10 |   |   send WISH(max(view + 1, view⁺)) to all;

11 when received WISH(v) from pⱼ
12 |   prev_v, prev_v⁺ ← view, view⁺;
13 |   if v > max_views[j] then max_views[j] = v;
14 |   view ← max{v|∃k.max_views[k] = v ∧ |{j|max_views[j] ≥ v}| ≥ 2f + 1};
15 |   view⁺ ← max{v|∃k.max_views[k] = v ∧ |{j|max_views[j] ≥ v}| ≥ f + 1};
16 |   if view⁺ = view ∧ view > prev_v then
17 |   |   stop_timer(timer_view);
       |   /* Δ-estimator is called when setting the timer        */;
18 |   |   start_timer(timer_view, 2 * Δᵢ);
19 |   |   trigger new_view(view);
20 |   if view⁺ > prev_v⁺ then
21 |   |   send WISH(view⁺) to all;
```

A.2   Correctness Proof

We assume that each process has access to a complete and accurate with constant $\mathcal{C}$ Δ-estimator. Let Δ_i^v be the output of the Δ-estimator at process p_i when it is called to enter view v. Let $t^\Delta \geq \mathsf{GST}$ be the time after which for every correct process p_i, the Δ-estimator is complete and accurate property, i.e. $\forall t \geq t^\Delta.\forall v' \leq v.\Delta \leq \Delta_i^v \leq \mathcal{C} \cdot \Delta$ for some fixed constant $\mathcal{C} \geq 0$.

Let $\Delta_{\max}^v = max\{\Delta_i^v\} \cdot 2$ and $\Delta_{\min}^v = min\{\Delta_i^v\} \cdot 2$ be the maximum and the minimum output of the Δ-estimator at the time it is called for entering view v.

We rewrite the lemmas related to the function $F(v)$ in [2]. As in [2], the *local view* of a process p_i at time t, denoted $\mathsf{LV}_i(t)$, is the latest view entered by p_i at or before t, or 0 if p_i has not entered any views by then. Thus, $\mathsf{GV}(t) = max\{\mathsf{LV}_i(t)|p_i$ is correct$\}$. We say that a process p_i attempts to advance from a view $v \geq 0$ at time t if at this time p_i executes the code in either line 3 or line 5, and $\mathsf{LV}_i(t) = v$. The *global view* at time t, denoted $\mathsf{GV}(t)$, be the maximum view entered by a correct process at or before t, or 0 if no view was entered by a correct process.

Definition 6. *Synchronizer properties are the following:*

1. $\forall i, v, v'.(E_i(v)$ *and* $E_i(v')$ *are defined* $) \wedge v < v' \Rightarrow E_i(v) < E_i(v')$
2. *There is a view* $\mathcal{V}$ *where synchronization starts and* $E_{\text{first}}(\mathcal{V}) \geq \text{GST}$
3. $\forall i.\forall v \geq \mathcal{V}.p_i$ *is correct* $\Rightarrow p_i$ *enters* v
4. $\forall v \geq \mathcal{V}.E_{\text{last}}(v) \leq E_{\text{first}} + 2\Delta$
5. $\forall v \geq \mathcal{V}.E_{\text{first}}(v+1) \geq E_{\text{first}}(v) + \Delta_{\max}^v$

Definition 7. *Synchronizer latency bounds are the following:*

A. $\forall v \geq \mathcal{V} . E_{\text{last}}(v+1) \leq E_{\text{first}}(v) + \Delta_{\max}^v + \Delta$
B. $S_{\text{first}} \geq \text{GST} \wedge t^\Delta \Rightarrow \mathcal{V} = 1 \wedge E_{\text{last}}(1) \leq S_{\text{last}} + \Delta$
C. Δ*-estimator is complete an accurate* $\wedge S_{f+1} \leq \text{GST} + \rho \Rightarrow \mathcal{V} = \text{GV}(\text{GST} + \rho) + 1 \wedge E_{\text{last}}(\mathcal{V}) \leq \text{GST} + \rho + \Delta_{\max}^{\mathcal{V}-1} \leq \text{GST} + \rho + C \cdot \Delta$

Lemma 22. *If a correct process enters a view* $v > 0$ *and* $E_{\text{first}}(v) \geq \text{GST}$, *then for all* $v' > v$, *no correct process attempts to advance from* $v' - 1$ *before* $E_{\text{first}}(v) + \Delta_{\min}^v$.

Proof. Proof by contradiction. Assume that there $\exists$ a time $t' < E_{\text{first}} + \Delta_{\min}^v$ and a correct process p_i that attempts to advance from $v' - 1 > v - 1$ at t'. Let us consider the time in which process p_i executes the code in line 5 (since the case in which line 3 is executed is not possible) and $\text{LV}_i(t') = 0 = v' - 1 > v - 1 \geq 0$. We have that $E_{\text{first}}(v' - 1) \leq E_i(v' - 1)$.

Since p_i.timer_view is not enabled at t', p_i must have entered $v' - 1$ at least $\Delta_{\min}^v$ before t' according to its local clock, then $E_i(v' - 1) \leq t' - \Delta_{\min}^v$. Since $v' - 1 \geq v$, by Corollary 20 in [2], it is true that $E_{\text{first}}(v' - 1) \geq E_{\text{first}}(v) \geq \text{GST}$. Therefore, given that after GST all processes clocks run a the same rate as real time, we have

$$E_{\text{first}}(v) \leq E_{\text{first}}(v' - 1) \leq E_i(v' - 1) \leq t' - \Delta_{\min}^v$$

Hence, $t' \geq E_{\text{first}}(v'-1) + \Delta_{\min}^v$, which contradicts our assumption. Therefore no correct process attempts to advance from $v' - 1$ before $E_{\text{first}}(v) + \Delta_{\min}^v$. □

Corollary 23. *Assume a correct process enters a view* $v > 0$ *and* $E_{\text{first}}(v) \geq \text{GST}$. *For all views* $v' > v$ *if there exists a correct process that enters* v', *then* $E_{\text{first}}(v') > E_{\text{first}}(v) + \Delta_{\min}^v$.

Proof. Since a correct process enters a view $v' > 0$, by Lemma 16 in [2], there exists a time $t < E_{\text{first}}(v')$ at which some correct process attempts to advance from $v' - 1$. By Lemma 22, we get $t \geq E_{\text{first}}(v) + \Delta_{\min}^v$ as required. □

Corollary 24. *Consider a view* v *and assume that* v *is entered by a correct process. If* $E_{\text{first}}(v) \geq \text{GST}$, *then a correct process cannot send a* WISH(v') *with* $v' > v$ *earlier than* $E_{\text{first}}(v) + \Delta_{\min}^v$.

Proof. Assume a correct process sends a WISH(v') with $v' > v$ at time t'. By Lemma 15 in [2], there $\exists s \leq t'$ such that some correct process p_i attempts to advance from $v' - 1 > v - 1$ at s. By Lemma 22, $s \geq E_{\text{first}}(v) + \Delta_{\min}^v$, which implies that $t' \leq s \leq E_{\text{first}}(v) + \Delta_{\min}^v$. □

Lemma 28. *For all v if some correct process enters v and*

(i) $E_{\text{first}}(v) \geq \text{GST}$,
(ii) $\text{postGST}(E_{\text{first}}(v))$ *holds, and*
(iii) Δ-*estimator is complete*

then all correct process enter v and $E_{\text{last}}(v) \leq E_{\text{first}}(v) + 2\Delta$

Proof. Since $E_{\text{first}}(v) \geq \text{GST}$ and $\Delta_{\min}^{v} > 2 \cdot \Delta$ for every $v' > v$, by Corollary 24, we have

(iv) no correct process sends $\text{WISH}(v')$ with $v' > v$ until after $E_{\text{first}}(v) + 2\Delta$

The rest of the proof is as in [2].   □

Corollary 29. *For all views v, if a correct process enters v, $E_{\text{first}}(v) > \text{GST} + \rho$ and the Δ-estimator is complete, then all correct processes enter v and $E_{\text{last}}(v) \leq E_{\text{first}}(v) + 2\Delta$.*

Lemma 34. *Assume a correct process enters a view v, $E_{\text{first}}(v) \geq \text{GST}$, the Δ-estimator is complete, and $\text{postGST}(E_{\text{first}}(v))$ holds. Then all correct processes enter the view $v + 1$ and $E_{\text{last}}(v + 1) \leq E_{\text{last}}(v) + \Delta_{\max}^{v} + \Delta$.*

Proof. Let $T = E_{\text{last}}(v) + \Delta_{\max}^{v}$. Assume that some correct process enters view $v + 1$ before T, then by Lemma 28, all correct processes enter view $v + 1$ and

$$E_{\text{last}}(v + 1) \leq E_{\text{first}}(v + 1) + 2\Delta \leq T + 2\Delta = E_{\text{last}}(v) + \Delta_{\max}^{v} + \Delta$$

as required.

Now assume that no correct process enters $v + 1$ before T. We have $T > E_{\text{first}}(v) \geq \text{GST}$. By Lemmas 33 and 18 in [2], eventually some correct process enters $v+1$, so by Corollary 24, $T \geq \text{GST}$ implies that no correct process can send $\text{WISH}(v')$ for any $v' > v + 1$ earlier than $T + \Delta_{\min}^{v+1}$. Then $\text{WISH}(v') > T + \Delta_{\min}^{v+1}$. Thus, given that $\text{WISH}(v') > T$ and $\Delta_{\min}^{v+1} > 2\Delta$ we get

$$\text{no correct process sends } \text{WISH}(v') \text{ with } v' > v + 1 \text{ before } T + 2\Delta \qquad (23)$$

By Lemma 28, all correct process enter v. Let p_i be a correct process that enters v at $E_i(v) \leq \text{GST}$, at this time p_i starts $p_i.\text{timer\_view}$ for the duration of Δ_i^{v}. Note that $\Delta_{\min}^{v} \leq \Delta_i^{v} \leq \Delta_{\max}^{v}$. Since by this time all clocks run a the same speed as real time, $p_i.\text{timer\_view}$ cannot last more than $E_i(v) + \Delta_i^{v} \leq E_i(v) + \Delta_{\max}^{v} \leq E_{\text{last}}(v) + \Delta_{\max}^{v}$. Let s_i be the time at which $p_i.\text{timer\_view}$ either expires or is stopped prematurely by executing the code in line 17; then $E_i(v) < s_i \leq E_{\text{last}}(v) + \Delta_{\max}^{v}$ and therefore

$$s_i \leq E_{\text{last}}(v) + \Delta_{\max}^{v} = (E_{\text{last}}(v) + \Delta_{\max}^{v} - \Delta) + \Delta = T + \Delta \qquad (24)$$

From here the proof follows exactly as in Lemma 34 in [2].   □

Corollary 35. *For all views v, if a correct process enters v, $E_{\mathrm{first}}(v) > \mathsf{GST} + \rho$, and the Δ-estimator is complete, then all correct processes enter the view $v + 1$ and $E_{\mathrm{last}}(v + 1) \le E_{\mathrm{last}}(v) + \Delta^v_{\max} + \Delta$.*

Theorem 36. *FastSync satisfies properties 1–5 in Definition 6 for $d = 2\Delta$.*

Proof. Let t^Δ be the time after which the Δ-estimator is complete. Property 1 is trivially satisfied. Let $\mathcal{V}$ be the first view such that a correct process enters $\mathcal{V}$, $E_{\mathrm{first}}(\mathcal{V}) \le t^\Delta > \mathsf{GST} + \rho$, the view $\mathcal{V}$ satisfies Property 2. Such a view exists because of the existence of a time in which the Δ-estimator is correct and Lemma 33 in [2] (global view keeps increasing). Since $E_{\mathrm{first}}(\mathcal{V}) \ge t^\Delta > \mathsf{GST}$, the view $\mathcal{V}$ satisfies Property 2. By Lemmas 18 and 33 in [2], a correct process enters every view $v \ge \mathcal{V}$. By Corollary 20 in [2]

$$E_{\mathrm{first}}(v) \ge E_{\mathrm{first}}(\mathcal{V}) > \mathsf{GST} \tag{26}$$

Since the Δ-estimator eventually satisfies completeness, $\Delta^v_{\min} > 2\Delta$ starting at some view v. Thus, by Corollary 29, all correct processes enter v and $E_{\mathrm{last}}(v) \le E_{\mathrm{first}}(v) + 2\Delta$ which validates Properties 3 and 4. To prove 5, fix a view $v \ge \mathcal{V}$. By (26), $E_{\mathrm{first}}(v) > \mathsf{GST}$, and therefore, by Corollary 23, we get $E_{\mathrm{first}}(v + 1) \ge E_{\mathrm{first}}(v) + \Delta^v_{\max}$ which implies Property 5. □

Theorem 38. *Let $\mathcal{V} = \mathsf{GV}(\mathsf{GST} + \rho) + 1$ and $d = 2\Delta$. Assume that $S_{f+1} \le \mathsf{GST} + \rho$ and Δ estimator is complete. Then FastSync satisfies properties 1–5 in Definition 6 and latency properties A–C in Definition 7.*

Proof. Property 1 is satisfied trivially. Let $W = \mathsf{GST} + \rho$ and $\mathcal{V} = \mathsf{GV}(W) + 1$. By Lemmas 18 and 33 from [2], some correct process enters $\mathcal{V}$. By Lemma 19 in [2], $\mathsf{GV}(E_{\mathrm{first}}(\mathcal{V})) = \mathcal{V}$. Since GV is non-decreasing and $\mathcal{V} > \mathsf{GV}(W)$, we have $E_{\mathrm{first}}(\mathcal{V}) > \mathsf{GST} + \rho \ge \mathsf{GST}$. Hence Property 2 holds. By Lemmas 18 and 33 from [2], some correct process enters every view $v \ge \mathcal{V}$. By Corollary 20 in [2], $v \ge \mathcal{V}$ implies that

$$E_{\mathrm{first}}(v) \ge E_{\mathrm{first}}(\mathcal{V}) \ge W \tag{28}$$

Since completeness is satisfied, $\forall v \ge \mathcal{V} \, . \, \Delta^v_{\min} \ge 2\Delta$. Thus, by Corollary 29, all correct processes enter v and $E_{\mathrm{last}}(v) \le E_{\mathrm{first}}(v) + 2\Delta$ which validates Properties 3 and 4.

To prove Properties 5 and A, fix a view $v \ge \mathcal{V}$. By (28), $E_{\mathrm{first}}(v) \ge \mathsf{GST}$, and therefore, by Corollary 23 we get $E_{\mathrm{first}}(v + 1) \ge E_{\mathrm{first}}(v) + \Delta^v_{\min}$, which implies Property 5. Since (28), $E_{\mathrm{first}}(v) \ge W$, by Lemma 26 in [2], $\mathsf{postGST}(E_{\mathrm{first}}(v))$ holds. We also have $\Delta^v_{\min}, \Delta^{\mathcal{V}}_{\min} \ge 2\Delta$. Thus, by Corollary 35, $E_{\mathrm{last}}(v + 1) \le E_{\mathrm{last}}(v) + \Delta^v_{\max} + \Delta$, and therefore, Property A holds. To prove Property C, we consider two cases:

Case 1: $\mathsf{GV}(W) = 0$. Hence $\mathcal{V} = 1$. Let

$$t_1 = max(S_{f+1}, W)$$

$$t_2 = max(S_{\mathrm{last}}, W)$$

$$T = max(min(S_{f+1}, S_{\text{last}} - \Delta), W)$$

Since $S_{f+1} \leq W$ and $min(W, S_{\text{last}} - \Delta) \leq W$, the above can be re-written as follows:

$$t_1 = max(S_{f+1}, W) = W$$

$$t_2 = max(S_{\text{last}}, W)$$

$$T = W$$

Then $\mathsf{GV}(T) = 0$. Since GV is non decreasing, $E_{\text{first}}(1) \geq \mathsf{GST}$. Thus by Corollary 24, no correct process can send $\mathtt{WISH}(v)$ for any $v > 1$ earlier than $T + \Delta_{\min}^1 > T + 2\Delta$. Since by Lemma 26 in [2] $\mathsf{postGST}(W)$ holds, by Lemma 31 in [2], $E_{\text{last}}(\mathcal{V}) \leq min(t_1 + 2\Delta, t_2 + \Delta) \leq t_1 + 2\Delta = \mathsf{GST} + \rho + 2\Delta$. Since $\Delta_{\max}^0 > 0$ we have

$$E_{\text{last}}(\mathcal{V}) \leq \mathsf{GST} + \rho + \Delta_{\max}^{\mathsf{GV}(W)} + 2\Delta$$

which implies the upper bound stated on Property C.

Case 2: $\mathsf{GV}(W) > 0$. Let $T = W + \Delta_{\max}^{\mathsf{GV}(W)} + \Delta$. Suppose first that some correct process enters $\mathsf{GV}(W) + 1$ before T. By Lemma 19 in [2], $\mathsf{GV}(E_{\text{first}}(\mathsf{GV}(W) + 1)) = \mathsf{GV}(W) + 1$. Since GV is non-decreasing, we have $E_{\text{first}}(\mathsf{GV}(W) + 1) > W$. Thus by Corollary 29, all correct processes enter $\mathcal{V}$ by $\mathsf{GST} + \rho + \Delta_{\max}^{\mathsf{GV}(W)} + 3\Delta$ as needed. Suppose now that no correct process enters $\mathcal{V}$ before T, so that $E_{\text{first}}(\mathcal{V}) \geq T \geq \mathsf{GST}$. Then, by Corollary 24,

no correct process can send $\mathtt{WISH}(v)$ for any $v > \mathcal{V}$ earlier that $T + \Delta_{\min}^{\mathcal{V}} > T + 2\Delta$ (29)

From Lemma 26 in [2], $\mathsf{postGST}(W)$ and therefore by Lemma 32 in [2], all correct processes send $\mathtt{WISH}(\mathcal{V})$ to all processes no later than $T + \Delta$. Since (29) holds, by Lemma 30 in [2], all correct processes enter $\mathcal{V}$, and $E_{\text{last}}(\mathcal{V}) \leq T + 2\Delta = \mathsf{GST} + \rho + \Delta_{\max}^{\mathsf{GV}(W)} + 3\Delta$ as needed. Since the Δ-estimator is accurate with constant $\mathcal{C}$

$$E_{\text{last}}(\mathcal{V}) \leq T + 2\Delta = \mathsf{GST} + \rho + (\mathcal{C} + 3)\Delta$$

is true too. $\square$

References

1. State machine replication in the libra blockchain. https://developers.libra.org/docs/assets/papers/libra-consensus-state-machine-replication-in-the-libra-blockchain.pdf
2. Bravo, M., Chockler, G.V., Gotsman, A.: Making byzantine consensus live. In: 34th International Symposium on Distributed Computing, DISC 2020, October 12–16, 2020, Virtual Conference, vol. 179. LIPIcs, pp. 23:1–23:17. Schloss Dagstuhl - Leibniz-Zentrum für Informatik (2020)

3. Buchman, E., Kwon, J., Milosevic, Z.: The latest gossip on BFT consensus. CoRR, abs/1807.04938 (2018)
4. Chandra, T.D., Toueg, S.: Unreliable failure detectors for reliable distributed systems. J. ACM **43**(2), 225–267 (1996)
5. Chefrour, D.: One-way delay measurement from traditional networks to SDN: a survey. ACM Comput. Surv. **54**(7), 156:1-156:35 (2022)
6. Chen, W., Toueg, S., Aguilera, M.K.: On the quality of service of failure detectors. IEEE Trans. Comput. **51**(1), 13–32 (2002)
7. Choi, J.-H., Yoo, C.: One-way delay estimation and its application. Comput. Commun. **28**(7), 819–828 (2005)
8. Dwork, C., Lynch, N.A., Stockmeyer, L.J.: Consensus in the presence of partial synchrony. J. ACM **35**(2), 288–323 (1988)
9. Fischer, M.J., Lynch, N.A., Paterson, M.: Impossibility of distributed consensus with one faulty process. J. ACM **32**(2), 374–382 (1985)
10. Gurewitz, O., Cidon, I., Sidi, M.: One-way delay estimation using network-wide measurements. IEEE Trans. Inf. Theory **52**(6), 2710–2724 (2006)
11. Halpern, J.Y., Suzuki, I.: Clock synchronization and the power of broadcasting. Distrib. Comput. **5**, 73–82 (1991)
12. Malkhi, D., Oprea, F., Zhou, L.: Ω meets Paxos: leader election and stability without eventual timely links. In: Fraigniaud, P. (ed.) DISC 2005. LNCS, vol. 3724, pp. 199–213. Springer, Heidelberg (2005). https://doi.org/10.1007/11561927_16
13. Mostéfaoui, A., Raynal, M.: Leader-based consensus. Parallel Process. Lett. **11**(1), 95–107 (2001)
14. Vakili, A., Grégoire, J.-C.: Accurate one-way delay estimation: limitations and improvements. IEEE Trans. Instrum. Meas. **61**(9), 2428–2435 (2012)
15. De Vito, L., Rapuano, S., Tomaciello, L.: One-way delay measurement: state of the art. IEEE Trans. Instrum. Meas. **57**(12), 2742–2750 (2008)
16. Yin, M., Malkhi, D., Reiter, M.K., Golan-Gueta, G., Abraham, I.: Hotstuff: BFT consensus with linearity and responsiveness. In: Robinson, P., Ellen, F., (eds.), Proceedings of the 2019 ACM Symposium on Principles of Distributed Computing, PODC 2019, Toronto, ON, Canada, July 29–August 2 2019, pp. 347–356. ACM (2019)

Mechanical Energy Minimization UAV-Mounted Base Station Path Plan for Public Safety Communication

Imane Chakour$^{(\boxtimes)}$ ⓘ, Cherki Daoui ⓘ, and Mohamed Baslam ⓘ

Information Processing and Decision Support Laboratory, Faculty of Sciences and Technics, Sultan Moulay Slimane University, Beni Mellal, Morocco
im.chakour@gmail.com

Abstract. The increasing number of situations in which wireless communication networks are damaged due to natural disasters has motivated researchers to utilize unmanned aerial vehicles (UAVs) to deliver fast and efficacious backup communication in post-disaster scenarios. UAVs are a logical option for public safety cellular networks due to their key features such as agility, mobility, flexibility, and adaptable altitude. There are exciting situations; for example, California and Turkey wildfires and UAVs can be integral to cellular networks beyond 5G as the technology rises and new efficient Scenarios are developed. In this paper, we investigate the use of a powered Feeder UAV to charge the batteries of UAVBSs, after which a UAV Relay can deliver backhaul connectivity to one of the UAVBSs, all UAVBSs can have hybrid FSO/RF link connections, and all UAVBSs has been designed within a disaster zone providing network coverage to users based on the latency-free communication. We compare a path planning design that uses ACO and Metropolis-hasting algorithms to find the optimal trajectory with the least propulsion energy required for the Feeder UAV to visit all UAVBSs, UAV relay, and return to a docking station that serves as a physical location where the Feeder UAV charges. In calculating the energy consumption, we consider both the hovering and the hardware of the Feeder UAV. According to simulation results, our proposed ACO design outperforms the proposed Metropolis-hasting design and the approach in the literature by up to 12% and 48%, respectively.

Keywords: UAV · Ant colony optimization · MCMC · Metropolis-hasting · Public safety communication · Trajectory optimization

1 Introduction

Natural disasters have an irreversible impact on the life of one person every second around the world [8]. As climate and environmental factors change, they are expected to result in more severe and common natural disasters, with serious

M.-A. Koulali and M. Mezini (Eds.): NETYS 2022, LNCS 13464, pp. 222–235, 2022.
https://doi.org/10.1007/978-3-031-17436-0_15

consequences for the well-being of people and the economies of nation states [16]. As a result, it is critical to employ the most cutting-edge communication technologies to provide the most effective public safety services possible [15].

Natural disasters including earthquakes, fires, or floods that interrupt the existing communications infrastructure or move large populations, overburdening what remains of the communications infrastructure [9], are examples of relevant scenarios. People in these situations need directions, guidance, and updates on the actual situation, and they frequently require sending requests for assistance or communicating their current location to emergency teams. In an ideal world, users need to be capable of contacting each other directly [4,14], despite the lack of cellular infrastructure, which is common in catastrophe situations. It is therefore essential to develop innovative solutions and approaches to replace or integrate existing communication infrastructures for the advantage of the damaged population and first responders [3].

Much of the effort is currently focused on: 1) catastrophe planning, 2) catastrophe assessment and 3) post-catastrophe recovery and response. The first two ways depend mainly on prediction recognition and surveillance. The post-catastrophe phase is primarily concerned with rescuing operations and facilitating the mission of first responders. The Integrated Drone Pilot Program was initiated in the United States in November 2017 as part of a White House Presidential Memorandum [2] to maximize the benefits of drone technologies to mitigate the safety and security risks to the public. The Memo was released following a previous successful drone mission to the latest disaster, the California and Turkey wildfires. The ABSOLUTE project in Europe aims to use hovering drones to improve the terrestrial network, especially for public safety and emergencies [1].

UAV-based communications are seen as a serious contender for widespread use of 5G. In addition, 3GPP intends to cover non-ground networks, such as drones and UAVs, in the second stage of the newly developed 5G radio standard, which is scheduled to be included in 3GPP's Rel-16 by mid-2022. Drone communications offer promising solutions for providing wireless connectivity to devices that lack infrastructure coverage, such as in the event of unplanned outages or damage to the communications infrastructure from malicious actions or natural disasters [17].

1.1 Literature Review

A further critical defy in UAV-based communication schemes is the optimal planning of the UAV trajectory. UAV trajectory optimization is necessary when used for intelligent cities, UAV-EUs, and caching scenarios. UAV path is heavily influenced by collision avoidance, ground user demands, energy constraints, and flight time. When researching UAV trajectories for performance optimization, for example, various critical issues must be considered, such as channel variability due to motion, UAV dynamics, UAV energy requirements, and flight restrictions.

The authors of [13] used reinforcement learning to design a data collection path from ground sensor nodes based on the shortest path technique. In addition, the authors of [21] developed an energy-efficient circuit for mobile drone crowd detection using a genetic algorithm (GA). The authors in [19] suggested an energy-efficacious path design in which a UAV attempts to maintain contact with a ground terminal. In [10], we applied machine learning to identify the optimum placement of divided UAV base stations to maximize the number of users covered in a catastrophe area. In addition, [11,12] demonstrated that drone base stations could supply succor to users by increasing network throughput and coverage when some base stations were down. [6] proposed a drone path design for emergency communication using delay tolerance and used GA to provide data to user groups.

This article's main contribution is to provide a rapid, productive, and low-cost deployment of post-disaster wireless communications. A UAV base station is diffused into clusters of users in a disaster area. To provide fast and facile network placement, it is supposed that the UAV base stations do not have any form of backhaul to the core network, so the UAV relay provides one of them a backhaul to connect using hybrid FSO/RF links and the UAVBS, and the UAVR does not have any form of load to guarantee their flight time.

The Feeder UAV begins at a docking station (the physical location from which the Feeder UAV charges), then travels to each UAV base station and UAV relay to charge them before returning to the docking station to recharge its batterie. This method is ideal for delay-tolerant communications, such as sending and receiving emergency messages, RSS feeds, emails, and text and multimedia messages.

We compare the ACO and MCMC solutions to find a path that can minimize the energy requirements of a drone power supply to charge the drone's base station batteries. Consider that this approach is a popularization of the famous Traveling Salesperson Problem (TSP), which determines the shortest distance route for a salesperson to visit all cities in a specified set of cities and get back to the source [18]. By funding the total energy usage of the Feeder UAV for any particular trajectory, which considers both the energy needs of the hovering and the hardware, as well as the energy needed to fly straight and to change the route of the Feeder UAV by turning flat to the next UAV, we illustrate that excluding the energy needs of the turns considerably underestimates the energy needs of the Feeder UAV. Thus, the case we represent differs from the typical TSP since the preceding and upcoming nodes targeted, the turn angle, affect the energy requirement.

To realize this objective, we evaluate the following key topics: In Sect. 2, we formulate our problem. In Sect. 3, we consider our energy minimization path planning algorithm based on ACO and Metropolis-hasting. In Sect. 4 describes the performance analysis of the algorithms, while Sect. 5 concludes the paper.

2   Problem Formulation

In Fig. 1, we Consider a geographical area exposed to a natural phenomenon where 100% of its ground cellular infrastructure is broken down. N UAV-mounted base stations are distributed to supply cellular coverage in the damaged areas where users could be clustered. The UAV-mounted base stations are linked using hybrid FSO/RF links, and one of them brings the backhaul connection from the UAV relay station.

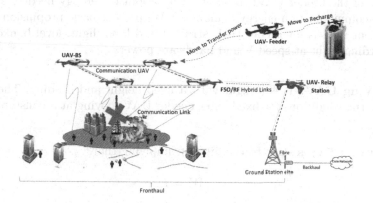

Fig. 1. UAV communication during post-disaster.

We formulate our problem in this architecture. It is worth noting that we have a set UB = {1, 2, ..., UB} of UAVBSs (base stations and relay UAVs) that we use to generate the necessary coverage for the damaged area.

2.1   Flight Altitude

The maximum height at which the load link between the Feeder UAV and the other UAVBS is significantly increased is given as [5] to ensure that all UAVBS are at the same altitude:

$$h = r \tan \theta, \tag{1}$$

By solving (2), we can find θ and r, representing the best elevation angle and the most effective coverage radius, respectively.

$$l = \frac{\eta_{\mathrm{LoS}} - \eta_{\mathrm{NLoS}}}{1 + \epsilon \exp\left(-\varsigma\left(\frac{180}{\pi}\vartheta - \epsilon\right)\right)} + 20 \log\left(\frac{r}{\cos\vartheta}\right) + \beta \tag{2}$$

In (2), LoS and λ are the line-of-sight and wavelength of the carrier, respectively, where $\beta = 20 \log(4\pi/\lambda) + \eta_{\mathrm{NLOS}}$. ϵ, ϑ, l, and NLoS are environment-dependent constants, the path loss threshold, and non-line-of-sight, respectively. Because of the additional losses to the free space propagation loss, LoS and NLoS are affected by the environment.

In this study, we assume that the N UAVBSs are randomly distributed in the relevant areas, with a least airspace separation of 2r between two UAVBSs and a height of h for the Feeder UAVs.

2.2   Feeder UAV Propulsion Energy Requirement

In general, a Feeder UAV's total energy consumption is subdivided into two components: 1) communication-attached energy and 2) propulsive energy. Propulsion energy is the mechanical energy requirements for the movement, hovering, and hardware of the Feeder UAV. In reality, the propulsion energy needed is higher than the communication energy demanded. We present basic propulsion energy requirement models for Feeder UAV straight and level flight, level banked turn in forwarding flight at speed V and hardware powers.

Fixed-Wing UAV. It is a flight with a fixed height and heading. The below describes the conditions for fixed-wing Feeder UAV moving at a constant speed [20]:

– The weight (W) is same to the lift (L), implying that,

$$W = L \tag{3}$$

– The drag (D) is the same as its thrust (Γ), that is,

$$D = \Gamma = \frac{1}{2}v^2 C_{D_0} S\rho(h) + \frac{2L^2}{\pi e_0 A_R S v^2 \rho(h)} \tag{4}$$

In (4), v, C_{D_0}, S, $\rho(h)$, e_0 and A_R are respectively the speed of the Feeder UAV, the drag coefficient at zero lift, the wing area, the air density at height h, the Oswald efficiency and the aspect ratio of the pavilion.

Considering that the energy is obtained by multiplying the force by the speed, the energy for a fixed-wing Feeer UAV, P_f, is defined as follows:

$$P_f = \Gamma v = \frac{1}{2}v^3 C_{D_0} S\rho(h) + \frac{2W^2}{\pi e_0 A_R S v \rho(h)} = a_1 v^3 + a_2/v \tag{5}$$

where

$$a_1 \triangleq \frac{1}{2}C_{D_0} S\rho(h), \text{ and } a_2 \triangleq \frac{2W^2}{\pi e_0 A_R S\rho(h)} \tag{6}$$

In (5), a_1 is referred to as the parasitic drag, which defines the energy needed to surmount the frictional drag and pressure on the Feeder UAV. In contrast, a_2 refers to the induced drag, which provides the energy required to surmount the lift-induced drag [20]. Considering the relationships between a_1, a_2 and v, we find that a1 dominates at fast speeds, while a_1 prevails at slow speeds. Finally, the propulsion energy consumption needed for straight-line level flight for a flight time T is the following:

$$E^F = (T - T_{move})P_f = (a_1 v^3 + a_2/v)(T - T_{move}) \tag{7}$$

where T_{move} is the time employed by Feeder UAV to travel from one UAV base station to another.

Rotay-wing UAV to change the Feeder UAV's heading, the aircraft must tilt by an angle such that the lift produces a component of acceleration that is proportional to the Feeder UAV's speed. The propulsion energy consumption required for Banked level turn UAV during time T given by:

$$
E^R = (T - T_{move})[a_1 \left(1 + \frac{3\,V^2}{q^2}\right) + a_2 \left(\sqrt{1 + \frac{V^4}{4v_o^4}} - \frac{V^2}{2v_o^2}\right)^{1/2}
$$
$$
\left[+\frac{1}{2}d_o\rho s A V^3\right]
$$
(8)

where a_1 and a_2 are constants that vary with the weight of the Feeder UAV, the rotor speed, the rotor disc size, the blade angular velocity, and the air density. The rotor tip speed is q, the fuselage drag ratio is d_o, the average rotor speed is v_o, the air density is ρ, the rotor strength is s, and the rotor disk area is A.

Hovering and Hardware Consumption. In our suggested solution, we have two types of unattached UAVs: 1) the Feeder UAV and 2) the UAVBSs. The Feeder UAV charges the batteries of the cUAVBS, the Feeder UAV consumes the hover and hardware energies. The energy levels of the hovering and hardware Feeder UAV, denoted by E_{hov}, E_{hard}, can be expressed, respectively, as:

$$
E_{hov} = E^F + E^R = \sqrt{\frac{(m_{tot}\,g)^3}{2\pi r_p^2 n_p \rho}}\,(T - T_{move})
$$
(9)

$$
E_{hard} = \left[\frac{P_{full} - P_{idle}}{v_{max}}v + P_{idle}\right](T_{move})
$$
(10)

The maximum speed of the Feeder UAV is given by v_{max}. P_{full}, P_{idle}, m_{tot}, g, ρ, r_p and n_p are respectively the hardware power levels when the UAV is travelling at full speed, when the Feeder UAV is in idle mode, the mass of the Feeder UAV, Earth's gravity, and air density, the radius and number of propellers of the Feeder UAV.

3   The Proposed Solution

In this section, we design a proposed energy minimization trajectory for the Feeder UAV to visit all the UAVBSs, the relay UAV and return to the docking station (source). Consider that this issue is combinatorial and NP-hard, and thus, challenging to be able to solve a major number of UAVBSs. As a result, we compare two combinations of trajectory search procedures with high-level strategies, trying to avoid local optimums and looking for solutions much nearer to the global optimum.

3.1   Ant Colony Optimization ACO

ACO [7] is a metaheuristic method grounded on the ants' foraging activity. Ants put pheromone in their paths, which makes the ants converge to the shortest path with the highest concentration of pheromone.

Fitness Function is the fitness value of the population p (group of all ants). We can calculate this value as the division of the full propulsion energy demanded Feeder UAV to take away from the docking station to all UAVBSs and return to the docking station, i.e., $\mathbf{Tr}_{p,1}$ by way of $\mathbf{Tr}_{p,2}, \ldots, \mathbf{Tr}_{p,N}$ and return to $\mathbf{Tr}_{p,1}$, for any path $\mathbf{Tr}_p$, $\forall p = 1, 2, \ldots, P$, and P refers to the number of populations. The fitness value f_p of the population p (N-group of ants) can be represented as follows:

$$f_p = \frac{1}{\exp[\sum_{i=1}^{N} \left(E_{hov}^i + E_{hard}^i \right)]} \tag{11}$$

Initialization is a step performed at the beginning of the process. We assume an appropriate size of ants in the colony (population N), a set of discrete allowable values m for each of the design variables (set size h), and we initialize all discrete values of the design variable into equal amounts of pheromones τ.

Build Tours from home, ants start traveling through the various paths and terminates at the destination node on each iteration (discrete value of design variables). The probability of selecting discrete values of design variable is:

$$P_{i,j}^{(k)} = \frac{\tau_{i,j}^{\alpha} \eta_{i,j}}{\sum_{i,j=1}^{m} \tau_{i,j}^{\beta} \eta_{i,j}} \tag{12}$$

with, (n^{th}) the number of ants (k^{th}) will move from node i to a node j following the probability displacement $P_{i,j}^{(n)}$.

Determine the cumulative probability areas related to different discrete values based on their probabilities. The specific discrete values are chosen by ant k will be selected using the roulette-wheel selection, generate N random numbers r in the area (0, 1), one for each ant, and then we define the discrete value by ant k for a variable as the one for which the cumulative probability area contains the random numbers.

Deposit and Update Trail - Once the Trajectory is Complete, the Ant Deposit Some Pheromone on the Trajectory. In this phase, we evaluate the fitness value of each ant and determine the best f_{best} and worst f_{worst} fitness function of the discrete value among ant.

– Update pheromone
  + Best ants reinforcement pheromones of the best path by:

$$\tau_{i,j}^{new} = \tau_{i,j}^{old} + \sum_k \Delta\tau_{i,j}^{(k)} \tag{13}$$

where

$$\Delta\tau_{i,j}^{(k)} = \frac{\zeta f_{best}}{f_{worst}} \tag{14}$$

  + Other ants: evaporate the pheromones of other paths by:

$$\tau_{i,j}^{new} = (1-\rho)\tau_{i,j}^{old} \tag{15}$$

where ζ and ρ represent the scaling parameter and evaporate rate respectively.

Termination the steps of ACO are iteratively repeated until the maximum number of iteration is achieved or a termination criterion is met and convergence; In the case where the locations of all the individuals converge to the same set of values, the method is assumed to have converged.

Our suggested ACO trajectory design is abstracted in Algorithm 1.

Algorithm 1. Propulsion Energy Minimization Feeder UAV Path plan

---

Input: Fitness function f, Upper bound u_b and lower bound l_b, population size N, number of iteration I, scaling parameter ζ, evaporate rate ρ, step size h (or number of discrete value m)

Initialization : Initialize all discrete value m of design variables equal amounts of pheromone ρ and t=1

Do

Loop :

Build Tours

For t=1,...,I
  – Find probability $P_{i,j}^{(k)}$ to select discrete value of design variables.
  – Determine the cumulative probability areas related to different discrete values based on its probabilities(Roulette-Wheel)

End

Deposit and update trail

For i=1,...,N

+ Generate a random numbers r

+ Find corresponding discrete value

+ Evaluate the fitness value $f_{x_{i,j}}$
  – Determine the best f_{best} and worst f_{worst} fitness value of discrete among ants.
  – Update best path by $\tau_{i,j}^{new} = \tau_{i,j}^{old} + \sum_k \Delta\tau_{i,j}^{(k)}$ and other paths by $\tau_{i,j}^{new} = (1-\rho)\tau_{i,j}^{old}$.

End

$T(t) = \max(f(t))$

t=t+1

While ($t > I$ and there is no convergence of the current solution)

Output: $T^*(t) = \max(T)$

3.2   Metropolis-Hasting Algorithm

The method used in this study is a method called Markov Chain Monte Carlo (MCMC). We use the Metropolis-Hasting algorithm. The underlying object of this algorithm is the Markov Chain. We call Markov Chain $(X_n)_{n \in \mathbb{N}}$ a process that, knowing all the path it has taken until this moment, look only at the place where he is to decide his next step, i.e.

Prob $(X_{n+1} = \alpha$ knowing all the paths traveled until the instant $n) =$ Prob $(X_{n+1} = \alpha$ knowing $X_n)$.

Our Markov Chain is the sequence of paths proposed by the Metropolis-Hasting algorithm.

First, we must define the function to be minimized. is the energy consumed during the charging of the UAVBSs. Let us note by S_N, the set of the paths that the Feeder UAV can cover. A path $\mathbf{Tr} \in S_N$ is of the form:

$$\mathbf{Tr} = (1, 3, 6, \ldots, N, \ldots) \tag{16}$$

In fact, a vector containing the ordered set of UAVBSs that the Feeder UAV visits.

$$\mathbf{Tr} = (\mathbf{Tr}(1), \mathbf{Tr}(2), \ldots, \mathbf{Tr}(N)) \tag{17}$$

where $\mathbf{Tr}(i)$ represents the ith UAVBS that the Feeder UAV traverses.

Thus the energy consumed of a path $\mathbf{Tr}$ is given by the relation:

$$E_{\mathbf{Tr}} = \sum_{i=1}^{N} [E_{\text{hov}}(\mathbf{Tr}(i), \mathbf{Tr}(i+1)) + E_{\text{hov}}(\mathbf{Tr}(N), \mathbf{Tr}(1)) \tag{18}$$
$$+ E_{\text{hard}}(\mathbf{Tr}(i), \mathbf{Tr}(i+1)) + E_{\text{hard}}(\mathbf{Tr}(N), \mathbf{Tr}(1))]$$

The function to be minimized is, therefore, the function:

$$f : \mathbf{Tr} \in S_N \rightarrow E_{\mathbf{Tr}} \tag{19}$$

The Metropolis-Hasting algorithm is as follows:

Step 0: choose a transition core Q. Choose a random path $\mathbf{Tr}_0$ (Initialization). Define a maximum number of iterations: Itermax.

Step 1: Simulate $\mathbf{Tr}_1$ according to the transition $Q(\mathbf{Tr}_0, \mathbf{Tr}_1)$.

Step 2: Calculate the Metropolis-Hastings ratio:

$$r(\mathbf{Tr}_0, \mathbf{Tr}_1) = \frac{f(\mathbf{Tr}_1) Q(\mathbf{Tr}_1, \mathbf{Tr}_0)}{f(\mathbf{Tr}_0) Q(\mathbf{Tr}_0, \mathbf{Tr}_1))}. \tag{20}$$

Step 3: Draw U according to a normal distribution on [0,1]. If $U \leq r(\mathbf{Tr}_0, \mathbf{Tr}_1)$, put $\mathbf{Tr}_0 = \mathbf{Tr}_1$, else if conserve $\mathbf{Tr}_0$. Repeat Itermax times the algorithm.

The function f corresponds to the stationary law of the Markov chain that we want to simulate by this algorithm. We take

$$f : \mathbf{Tr} = \exp\left(-E_{\mathbf{Tr}}\right) \tag{21}$$

By choosing this function, we ensure the convergence of the algorithm to the minimum. In our approach, we will choose asymmetrical transition core, i.e. that

$$Q\left(\mathbf{Tr}_0, \mathbf{Tr}_1\right) = Q\left(\mathbf{Tr}_1, \mathbf{Tr}_0\right), \forall \mathbf{Tr}_0, \mathbf{Tr}_1 \in S_N \tag{22}$$

The Metropolis-Hastings report thus becomes:

$$r\left(\mathbf{Tr}_0, \mathbf{Tr}_1\right) = \exp\left(\mathbf{Tr}_1 - \mathbf{Tr}_0\right) \tag{23}$$

Algorithm 2. Feeder UAV Trajectory Optimization

1: Select initial value $\mathbf{Tr}_0$ and Itermax
2: For i=1,...,N, repeat:
3:    1. Draw candidate $\mathbf{Tr}* \sim Q\left(\mathbf{Tr}^* \mid \mathbf{Tr}_{i-1}\right)$.
    2. $\alpha = \dfrac{f\left(\mathbf{Tr}^*\right)/Q\left(\mathbf{Tr}^*|\mathbf{Tr}_{i-1}\right)}{f\left(\mathbf{Tr}_{i-1}\right)/Q\left(\mathbf{Tr}_{i-1}|\mathbf{Tr}^*\right)} = \dfrac{f\left(\mathbf{Tr}^*\right)Q\left(\mathbf{Tr}_{i-1}|\mathbf{Tr}^*\right)}{f\left(\mathbf{Tr}_{i-1}\right)Q\left(\mathbf{Tr}^*|\mathbf{Tr}_{i-1}\right)}$
    3. $\alpha \geqslant 1$ accept $\mathbf{Tr}^*$ and set $\mathbf{Tr}_i \leftarrow \mathbf{Tr}^*$
4: $0 < \alpha < 1$

    – accept $\mathbf{Tr}^*$ and set $\mathbf{Tr}_i \leftarrow \mathbf{Tr}^*$ with prob α
    – reject $\mathbf{Tr}^*$ and set $\mathbf{Tr}_i \leftarrow \mathbf{Tr}_{i-1}$ with prob 1-α

---

4 Numerical Results

In this part, we evaluate the performance of our proposed algorithms versus [21]. In place of having the fitness function of [21] in our suggested programs, which considers the amount of energy consumption associated with communication, we take our fitness function. The latter uses propulsion energy which refers to the mechanical energy required for the movement of the UAV. Our fitness function considers the simultaneous consumption of hovering and hardware energy of the Feeder UAV during the flight. In general, the energy requirement for propulsion is much higher than the energy consumption for communication. In Fig. 1, we illustrate the UAVs' mounted base station topology and optimal flight trajectory for ACO and Metropolis-hasting, respectively. The green dashed segment represents the ideal path proposed by the MCMC method, and the red dashed ones indicate the optimal trajectory design obtained by ACO.

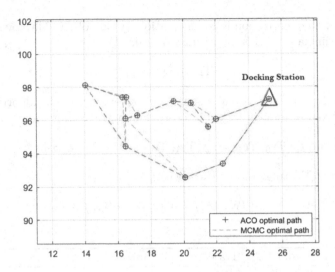

Fig. 2. Trajectory optimization.

In Fig. 2, we compare the GA algorithm based on [21] with the energy consumption of our paths planning proposal as a function of Feeder UAV speed for N = 18 UAVBSs. As we can see, as the velocity of the Feeder UAV grows, the energy requirements of all the algorithms decrease until they reach a minimum velocity of 31 m/s, at which point they start accelerating one more time. This demeanor is related to surmount parasitic drag and lift-induced drag and is coherent with the energy level of the aircraft. At a high Feeder UAV rate, we can observe that the suggested ACO conception surpasses the algorithm based on [21] and the proposed MCMC algorithm by more than 38% and 14%, respectively. This is due to the superiority of our ACO, which performs path updates on a defined population percent every generation and only swaps in new paths if they get a greater fitness value than the other ants. Furthermore, unlike the Metropolis-hasting and GA algorithms, our algorithm considers the energy charge of traveling to every base station on the path while depositing pheromone. As shown in the algorithm in [21], when the total energy requirement is considered, i.e., the hardware energy demand is also assumed in the definition of our fitness function. When the power UAV rate increases, the resulting energy demand is lower than when just the hover energy is considered, by about 1–6 percent. Nonetheless, our ACO outperforms the algorithm in [21] by more than 30%. This validates our ACO design's superiority over the algorithms in our Metropolis-hasting and [21] experiments.

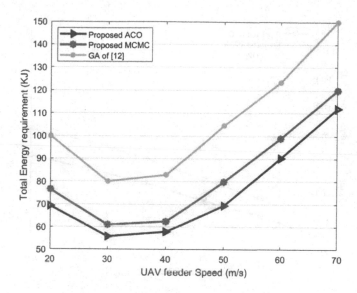

Fig. 3. Comparison of Feeder UAV energy requirements of our proposed algorithms trajectories design versus genetic algorithm for increasing UAV speed.

Figure 3, shows the energy consumption of the trajectories design of our proposed algorithms when the number of base stations becomes larger compared to the GA algorithm, with v = 31 m/s and P = [250; 350; 430; 520; 650; 800]. Since the number of UAV base stations augments the search space for trajectories, P in our proposed designs and the GA algorithm were set to change with thenumber of UAV base stations. All of the algorithms' energy requirements increase with the number of UAVBSs, as expected. This is due to the growth in flight time and the number of rounds necessary for the Feeder UAV to achieve all the UAVBSs when the number of UAVBSs augments. As the number of UAVBSs becomes larger, the achievement gap between our suggested ACO and our Metropolis-hasting conception on the one hand and the algorithm in [21], on the other hand, grows. This is attributable to our criteria for selecting the best fitness and our update trail, which is based on the raw energy consumption of each UAVBS. As a result, our ACO algorithm outperforms the algorithm in [21] by 24% to 42% for both a high and low number of UAVBS, while getting 13% less energy consumption than our Metropolis-hasting algorithm. When the total energy consumption is considered in the algorithm of [21], the difference is about 6 (Fig. 4).

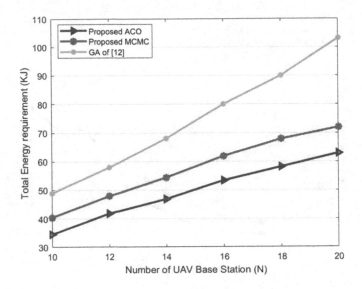

Fig. 4. Comparison of Feeder UAV energy needs of our suggested trajectory design algorithms versus the genetic algorithm for an augmenting number of UAVBS.

5   Conclusion

In this paper, we compared a trajectory design based on the ACO algorithm and the metropolis-hasting algorithm for moving of the Feeder UAV to charge the batteries of UAVBSs deployed around a disaster area and returning to a docking station. To calculate the energy requirements of the Feeder UAV, the design of the path considers both the hover and the material. In terms of total energy requirements, simulation results show that the suggested solutions outperform a parh algorithm based on [21]. We intend to use optimal transport theory in the future to derive optimal cell combinations and resource management designs that maximize system behavior in terms of energy efficiency, throughput, and delay under explanatory time-of-flight constraints on the UAVBSs.

References

1. Aerial Base-Stations with Opportunistic Links for Unexpected and Temporary Events: ABSOLUTE. http://www.absoluteproject.eu
2. Presidential memorandum for the secretary of transportation, November 2017. https://www.whitehouse.gov/presidentialactions/presidential-memorandum-secretary-transportation/
3. Al-Hourani, A., Kandeepan, S., Jamalipour, A.: Stochastic geometry study on device-to-device communication as a disaster relief solution. IEEE Trans. Veh. Technol. **65**(5), 3005–3017 (2015)

4. Ali, K., Nguyen, H.X., Shah, P., Vien, Q.-T., Bhuvanasundaram, N.: Architecture for public safety network using D2D communication. In: 2016 IEEE Wireless Communications and Networking Conference Workshops (WCNCW), pp. 206–211. IEEE (2016)
5. Alzenad, M., El-Keyi, A., Lagum, F., Yanikomeroglu, H.: 3-D placement of an unmanned aerial vehicle base station (UAV-BS) for energy-efficient maximal coverage. IEEE Wireless Commun. Lett. **6**(4), 434–437 (2017)
6. Anazawa, K., Li, P., Miyazaki, T., Guo, S.: Trajectory and data planning for mobile relay to enable efficient internet access after disasters. In: 2015 IEEE Global Communications Conference (GLOBECOM), pp. 1–6. IEEE (2015)
7. Châari, I., Koubaa, A., Bennaceur, H., Trigui, S., Al-Shalfan, K.: smartPATH: a hybrid ACO-GA algorithm for robot path planning. In: 2012 IEEE Congress on Evolutionary Computation, pp. 1–8. IEEE (2012)
8. Erdelj, M., Natalizio, E.: UAV-assisted disaster management: applications and open issues. In: 2016 International Conference on Computing, Networking and Communications (ICNC), pp. 1–5. IEEE (2016)
9. Gomez, K., Goratti, L., Rasheed, T., Reynaud, L.: Enabling disaster-resilient 4G mobile communication networks. IEEE Commun. Mag. **52**(12), 66–73 (2014)
10. Klaine, P.V., Nadas, J.P.B., Souza, R.D., Imran, M.A.: Distributed drone base station positioning for emergency cellular networks using reinforcement learning. Cogn. Comput. **10**(5), 790–804 (2018)
11. Kumbhar, A., Guvenc, I., Singh, S., Tuncer, A.: Exploiting LTE-advanced HetNets and FeICIC for UAV-assisted public safety communications. IEEE Access **6**, 783–796 (2017)
12. Merwaday, A., Guvenc, I.: UAV assisted heterogeneous networks for public safety communications. In: 2015 IEEE Wireless Communications and Networking Conference Workshops (WCNCW), pp. 329–334. IEEE (2015)
13. Pearre, B., Brown, T.X.: Model-free trajectory optimization for wireless data ferries among multiple sources. In: 2010 IEEE Globecom Workshops, pp. 1793–1798. IEEE (2010)
14. Shklovski, I., Palen, L., Sutton, J.: Finding community through information and communication technology in disaster response. In: Proceedings of the 2008 ACM Conference on Computer Supported Cooperative Work, pp. 127–136 (2008)
15. Smith, P.C., Simpson, D.M.: Technology and communications in an urban crisis: the role of mobile communications systems in disasters. J. Urban Technol. **16**(1), 133–149 (2009)
16. Van Aalst, M.K.: The impacts of climate change on the risk of natural disasters. Disasters **30**(1), 5–18 (2006)
17. Vattapparamban, E., Güvenç, I., Yurekli, A.I., Akkaya, K., Uluağaç, S.: Drones for smart cities: issues in cybersecurity, privacy, and public safety. In: 2016 International Wireless Communications and Mobile Computing Conference (IWCMC), pp. 216–221. IEEE (2016)
18. Weisstein, E.W.: Traveling salesman problem. http://mathworld.wolfram.com/TravelingSalesmanProblem.html
19. Zeng, Y., Zhang, R.: Energy-efficient UAV communication with trajectory optimization. IEEE Trans. Wireless Commun. **16**(6), 3747–3760 (2017)
20. Zeng, Y., Zhang, R.: Energy-efficient UAV communication with trajectory optimization. IEEE Trans. Wireless Commun. **16**(6), 3747–3760 (2017)
21. Zhou, Z., et al.: When mobile crowd sensing meets UAV: energy-efficient task assignment and route planning. IEEE Trans. Commun. **66**(11), 5526–5538 (2018)

Dynamics Analysis for a Duopoly Game with Bounded Rationality in Cognitive Radio Network

Lhoussaine Daoudi[1]($\boxtimes$)(iD), Mohamed Baslam[1](iD), and Said Safi[2](iD)

[1] TIAD Laboratory, FST, Sultan Moulay Sliman University, Benimellal, Morocco
lhoussainedaoudi@gmail.com
[2] LIMATI Laboratory, Department of Mathematics and Computer Sciences,
Sultan Moulay Slimane University, Beni Mellal, Morocco

Abstract. The cognitive radio is considered as a solution to share frequency bands for the purpose of maximizing the utilization of radio spectrum in wireless networks. In this present document, we consider the issue of spectrum sharing behavior when secondary users are willing to allocate underutilized frequency spectrum by a primary user or certified organization. In addition, earlier studies show that the spectrum sharing is beneficial when set in a cooperative manner between users. However, creating a trustworthy relation between secondary users is the main issue in the aspects of sharing fairness. We formulate this selfish behavior problem as a Cournot bounded rationality game to obtain the desired spectrum allocation for all secondary users. The evolution over time of this non-cooperative game is analyzed. The Nash equilibrium existence and uniqueness of the game are derived. Then, the local stability analysis of the fixed points has been carried out. The analysis showed that users using bounded rationality are more likely to reach the Nash equilibrium point which is considered as the solution of this game. To prove our theoretical analysis, we perform numerical simulations such us bifurcation diagrams which were used to show the impact of the bounded rationality learning rate and then basin of attraction to examine the global stability of the Nash equilibrium.

Keywords: Spectrum sharing · Cournot duopoly · Non-cooperative game · Discreet dynamical system · Bounded rationality · Nash equilibrium · Stability analysis

1 Introduction

In cognitive radio network some frequency bands are partially occupied (the occupation of the bands is between 15% and 85%) in specific locations and at specific time [1]. In general, radio spectrum is managed in a static manner by agencies which are responsible for allocating frequencies to users. The radio band is broken down into several blocks. Each block is dedicated to specific uses and

M.-A. Koulali and M. Mezini (Eds.): NETYS 2022, LNCS 13464, pp. 236–251, 2022.
https://doi.org/10.1007/978-3-031-17436-0_16

the use of these frequencies, therefore, requires a license that is not required in the case of so-called free ISM bands (industrial, scientific and medical). This static and non-optimized spectrum management has led researchers to find solutions to optimize spectral reuse without disrupting the already established regulations. The idea of such dynamic spectrum management is based on observation that it is possible to exploit the free or underutilized spaces of the spectrum. In order to function this, the secondary users use the cognitive radio to sense the spectrum holes then to share the wanted band with a so-called primary user in a dynamic way. The idea is that a cognitive radio interface can itself adapt its own behavior based on the environment in which it operates and thus adjust its operating parameters dynamically and autonomously to optimize the use of available radio frequencies, while minimizing interference with other users.

One of the major challenges is to be able to propose an allocation scheme, which not only give an optimization of the spectral use, but also it reduces the interference caused by primary users and secondary users. In order to address this problem, game theory is an effective tool for modeling behaviors of secondary users cooperative and non cooperative behaviors. We consider the competition between secondary users in this way, each user seeks to maximize the amount of frequency to be allocated, according to the price of frequency spectrum unit specified by the primary user who shares the free frequency bands.

We formulate this spectrum sharing behavior as an oligopoly game in which a few firms compete with each other for maximum profit. In this case, the secondary users are similar to the firms that are competing for the allocation of the spectrum offered by the primary user to maximize their profits. We use a non-cooperative dynamic game in which a secondary user's strategy change is based on price information obtained from the primary user. Based on this information, the secondary user's share of the spectrum is controlled by the bounded rationality learning rate. Through this dynamic spectrum management mechanism, we analyze the stability condition of the Nash equilibrium by employing local stability analysis. In addition, the sensitivity of the initial strategy selection, which influences the global stability, is evaluated using the concept of basin of attraction [2].

Our work aims at establishing a dynamic Cournot duopoly game model where secondary users can iteratively adapt their strategy in terms of requested spectrum size. The local and global stability properties of the Nash equilibrium solution of this spectrum allocation game are studied in detail in this work. The main aspects of this paper are as follows:

- A model of competitive frequency sharing between sub users in cognitive radio networks is suggested and described according to the non-cooperative game mechanism with bounded rationality.
- A distributed dynamic strategy adaptation model is proposed and the stability features (e.g. convergence, bifurcation, stability region and chaotic behavior) of this scheme are studied, and
- The performance of the spectrum allocation pattern is evaluated based on various system settings (e.g., the quality of the radio channel and the bounded rationality learning rate).

This article is structured as follows. After this introduction, we will present works related to this theme in Sect. 2, after that we briefly describe the duopoly game with bounded rationality in the Sect. 3, then in Sect. 4, we will analyze the dynamics of this duopoly game with bounded rationality. Then, we provide explicit conditions on its parameters, like the existence and local stability conditions of the equilibrium points. In Sect. 5, we will present numerical simulations, which will allow us to validate our results acquired through our analysis in order to verify the global stability of the Nash equilibrium point. Finally, some thoughts are restrained to the conclusion Sect. 6.

2 Related Works

Cognitive radio technologies are introduced in the following paper [3] where the basic tasks as well as behavior emerging from the cognitive radio were covered. The duopoly game have many application, M. Baslam et al. provide a set-theoretic structure for the dynamic behaviors of a duopoly game in the telecommunications service provider environment [4]. Also, multiplayer game design may be used to obtain an individual optimal solution for managing resources in wireless networks. For example, game theory that has been, used for channel allocation [5] and pricing [6]. Likely in [7], an adaptive channel allocation scheme based on game theory has been proposed for cognitive radio networks. More specifically, a game has been formulated in order to capture both selfish and cooperative player's behaviors. The players are the wireless nodes and their strategies are defined in terms of channel selection. In [8], the study of the convergence of different types of dynamic games in cognitive radio has been investigated (i.e. coordinated behavior, best response and best response for potential repetitive games). Furthermore, a game theoretic framework has been proposed for distributed power control to achieve flexibility in the use of spectrum in a cognitive radio network. However, the dynamic behavior of the strategy adaptation was not addressed in this work. The spectrum sharing problem was formulated as a potential game, and the Nash equilibrium of this game was obtained by a distributed sequential game [9], but the price issue has been ignored. Therefore, D. Niyato et al. in their paper studied a model of oligopolistic competition game on spectrum sharing in two cases: static and dynamic [10]. However, the behavior of spectrum allocation may be either cooperative or non-cooperative. Dludla et al. [11] discussed these two behaviors, particularly in the case of licensed shared access (LSA) (non-cooperative) and television white space (TVWS) (cooperative). As a result, the spectrum sharing problem can be modeled as a dynamic non-cooperative game with bounded rationality.

3 System Model and Assumption

We consider a cognitive radio wireless network based on spectrum overlay having one primary users and two concurrent secondary users (Fig. 1). The primary user is required to share a specific amount of the spectrum (q_i) with each secondary user, i.e. *i*one with the following spectrum unit cost function:

$$C(q_T) = a + bq_T, \tag{1}$$

where a and b are non-negative constants, and $q_T = q_1 + q_2$, refers to the total amount of spectrum that can be shared by all secondary users. Following the allocation decision, the secondary user transmits the allocated spectrum using adaptive modulation to improve the transmission performance.

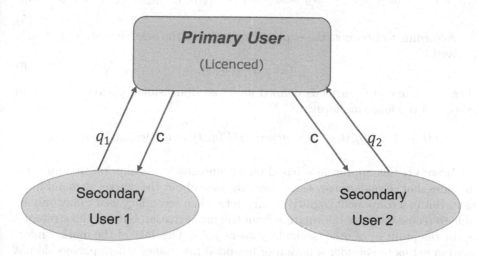

Fig. 1. System model

So let $\mathbf{G} = \{\mathbb{P}, \mathbb{A}, \mathbb{U}\}$ be the spectrum non-cooperative allocation game, in which $\mathbb{P} = \{1, 2\}$, is the set of secondary users, and $\mathbb{A}$ denote the set of their strategies $\mathbb{A} = \{q_1, q_2\}$, and $\mathbb{U} = \{u_1, u_2\}$, is the set of all benefits of those secondary users.

The cost function of the secondary user i:

$$c_i(q_i) = q_i C(q_T),$$

which can be written as an increasing dual differential function:

$$c_i(q_i) = q_i(a + b(q_i + q_j)), \qquad i, j = 1, 2 \qquad i \neq j. \tag{2}$$

Let $R(q_i)$ the revenue function of the secondary user i then the profit of ith secondary user from the game above is expressed as follows:

$$u_i(t) = R(q_i(t)) - c_i(q_i(t)), \qquad i, j = 1, 2 \qquad i \neq j. \tag{3}$$

Or the cost function of the secondary user (CRi) at the time step t is defined bye:

$$c_i(q_i(t)) = q_i(a + b(q_i + q_j)),$$

where $q_j(t)$ is the expected frequency band of the secondary user (Crj), $j \neq i$, $i, j \in \{1, 2\}$ then, the profit of secondary user i become:

$$u_i(t) = R(q_i(t)) - q_i(t)C(q_i(t) + q_j(t)), \qquad i, j \in \{1, 2\} \qquad i \neq j. \qquad (4)$$

If we consider that the size of the spectrum q_j shared by the other secondary user is known, the best response function of the secondary user i is defined as follows:

$$q_i(t+1) = r_i(q_j^e(t+1)) = arg \max_{q_i}[u_i(t) = R(q_i(t)) - q_i(t)c_i(q_i(t) + q_j^e(t+1))].$$
$$(5)$$

According to Cournot, the expected quantity in the next time step $(q_j^e(t+1))$ is given by:

$$q_j^e(t+1) = q_j(t), \qquad (6)$$

then, the game of Cournot is defined as a two dimensional discrete dynamical system of the following form:

$$q_i(t+1) = r_i(q_j^e(t+1)) = arg \max_{q_i}[R(q_i(t)) - q_i(t)c_i(q_i(t) + q_j(t))]. \quad (7)$$

However, this approach is based on an unrealistic assumption: it implicitly assumes that secondary users are knowledgeable about the market demand function. But in a convenient cognitive radio network, a secondary user i may only be able to recipe the price information from the primary user, but not the strategies q_j, or the profit u_j of other secondary users $j \neq i$. This lake of the market information led us to consider a notion of bounded rationality where players do not immediately adjust their strategies to the optimal quantity by solving a profit maximization problem. However, complete and accurate information about the network would be required for this. We assume that players (secondary users) in this game adjust their strategies gradually based on the current pricing information i.e., each secondary user (say ith one) modifies its frequency allocation spectrum (q_i) according to its marginal profit:

$$\frac{\partial u_i(q_i(t), q_j^e(t+1))}{\partial q_i}, \qquad i = 1, 2, \ i \neq j. \qquad (8)$$

Thus, the dynamic system with bounded rationality becomes:

$$\begin{cases} q_1(t+1) = q_1(t) + \theta_1 q_1(t) \frac{\partial u_1(q_1(t), q_2^e(t+1))}{\partial q_1} \\ q_2(t+1) = q_2(t) + \theta_2 q_2(t) \frac{\partial u_2(q_1^e(t+1), q_2(t))}{\partial q_2}, \end{cases} \qquad (9)$$

where θ_i, $i = 1, 2$, is the learning rate (i.e. the adjustment speed parameter) this means that when the marginal profit is positive/negative, he increases/decreases his sharing spectrum q_i in the next allocation. Then, we put the revenue of the secondary user CRi in the form $R_i(q_i) = \gamma_i q_i$ where $\gamma_i = \zeta_i \delta_i$, denote signal gain (or channel quality), ζ_i denote the average transmission rate and δ_i is the revenue per unit of transmission rate. It is obvious that R_i is a linear and increasing function. We set the unit cost function for both players as a convex function defined by:

$$C(q_i + q_j) = a + b \times (q_i + q_j), \tag{10}$$

where a and b are two non-negative constants. Therefore, the profit of the ith secondary user can be rewritten as follows:

$$u_i = q_i \times \gamma_i - q_i \times (a + b \times (q_i + q_j)), \quad i, j = 1, 2 \quad i \neq j. \tag{11}$$

The marginal profit function for the secondary user CRi can then be obtained from

$$\frac{\partial u_i(q_i, q_j)}{\partial q_i} = \gamma_i - a - 2bq_i - bq_j \quad where \quad i, j = 1, 2 \quad et \quad i \neq j. \tag{12}$$

This marginal profit can be rewritten in terms of the unit cost $C(q_T)$ offered by the primary user as follows:

$$\frac{\partial u_i(q_i, q_j)}{\partial q_i} = \gamma_i - bq_i - [a + b(q_i + q_j)] \quad where \quad i, j = 1, 2 \quad et \quad i \neq j. \tag{13}$$

Thus, the two secondary users adjust their strategies according to the unit spectrum price function $C(q_1 + q_2)$. We assume that the strategy expected at the upcoming period is $q_j^e(t+1) = q_j(t)$ we substitute in Eq. (9) then, the duopoly game with bounded rationality is given by:

$$\begin{cases} q_1(t+1) = q_1(t) + \theta_1 q_1(t)(\gamma_1 - a - 2bq_1(t) - bq_2(t)), \\ q_2(t+1) = q_2(t) + \theta_2 q_2(t)(\gamma_2 - a - 2bq_2(t) - bq_1(t)). \end{cases} \tag{14}$$

4   Dynamics of Spectrum Allocation Game with Bounded Rationality

4.1   Equilibrium Points and Local Stability

At the equilibrium, we have $q_i(t+1) = q_i(t) = q$, $i = 1, 2$ then from equations in dynamical game (14) we have

$$\begin{cases} \theta_1 q_1(t)(\gamma_1 - a - 2bq_1(t) - bq_2(t)) = 0, \\ \theta_2 q_2(t)(\gamma_2 - a - 2bq_2(t) - bq_1(t)) = 0 \end{cases} \tag{15}$$

from this two equations we have four fixed points:

$$\begin{cases} E_0 = (0, 0) \\ E_1 = (\frac{\gamma_1 - a}{2b}, 0) \\ E_2 = (0, \frac{\gamma_2 - a}{2b}) \\ E_* = (\frac{2(\gamma_1) - \gamma_2 - a}{3b}, \frac{2(\gamma_2) - \gamma_1 - a}{3b}) \end{cases} \tag{16}$$

obviously, E_0, E_1 and E_2 are limit equilibrium points. The fixed point E_* is the Nash equilibrium point and has a meaning for the network in case:

$$\begin{cases} 2\gamma_1 - \gamma_2 - a > 0 \\ 2\gamma_2 - \gamma_1 - a > 0 \end{cases} \quad means \quad \begin{cases} 2\gamma_1 - \gamma_2 > a \\ 2\gamma_2 - \gamma_1 > a. \end{cases}$$

Theorem 1. *The Nash Equilibrium point E_* exist and it is unique.*

Proof. In order to prove existence, we note that the strategy space q_i of each secondary user CRi is defined by all bands in the closed interval restricted by the minimum and maximum frequency band. Thus, the strategy space $\mathbb{A}$ is a non-empty, convex and compact subset of the Euclidean space $\mathbb{R}^N$. Furthermore, the utility is concave with respect to the frequency band, as shown by the second derivative test: from the expression of marginal profit (13) of each secondary users we have $\frac{\partial^2 u_i(q_i,q_j)}{\partial q_i^2} = -2b < 0$, which guarantees the existence of a NE [12].

We use the following proposition, which is valid for any concave game [13]: When a concave game respect the dominance solvency condition:

$-\frac{\partial^2 u_i(q_i,q_j)}{\partial q_i^2} - \sum_{j=1,j\neq i}^{2} \mid \frac{\partial^2 u_i(q_i,q_j)}{\partial q_i \partial q_j} \mid \geq 0$, Then the game G has a unique NE. We have the mixed partial derivative which is written as follows: $\frac{\partial^2 u_i(q_i,q_j)}{\partial q_i \partial q_j} = -b$,

therefor, $-\frac{\partial^2 u_i(q_i,q_j)}{\partial q_i^2} - \sum_{j=1,j\neq i}^{2} \mid \frac{\partial^2 u_i(q_i,q_j)}{\partial q_i \partial q_j} \mid = 2b - b = b > 0$, then fixed band frequency NE point is then unique. ∎

To explore the local stability of the equilibrium points E_0, E_1, E_2 and E_* we determine the Jacobian matrix of the mapping Q deduced from the dynamic game:

$$Q \begin{cases} Q_1(q_1,q_2) = q_1 + \theta_1 q_1 \{\gamma_1 - a - 2bq_1 - bq_2\} \\ Q_2(q_1,q_2) = q_2 + \theta_2 q_2 \{\gamma_2 - a - 2bq_2 - bq_1\}. \end{cases} \tag{17}$$

The Jacobian matrix of the mapping Q is found as follows:

$$J(q_1,q_2) = \begin{bmatrix} 1 + \theta_1(\zeta_1\delta_1 - a - 4bq_1 - bq_2) & -b\theta_1 q_1 \\ -b\theta_2 q_2 & 1 + \theta_2(\zeta_2\delta_2 - a - 4bq_2 - bq_1) \end{bmatrix} \tag{18}$$

Then, the stability condition is applied. By definition, the fixed point is stable if and only if the eigenvalues say λ_i of the Jacobian matrix at this point are all inside the unit circle of the complex plane (i.e., $\mid \lambda_i \mid < 1$) [14,15].

We now study the stability condition at each fixed point starting with the equilibrium point E_0, we obtain the associated Jacobian matrix which is written as follows:

$$J(0,0) = \begin{bmatrix} 1 + \theta_1(\gamma_1 - a) & 0 \\ 0 & 1 + \theta_2(\gamma_2 - a) \end{bmatrix} \tag{19}$$

according to stability condition the point E_0 is stable if the following conditions are true: $\mid 1 + \theta_1(\gamma_1 - a) \mid < 1$ and $\mid 1 + \theta_2(\gamma_2 - a) \mid < 1$.

First we consider the case $\begin{cases} 1 + \theta_1(\gamma_1 - a) > -1 \\ 1 + \theta_2(\gamma_2 - a) > -1 \end{cases}$ or equivalently

$\begin{cases} \theta_1(\gamma_1 - a) > -2 \\ \theta_2(\gamma_2 - a) > -2 \end{cases}$

which are verified. Now, we consider the case

$$\begin{cases} 1 + \theta_1(\gamma_1 - a) < 1 \\ 1 + \theta_2(\gamma_2 - a) < 1 \end{cases}$$

from which we obtain the E_0 stability conditions as follows:

$$\begin{cases} \gamma_1 < a, \\ \gamma_2 < a. \end{cases}$$

when the cost of spectrum at the outset (10) is higher than the revenue earned from the allocated spectrum, a secondary user is prepared to keep out of the competition.

For the fixed point E_1, the corresponding Jacobian matrix takes the following form:

$$J(\frac{\gamma_1 - a}{2b}, 0) = \begin{bmatrix} 1 + \theta_1(-\gamma_1 + a) & \theta_1 \frac{\gamma_1 - a}{2} \\ 0 & 1 + \theta_2 \frac{1}{2}(2\gamma_2 - \gamma_1 - a) \end{bmatrix} \qquad (20)$$

the stability condition on the first eigenvalue $\lambda_1 = 1 + \theta_1(-\gamma_1 + a)$ give us:

$$\begin{cases} |1 + \theta_1(-\gamma_1 + a)| < 1 \\ |1 + \frac{1}{2}\theta_2(2\gamma_2 - \gamma_1 - a)| < 1 \end{cases}$$

the first condition is satisfied since $\gamma_1 > a$ then the stability condition is $|1 + \frac{1}{2}\theta_2(2\gamma_2 - \gamma_1 - a)| < 1$
again, since $q_2^* = \frac{2(\zeta_2\delta_2) - \zeta_1\delta_1 - a}{3b}$ of the Nash equilibrium is non negative and b is non-negative, we consider only the condition $2\gamma_2 - \gamma_1 - a > 0$ for the second eigenvalue. So for the fixed point E_1 we have two conditions:

i) $\gamma_1 > a$ the signal gain in the revenue function of the first secondary user is greater than the spectrum cost at the beginning.
ii) $2\gamma_2 > \gamma_1 + a$: the value γ_1 in the revenue function of the first secondary user is much smaller than that of the other secondary user.

In the same way with the fixed point $E_2 = (0, \frac{\gamma_2 - a}{2b})$, we have by the symmetry reason in the model the stability conditions:

i) $\gamma_2 > a$ the signal gain in the revenue function of the second secondary user is greater than the spectrum cost at the beginning.
ii) $2\gamma_1 > \gamma_2 + a$: the value of γ_2 in the revenue function of the first secondary user is much smaller than that of the other secondary user.

Now we investigate the local stability of Nash equilibrium point E_* (16) the corresponding Jacobian matrix is writing as follows:

$$J(q_1^*, q_2^*) = \begin{bmatrix} 1 - 2\theta_1(\frac{2\gamma_1 - \gamma_2 - a}{3}) & -\theta_1(\frac{2\gamma_1 - \gamma_2 - a}{3}) \\ -\theta_2(\frac{2\gamma_2 - \gamma_1 - a}{3}) & 1 - 2\theta_2(\frac{2\gamma_2 - \gamma_1 - a}{3}) \end{bmatrix}. \qquad (21)$$

The characteristic equation to obtain the eigenvalue is given as follows:

$$det(J - \lambda I) = \lambda^2 - \lambda(j_{1,1} + j_{2,2}) + (j_{1,1}j_{2,2} - j_{1,2}j_{2,1}) = 0.$$

Since the discriminant is non negative ($\Delta_\lambda = 4j_{1,2}j_{2,1} + (j_{1,1} - j_{2,2})^2$). Then the two eigenvalues associated to the Nash equilibrium point are:

$$(\lambda_1, \lambda_2) = \frac{(j_{1,1} + j_{2,2}) \overset{+}{\underset{-}{}} \sqrt{4j_{1,2}j_{2,1} + (j_{1,1} - j_{2,2})^2}}{2} \tag{22}$$

where:

$$\begin{cases} j_{1,1} = 1 - 2\theta_1 \frac{2\gamma_1 - \gamma_2 - a}{3}, \\ j_{2,2} = 1 - 2\theta_2 \frac{2\gamma_2 - \gamma_1 - a}{3}, \\ j_{1,2} = -\theta_1 \frac{2\gamma_1 - \gamma_2 - a}{3}, \\ j_{2,1} = -\theta_2 \frac{2\gamma_2 - \gamma_1 - a}{3}. \end{cases} \tag{23}$$

The Nash fixed point stability condition that is all eigenvalues of the corresponding Jacobian matrix λ_1 and λ_2 are inside the unit circle of the complex plane [14, 15]. Basically, given γ_1, γ_2, a and b, the above stability condition can be written as a system of equations with two variables θ_1 and θ_2:

$$\begin{cases} \left| \frac{(j_{1,1}+j_{2,2})+\sqrt{4j_{1,2}j_{2,1}+(j_{1,1}-j_{2,2})^2}}{2} \right| < 1 \quad and \\ \left| \frac{(j_{1,1}+j_{2,2})-\sqrt{4j_{1,2}j_{2,1}+(j_{1,1}-j_{2,2})^2}}{2} \right| < 1. \end{cases} \tag{24}$$

Note that the above local stability analysis is usable only for the case where the initial strategies $q_i(t = 0)$, $i = 1$, 2, are closes to the Nash equilibrium. On the other hand, when the starting strategies are arbitrarily chosen, they may be too far from the Nash equilibrium and the strategic adaptation may not converge.

To study the global stability of the dynamical system. We employ the concept of basin of attraction. The basin of attraction defines the set of initial strategies from which the dynamic behavior of the game converges to the Nash equilibrium.

Definition 1. *Let E denote the open set of points (e.g. equilibrium points) which are generating a convergent trajectory to q_i^*, for map $Q : (q_i) \to (q_i^{'})$ the basin of attraction is thus defined: $B(E) = \{(q_i)/Q(q_i(t)) \to (q_i^*), \quad t \to \infty\}$ where t it is time (i.e., iteration).*

5   Performance Evaluation

5.1   Cognitive Radio Environment

We examine our analytical results in a cognitive radio environment, where a primary user shares the frequency spectrum of size 16 MHz with two secondary users. Then the target average **PER** for all users in all transmission modes is $P\bar{E}R_s = 0.03$. We use the same parameter and the same method as in [16] to obtain the probability $P_r(s)$ and the transmission rate δ_i. For the cost function, we set $a = 10$ and $b = 0.5$. The revenue of a secondary user for a unit of transmission rate is as follows $\zeta_1 = \zeta_2 = 10$.

5.2   Dynamic Behavior

We set the initial strategies (i.e. strategies at time zero) to $q_1(t = 0) = 5$ MHz, $q_2(t = 0) = 1$ MHz and the channels quality to $\gamma_1 = 17$ dB and $\gamma_2 = 15$ dB. For these parameters, the Nash equilibrium is found at $q_1^* = 6$ MHz and $q_2^* = 2$ MHz.

We now investigate the dynamic behavior over time of the above game.

As is evident from (Fig. 2) and (Fig. 3), with the proper setting of the learning rates of bounded rationality θ_1 and θ_2, the spectrum sharing will progressively reach the Nash equilibrium(e.g. $\theta_1 = \theta_2 = 0.291$ red graph). On the other hand,

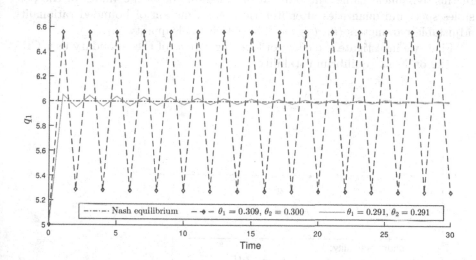

Fig. 2. Dynamic behavior of CR1 stable and unstable cases (Color figure online)

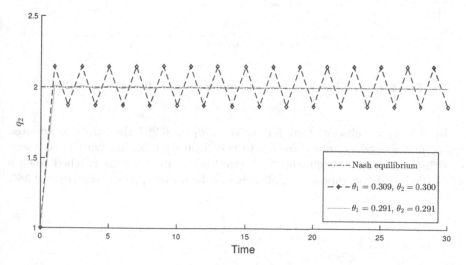

Fig. 3. Dynamic behavior of CR2 stable and unstable cases (Color figure online)

if the adjustment speed is important (e.g., $\theta_1 = 0.309$, $\theta_2 = 0.300$ blue graph), the strategies of the two secondary users oscillate between two values and may never reach the Nash equilibrium. Indeed, as the learning rate is too high, a secondary user relies heavily on recent information (i.e., cost) obtained from the primary user, and as a result, the strategies are adjusted by steps to widely achieve the Nash equilibrium.

5.3   Bifurcation Diagram

In this dynamical game, the bifurcation diagram shows the values of the possibles spectrum quantities after iteration as a function of bounded rationality adjustable parameters (θ_1, θ_2) for different channels quality (γ_1, γ_2).

First, we investigate the effect of learning rate θ_i of the secondary user CRi, $i = 1, 2$ on Nash equilibrium stability.

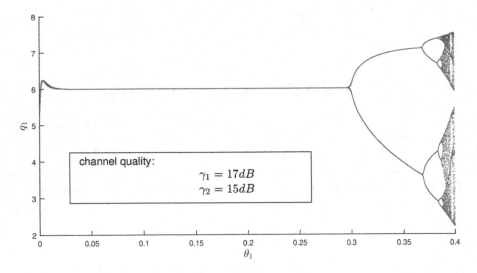

Fig. 4. CR1, Bifurcation Diagram under $\gamma_1 = 17\,\text{dB}$ and $\gamma_2 = 15\,\text{dB}$

In (Fig. 4) we observe that for $0.037 < \theta_1 < 0.294$ the strategy adopted by the first secondary user converge to the Nash equilibrium. On the contrary, for $0.294 < theta_1 < 0.369$, the Nash equilibrium may not be reached, then a bifurcation doubling appears. Finally, chaotic behavior appears when $\theta_1 > 0.385$.

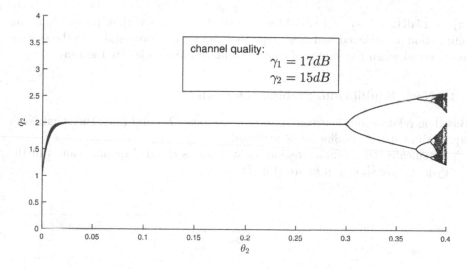

Fig. 5. CR2, Bifurcation Diagram under $\gamma_1 = 17$ dB and $\gamma_2 = 15$ dB

The same thing with the second secondary user CR2, the figure (Fig. 5) show that the Nash equilibrium is reached when $0.099 < \theta_2 < 0.291$ and bifurcation doubling appears at $\theta_2 = 0.292$ and chaotic behavior appears when $\theta_2 > 0.371$.

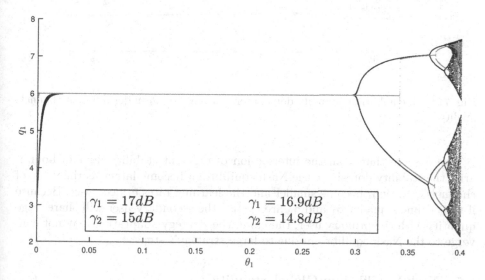

Fig. 6. CR1, Bifurcation Diagram under different channels quality γ_i (Color figure online)

The figure (Fig. 6) show the bifurcation diagram of secondary user (CR1) with different channel quality ($\gamma_1 = 16.9$ dB and $\gamma_2 = 14.8$ dB red graph) and

($\gamma_1 = 17\,$dB and $\gamma_2 = 15\,$dB blue graph). One can see that period-doubling bifurcation are delayed and Nash equilibrium become more stable in the system as expected when the values of channel quality are smaller (red graph).

5.4   Nash Equilibrium Stability Domain

Based on relationship between θ_1 and θ_2 (see Eqs. (24) and (23)) such that Nash equilibrium spectrum Sharing is achieved.

Specifically, the stability region under various channel quality values in the θ_1, θ_2-plane are shown in figure (Fig. 7).

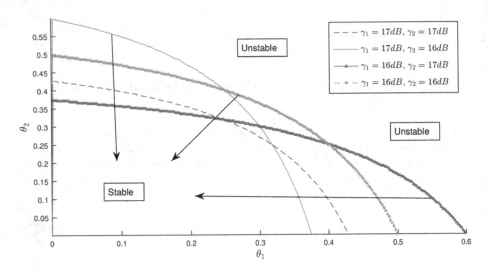

Fig. 7. Nash equilibrium stability domain for learning rate θ_i under different channels quality γ_i

We observe that from the intersection of different stability domain boundaries the stability domain of the Nash equilibrium become larger as the value of channels quality γ_i become smaller and the learning rates θ_i decreases. Because if the channels quality γ_1 and γ_2 are better, the secondary user will share large quantity with the primary user, therefore, the strategy adaptation may not converge to the Nash equilibrium due to large strategy's steps.

5.5   Nash Equilibrium Global Stability

In dynamical systems the stability of the fixed point is sensitive to initial strategy setting in fact figure (Fig. 8) show the domain of initial strategies (red graph) where the strategy adaptation converge (i.e., or is attracted) to the Nash equilibrium when the spectrum sharing scheme is iterated.

Yet, if the initial choice of strategy is outside the basin of attraction, and even if the learning rate is picked in the stability region, the adaptation of the strategy will be pushed out to infinity.

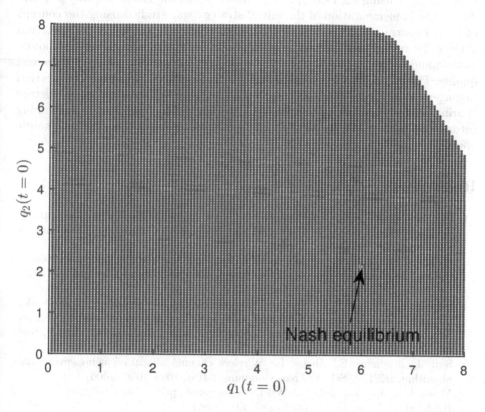

Fig. 8. Nash equilibrium Basin of attraction

We observe that as in the case of the stability region when the learning rate becomes higher, the size of the basin of attraction becomes smaller due to the destabilization effect. On the other hand, when the quality of the channel improves, the basin of attraction becomes larger. This is because when the channel quality improves, secondary users share larger spectrum size. Therefore, initial strategies that are nearer to the Nash equilibrium will converge quickly to the wanted solution.

6 Conclusion

We have proposed a game theoretical competitive spectrum sharing model in a cognitive radio network composed of a primary user and several secondary users sharing the same radio spectrum. This scheme is based on a dynamic game in which each secondary user adapts its spectrum sharing strategy by only observing the marginal profit which is a cost function of the spectrum offered by the primary user. So far, we have studied analytically the stability of this dynamic game using the local stability theory. Thus, the global stability problem due to the implementation of the initial strategy was studied using the concept of basin of attraction. The Nash equilibrium offers a fair solution for spectrum sharing. However, for the stability of this solution, the numerical results showed chaotic and bifurcated behavior due to changes in learning rates and channel quality. Therefore, the spectrum sharing scheme above will be useful for spectrum management in future generations of cognitive radio systems and infrastructure sharing between network operators. Other papers will be published in the coming future with further details on oligopoly games and control tools for the chaotic effects.

References

1. FCC Spectrum Policy Task Force. Report of the spectrum efficiency working group. Technical report No. 02-135, Federal Communication Commission, Washington, DC, November 2002
2. Boccaletti, S.: The Control of Chaos: Theory and Applications. Elsevier (2000)
3. Haykin, S.: Cognitive radio: brain empowered wireless communications. IEEE J. Sel. Areas Commun. 23(2), 201–220 (2005)
4. Baslam, M., El-Azouzi, R., Sabir, E., Bouyakhf, E.H.: New insights from a bounded rationality analysis for strategic price-QoS war. In: 6th International ICST Conference on Performance Evaluation Methodologies and Tools (2012). https://doi.org/10.4108/valuetools.2012.250410
5. Sun, J., Modiano, E., Zheng, L.: Wireless channel allocation using an auction algorithm. IEEE J. Select. Areas Commun. 24(5), 1085–1096 (2006)
6. Musacchio, J., Walrand, J.: WiFi access point pricing as a dynamic game. IEEE/ACM Trans. Netw. 14(2), 289–301 (2006)
7. Comaniciu, C., Nie, N.: Adaptive channel allocation spectrum etiquette for cognitive radio networks. In: First IEEE International Symposium on New Frontiers in Dynamic Spectrum Access Networks, DySPAN 2005 (2005)
8. Neel, J.O., Reed, J.H., Gilles, R.P.: Convergence of cognitive radio networks. In: Proceedings of IEEE WCNC 2004, vol. 4, pp. 2250–2255, March 2004
9. Xing, Y., Mathur, C.N., Haleem, M.A., Chandramouli, R., Subbalakshmi, K.P.: Real-time secondary spectrum sharing with QoS provisioning. In: Proceedings of IEEE CCNC 2006, vol. 1, pp. 630–634, January 2006
10. Niyato, D., Hossain, E.: Competitive spectrum sharing in cognitive radio networks: a dynamic game approach. IEEE Trans. Wireless Commun. 7(7), 2651–2660 (2008)
11. Dludla, G., Mfupe, L., Mekuria, F.: Overview of spectrum sharing models: a path towards 5G spectrum toolboxes. In: Mekuria, F., Nigussie, E.E., Dargie, W., Edward, M., Tegegne, T. (eds.) ICT4DA 2017. LNICST, vol. 244, pp. 308–319. Springer, Cham (2018). https://doi.org/10.1007/978-3-319-95153-9_28
12. Rosen, J.B.: Existence and uniqueness of equilibrium points for concave N-person games. Econometrica 33(3), 520–534 (1965)
13. Lasaulce, S., Debbah, M., Altman, E.: Methodologies for analyzing equilibria in wireless games. IEEE Signal Process. Mag. 26, 41–52 (2009)

14. Agiza, H.N., Bischi, G.-I., Kopel, M.: Multistability in a dynamic cournot game with three oligopolists. Math. Comput. Simul. **51**, 63–90 (1999)
15. Kar, I.: Stability Analysis of Discrete Time Systems, Digital Control Module 3. https://nptel.ac.in/content/storage2/courses/108103008/PDF/module3/m3_lec1.pdf
16. Liu, Q., Zhou, S., Giannakis, G.B.: Queuing with adaptive modulation and coding over wireless links: cross-layer analysis and design. IEEE Trans. Wireless Commun. **4**(3), 1142–1153 (2005)

IoT Based Prediction of Active and Passive Earth Pressure Coefficients Using Artificial Neural Networks

Salima Attache[1]●, Ikram Remadna[2]●, Labib Sadek Terrissa[2(✉)]●,
Ikram Maouche[2]●, and Noureddine Zerhouni[3]●

[1] LRGC Laboratory, Biskra University, BP 145 RP, 07000 Biskra, Algeria
`salima.attache@univ-biskra.dz`
[2] LINFI Laboratory, Biskra University, BP 145 RP, 07000 Biskra, Algeria
`{ikram.remadna,terrissa,ikram.maouche}@univ-biskra.dz`
[3] FEMTO-ST Institute (UMR CNRS 6174), Bourgogne Franche-Comte University,
Besançon, France
`zerhouni@ens2m.fr`

Abstract. Internet of Things (IoT) combined with Artificial intelligence (AI) applied to data-centric systems has demonstrated excellent predictive capabilities compared to conventional civil engineering methodologies. Consequently, it is commonly used to model the complex behaviour of the majority of geotechnical engineering materials. This research aims to build a fast and accurate solution for predicting the lateral earth pressure applied to a retaining wall using IoT technologies and artificial neural networks. We used a Multilayer Neural Network (MLNN) to predict both active (Ka) and passive (Kp) earth pressure coefficients for various geometric configurations on frictional soil. The correlation coefficient and root mean square error have been used to evaluate the artificial neural network's performance. The correlation coefficients for Ka and Kp were close to one. Consider the root mean square; our model predicted Ka to be 0.006 and Kp to be 0.05. The resulting values are compared to those produced using the analytical and numerical technique. This method has been shown to provide more accurate results than analytical and numerical approaches.

Keywords: Artificial Intelligence · Machine learning · Passive and active earth pressure coefficients · Retaining walls

1 Introduction

The estimation of the active and passive earth pressure coefficients is one of the important problems in the field of geotechnical engineering. Several researchers have established numerous theoretical techniques, including slip line technique, limit equilibrium method [15, 20, 23, 26, 27, 31, 34, 36, 37], limit analysis [10–12, 33, 35], the method of characteristics [14, 19, 32], as well as various numerical techniques, such as the finite difference method [7] and the finite element

© The Author(s), under exclusive license to Springer Nature Switzerland AG 2022
M.-A. Koulali and M. Mezini (Eds.): NETYS 2022, LNCS 13464, pp. 252–262, 2022.
https://doi.org/10.1007/978-3-031-17436-0_17

method [4,16]. In recent years, many approaches for determining the safety factors of wall design in a shorter time have gained importance. The techniques are mainly used to estimate some factors that are difficult to be measured directly or accurately.In addition, they need much less computing time than the conventional trial-and-error technique [24]. The artificial neural networks method is one of these different methods commonly used to solve many engineering problems [17,29,39]. Artificial neural networks (ANNs), based on complex mathematical models and advanced software tools, may evaluate all reliable choices for a given project outcome. However, relatively few research have been conducted on artificial neural networks' applicability for estimating retaining structure behaviors. [25] focused on the pile-anchor retaining structure's deformation prediction [22] investigated the use of neural networks to predict the displacement of a deep foundation pit retaining structure. [13] used artificial neural networks to predict the deformation properties of pile displacement. [38] employed artificial neural networks to estimate the liquefication of the sand resistance. In [6], the authors were interested in intelligent systems driven by IoT technology. They have suggested a novel solution based on IoT and cloud computing technologies that allows the connection and enhancement of traditional systems (industrial, healthcare, etc.) through dashboards for monitoring, supervising, and managing a large number of distributed objects. A prognostics and Health management system in Industry 4.0, using IoT and cloud computing to solve maintenance issues has been proposed in [5]. The proposed research aims to provide a rapid and accurate solution based on IoT technology for predicting active and passive earth pressure coefficients for a vertical wall that retains a horizontal cohesionless backfill without surcharge loading while ignoring the impact of soil unit weight. A multilayer artificial neural network was designed and tested for this goal. The obtained results were compared to numerical and analytical results. Our approach has shown several advantages for pressure coefficient estimation. It is a precise, less disruptive, and less expensive approach. It allows the avoidance of very costly experimental procedures of materials and time consuming. At the same time, the numerical methods in this field require a high level of problem design and programming and also high-performance computing resources. Furthermore, the application of artificial neural networks has great value when it is difficult or impossible to uncover relationships.

This article is structured as follows: We begin by providing a quick overview of our study via a literature review. Section 2 provided the main fundamentals of our research. In Sect. 3, we discuss the whole architecture, as well as the model and data. Section 4 summarizes and discusses the results. Finally, in Sect. 5, we conclude with a conclusion.

Algorithm 1. Sending

---

while *Running* **do**
    Sensing data (Ai)
    Send to sink (Ai)
end while

Algorithm 2. Data Receive

---

while *Running* **do**
    Receive commands from principal sink
    $Ak = Select\ action\quad (Ti)$
    Run actuators (Ak)
end while

Algorithm 3. Publishing

---

while *Running* **do**
    topic = generate topic (Ai)
    MQTT.publish (*topic, broker network address*)
end while

Algorithm 4. Data subscriber

---

while *Running* **do**
    $Wi=message\ (MQTT\ subscriber\ topic)$
    Send to Sink(Ti)
end while

---

2 IoT Based Prediction System Architecture

This section describes the overall architecture and technical specifications of active and passive earth pressure coefficients prediction model. The model as well as the used dataset have been detailed.

The architecture of the suggested solution is briefly described in this section. Figure 1 depicts an intelligent prediction system for active and passive earth pressure coefficients using IoT technology. The architecture is divided into two parts: a data side that collects and stores data at the edge, and a processing side that processes the data in the cloud to predict pressure coefficients.

The data is gathered with the use of "Algorithm 1" which is deployed on the sink. Mi denotes a message that includes the asset or device's identify, the sensor's identifier, the sensed data, and the time of transmission. The second and third algorithms are used to send and receive data as a broker MQTT publisher on the edge. Data is sent and received using the second and third algorithms (Algorithm 3, 4). The prediction system is located on the processing side. It consists of two distinct stages: offline and online. We analyze, train, and evaluate the model using several metrics (best errors) and finally we test it.

Once the model has been optimized and validated, it will be stored, allowing for the online prediction of active and passive earth pressure coefficients. As a consequence, the database will be updated.

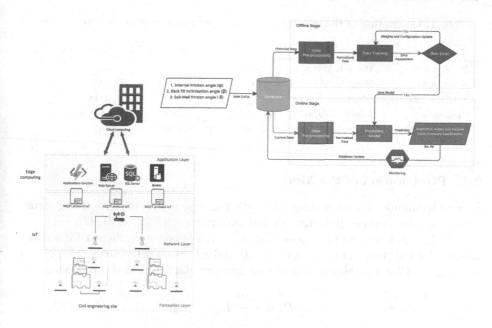

Fig. 1. IoT based prediction system architecture.

In order to build the MLNN model, a potential set of hyper-parameters must be defined, such as the number of hidden layers, the number of neurons, batch size, number of epochs, learning rate, and other parameters. Their optimization can highly affect MLNN performance. Selecting the optimal hyper-parameters values manually (trial-and-error approach) is difficult and can be time-consuming and error-prone due to a lack of understanding of the impacts of parameters. An automatic Hyperparameters Selection (AHPS) algorithm has been used to overcome these challenges [3, 8, 30]. Optuna, is a software framework for automating the optimization process of these hyperparameters, enabling efficient hyperparameter optimization by adopting state-of-the-art algorithms for sampling hyperparameters and pruning efficiently unpromising trials [1, 2]. In this study, an automated search for optimal hyperparameters was carried out using optuna with Median Pruner with Random Sampler algorithms to maximize efficiency.

The range of the hyperparameters detailed in Table 1, with the selected by Optuna for the ka and kp model. These most sensitive hyperparameters are chosen due to their highest impact on the performance.

Table 1. Description of the hyperparameters, their range and the selected values.

Name	Range	Selected for Kp	Selected for Ka
N° of layers	Min =1, Max = 6, step = 1	4	2
N° of units	Min = 1, Max = 128, step = 1	(79, 71, 79, 77)	(10, 15)
Activation function	relu, tanh, logistic	relu	relu
Optimizer	Adam, SGD, RMSprop	Adam	Adam
Learning rate	Min = 1e–3, Max = 0.1, step = 0.005	0.0101	0.01

2.1 Presentation of the Model

Several techniques for estimating the earth pressure acting on a retaining structure have been suggested during the last half-century [9,15,18,21,27].

The lateral force can be expressed as an earth pressure coefficient for a cohesionless backfill with no surcharge ($q = 0$ and $c = 0$). These forces (Fig. 2) can be computed for a retaining wall of unit length with Eqs. 1 and 2 respectively.

$$P_a = \frac{\gamma H^2}{2} K_{a\gamma} \tag{1}$$

$$P_p = \frac{\gamma H^2}{2} K_{p\gamma} \tag{2}$$

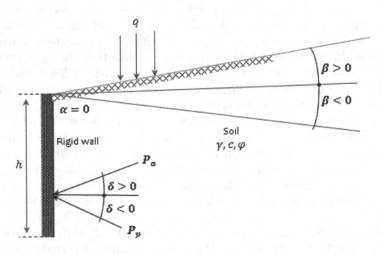

Fig. 2. Earth pressure problem notation.

2.2 Dataset Description

The database for this investigation was created from rigid retaining structures. It is commonly used by the scientific community and available from [35]. We have drawn up Table 2 to describe this dataset. In this study, we have dressed a CSV file with a total of 100 point dataset including the index properties of soil and wall ($\lambda, \beta, \delta, \phi,\ h,\ b$), in our prediction system. These features were used as input variables, whereas the output variables are active and passive earth pressure coefficients (K_a, K_p).

Table 2. Dataset description.

Attributes	Category	Description
ϕ	Numerical	Soil internal friction angle
δ	Numerical	Soil-wall interface friction angle
β	Numerical	Back fill inclination angle
λ	Numerical	Wall inclination
K_p	Numerical	Passive earth pressure coefficient
K_a	Numerical	Active earth pressure coefficient
h	Numerical	Wall height
b	Numerical	Wall breadth

3   Experiments and Results

In this section, we introduce the experimental conditions and analyze the experimental results, mainly comparing the prediction coefficients (k_a, k_p) with analytical and numerical (Flac 3D) approaches (As shown in Table 4). All of the tests were performed on a PC with an Intel Core i7- 8700k (3.70 GHz) processor and 16 GB of RAM, using Python 3.5 and the Keras Deep Learning Library. The Root Mean Square Error ($RMSE$) and R-squared (R^2), which are typically used to determine the difference between original and predicted data, were considered objective performance measures for evaluating the performance of the active and passive earth pressure coefficients estimation [28].

The RMSE is given by Eq. 3.

$$RMSE = \sqrt{\frac{1}{N}\Sigma_{i=1}^{N}\left(z_c - z_e\right)^2} \tag{3}$$

where N is the total number of samples, z_c is the actual coefficient value and z_e is the estimated coefficient value of the testing dataset.

Whereas the R-squared is given by Eq. 4.

$$R^2 = 1 - \frac{SSE}{TSS} \tag{4}$$

where SSE is the sum of squared errors, and TSS is the total sum of squares.

We noticed that the main goal is to obtain the maximum highest level of accuracy by minimizing as much as possible the the RMSE and maximizing R^2 as shown in Table 3 and Fig. 3. For the purpose of splitting dataset, we partitioned the database into two subsets in our contribution. The first subset is used to fit the model and is referred to as the training dataset. The second is used to evaluate the fit learning model and it is referred to as the test dataset. The objective is to estimate the performance of the machine learning model on new data that was not used to train the model.

Table 3. $RMSE$ and $R2$ values for Training, Testing,and Validating.

K_a						K_p					
Train		Test		Validation		Train		Test		Validation	
RMSE	R^2	RMSE	R^2	RMSE	R^2	RMSE	R^2	RMSE	R^2	RMSE	R^2
0,005	0,99	0,025	0,91	0,012	0,97	0,068	0,99	0,0478	0,99	0,156	0,98

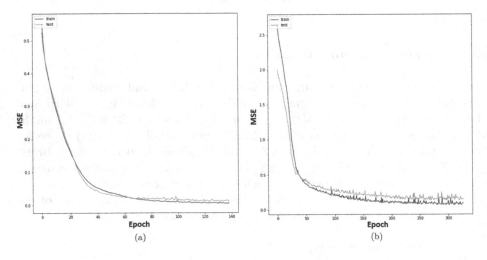

(a)   (b)

Fig. 3. MSE for: (a) Ka and (b) Kp Model.

Table 4 shows Kp and Ka values for analytical, predicted and numerical approaches for the same parameters ($\lambda, \beta, \delta, \phi,\ h,\ b$). One can observe easily in Fig. 4 that our MLNN-based prediction system overperforms significantly those obtained by [7, 35].

This improvement is about 14,97% and 16,38% for Kp when compared to analytical and numerical methods, respectively, and around 11,29% and 6,73% for Ka when compared to analytical and numerical methods, respectively.

Table 4. Comparison of K_p and K_a (Analytical[14] vs. Predicted vs. Numerical[18]) methods.

K_p						K_a					
σ/φ	β/φ	φ	(1)	(2)	(3)	σ/φ	β/φ	φ	(1)	(2)	(3)
1	0	20	3.13	3.093	/	1	0	25	0.363	0.335	/
0	−2/3	20	1.39	1.372	1.435	0	1/3	20	0.54	0.498	0.524
1/3	−1/3	40	4.1	3.884	4.219	2/3	2/3	40	0.29	0.272	0.27
1/3	−1/3	35	3.35	3.033	3.426	2/3	2/3	35	0.35	0.318	0.333
1/2	−1/2	25	2.13	1.811	2.166	0	0	35	0.27	0.273	0.271
1/3	−2/3	20	1.51	1.452	1.546	1	2/3	40	0.31	0.275	/
1	−2/3	30	2.62	2.552	/	1/3	1/3	30	0.35	0.351	0.349
0	−1/3	40	2.83	2.839	3.046	1/2	2/3	25	0.49	0.455	0.482
2/3	−2/3	20	1.66	1.636	1.672	2/3	2/3	20	0.57	0.526	0.564
1	0	25	4.54	3.983	/	1/2	0	20	0.45	0.430	0.443

(1): Analytical (2): Predicted (3): Numerical

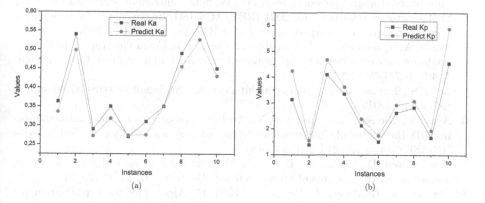

Fig. 4. Analytical, predicted and numerical values for: (a) Ka and (b) Kp.

4   Conclusion

Evaluating active and passive earth pressure coefficients is essential for geotechnical structure and construction design. On the other hand, the shear strength experiment is time consuming. Additionally, it necessitates the purchase of expensive laboratory equipment. Thus, using advanced machine learning methods to predict active and passive earth pressure coefficients is a cost-effective method for rapidly determining and estimating active and passive earth pressure coefficients. This research proposes and tests an active and passive earth pressure coefficient intelligent prediction system based on IoT technology. We investigated rigid retaining structures with soil and wall index properties ($\lambda, \beta, \delta, \phi,\ h$, and b). We have dressed and structured a dataset collected through the IoT layer.

This study consists of two stages: data collection and processing. The predicted coefficients are compared to those obtained analytically and numerically. It has been demonstrated that data-driven systems based on IoT technology and artificial intelligence approaches perform well when estimating such coefficients. In future work, we will add more data to our prediction system and use new machine learning techniques to improve it.

References

1. Akiba, T., Sano, S., Yanase, T., Ohta, T., Koyama, M.: Optuna: a next-generation hyperparameter optimization framework. In: Proceedings of the 25th ACM SIGKDD International Conference on Knowledge Discovery & Data Mining, pp. 2623–2631 (2019)
2. Ammari, A., Mahmoudi, R., Hmida, B., Saouli, R., Bedoui, M.H.: A review of approaches investigated for right ventricular segmentation using short-axis cardiac MRI. IET Image Proc. **15**(9), 1845–1868 (2021)
3. Ammari, A., Mahmoudi, R., Hmida, B., Saouli, R., Bedoui, M.H.: Slice-level-guided convolutional neural networks to study the right ventricular segmentation using MRI short-axis sequences. In: 2021 IEEE/ACS 18th International Conference on Computer Systems and Applications (AICCSA), pp. 1–6. IEEE (2021)
4. Antão, A.N., Santana, T.G., Vicente da Silva, M., da Costa Guerra, N.M.: Passive earth-pressure coefficients by upper-bound numerical limit analysis. Can. Geotech. J. **48**(5), 767–780 (2011)
5. Ayad, S., Terrissa, L.S.: A generic architecture for intelligent systems based on IoT technology (2019)
6. Ayad, S., Terrissa, L.S., Zerhouni, N.: An IoT approach for a smart maintenance. In: 2018 International Conference on Advanced Systems and Electric Technologies (IC_ASET), pp. 210–214. IEEE (2018)
7. Benmeddour, D., Mellas, M., Frank, R., Mabrouki, A.: Numerical study of passive and active earth pressures of sands. Comput. Geotech. **40**, 34–44 (2012)
8. Bergstra, J., Bardenet, R., Bengio, Y., Kégl, B.: Algorithms for hyper-parameter optimization. In: 25th Annual Conference on Neural Information Processing Systems (NIPS 2011). vol. 24. Neural Information Processing Systems Foundation (2011)
9. Caquot, A., Kérisel, J.L.: Traité de mécanique des sols. Gauthier-Villars (1956)
10. Chen, W.F.: Limit Analysis and Soil Plasticity. J. Ross Publishing (2007)
11. Chen, W.F., Liu, X.: Limit analysis in soil mechanics. Elsevier (2012)
12. Chen, W., Rosenfarb, J.: Limit analysis solutions of earth pressure problems. Soils Found. **13**(4), 45–60 (1973)
13. Chen, Y.H., Wang, Y.W.: The analysis on the deformation predition of pile-anchor retaining structure in deep foundation pit in kunming. In: Applied Mechanics and Materials, vol. 166, pp. 1222–1225. Trans Tech Publications (2012)
14. Cheng, Y.M.: Seismic lateral earth pressure coefficients for c-φ soils by slip line method. Comput. Geotech. **30**(8), 661–670 (2003)
15. Coulomb, C.A.: Essai sur une application des regles de maximis et minimis a quelques problemes de statique relatifs a l'architecture (essay on maximums and minimums of rules to some static problems relating to architecture) (1973)

16. Elsaid, F.: Effect of retaining walls deformation modes on numerically calculated earth pressure. In: Numerical Methods in Geotechnical Engineering, pp. 12–28 (2000)
17. Hsu, K.l., Gupta, H.V., Sorooshian, S.: Artificial neural network modeling of the rainfall-runoff process. Water Resour. Res. **31**(10), 2517–2530 (1995)
18. Kérisel, J., Absi, É.: Active and Passive Earth Pressure Tables. Routledge (2017)
19. Kumar, J., Chitikela, S.: Seismic passive earth pressure coefficients using the method of characteristics. Can. Geotech. J. **39**(2), 463–471 (2002)
20. Kumar, J., Rao, K.S.: Passive pressure coefficients, critical failure surface and its kinematic admissibility. Géotechnique **47**(1), 185–192 (1997)
21. Lancellotta, R.: Analytical solution of passive earth pressure. Géotechnique **52**(8), 617–619 (2002)
22. Li, Y., Yao, Q., Qin, L.: The Application of Neural Network to Deep Foundation Pit Retaining Structure Displacement Prediction. World Acad Union-World Acad Press, Liverpool (2008)
23. Luan, M., Nogami, T.: Variational analysis of earth pressure on a rigid earth-retaining wall. J. Eng. Mech. **123**(5), 524–530 (1997)
24. McCormac, J.C., Brown, R.H.: Design of Reinforced Concrete. John Wiley & Sons, New York (2015)
25. Moayedi, H., Mosallanezhad, M., Rashid, A.S.A., Jusoh, W.A.W., Muazu, M.A.: A systematic review and meta-analysis of artificial neural network application in geotechnical engineering: theory and applications. Neural Comput. Appl. **32**(2), 495–518 (2020)
26. Patki, M.A., Mandal, J.N., Dewaikar, D.M.: Computation of passive earth pressure coefficients for a vertical retaining wall with inclined cohesionless backfill. Int. J. Geo-Eng. **6**(1), 1–17 (2015)
27. Rankine, W.J.M.: II. On the stability of loose earth. Philos. Trans. R. Soc. Lond. **147**, 9–27 (1857)
28. Remadna, I., Terrissa, S.L., Zemouri, R., Ayad, S.: An overview on the deep learning based prognostic. In: 2018 International Conference on Advanced Systems and Electric Technologies (IC_ASET), pp. 196–200. IEEE (2018)
29. Remadna, I., Terrissa, S.L., Zemouri, R., Ayad, S., Zerhouni, N.: Unsupervised feature reduction techniques with bidirectional gru neural network for aircraft engine rul estimation. In: Ezziyyani, M. (ed.) AI2SD 2019. AISC, vol. 1105, pp. 496–506. Springer, Cham (2020). https://doi.org/10.1007/978-3-030-36674-2_50
30. Remadna, I., Terrissa, S.L., Zemouri, R., Ayad, S., Zerhouni, N.: Leveraging the power of the combination of CNN and bi-directional LSTM networks for aircraft engine RUL estimation. In: 2020 Prognostics and Health Management Conference (PHM-Besançon), pp. 116–121. IEEE (2020)
31. Shields, D.H., Tolunay, A.Z.: Passive pressure coefficients by method of slices. J. Soil Mech. Found. Div. **99**(12), 1043–1053 (1973)
32. Sokolovskii, V.V.: Statics of Granular Media. Elsevier (2016)
33. Soubra, A.H.: Static and seismic passive earth pressure coefficients on rigid retaining structures. Can. Geotech. J. **37**(2), 463–478 (2000)
34. Soubra, A.H., Kastner, R., Benmansour, A.: Passive earth pressures in the presence of hydraulic gradients. Géotechnique **49**(3), 319–330 (1999)
35. Soubra, A.H., Macuh, B.: Active and passive earth pressure coefficients by a kinematical approach. Proc. Inst. Civil Eng. Geotech. Eng. **155**(2), 119–131 (2002)
36. Subba Rao, K., Choudhury, D.: Seismic passive earth pressures in soils. J. Geotech. Geoenviron. Eng. **131**(1), 131–135 (2005)

37. Terzaghi, K.: Theoretical Soil Mechanics 1943, vol. 19. Wiley, New York (2007)
38. Young-Su, K., Byung-Tak, K.: Use of artificial neural networks in the prediction of liquefaction resistance of sands. J. Geotech. Geoenviron. Eng. **132**(11), 1502–1504 (2006)
39. Zemouri, R., et al.: Hybrid architecture of deep convolutional variational auto-encoder for remaining useful life prediction. In: Proceedings of the 30th European Safety and Reliability Conference and the 15th Probabilistic Safety Assessment and Management Conference, pp. 3591–3598. Research Publishing Services, Singapore (2017)

Verification

Applying Custom Patterns in Semantic Equality Analysis

Viktor Malík[1,2](✉)[iD], Petr Šilling[1][iD], and Tomáš Vojnar[1][iD]

[1] Faculty of Information Technology, Brno University of Technology,
Brno, Czech Republic
{xmalik11,xsilli01,vojnar}@vut.cz, xmalik11@fit.vut.cz
[2] Red Hat Czech, Brno, Czech Republic

Abstract. This paper develops a novel approach to using code change patterns in static analysis of semantic equivalence of large-scale software. In particular, we propose a way to define custom code change patterns, describing changes that do change the semantics but in a safe way, and a graph-based algorithm to efficiently detect occurrences of such patterns between two versions of software. The proposed method allows one to reduce the number of false positive results generated by static code-pattern-based analysis of semantic equivalence by specifying which patterns of changes should be considered semantically equivalent. Our experiments with the Linux kernel show that it is possible to eliminate a substantial number of detected differences with just a small number of patterns, while maintaining a very high scalability of the overall analysis. Furthermore, the proposed concept allows for a possible future combination with automatic inference of patterns, which promises significant improvements in the area of static analysis of semantic equivalence.

1 Introduction

Semantic stability is a crucial quality of many successful software projects. While in some cases it is sufficient to only preserve the API, other cases require full functional stability (of at least some of the core parts). In order to decrease the risk of potential stability breakage, projects often use various automated ways to detect (undesirable) semantic changes every time a new version is released. Testing, while being the most widely used one, suffers from the possibility of not covering all possible cases. Methods of static analysis of semantic equivalence eliminate this problem, however, usually for the price of a higher time and resource consumption. Aiming at these issues, our previous work [13] introduced a new framework called DIFFKEMP, which allows to quickly and automatically analyse large-scale C projects for full semantic equivalence.

Methods of semantic equivalence detection suffer from other problems than scalability, though. One of the common ones is that software projects usually need to introduce semantic changes even to the parts which should remain stable. This happens, for example, when fixing bugs and security issues. Such changes

M.-A. Koulali and M. Mezini (Eds.): NETYS 2022, LNCS 13464, pp. 265–282, 2022.
https://doi.org/10.1007/978-3-031-17436-0_18

are desirable, however, they change the semantics and hence pollute the output of semantic equality checks. Eliminating this problem is quite difficult as the changes are often project-specific: a change that is considered safe for one project needs not to occur or, even worse, may be considered unsafe in another one.

In this work, we introduce a simple novel approach to describe code changes using so-called *custom change patterns* and a highly scalable method to detect such changes during analysis of semantic equivalence of real-world software. This allows users of semantic-equality analysers to specify which kinds of differences they wish to ignore (i.e., to consider safe). We develop our approach as an extension of the DIFFKEMP project that we introduced in our previous work [13]. Our approach is based on describing code changes through parametrised control-flow graphs and on using a specific graph algorithm to match occurrences of change patterns between a pair of software versions.

Our experiments, which we performed on various versions of the Red Hat Enterprise Linux kernel, show that the proposed method allows to eliminate tens of false positive results by supplying just few change patterns. At the same time, we show that our pattern detection method is very scalable as it does not disrupt the DIFFKEMP's ability to analyse hundreds of thousands of lines of code in the order of minutes.

Overall, we may summarize the contributions of this work as follows:

1. We introduce a novel representation of patterns of code changes using parametrised control-flow graphs.
2. We propose a highly scalable method to match such patterns on pairs of versions of large-scale real-life software.
3. We implement the proposed solution within the DIFFKEMP framework and show that our approach is able to substantially decrease the number of false positive results detected by a semantic equivalence analysis algorithm, while still maintaining a high scalability of the analysis.

1.1   Related Work

The idea of using code pattern matching in static analysis is not new and there exists a handful of successful applications. One of the areas is bug finding represented by tools such as FINDBUGS and its successor SPOTBUGS [5] for Java or CPPCHECK [14] for C/C++. These tools analyse programs on the level of abstract syntax trees (AST) or bytecode and try to identify pre-defined patterns which typically lead to incorrect or malicious behaviour. Our patterns differ from these in a way that they always work with a pair of programs (instead of a single one), since they have to describe a code change.

Pairs of program versions are also compared by works aimed at automatic extraction of bugfix patterns [10,12]. These works extract patterns of changes from software patches using convolutional neural networks [10] or a patch generalization algorithm [12]. Especially the latter work uses patterns similar to ours—while the authors propose to use parametrized ASTs, we rely on parametrized control-flow graphs which better suit our use-case of checking functional equivalence. The main difference is that our goal is to take an existing pattern and detect its instance in a pair of versions, whereas these works take an existing set of patches and infer a set of patterns. The inferred patterns are then used to introduce new bug classes for FINDBUGS or for automatic program repair [11].

Similar to these are works aimed at summarizing differences between programs [1,6,18] which produce a description of differences done between two versions of a software. The produced output in some way corresponds to our patterns, however, such descriptions are typically not suited for further processing. This is also the case for a group of works aimed at identification of structural and API refactorings [2,17,20]. These try to analyse programs and find occurrences of refactorings from some pre-defined list, typically the Fowler's catalogue [3].

Perhaps the closest work to ours is the COCCINELLE tool [16] whose original purpose is to detect and apply collateral evolutions in Linux drivers. The tool uses a custom specific language SMPL [15] to represent patterns of code changes. SMPL is based on semantic patches which are translated to the CTL logic. These are then matched against a CFG of a program (using model checking) to obtain a version of the code after the patch is applied. COCCINELLE deals with a slightly different problem than we do—it applies a single patch to a single program version to obtain a new version, while we deal with two existing program versions and have to match the observed changes with one of the existing patterns. In addition, COCCINELLE uses a more heavy-weight approach compared to our light-weight and fast graph matching algorithm capable of matching a large number of patterns on huge code-bases in the matter of minutes.

To the best of our knowledge, the work presented in this paper is the first one which attempts to deal with arbitrary code change patterns in the context of semantic equality analysis. There exist other tools for static analysis of semantic equivalence such as RVT [4], SYMDIFF [8], LLREVE [7], or UC-KLEE [19]. These are able to deal with arbitrary code changes, however, the changes must be semantics-preserving (which is not a requirement for our patterns), and they use a rather complex and slow methods to analyse programs, not suitable for large-scale software.

2   Pattern-Based Analysis of Semantic Equality

The work presented in this paper is based on our recently introduced framework for scalable static analysis of semantic differences called DIFFKEMP [13]. Since the algorithms and concepts that we propose in this paper are suited for DIFFKEMP, we first introduce its basic principles in this section.

DIFFKEMP is a framework implementing a highly scalable automated method for comparing the semantics of two versions of a program, with special focus on large-scale programs written in C, such as the Linux kernel. In order to achieve scalability to hundreds of thousands of lines of code, the method builds on three basic principles:

- First, wherever possible, it performs *instruction-by-instruction* comparisons on the level of the LLVM intermediate code representation. Since the compared versions are expected to be similar, this is a fast comparison step which often succeeds to show semantic equality of large parts of the code.
- Of course, a simple per-instruction comparison would not be sufficient in many cases. In order to partially eliminate this problem, the compared programs are *pre-processed* using various static analyses and code transformations (e.g., constant propagation or dead code elimination) which bring the compared versions to a form when the per-instruction comparison can be used as often as possible.
- Last, the method uses a set of pre-defined *semantics-preserving change patterns (SPCPs)*. These are used to check whether the observed code change matches some change pattern that has already been shown to preserve semantics. Examples of such patterns are *moving code into functions* or *changing structure types*.

One of the potential problems of the method is that the set of SPCPs is hard-coded into DIFFKEMP, and it is very likely unable to cover a number of semantics-preserving changes that may occur in real-life software. In this paper, we address this problem by introducing a new method which allows DIFFKEMP to dynamically load and use change patterns defined by users.

The proposed method builds on the existing concepts of DIFFKEMP, hence we describe the most important ones in the rest of this section. In particular, we focus on the LLVM intermediate representation (which is used to represent the compared programs), we present the main algorithm for checking semantic equivalence, and we describe how SPCPs are incorporated into this algorithm.

2.1   Program Representation

Before comparing any programs, DIFFKEMP translates them into the LLVM intermediate representation (LLVM IR). Then, all the comparisons are done on the level of this representation. In this section, we introduce its basic components.

In LLVM IR, each function of a program is represented using a single *control-flow graph (CFG)*. A CFG is composed of basic blocks connected by edges which represent program branching. A basic block is a list of instructions satisfying the property that all incoming edges are directed to the first instruction and all outgoing edges are directed from the last instruction.

An *instruction* performs an operation over a (potentially empty) list of operands and it may produce an output. LLVM IR fulfills the single static assignment (SSA) property, hence, if an instruction produces an output, it is stored in a newly introduced local variable (sometimes also called a register). The set of all instruction operations can be found in [9]. An instruction operand can be of multiple kinds: a local variable (i.e., a result of another instruction), a global variable, a constant, or a function (in the case of `call` instructions and instructions working with function pointers). In the rest of this paper, we use the following notation to represent an instruction performing an operation *op* over operands $o_1, \ldots, o_n$ and creating a variable v:

$$v = op(o_1, \ldots, o_n). \tag{1}$$

The CFGs in LLVM IR are typed – each value has its own type. The complete type system is defined by [9]. For convenience, we introduce the function *typeof* which returns the type of any value. In this work, we deal with user-defined structure types which may be named, hence we introduce the function *typename* which for each named structured type returns its name.

Each instruction of a basic block, except for the last instruction, has a single successor which is the instruction immediately following it inside the block. The last instruction of a block may be a *branching* or a *terminator* instruction. Terminator instructions immediately exit the function and potentially return a value (if the function returns one). Branching instructions may have one or two successors which are always initial instructions of basic blocks within the same function. Depending on the number of successors, we speak about *unconditional* (one successor) or *conditional* (two successors) branches. Conditional branches contain a boolean condition which selects the branch to follow. To simplify the presentation, we introduce three functions related to instruction successors:

- *succ* defines for each non-branching and each unconditional branching instruction its only successor,
- *succT* and *succF* define for each conditional branching instruction the successor instructions which will be followed if the branching condition is evaluated to true and false, respectively. We refer to these successors as to the *true-case* and the *false-case* successors.

2.2 Analysis of Function Equality

We now present the main algorithm for comparing semantic equality of functions introduced in [13]. The main idea of the algorithm is to split each of the compared functions into the same number of chunks using so-called *synchronisation points* and then check that the code between pairs of corresponding synchronisation points is semantically equal. This approach allows to reduce the complexity of the comparison as only small pieces of the code must be compared at a time. As outlined before, synchronisation points are typically (but not always) placed after each instruction. In addition, multiple semantics-preserving transformations of the functions are run prior to the actual comparison, which allows to use per-instruction synchronisation more often.

Checking of semantic equality is facilitated by building two bijective functions (maps) denoted *smap* and *varmap*. The *smap* function represents a mapping between synchronisation points of the two compared functions. On the other hand, *varmap* represents a mapping between variables (or memory locations in general) of the compared functions.

Using these two maps, DIFFKEMP is able to check for semantic equality of the entire functions. The main idea is the following: for each synchronisation point s in one function, we find the corresponding synchronisation point in the other function (using $smap(s)$) and check that the program states reachable at s and $smap(s)$ are equal under the mapping $varmap$. The main complexity of the algorithm lies in building both synchronisation maps. In order to do this efficiently, DIFFKEMP builds the maps lazily while traversing the control-flow.

We now present a simplified version of the algorithm. At the beginning of the comparison, one synchronisation point is placed at the entry of each function and these are initially synchronised in $smap$. In addition, function parameters and global variables used in the compared functions are synchronised in $varmap$. Then, for each yet unvisited synchronised pair, the algorithm performs the following steps:

1. **Pattern detection.** This step decides whether a built-in SPCP is applicable at this point. This is usually done by a very quick analysis of the instructions immediately following the current synchronisation points. The efficiency of this step is important as it is potentially performed for each pair of synchronisation points for each supported SPCP.
2. **Determine successor synchronisation pairs.** This second step finds the following pairs of synchronised points, i.e., points from where the analysis will continue after the currently analysed pieces of code are compared as semantically equal. If some built-in SPCP is applicable, it must define the set of the following synchronisation pairs. Otherwise, the new points are placed right after the following instructions using the successor functions $succ$ (for the case of non-branching and unconditional branching instructions) or $succT$ and $succF$ (for the case of a conditional branching instruction).
3. **Semantic equality detection.** We now check that the pieces of code between the current and each of the following pair of synchronisation points are semantically equal. Compared to Step 1, this is usually a more thorough check. It is done either by using a pattern-specific comparison or by comparing the semantics of single instructions. In the latter case, the algorithm checks that the instructions perform the same operation over operands which are the same or mapped via $varmap$.
4. **Update variable mapping.** If the compared pieces of code produce some outputs (e.g., instructions introduce new local variables), the corresponding outputs are made synchronised in $varmap$.
5. **Schedule following comparison.** Finally, the new synchronisation points from Step 2 are scheduled for a subsequent comparison and the algorithm continues with Step 1.

For a more detailed and formalised description of the algorithm, see [13].

3   Representation of Custom Change Patterns

We now proceed to our proposal of a method allowing one to incorporate custom change patterns to the semantics equivalence comparison method described in Sect. 2. The existing method already handles several built-in change patterns, hence we adopt and extend the current approach. While the method currently addresses the semantics-preserving change patterns (SPCPs) only, we want our extension to allow also patterns altering the semantics. With respect to this, we denote the new custom patterns introduced in this paper as *custom change patterns (CCPs)*.

In this section, we introduce a formal definition of CCPs. The algorithm for matching CCPs in the compared programs is described next in Sect. 4. We require CCPs to be able to describe arbitrary changes that may occur in programs supported by DIFFKEMP (i.e., any programs compilable to LLVM IR). To this end, our pattern definition is inspired by and based on the program representation that we use.

With respect to the way patterns are currently handled in DIFFKEMP, we require our CCP representation to allow for the following:

- describe a code change between two compared versions of a program,
- parametrise the pattern so that it can be matched to a larger set of actual changes, and
- express which memory locations should be synchronised after the pattern is successfully matched to an observed change.

3.1 Formal Definition of Custom Change Patterns

We represent our patterns with the help of *parametrised control-flow graphs*. A parametrised CFG c is a triple:

$$c = (in, cfg, out). \tag{2}$$

Here, cfg is a control-flow graph which can be parametrised using undefined local variables and undefined structure types, representing the input values and types of the CFG, respectively. The component in of c is the set of all input variables and types used in cfg. Last, out denotes the set of "outputs" of the parametrised CFG, i.e., the set of local variables which may be used outside of c. With respect to this, we define a code change pattern as a tuple

$$p = (c_o, c_n, imap, omap) \tag{3}$$

where c_o and c_n are parametrised CFGs corresponding to the old and the new version of the code change that is represented by p, respectively. Let

$$c_o = (in_o, cfg_o, out_o) \tag{4}$$
$$c_n = (in_n, cfg_n, out_n). \tag{5}$$

Then, $imap : in_o \leftrightarrow in_n$ is a mapping between the inputs of the parametrised CFGs c_o, c_n expressing which values and types in the compared programs must have the same semantics in order to successfully match the pattern. Analogically, $omap : out_o \leftrightarrow out_n$ is a mapping between output variables of the parametrised CFGs expressing which variables of the compared programs will be mapped (i.e., will have the same semantics) after the pattern is successfully matched.

The above definition of CCPs allows us to seamlessly incorporate them into the current comparison algorithm. We do this by defining generic implementations of the pattern-specific operations required by the algorithm introduced in Sect. 2.2.

3.2 Encoding Change Patterns with LLVM IR

To be able to use CCPs in practice, we need them to be encoded in a form that DiffKemp is able to use. As patterns are represented by parametrised CFGs, LLVM IR is the natural choice.

In particular, we encode each pattern using two LLVM IR functions, one for each parametrised CFG of the pattern (c_o and c_n). The sets of input values from in_o and in_n are encoded using LLVM function parameters and their mapping (for $imap$) is determined based on the parameters' order. For type parameters, the patterns contain a custom type prefixed with `diffkemp.type`. This custom type is then used in both c_o and c_n, hence no explicit encoding of the mapping is necessary.

The sets of output variables (out_o and out_n) and their mapping $omap$ are represented by introducing a special function `diffkemp.mapping` which is called in each pattern function just before its exit. The call contains a list of variables representing out_o and out_n and the mapping is determined automatically based on their order.

The pattern matching algorithm that we introduce in the following section requires our patterns to encode some additional information. These are typically encoded in LLVM IR using LLVM metadata. More details on LLVM metadata can be found in [9].

4 Custom Change Pattern Matching

We now propose a method to detect occurrences of custom change patterns in the compared programs. Since our goal is to utilise this method in the comparison described in Sect. 2.2, we use the same approach as is already used for the semantics-preserving change patterns. In particular, we provide definitions for pattern-specific operations required by the algorithm described in Sect. 2.2. These definitions are generic, which means that they can be used for any custom change pattern having the form defined in the previous section.

To simplify the presentation in the rest of this section, we assume the following situation:

- two versions of a function f, denoted f_o and f_n (the old and the new version, respectively), are being compared using the algorithm from Sect. 2.2,
- f_o and f_n are represented using CFGs as described in Sect. 2.1, and we refer to them as to *compared-function CFGs*,
- the comparison algorithm is at the point of processing a pair of synchronisation points s_o and s_n, and

- the goal is to check if a custom change pattern $p = (c_o, c_n, imap, omap)$ is applicable and, if so, to apply it. We also let $c_o = (in_o, cfg_o, out_o)$ and $c_n = (in_n, cfg_n, out_n)$ and we refer to cfg_o and cfg_n as to *pattern CFGs*.

In the following subsections, we propose definitions of functions required by the individual steps of the main comparison algorithm as presented in Sect. 2.2.

4.1 Pattern Detection

The purpose of this step is to check if a pattern can be applied from the current pair of synchronisation points. As the check may be executed for each pattern at each synchronisation points pair, it is necessary that it is done in a very quick and efficient way. On the other hand, custom change patterns may describe arbitrary changes, hence the largest part of the matching must be done in this step.

For a custom change pattern p, we need to check that cfg_o is a subgraph of f_o and cfg_n is a subgraph of f_n. Checking of subgraph isomorphism is generally expensive, however, we are dealing with CFGs in a specific situation which allows us to use a rather efficient approach. In particular, we build on assumptions that (1) each CFG has a single entry point and (2) we only need to match the pattern CFG starting from the current synchronisation point in the compared-function CFG. Hence, there is a unique point where the matching must start, and we can use a straightforward control-flow traversal to check whether all instructions of the pattern CFG match instructions in the compared-function CFG.

Even though the problem is now much reduced, two major issues remain:

1. We still need to perform the full CFG comparison from each pair of synchronisation points for each pattern. Even though the matching algorithm is efficient, running it so many times may cause problems with scalability, which is DIFFKEMP's main concern.
2. The occurrence of a pattern CFG in the corresponding compared function CFG may be interleaved with non-related instructions. This is a common situation as the LLVM compiler often reorders non-conflicting instructions.

To address the first issue, we always start the CFG matching from the first pair of instructions which differ between the pattern CFGs cfg_o and cfg_n. These are required to be marked explicitly in the pattern (we use LLVM metadata to do that) and we denote them as *the first differing instruction pair*. Thanks to that, the pattern can only be matched if f_o and f_n contain a synchronised pair of differing instructions and, in addition, that pair matches the first differing pair of the pattern. In practice, this heuristic quickly eliminates most of the non-matching pattern candidates for most of the synchronisation points.

Note that the pattern CFGs may start with sequences of instructions which are the same for both cfg_o and cfg_n and which will be not be initially compared. Such instructions denote a *context* in which the pattern must be applied—they define how some of the variables used inside the pattern must be created. We denote the sets of such variables ctx_o and ctx_n for the old and the new version of the pattern CFG, respectively. Naturally, it is necessary to check that

Input: $c_x = (in_x, cfg_x, out_x)$: pattern CFG
$\quad\quad\quad f_x$: compared function CFG
$\quad\quad\quad s_x$: current synchronisation point in f_x
Result: $match_x$: mapping between values and types of cfg_x and f_x
1 $\,e_p =$ first differing instruction of cfg_x
2 $\,e_f =$ instruction immediately following s_x in f_x
3 $\,Q = \{(e_p, e_f)\}$
4 $\,match_x = \{\}$
5 **while** Q *is not empty* **do**
6 $\quad$ take any (i_p, i_f) from Q
7 $\quad$ **if** $\neg cmpInst(i_p, i_f, in_x)$ **then** // updates $match_x$
8 $\quad\quad$ **if** $succ(i_f)$ *is defined* **then**
9 $\quad\quad\quad$ add $(i_p, succ(i_f))$ to Q // instruction skipping
10 $\quad\quad\quad$ **continue**
11 $\quad\quad$ **else return** $\emptyset$
12 $\quad$ **if** i_p *is conditional branch* **then**
13 $\quad\quad$ add $(succT(i_p), succT(i_f))$ to Q
14 $\quad\quad$ add $(succF(i_p), succF(i_f))$ to Q
15 $\quad$ **else** add $(succ(i_p), succ(i_f))$ to Q
16 **if** $\neg checkContext(match_x, ctx_x, in_x)$ **then**
17 $\quad$ **return** $\emptyset$
18 **return** $match_x$

Algorithm 1: Matching pattern CFG to one of the compared functions

the same context appears in the compared functions, i.e., that the variables of the compared functions matched with the context variables were created using equivalent instructions. This is done as the last step of our matching method.

To address the second issue, we allow our matching algorithm to "skip" instructions on the side of the function CFGs. These instructions will need to be compared using the default comparison, which is a problem that we address later in this section.

With respect to all the described mechanisms, our algorithm for detecting an occurrence of a pattern is shown in Algorithm 1. This algorithm must be run separately for both versions of the compared program and their corresponding pattern CFGs. Hence, we use the subscript $x \in \{o, n\}$ as a placeholder for either the old or the new version. If both comparisons succeed, the pattern is considered as applicable.

The algorithm simply traverses the control-flow of cfg_x and f_x, starting from the first differing instruction in cfg_x and from the instruction immediately following the current synchronisation point s_x in f_x. For each instruction pair, it uses the $cmpInst$ function to check that the instructions match. If they do not, the algorithm allows to skip instructions in f_x if they have a single successor which may be followed. We do not allow to skip conditional branching instructions. If the algorithm succeeds, it performs the context validation step and returns $match_x$, which is a map (a set of pairs) of semantically equivalent values and types between cfg_x and f_x.

Input: $i_p : v_p = op_p(o_p^1, \ldots, o_p^m)$ (pattern instruction),
   $i_f : v_f = op_f(o_f^1, \ldots, o_f^n)$ (compared-function instruction),
   in_x (pattern inputs)
   ctx_x (pattern context)
Output: *true* if i_p matches i_f, *false* otherwise

1 **if** $op_p \neq op_f$ **then return** false // ensures $m = n$
2 **for** $1 \leq i \leq n$ **do**
3   **if** $typeof(o_p^i) \in in_x$ **then**
4   add $(typeof(o_p^i), typeof(o_f^i))$ to $match_x$
5   **else if** $typeof(o_p^i) \neq typeof(o_f^i)$ **then**
6   **return** false
7   **if** $o_p^i \in in_x \vee o_p^i \in ctx_x$ **then**
8   add (o_p^i, o_f^i) to $match_x$
9   **else if** $\neg(o_p^i = o_f^i \vee name(o_p^i) \approx name(o_f^i) \vee match_x(o_p^i) = o_f^i)$ **then**
10   **return** false
11 $match_x(v_p) = v_f$
12 **return** true

Algorithm 2: Definition of the *cmpInst* function

The $match_x$ map is created by the *cmpInst* function, whose definition is shown in Algorithm 2. At its entry, the function takes two instructions (using the notation from Eq. (1)) and the set of the corresponding pattern inputs. It checks whether the instructions perform the same operation over semantically equivalent operands. Operands are considered semantically equivalent if both their types and values match. This matching is checked in multiple steps:

1. If the type of the pattern instruction operand is a part of the pattern input, we create a new matching with the type of the corresponding operand from the compared function (lines 3–4). In other words, this step marks which types of the compared funtion are mapped to which input types of the pattern CFG. Later, during the *semantic equality detection* step (Sect. 4.3), we check that the types of the old and the new compared functions which were mapped to semantically equivalent pattern inputs are also semantically equivalent.
2. If the types do not match (and one of them is not an input), operands are considered as semantically different (lines 5–6).
3. A check similar to point 1 is done for the operand values, except that they may also be parts of the pattern context (lines 7–8).
4. Last, a check similar to point 2 is done for the operand values (lines 9–10). For values, the equality check is more complex than for types and it depends on the operand kind. For constants, we check for direct equality. For functions and global variables, we check for name match. Besides pure name equality, we allow patterns to specify *renaming rules* which describe how called function names may differ between the versions (this is expressed by $\approx$ in the algorithm). Last, for local variables, we check if the values have already been mapped via $match_x$. These checks are handled by the individual disjuncts at line 9 of the algorithm.

If the comparison succeeds, *cmpInst* accordingly updates the mapping $match_x$. The mappings created by comparing the two given program versions against the

Input: $match_x$: matching of values between cfg_x and f_x
ctx_x: the set of pattern context variables
in_x (pattern inputs)

1 **do**
2   **for** $(v_p, v_f) \in match_x$ **do**
3   **if** $v_p \in ctx_x$ **then**
            // Let i_p and i_f be instructions creating v_p and v_f, resp.
4   **if** $\neg cmpInst(i_p, i_f, in_x)$ **then** // may update $match_x$
5   **return** false
6 **while** $match_x$ *is updated*
7 **return** true

Algorithm 3: *checkContext*: matching context instructions between the pattern and the compared function CFGs

different sides of a change pattern (i.e., $match_o$ and $match_n$) will be used later during the *semantic equality detection* step.

The last step of Algorithm 1 is *context validation*. As mentioned before, so-called pattern context instructions are initially not matched for optimisation purposes. In this step, we check that the values created by such instructions (the set of these values is denoted ctx_x) are created in the same way in the pattern and in the compared function. This check is performed by Algorithm 3.

The algorithm checks that variables created by context instructions which should have the same semantics (as they are in $match_x$) are created by semantically equivalent instructions. Running $cmpInst$ may again update $match_x$, hence the check must be run while $match_x$ changes.

4.2   Determining Successor Synchronisation Points

The purpose of this step is to determine where the analysis continues from, after the comparison of the current code chunks succeeds. For custom change patterns, we continue from (i.e., place a successor synchronisation point to) each instruction i of the compared function which has not been matched to the pattern CFG but which is immediately following some instruction matched to the pattern CFG. However, there may be several such instructions, due to two reasons:

- the pattern CFG is not required to have a single exit point, hence matching may end in multiple basic blocks and
- as explained in the previous section, we allow to skip instructions in the compared-function CFG, and these must be compared after the pattern is successfully matched.

Due to these, there may be a large number of instructions to continue from, hence we introduce an additional limitation. We only place a synchronisation point at each instruction i if there is no other synchronisation point already placed at an instruction i' such that i is reachable from i'. This is safe to do as if there is such an instruction i', i will be eventually analysed using the default comparison method which follows the control flow.

During the subsequent comparison, we make the main algorithm ignore instructions that were already matched by the pattern.

4.3   Semantic Equality Detection

Once the pattern is determined as applicable (i.e., a matching sub-CFG can be found in the corresponding function), it is still necessary to check that it is applied on semantically equivalent values and types of the compared-function CFGs. In other words, we need to check that the values and the types that were matched to the inputs of the pattern CFGs have the same semantics in both compared function versions.

To do this, we make use of the mapping functions created during the pattern detection, in particular $imap$ which maps semantically equivalent inputs of the pattern CFGs and $match_o$ and $match_n$ which map variables and types of pattern CFGs to variables and types of the compared-function CFGs as determined during pattern detection. Using these mappings, we check if the following holds:

$$\forall (i_o, i_n) \in imap :$$
$$match_o(i_o) = match_n(i_n) \vee \qquad \text{(covers constants)} \quad (6)$$
$$varmap(match_o(i_o)) = match_n(i_n) \vee \qquad \text{(covers variables)} \quad (7)$$
$$typename(match_o(i_o)) = typename(match_n(i_n)) \quad \text{(covers struct types)} \quad (8)$$

That is, we check that pattern inputs which should be semantically equivalent (via $imap$) are matched to values and types in the compared functions which are also semantically equivalent. Semantic equivalence in the compared functions is done based on the kind of the compared value: constants are compared by value, variables are compared using $varmap$, and structure types are compared by name.

4.4   Updating the Variable Mapping

The last step of handling change patterns in the comparison method introduced in Sect. 2.2 is to determine which variables created by the pattern have the same semantics for the following comparison. This is done by updating the $varmap$ function. For our custom change patterns, we again use the maps $match_o$ and $match_n$ created during the pattern detection step along with the pattern outputs mapping $omap$. In particular, we update $varmap$ so that:

$$\forall (o_o, o_n) \in omap : varmap(match_o(o_o)) = match_n(o_n) \qquad (9)$$

That is, for each pair of semantically equivalent pattern outputs (determined via $omap$), we let the values matched in the compared functions to be also semantically equivalent (via $varmap$).

5   Implementation and Evaluation

We implemented the proposed method as an extension of the DIFFKEMP tool. It is available from https://github.com/viktormalik/diffkemp/releases/tag/patterns. Currently, patterns must be specified manually using LLVM functions. Examples of patterns can be seen in the regression test suite of the project. We performed several experiments with our implementation, in order to evaluate usefulness and performance of the solution. All experiments were done on an 8-core Intel i7-1185 machine with 32 GB of RAM.

In our first experiment, we demonstrate practical usability of the approach by applying several custom patterns on a real-life project. We chose the Linux kernel (the main target of DIFFKEMP), in particular we investigated changes done between pairs of the recent releases of the Red Hat Enterprise Linux kernel. First, we identified five patterns of changes which repeat often across versions and although they alter the semantics, the changes are safe to be done. These include, e.g., modifications of the compiler behaviour concerning ordering or speculative execution of commands. A complete description of the used patterns can be found in Appendix A. Then, for each pair of succeeding versions of RHEL 8 (and the last pair of versions of RHEL 7), we performed a semantic comparison of all functions from a so-called *kernel application binary interface (KABI)*[1]. We performed each comparison twice—once without the proposed patterns and once with them. A comparison of the obtained results is shown in Table 1.

Table 1. Results of KABI analysis with and without custom patterns

RHEL versions	Differing functions		Pattern occurrences				
	w/o patterns	With patterns	P1	P2	P3	P4	P5
7.8/7.9	20	18		✓			✓
8.1/8.2	137	132	✓	✓	✓		✓
8.2/8.3	150	145	✓	✓	✓		
8.3/8.4	173	172				✓	
8.4/8.5	150	144		✓		✓	

The table shows numbers of functions identified as semantically differing with and without usage of patterns. Note that these are not necessarily KABI functions but may be called by one of them. We may observe that using 5 patterns removed 19 detected differences, i.e., each pattern was able to eliminate almost 4 differences on average. While this may not seem a lot, note that every difference should be reviewed manually. Hence, removing even a small number of differences may substantially reduce the amount of human work needed. In this case, the removed functions were often called from multiple KABI symbols and the overall output was shortened by 40 diff chunks comprised of 816 lines.

---

[1] A list of functions which are guaranteed to remain stable across minor RHEL releases.

Another important part of this experiment is in the second part of the table, which shows that each pattern was successfully applied in at least two different pairs of versions (some were applied even across major releases). This demonstrates that the patterns are generic enough to be defined just once and then can be reused within a project for its lifetime.

In our second experiment, we demonstrate high scalability of our pattern matching algorithm. Scalability is one of the main properties of DIFFKEMP, allowing it to be applied in practice. In this experiment, we again perform an analysis of KABI functions of the recent RHEL versions, however, this time, we apply as many as 24 patterns (taken from the first experiment and from our regression tests). Naturally, most of these will never be matched, however, the algorithm must try to match every pattern for every difference found. Hence, this experiment shows that even this larger number of patterns does not affect scalability of the overall analysis. The results are displayed in Table 2.

Table 2. Comparison of runtime with and without pattern matching

RHEL versions	Run time		KABI functions	Compared functions
	w/o patterns	with 24 patterns		
8.0/8.1	2 m 43 s	2 m 41 s	471	3446
8.1/8.2	3 m 30 s	3 m 29 s	521	3643
8.2/8.3	4 m 36 s	4 m 24 s	628	3978
8.3/8.4	5 m 36 s	5 m 35 s	631	3607
8.4/8.5	5 m 24 s	5 m 24 s	640	4002

We may observe that for all versions, the run time of the analysis is equal or even slightly shorter when using patterns. This shows that our matching algorithm is truly efficient. Each run time was obtained as an average wall time of 5 runs. The reason why times are shorter with patterns is that patterns cause more functions to be compared as equal, eliminating the necessity for further computations, such as precise difference localisation. To highlight the performance of the overall comparison, we give the number of KABI symbols and the number of total unique functions compared for each pair of versions.

6   Conclusions and Future Work

In this work, we proposed to apply code pattern matching in the context of analysis of semantic equivalence of programs. We introduced a new encoding of patterns of code changes based on parametrised control-flow graphs and an algorithm to detect occurrences of these patterns between two versions of a software. Our method is aimed at light-weight and scalable analysers, specifically at the DIFFKEMP framework introduced in one of our previous works. Lightweight analysers often suffer from a number of false positive results, which may be eliminated using custom patterns. In addition, to the best of our knowledge, our approach is the only one which allows to eliminate even differences which alter semantics but which are known to be safe and necessary. We demonstrate this capability in one of our experiments with the Linux kernel. Additionally, we show that our approach is highly scalable as it allows to efficiently apply tens of patterns during analysis of hundreds of thousands of lines of code.

The main drawback of the proposed solution is that the patterns must be specified manually at this moment, which may be cumbersome for some applications. Hence, one of the possible future improvements could be automatic inference of patterns which, when combined with our solution, could substantially improve the area of scalable analysis of semantic equivalence of software.

Acknowledgement. The authors were supported by the project 20-07487S of the Czech Science Foundation and the FIT BUT internal project FIT-S-20-6427.

A   Patterns Used in Experiments

Here, we present details on patterns that we used for our first experiment. For each pattern, we give an example of a real usage of the pattern within the RHEL kernel. Even though our patterns are defined in LLVM IR, we give examples in C, as it is much more readable. The LLVM IR representations of the patterns can be found in the DIFFKEMP repository. In our experiment, we defined 5 patterns:

P1: Use READ_ONCE for a memory read
Usage of the READ_ONCE macro prevents compiler from merging of refetching memory reads. This pattern describes a situation when a simple memory read is replaced by a memory read through the macro. For example:

$$p \to cpu \quad \to \quad READ\_ONCE(p \to cpu)$$

The pattern is parametrised by 3 inputs: (1) the pointer to read from, (2) the field to read, and (3) the type of the pointer.

P2: Use WRITE_ONCE for a memory write
The WRITE_ONCE macro is analogical to READ_ONCE, except that it is suited for memory writes. This pattern describes a situation when a simple memory write is replaced by a write through the macro. For example:

$$p \to cpu = cpu \quad \to \quad WRITE\_ONCE(p \to cpu, cpu)$$

This pattern is parametrised by 4 inputs: (1) the pointer and (2) the field to write to, (3) the type of the pointer, and (4) the value to write.

P3: Use unlikely for a condition
Usage of the unlikely macro tells the compiler that certain condition will evaluate to true only in a very small number of cases. The compiler can use this information to, e.g., perform a more efficient ordering of instructions.

This pattern reflects a situation when the `unlikely` macro is added to a condition. For example:

$$\texttt{if(sched\_info\_on())} \quad \rightarrow \quad \texttt{if(unlikely(sched\_info\_on()))}$$

The boolean condition is the single input of the pattern.

P4: Replace `spin_(un)lock` by `raw_spin_(un)lock`

The Linux kernel provides multiple functions for locking. This pattern describes a situation when usage of `spin_lock` is replaced by `raw_spin_lock`. For example:

$$\texttt{spin\_lock(\&last\_pool->lock)} \quad \rightarrow \quad \texttt{raw\_spin\_lock(\&last\_pool->lock)}$$

The same situation may happen with unlocking, hence we would normally need 2 patterns. Thanks to the possibility to specify renaming rules (see Sect. 4.1), our approach allows to handle both locking and unlocking using a single pattern.

P5: Replace `RECLAIM_DISTANCE` by `node_reclaim_distance`

The `RECLAIM_DISTANCE` macro and the `node_reclaim_distance` global variable are two ways of setting a maximum distance between CPU nodes used for load balancing. This pattern describes a situation when the usage of the macro is replaced by the usage of the global variable. Since this is just a simple replacement of one identifier by another, we leave this pattern without an example.

References

1. Apiwattanapong, T., Orso, A., Harrold, M.J.: A differencing algorithm for object-oriented programs. In: Proceedings of the 19th IEEE/ACM International Conference on Automated Software Engineering, pp. 2–13. IEEE (2004)
2. Dig, D., Comertoglu, C., Marinov, D., Johnson, R.: Automated detection of Refactorings in evolving components. In: Thomas, D. (ed.) ECOOP 2006. LNCS, vol. 4067, pp. 404–428. Springer, Heidelberg (2006). https://doi.org/10.1007/11785477_24
3. Fowler, M.: Refactoring: Improving the Design of Existing code. Addison-Wesley Professional, Boston (2018)
4. Godlin, B., Strichman, O.: Regression verification. In: Proceedings of the 46th, pp. 466–471. Association for Computing Machinery, New York, NY, USA (2009)
5. Hovemeyer, D., Pugh, W.: Finding bugs is easy. ACM sigplan notices **39**(12), 92–106 (2004)
6. Jackson, D., Ladd, D.A.: Semantic diff: A tool for summarizing the effects of modifications. In: Proceedings 1994 International Conference on Software Maintenance, pp. 243–252. USA (1994)
7. Kiefer, M., Klebanov, V., Ulbrich, M.: Relational program reasoning using compiler IR. J. Autom. Reason. **60**, 337–363 (2018). https://doi.org/10.1007/s10817-017-9433-5

8. Lahiri, S.K., Hawblitzel, C., Kawaguchi, M., Rebêlo, H.: SYMDIFF: a language-agnostic semantic diff tool for imperative programs. In: Madhusudan, P., Seshia, S.A. (eds.) CAV 2012. LNCS, vol. 7358, pp. 712–717. Springer, Heidelberg (2012). https://doi.org/10.1007/978-3-642-31424-7_54

9. Lattner, C., Adve, V.: LLVM Language Reference Manual (2022). https://llvm.org/docs/LangRef.html

10. Liu, K., Kim, D., Bissyandé, T.F., Yoo, S., Le Traon, Y.: Mining fix patterns for findbugs violations. IEEE Trans. Softw. Eng. **47**(1), 165–188 (2018)

11. Liu, K., Koyuncu, A., Kim, D., Bissyandé, T.F.: Avatar: fixing semantic bugs with fix patterns of static analysis violations. In: 2019 IEEE 26th International Conference on Software Analysis, Evolution and Reengineering (SANER), pp. 1–12. IEEE (2019)

12. Long, F., Amidon, P., Rinard, M.: Automatic inference of code transforms for patch generation. In: Proceedings of the 2017 11th Joint Meeting on Foundations of Software Engineering, pp. 727–739 (2017)

13. Malík, V., Vojnar, T.: Automatically checking semantic equivalence between versions of large-scale C projects. In: 2021 14th IEEE Conference on Software Testing, Verification and Validation (ICST), pp. 329–339. IEEE (2021)

14. Marjamäki, D.: Cppcheck: a tool for static c/c++ code analysis (2022). https://cppcheck.sourceforge.io/

15. Padioleau, Y., Hansen, R.R., Lawall, J.L., Muller, G.: Semantic patches for documenting and automating collateral evolutions in Linux device drivers. In: Proceedings of the 3rd Workshop on Programming Languages and Operating Systems: Linguistic Support for Modern Operating Systems, pp. 10-es (2006)

16. Padioleau, Y., Lawall, J.L., Muller, G.: Understanding collateral evolution in linux device drivers. In: Proceedings of the 1st ACM SIGOPS/EuroSys European Conference on Computer Systems 2006, pp. 59–71 (2006)

17. Prete, K., Rachatasumrit, N., Sudan, N., Kim, M.: Template-based reconstruction of complex refactorings. In: Proceedings of the 2010 IEEE International Conference on Software Maintenance, pp. 1–10 (2010)

18. Raghavan, S., Rohana, R., Leon, D., Podgurski, A., Augustine, V.: Dex: a semantic-graph differencing tool for studying changes in large code bases. In: 20th IEEE International Conference on Software Maintenance, 2004, pp. 188–197. USA (2004)

19. Ramos, D.A., Engler, D.R.: Practical, low-effort equivalence verification of real code. In: Gopalakrishnan, G., Qadeer, S. (eds.) CAV 2011. LNCS, vol. 6806, pp. 669–685. Springer, Heidelberg (2011). https://doi.org/10.1007/978-3-642-22110-1_55

20. Weißgerber, P., Diehl, S.: Identifying refactorings from source-code changes. In: Proceedings of the 21st IEEE/ACM International Conference on Automated Software Engineering, pp. 231–240. IEEE (2006)

Verifying Reachability for TSO Programs with Dynamic Thread Creation

Parosh Aziz Abdulla[1], Mohamed Faouzi Atig[1(✉)], Ahmed Bouajjani[2],
K. Narayan Kumar[3], and Prakash Saivasan[4]

[1] Uppsala University, Uppsala, Sweden
mohamed_faouzi.atig@it.uu.se
[2] University of Paris, Paris, France
[3] Chennai Mathematical Institute, CNRS UMI ReLaX, Chennai, India
[4] The Institute of Mathematical Sciences, HBNI, CNRS UMI ReLaX, Chennai, India

Abstract. The verification of reachability properties for programs under weak memory models is a hard problem, even undecidable in some cases. The decidability of this problem has been investigated so far in the case of static programs where the number of threads does not change during execution. However, dynamic thread creation is crucial in asynchronous concurrent programming. In this paper, we address the decidability of the reachability problem for dynamic concurrent programs running under TSO. An important issue when considering a TSO model in this case is maintaining causality precedence between operations issued by threads and those issued by their children. We propose a general TSO model that respects causality and prove that the reachability problem for programs with dynamic creation of threads is decidable.

1 Introduction

Automatic verification of (shared-memory) concurrent programs running under weak memory models is an important and challenging problem. For performance reasons, modern hardware and compilers ensure memory models that do not guarantee strong consistency, i.e., the fact that every update is immediately visible to all concurrent threads, which is ensured in this context only by the sequential consistency model (SC). Rather, they ensure models with relaxed consistency guarantees, allowing operations issued by a same thread to be reordered. This makes the behaviors of concurrent programs running over these models unintuitive and complex, and reasoning about their correctness very hard. A fundamental issue in this context is the decidability of verification problems such as the reachability problem. This problem has been investigated for several weak memory models such as TSO, Power, C/C++11, etc. (e.g., [2,3,6,11,12,17]). This problem is difficult because, roughly, weak memory models have the capacity of reordering events (reads and writes) and moving them arbitrarily far w.r.t their original position in a (sequentially consistent) computation. Reasoning about such reorderings requires considering arbitrarily long

M.-A. Koulali and M. Mezini (Eds.): NETYS 2022, LNCS 13464, pp. 283–300, 2022.
https://doi.org/10.1007/978-3-031-17436-0_19

partial orders between events or operational models using unbounded buffers, which leads to the consideration of infinite-state models for which the decidability of verification problem is not trivial. It has been shown that for some models such as TSO, the Strong Release/Aquire and the relaxed fragments of C/C++11, the reachability problem is decidable [6,11,12,17], while it is undecidable for other models such as Power and the Release/Aquire fragment of C/C++ [2,3,6].

All the existing work addressing the verification of reachability problem under weak memory models consider that the number of threads is static, fixed in the beginning of the program execution and does not change dynamically afterwards. However, dynamic thread creation is a crucial feature in asynchronous concurrent programming where new threads are created in order to execute in parallel different tasks. In this paper, we investigate the problem of verifying concurrent programs with dynamic thread creation running under TSO.

Before tackling this verification problem, a first important question to address is what is the semantics of such concurrent programs. For a program with a static number of threads, the semantics under TSO is defined using a FIFO store buffer for each thread. The store buffers are initially empty and a write operation issued by a thread is sent to its buffer where it will be pending until it can be committed to the main memory. A read operation from a variable x by a thread t first fetches, if it exists, the last value written on x by t that is still pending in its store buffer, and if this value does not exist, the read operation takes the value of x in the main memory. So, in the TSO model, read operations can overtake write operations issued by the same thread when they are on different variables and access stale values w.r.t. values written by other threads and not yet visible. Observe that in the TSO model, write operations issued by the same thread are never reordered (even if they are on different variables).

A possible extension of this semantics to programs with dynamic thread creation would be to associate with each newly created thread a store buffer, initially empty. This is for instance the semantics adopted in [18]. However, while this semantics (called here the *empty-create* semantics) looks natural, it has a serious problem, namely it does not respect causality between write operations. Indeed, a write operation pending in the store buffer of a thread at the moment it creates a new child can be committed after a write issued by that child. To see that, consider for instance the execution of the program shown in Fig. 1 where thread t starts by issuing the operation $x := 1$ at line 1, and then creates t' at line 2 while the previously issued write operation is still pending in its store buffer. Then, thread t' starts execution at line 3 by reading the value 0 from the memory since the write at line 1 is still not visible to it. This execution violates causality since the instruction $x := 1$ at line 1 was not visible to thread t' and thus the instruction at line 3 by t' was executed without taking into account the instruction $x := 1$.

Initially: x = y = 0

Thread t	Thread t'
1: x := 1	3: r2 := x
2: create (t')	

Fig. 1. Violating the causality

Allowing such behaviors is an undesirable feature that is explicitly discarded in general by the semantics of programming languages such as Java [19].

Moreover, the *empty-create* semantics does not respect the fundamental DRF property [10] (i.e., if the program is DRF under SC, then it will not exhibit non-SC behavior under TSO). To see that, consider the program in Fig. 1. This is a DRF program under SC however it exhibits a non-SC behavior under the *empty-create* semantics where the created thread can read the initial value of x.

Thus, a model that enforces causality must be considered. The most permissive way for doing this is to ensure that, while the parent and its child can run in parallel, no write issued by a child can be committed before writes issued before its birth by its parent. For that, we need to distinguish (in the store buffer) between writes issued by the parent before the creation of its child and writes issued after that creation. Since the number of thread creations is unbounded at all levels, a natural way to proceed is to maintain a tree-like dynamic structure of store buffers: If a thread t, with a current store buffer content $b(t)$, creates a thread t', then two new buffers $b(t')$ and $b'(t)$ are added to the tree structure, $b(t')$ is the buffer of t' used to store all writes issued by t', and $b'(t)$ is a new buffer of t used to store all the future write operations issued by t. Both $b(t')$ and $b'(t)$ are children of the buffer $b(t)$ in the buffer structure. From the point of view of t, the whole store buffer is actually the concatenation of the two buffers $b'(t)$ and $b(t)$, i.e., new writes are added to $b'(t)$ and writes are committed first from $b(t)$ until it becomes empty, and only by then from $b'(t)$. From the point of view of t', the store buffer (for reading its own writes) is $b(t')$ concatenated with $b(t)$. The fact that $b(t')$ is a child of $b(t)$ in the structure is used to ensure (1) that t' can read from writes issued by the parent before t' creation (when it is the last write to the considered variable stored in $b(t') \cdot b(t)$), and (2) that no write from $b(t')$ is committed before $b(t)$ is empty. A fence instruction issued by t' has the effect of flushing both $b(t')$ and $b(t)$ (in general all the buffers in the tree structure on the path from $b(t')$ to the root). The resulting model (called *clone-create* semantics) will forbid that the thread t' reads the initial value of x in the program shown in Fig. 1 and hence preserving the causality.

Our main result in this paper is the proof of the decidability of the reachability problem of concurrent program under the *clone-create* semantics. For technical reasons, we use in the paper an equivalent version of this model where the buffer tree structure is encoded as a sequence of buffers using duplication and synchronization mechanisms. Our approach for establishing the decidability of the reachability problem is based on using the framework of well-structured systems [9,15]. This is a generic framework allowing to prove the decidability of the reachability problem for infinite-state systems provided they enjoy some particular properties. Basically, it consists in showing that the transition system is monotonic w.r.t. a well-quasi ordering (WQO), which means that there is a WQO which is a simulation relation on the state space of the system: If two states s_1 and s_2 are related by the WQO, then whenever the system can move from s_1 to another state s_1' by executing some operation, it is possible to move in a number of steps from s_2 to another state s_2' s.t. s_2 and s_2' are related by the WQO. It has been shown that for such systems, the control state reachability problem (or reachability of an upward closed set of states) is decidable [9,15].

A major difficulty for adopting this approach in the case of our systems is that it is hard, if not impossible, to establish monotonicity in the presence of store buffers w.r.t. usual WQO ordering on word/tree structures. Roughly, these WQO's are based on the idea of structure embeddings, and it is clear that given a state s_1, adding naively write operations in store buffers in s_1 to get a larger state s_2 in the WQO can disallow the execution of some read operations that are possible from s_1, which leads to a violation of monotonicity. Therefore, to achieve our decidability result, the main challenge is to transform our operational model to another one that induces for each given program a transition system that is monotonic w.r.t. a suitable WQO on the state space. This is conceptually and technically non-trivial. To obtain a monotonic model we propose a new variant dual semantics based on load buffers where data flows in the reverse order, from the memory to the threads, simulating the fact that reads can access to stale values reaching them with some delay. We prove that this dual semantics is equivalent to the original one (w.r.t. state reachability). The advantage of such semantics is that adding loads to load buffers cannot harm since they can also be dropped. We show that, by using load buffers instead of store buffers, it is indeed possible to define an alternative operational model that has the desired properties for proving well-structuredness. While the idea of TSO load buffers has already been used in the literature [5], the definition of a load buffer TSO semantics for programs with dynamic thread creation that preserves causality poses several new hard technical problems for which subtle solutions had to be found (see Sect. 4 for more details).

Related Work. Boudol et al. proposed in [14] a tree-based operational semantics for weak memory models satisfying the DRF property and supporting thread creation. Their model is more relaxed than our *clone-create* semantics. Lui et al. adopted in [18] a TSO semantics where each new thread is created with an empty buffer. Batty et al. proposed in [13] a memory model for C11 that has a relation called *"additional synchronizes with"*, which keeps track of the causality between the parent and its descendants. Kaiser et al. proposed also in [16] a model for a fragment of C11 where child thread should be created with a view equal to that of its parent. The two proposed semantics for the C11 memory model are close in the spirit to our *clone-create* semantics for TSO. However, they are formally different due to the difference of the considered memory models.

The decidability and complexity for the verification problems of safety properties for programs under weak memory models has been addressed for TSO [4,5,11,12], PSO [7], POWER [3], RA [2], SRA [17], and promising semantics [6]. All these works consider static programs where the number of threads does not change during execution. The load-buffer semantics was first proposed in [4,5] but its extension to thread creation poses many challenges, in particular (1) the design of an equivalent dual semantics for the tree-like dynamic structure of store buffers under TSO and (2) finding a suitable WQO that can be used to show the monotonicity of the resulting transition system.

Finally, the parameterized verification of programs running under TSO has been addressed in [4,5,8]. This problem consists in the verification of an arbitrary number of identical threads running under TSO. Observe that parametrized verification still deals with *static* programs since the number of involved threads does not change during the execution. The decidability of the parameterized verification is a corollary of our decidability result since a program can start its execution by creating an arbitrary number of threads that will run statically.

2   Preliminaries

In this section, we present the notations that we use in the rest of the paper.

We use $\mathbb{N}$ to denote the set of natural numbers. For a finite set A, we define $|A|$ to be the size of A. For sets A and B, we use $[A \to B]$ to denote the set of functions from A to B and write $f : A \to B$ to denote that $f \in [A \to B]$. Given an element a and $a' \in B$, we use $f[a \leftarrow a']$ to denote the function $g : (A \cup \{a\}) \to B$ such that $g(a) = a'$, and $g(b) = f(b)$ if $b \neq a$.

For a set A, we define $A^{\circledast}$ to be the set of finite multisets over A. We view a multiset M over A as a function $M : A \to \mathbb{N}$. Sometimes, we write multisets as lists, so if $a, b \in A$, then $[a, a, a, b, b]$ represents a multiset M such that $M(a) = 3$, $M(b) = 2$, and $M(x) = 0$ if $x \notin \{a, b\}$.

We use A^* to denote the set of finite words over A. For a word $w \in A^*$, we use $|w|$ to denote the length of w. For $i : 1 \leq i \leq |w|$, we use $w[i]$ to denote the ith element of w. We use $a \in w$ to denote that $w[i] = a$ for some $i : 1 \leq i \leq |w|$. For words $w_1, w_2 \in A^*$, we use $w_1 \cdot w_2$ to denote their concatenation. We write $w_1 \preceq_A^{\text{word}} w_2$ if w_1 is a (not necessarily contiguous) sub-string of w_2.

3   Total Store Order

In this section, we extend the classical definition of Total Store Order (TSO) [20, 21] to thread creation settings. We first define the syntax of the class of programs we consider and then describe its operational semantics under the TSO memory model. We assume that programs can dynamically create threads. We propose a thread creation semantics (called *clone-create*) that respects the causality between the created thread and its parent.

Syntax. We assume a finite set of shared variables $\mathbb{X}$ whose values range over a finite domain $\mathbb{D}$ of data values. We assume that the data domain $\mathbb{D}$ contains the initial value 0. A thread P is simply a tuple of the form $\langle Q, q^{init}, \Delta \rangle$. Here Q is a finite set of states, $q^{init} \in Q$ is the initial state and Δ is the finite transition relation. A transition $\delta \in \Delta$ is a triple of the form $\langle q, \text{instr}, q' \rangle$, where $q, q' \in Q$ are the states of the transition and the instr is an instruction. We assume w.l.o.g. that q' is different from q. The instruction can be one of skip skip, read $\text{r}(x, d)$, write $\text{w}(x, d)$, atomic-read-write $\text{arw}(x, d, d')$, fence mf or the thread create instruction $\text{create}(q'')$. Without loss of generality, we assume that all threads involved have the same description $\langle Q, q^{init}, \Delta \rangle$.

TSO Configurations. A TSO configuration is a tuple of the form $\langle \mathcal{P}, \mathcal{Q}, \mathcal{B}, \mathcal{M} \rangle$ where $\mathcal{P}$ is the set of thread names (or threads for short), $\mathcal{Q} : \mathcal{P} \mapsto Q$ is a function that maps each thread to a state, $\mathcal{M} : \mathbb{X} \mapsto \mathbb{D}$ is the main memory and

$\mathcal{B} : \mathcal{P} \mapsto (\mathbb{X} \times \mathbb{D} \times \mathcal{P})^*$ is a per thread store buffer containing the writes performed by the thread. In addition to storing the writes, the store buffer also tags these writes with the information on the originator of the write. The originator of the write is the thread that first inserted the element into the store buffer as a consequence of issuing a write instruction. This is required to distinguish the elements of store buffer inserted due to duplication during the thread creation. This will become clear when we describe the various semantics of thread creation.

The initial TSO configuration is given by $\gamma_{in} = \langle \mathcal{P}^{init}, \mathcal{Q}^{init}, \mathcal{B}^{init}, \mathcal{M}^{init} \rangle$, where $\mathcal{P}^{init} = \{p_0\}$ is an unique initial thread, $\mathcal{Q}^{init}$ assigns the initial state q^{init} to the single initial thread (i.e., $\mathcal{Q}^{init}(p_0) = q^{init}$), $\mathcal{B}^{init}$ assigns an empty store to the initial thread (i.e., $\mathcal{B}^{init}(p_0) = \epsilon$) and $\mathcal{M}^{init}$ assigns the initial value 0 to all variables (i.e., $\mathcal{M}^{init}(x) = 0$ for $x \in \mathbb{X}$).

Clone-Create Semantics. In the following, we present the *clone-create* semantics for TSO with thread creation. The TSO transition relation $\rightarrow_{TSO_c}$ of the *clone-create* semantics between the TSO configurations is described by the inference rules in Fig. 2. Consider a transition $\delta = \langle q, \mathtt{instr}, q' \rangle$, performed by a thread p from a configuration $\gamma = \langle \mathcal{P}, \mathcal{Q}, \mathcal{B}, \mathcal{M} \rangle$. For such a transition to be performed, we should have $\mathcal{Q}(p) = q$. Execution of the transition entails a state change for the thread p to q'. In addition, other parts of the configuration can be changed depending on $\mathtt{instr}$.

If $\mathtt{instr} = \mathtt{w}(x, d)$ i.e. the instruction was a *write*, then the transition relation is defined by the rule Write. In this case, the value $\langle x, d, p \rangle$ is appended to the store buffer $\mathcal{B}(p)$ of the thread p. Note that the element inserted into the store buffer is tagged with p, indicating an original write.

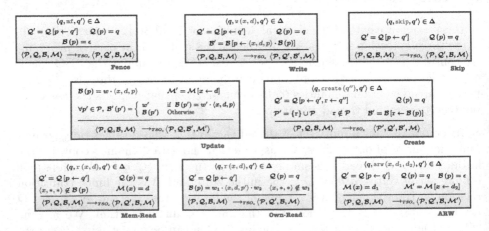

Fig. 2. The inference rules for TSO

If $\mathtt{instr} = \mathtt{arw}(x, d_1, d_2)$ i.e. the instruction was an *atomic-read-write*, then the transition relation is defined by the rule ARW. In this case, the transition is executed only if the store buffer of the thread p is empty i.e. $\mathcal{B}(p) = \epsilon$ and the current memory of x has the correct value i.e. $\mathcal{M}(x) = d_1$. On successful execution, the value in memory for x is updated to d_2.

If $\mathtt{instr} = \mathtt{r}\,(x, d)$, then the rules Mem-Read and Own-Read are used to define the transition relation. These transitions only affects the states of the configuration. The Own-Read is used when there are values for x in the p-store buffer i.e. $\langle x, *, * \rangle \in \mathcal{B}\,(p)$, in this case the transition is enabled if the latest written value to x is d. In case there is no values of x in $\mathcal{B}\,(p)$, then the rule Mem-Read is used. In this case the transition is enabled only if the value of x in the memory is d.

If $\mathtt{instr} = \mathtt{skip}$, then the rule Skip is used. In this case, only the state of the thread changes and no other components are affected. If $\mathtt{instr} = \mathtt{mf}$, then the rule Fence is used. The transition is enabled only if the store buffer of the thread p is empty i.e. $\mathcal{B}\,(p) = \epsilon$. In this case also, only the state of the thread changes, no other values are affected.

If $\mathtt{instr} = \mathtt{create}\,(q'')$, then the rule Create creates a new thread and its state is initialized to the state (i.e., q'') specified in the instruction. The store buffer of the newly created child thread is initialised by duplicating the store buffer of its parent thread. In doing so, we restrict the communication between the parent and the child thread and preserve the causality. As we will see in the next paragraph, removing a duplicate write from the store buffer is always synchronised with removing the originator of that write. This is done in order to avoid updating the memory multiple times due to the duplication. Observe that the semantics allows parallel execution of the created thread. However, for the variables that are present in its store buffer the child thread is only allowed to read the last written value (inherited from the parent or subsequently written by the child). It should also be noted that the inherited writes of a child thread may include those inherited by its parent (and so on). This in-turn restricts the communication between the parent and the child to the last written value for each variable that was in the parent's buffer during the thread creation.

The rule Update facilitates moving the values from the store buffer to the main memory. This rule non-deterministically updates the main memory with an original write in the head of the store buffer. Recall that a write in the store buffer of thread p is called original if it is of the form $\langle x, d, p \rangle$ for some x, d. In this case the value of x in memory is updated with the value d. In addition, the rule identifies the set of all duplicates of this original write and deletes them. A write, in the store buffer of a thread p', is a duplicate if it is of the form $\langle x, d, p \rangle$ for $p \neq p'$. Thus it was inherited from its parent. Note that the duplication of a buffer does not alter the order of the pending writes. This ensures that when an original write is at the head of the store buffer, then its duplicates will also be at the head of the store buffers of the respective threads that have inherited it.

The TSO Reachability Problem. We say that a TSO configuration γ is TSO_c-reachable if there are TSO configurations $\gamma_0, \ldots, \gamma_n$ such that $\gamma_{in} = \gamma_0 \rightarrow_{TSO_c} \gamma_1 \rightarrow_{TSO_c} \cdots \rightarrow_{TSO_c} \gamma_n = \gamma$, and denote it by $\gamma_{in} \xrightarrow{*}_{TSO_c} \gamma$. Given a state $q \in Q$, we say it is TSO_c-reachable if there is a configuration $\gamma = \langle \mathcal{P}, \mathcal{Q}, \mathcal{B}, \mathcal{M} \rangle$ such that $\gamma_{in} \xrightarrow{*}_{TSO_c} \gamma$ and there is a $p \in \mathcal{P}$ such that $\mathcal{Q}\,(p) = q$ and $\mathcal{B}\,(p') = \epsilon$ for all $p' \in \mathcal{P}$. We call the problem of checking whether a given state is TSO_c-reachable, the state TSO_c reachability problem.

4   Load-Buffer Semantics for TSO with Thread Creation

In this section, we propose a new variant of the load-buffer semantics presented in [4,5] for programs with thread creation. Then, we define its corresponding reachability problem. Finally, we show the equivalence between the *clone-create* semantics and the load buffer semantics in terms of the set of reachable states.

In the original model of load-buffer semantics, a load FIFO buffer is associated with each thread [4,5]. The sequence of messages inside a load buffer of a thread corresponds to the sequence of potential values that will be read by that thread. This means that the flow of information is now in the opposite direction (i.e., from the memory to threads). The write instructions take effect immediately in the shared memory while potential read values are propagated, in non-deterministic manner, from the memory to the thread through the load buffer. Any write instruction executed by a thread updates instantaneously the memory and is added to the tail of its load buffer. This newly added self-written value takes precedence over all other pending values in the load buffer on the same variable. To execute a read instruction, a thread first checks its load buffer for a self-written value on the same variable as the read, if such a self-written message exists then the thread reads the last propagated self-write; otherwise the thread reads the value at the head of the buffer if it is on the same variable.

There are three main challenges that we need to address in order to adapt the load-buffer semantics to programs with thread create. The first challenge is to find an equivalent rule to the `Create` one of Fig. 2. Surprisingly, we show that this rule can be simulated by duplicating the load buffer of the parent thread without the need of any kind of synchronisation (between the different load buffers) when removing a value from a load buffer (in contrast with the store buffer case). The second challenge is that the sequence of values in the load buffer of a thread corresponds to the sequence of values that will be potentially read by that thread. In the presence of duplication (due to thread creation), this means that the sequence of values should also match the sequence of values that will be read by all its descendants. To address this challenge, the load buffer will contain sequence of memory snapshots that will be added to all load buffers when a write instruction is performed. This memory snapshots can be read multiple times by a thread if they are at the head of its load buffer. The third challenge is related to the thread identifiers that are components of the messages in the store buffers. The set of thread identifiers can be unbounded (due to thread creation) and this poses many challenges when it comes to prove the decidability of the state reachability problem for programs running under the load-buffer semantics. We show that there is no need to keep thread identifiers as part of the messages in the load buffers and it is sufficient to replace them with a finite set of tags to identify the last memory snapshot due to the execution of a write instruction by the thread itself or by one of its ancestors. Finally, the tree-like dynamic structure required in the *clone-create* semantics is surprisingly not needed when defining the equivalent load-buffer semantics. This will be very useful in proving the decidability of the state reachability problem since coming up with a monotonic well-quasi ordering for tree-like structure is difficult.

In the rest of this section, we assume a finite set of shared variables $\mathbb{X}$ and a finite data domain $\mathbb{D}$ (with $0 \in \mathbb{D}$). We also assume that threads are defined by the following tuple $P = \langle Q, q^{init}, \Delta \rangle$.

Load-Buffer Configurations. A configuration γ in the load-buffer semantics (or simply an LB configuration) is a tuple of the form $\langle \mathcal{P}, \mathcal{Q}, \mathcal{B}, \mathcal{M} \rangle$ describing a set of threads and the states of the three parts of the load buffer architecture. We explain the elements of the tuple one by one.

As in the case of TSO configurations, $\mathcal{P}$ is the finite set of threads. The thread state mapping $\mathcal{Q} : \mathcal{P} \mapsto Q$ defined the local state of each thread $p \in \mathcal{P}$. The memory state $\mathcal{M} : \mathbb{X} \mapsto \mathbb{D}$ defines the value of each shared variable. There is an unbounded *load buffer*, (an *lbuffer*, for short), between each thread $p \in \mathcal{P}$ and the shared memory. The load buffer is a FIFO buffer, the tail of the buffer is to the right and the head to the left. We use this notation to indicate the direction in which the information travels i.e. from the memory to the threads. We refer to the lbuffer of p as the p-lbuffer. A message inside the p-lbuffer can be of one of two types, namely (i) a *self-read* message $\langle \text{srd}, \mathcal{N}, x \rangle$ corresponding to a memory snapshot $\mathcal{N} : \mathbb{X} \mapsto \mathbb{D}$ that was obtained by executing a write instruction on the variable x by the thread itself or one of its ancestors and inherited at creation, or (ii) an *other-read* message $\langle \text{ord}, \mathcal{N}, x \rangle$ corresponding to a memory snapshot that was obtained by executing a write instruction on the variable x by another thread. Our semantics maintains the invariant that the contents of the lbuffers are *lb-words*. An *lb-word* is a word $w \in (\{\text{ord}, \text{srd}\} \times [\mathbb{X} \to \mathbb{D}] \times \mathbb{X})^*$ s.t. for any variable $x \in \mathbb{X}$, there is at most one message of the form $\langle \text{srd}, \mathcal{N}, x \rangle$ in w.

We let Σ_L to denote the set of lb-words. The lbuffer state $\mathcal{B} : \mathcal{P} \to \Sigma_L^*$ defines the content of the p-lbuffer for each thread $p \in \mathcal{P}$. For a word $w \in \Sigma_L^*$, a variable $x \in \mathbb{X}$, and a memory snapshot $\mathcal{N} \in [\mathbb{X} \to \mathbb{D}]$, we define $w \odot \langle \text{srd}, \mathcal{N}, x \rangle :=$ $w' \cdot \langle \text{srd}, \mathcal{N}, x \rangle$, where $w' \in \Sigma_L^*$ is the word we get by replacing in w all messages of the form $\langle \text{srd}, \mathcal{N}', x \rangle$ by $\langle \text{ord}, \mathcal{N}', x \rangle$. We will later use this operation, to update the content of lbuffers. This is done by making all self-read messages on x in the buffer of a thread $p \in \mathcal{P}$ as other-read messages and adding a single self-read message on x with the memory snapshot $\mathcal{N}$ at the tail of the lbuffer. Observe that, by the above mentioned invariant, there will be at most one self-read message per variable in w.

An LB configuration $\beta_{in} = \langle \mathcal{P}^{init}, \mathcal{Q}^{init}, \mathcal{B}^{init}, \mathcal{M}^{init} \rangle$ is *initial* if and only if $\mathcal{P}^{init} = \{p_0\}$ is the unique initial thread, $\mathcal{Q}^{init}(p_0) = q^{init}$ (i.e., assigning the initial state q^{init} to the single initial thread), $\mathcal{M}^{init}(x) = 0$ for $x \in \mathbb{X}$ (i.e., assigning the initial value 0 to all the variables) and $\mathcal{B}^{init}(p_0) = \langle \text{ord}, \mathcal{M}^{init}, x \rangle$ is the initial content of the p_0-lbuffer. Let Γ denote the set of all LB configurations.

The Load-Buffer Transition Relation. The transition relation $\to_{TSO_{lb}}$ between two LB configurations is defined in Fig. 3. As in the case of the TSO semantics, any transition $\delta = \langle q, \text{instr}, q' \rangle$ performed by a thread p on a LB configuration $\gamma = \langle \mathcal{P}, \mathcal{Q}, \mathcal{B}, \mathcal{M} \rangle$ is enabled if and only if $\mathcal{Q}(p) = q$. The execution of the transition entails a state change along with possible change to other components of the configuration.

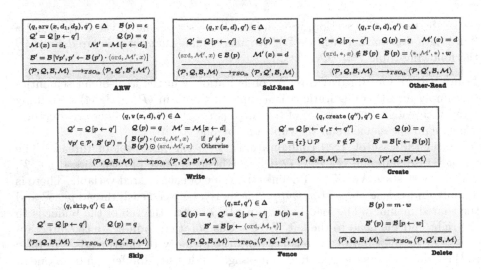

Fig. 3. The load-buffer semantics

If $\mathtt{instr} = \mathtt{w}\,(x,d)$ i.e. the instruction was a write, then the rule $\mathtt{Write}$ of Fig. 3 is used. In this case, the write instruction is applied to the main memory immediately and the resulting memory is appended to the tail of the load-buffer of all existing threads. For the thread that performed the operation, the memory snapshot is marked as a $\mathtt{srd}$ (self-read) to the variable x.

If $\mathtt{instr} = \mathtt{arw}\,(x, d_1, d_2)$ i.e. the instruction was an *atomic-read-write*, then the rule $\mathtt{ARW}$ is used. The rule requires that the load buffer $\mathcal{B}(p)$ of the executing thread p is empty and the current value for x in the main memory is d_1. On successful execution of the instruction, the value of x in the main memory is updated with d_2 and the resulting memory is appended to the tail of all the existing threads. We note that this is the only instance when the memory is directly read. While this can be easily eliminated, we use this to keep the semantics simple.

If $\mathtt{instr} = \mathtt{r}\,(x,d)$ i.e. the instruction was a *read*, then one of the rules $\mathtt{Self}\text{-}\mathtt{Read}$ or $\mathtt{Other}\text{-}\mathtt{Read}$ is used. In the case of a memory snapshot $\mathcal{M}'$ with a $\mathtt{srd}$ tag for the variable x is present in the buffer, then the rule $\mathtt{Self}\text{-}\mathtt{Read}$ is used. This rule is executed only if the value of the variable x in the memory snapshot $\mathcal{M}'$ is d. We note that the memory snapshot needs not be at the head of the load buffer for the instruction to be performed. The rule $\mathtt{Other}\text{-}\mathtt{read}$ is used when there is no memory snapshot with a $\mathtt{srd}$ tag for the variable x. In this case the transition is executed only if the value of the variable x in the memory snapshot $\mathcal{M}'$, that is at the head of the load buffer, is d. Both of these rules only affect the state component of the configuration.

In order to let the memory snapshots inside the p-lbuffer flow, we use the rule $\mathtt{Delete}$ to remove the memory snapshot at the head of the p-lbuffer, and thus give p the possibility of reading the next memory snapshot in the p-lbuffer.

If $\mathtt{instr} = \mathtt{create}$, then the rule $\mathtt{Create}$ is used. Here, the state of the executing thread is changed, a new thread is spawned and the load buffer of the new thread is initialised by copying the load buffer of its parent thread.

If $instr = skip$, then the rule Skip is used. In this case, only the state of the executing thread changes. If $instr = mf$, then the rule Fence is used. In this case, the transition is enabled only when the load buffer of the executing thread is empty. As a result of executing the transition, the current shared memory is copied to the load buffer. Note that we can replace the operation of copying the shared memory to the load buffer by requiring that the load buffer of the executing thread is of size 1. We only use this for the sake of simplicity.

The Load-Buffer Reachability Problem. We say that an LB configuration β is TSO_{lb}-reachable if there are $\beta_0, \ldots, \beta_n \in \Gamma$ such that $\beta_{in} = \beta_0 \rightarrow_{TSO_{lb}} \beta_1 \rightarrow_{TSO_{lb}} \cdots \rightarrow_{TSO_{lb}} \beta_n = \beta$, we denote it by $\beta_{in} \xrightarrow{*}_{TSO_{lb}} \beta$. Given a state $q \in Q$, we say it is TSO_{lb}-reachable if there is an LB configuration $\beta = \langle \mathcal{P}, \mathcal{Q}, \mathcal{B}, \mathcal{M} \rangle$ such that $\beta_{in} \xrightarrow{*}_{TSO_{lb}} \beta$ and there is a $p \in \mathcal{P}$ such that $\mathcal{Q}(p) = q$ and $\mathcal{B}(p') = \epsilon$ for all $p' \in \mathcal{P}$. We call the problem of checking whether a given state is TSO_{lb}-reachable, the state TSO_{lb} reachability problem.

Theorem 1. *Given a thread $P = \langle Q, q^{init}, \Delta \rangle$ and a state $q \in Q$, q is TSO_c-reachable if and only if it is TSO_{lb}-reachable.*

5   Well-Structured Transition Systems

In this section, we recall some basic concepts from the framework of well-structured transition systems [1,9,15] that we will use to show the decidability of the state reachability problem for programs under the load-buffer semantics. In particular, we introduce monotonic transition systems and furthermore describe a method for building new well quasi-orders from existing ones.

Monotonic Transition Systems. Fix a set A. A binary relation $\preceq \subseteq A \times A$ on A is a *quasi-order* (or simply an *ordering* if it is reflexive and transitive). We say that $\preceq$ is a *well quasi-order (wqo)* on A if (i) it is a quasi-order, and (ii) for any infinite sequence $a_0 a_1 a_2 \cdots$ of elements from A, there are $1 \leq i < j$ such that $a_i \preceq a_j$. Often, we call the pair $\langle A, \preceq \rangle$ a quasi-order (or a wqo), if $\preceq$ is a quasi-order (or a wqo) on A. A set $U \subseteq A$ is *upward closed* if for every $a \in U$ and $b \in A$ with $a \preceq b$, we have $b \in U$. The upward closure of a set $U \subseteq A$ is $U\uparrow = \{b \mid \exists a \in U, a \preceq b\}$. It is well-known that every upward closed set $U \subseteq A$ can be characterized by a finite set $M \subseteq U$ (called minor set of U) such that (i) $M\uparrow = U$ and (ii) if a and b are in M such that $a \preceq b$ then $a = b$. We use min to denote the function that returns the minor set of a given upward closed set U.

A *Monotonic Transition System (MTS)* is a tuple $\langle \Gamma, \Gamma^{init}, \preceq, \rightarrow \rangle$ where: (1) Γ is a (potentially infinite) set of *configurations*, (2) $\Gamma^{init} \subseteq \Gamma$ is the set of *initial configurations*, (3) $\preceq$ is a wqo on Γ, (4) $\preceq$ is computable, i.e., for each pair $\gamma_1, \gamma_2 \in \Gamma$, we can effectively check whether $\gamma_1 \preceq \gamma_2$, (5) $\rightarrow$ is a binary transition relation on Γ (we use $\gamma \rightarrow \gamma'$ to denote that $\langle \gamma, \gamma' \rangle \rightarrow$), and (6) the transition relation $\rightarrow$ is *monotone* wrt. $\preceq$, i.e., given configurations $\gamma_1, \gamma_2, \gamma_3 \in \Gamma$, where $\gamma_1 \rightarrow \gamma_2$ and $\gamma_1 \preceq \gamma_3$, there is a configuration $\gamma_4 \in \Gamma$ such that $\gamma_3 \xrightarrow{*} \gamma_4$ and $\gamma_2 \preceq \gamma_4$ where $\xrightarrow{*}$ to denote the reflexive transitive closure of $\rightarrow$.

For sets of configurations $G_1, G_2 \subseteq \Gamma$, we use $G_1 \xrightarrow{*} G_2$ to denote that there are $\gamma_1 \in G_1$ and $\gamma_2 \in G_2$ such that $\gamma_1 \xrightarrow{*} \gamma_2$. For a set $G \subseteq \Gamma$, we define $\mathtt{Pre}(G) := \{\gamma | \exists \gamma' \in G. \gamma \to \gamma'\}$, i.e., it is the set of configurations that can reach G through a single step of the transition relation. We define $\mathtt{Pre}^*(G) := \{\gamma | \exists \gamma' \in G. \gamma \xrightarrow{*} \gamma'\}$, i.e., it is the set of configurations that can reach G.

The reachability problem MTSREACH consists in checking whether, for a given an MTS $\langle \Gamma, \Gamma^{init}, \preceq, \to \rangle$ and an upward-closed set $U \subseteq \Gamma$, $\Gamma^{init} \xrightarrow{*} U$. The following theorem follows from [1,9,15].

Theorem 2. MTSREACH *is decidable if for each configuration* $\gamma \in \Gamma$: (1) *we can effectively check whether* $\gamma\!\uparrow \cap \Gamma^{init} \neq \emptyset$, *and* (2) *we can compute a finite set of configurations* A *such that* $\mathtt{Pre}(\gamma\!\uparrow) \subseteq A\!\uparrow\subseteq \mathtt{Pre}^*(\gamma\!\uparrow)$.

Deriving New Well Quasi-orders. Let $\langle A, \preceq \rangle$ be a quasi-order. We show how to extend $\preceq$ to tuples, multi-sets, and words. Consider k quasi-orders $\langle A_1, \preceq^{\textcircled{1}} \rangle, \ldots, \langle A_k, \preceq^{\textcircled{k}} \rangle$. Define the quasi-order $\preceq^{\otimes}$ on the Cartesian product $A_1 \times \cdots \times A_k$ such that, for tuples $a = \langle a_1, a_2, \ldots, a_k \rangle$ and $b = \langle b_1, b_2, \ldots, b_k \rangle$ we have that $a \preceq^{\textcircled{k}} b$ if $a_i \preceq^{\textcircled{\scriptsize$i$}} b_i$, for all $i : 1 \leq i \leq k$. We define the quasi-order $\langle A^{\circledast}, \preceq^{\textcircled{\circledast}} \rangle$, where $A^{\circledast}$ is the set of finite multisets over A as follows: If $M_1 = [a_1, \ldots, a_m]$ and $M_2 = [b_1, \ldots, b_n]$ are multisets over A, then we write $M_1 \preceq^{\textcircled{\circledast}} M_2$ to denote that there is an injection $g : \{1, \ldots, m\} \to \{1, \ldots, n\}$, such that $a_i \preceq b_{g(i)}$ for all $i : 1 \leq i \leq m$. Finally, we define the quasi-order $\langle A^*, \preceq^{\circledast} \rangle$, where A^* is the set of finite words over A as follows. Let $w_1, w_2 \in A^*$ be words over A whose lengths are $m = |w_1|$ and $n = |w_2|$ respectively. We write $w_1 \preceq^{\circledast} w_2$ to denote that there is an injection $f : \{1, \ldots, m\} \to \{1, \ldots, n\}$ such that $w_1(i) \preceq (w_2(f(i)))$, for all $i : 1 \leq i \leq m$. Notice that $\preceq^{\mathtt{word}} = (=)^{\circledast}$. The following theorem follows from the definition of wqos (see, e.g., [1].)

Theorem 3. 1. $\langle A, = \rangle$ *is a wqo if* A *is finite.*

2. *If* $\langle A_1, \preceq^{\textcircled{1}} \rangle, \ldots, \langle A_k, \preceq^{\textcircled{k}} \rangle$ *are wqos, then* $\langle A^1 \times \cdots \times A^k, \preceq^{\otimes} \rangle$ *is a wqo.*

3. *If* $\langle A, \preceq \rangle$ *is a wqo then* $\langle A^{\circledast}, \preceq^{\textcircled{\circledast}} \rangle$ *and* $\langle A^*, \preceq^{\circledast} \rangle$ *are wqos.*

4. *If* $\langle A, \preceq_1 \rangle$ *is a wqo and* $\preceq_1 \subseteq \preceq_2 \subseteq A \times A$ *then* $\langle A, \preceq_2 \rangle$ *is a wqo.*

6   The Decidability of the LB Reachability Problem

In this section, we show the decidability of the state TSO_{lb}-reachability problem.

Theorem 4. *The state* TSO_{lb}-*reachability problem is decidable.*

To prove the above theorem we instantiate the framework of Sect. 5. We show that $\langle \Gamma, \Gamma^{init}, \preceq^{\mathtt{conf}}, \to_{TSO_{lb}} \rangle$ is an MTS where Γ is the set of LB configurations, $\Gamma^{init} = \{\beta_{in}\}$ is the initial LB configuration, $\preceq^{\mathtt{conf}}$ is an wqo on the set of LB configurations such that it is computable, and the transition relation $\to_{TSO_{lb}}$ is monotone wrt. $\preceq^{\mathtt{conf}}$. Then, we show the two conditions for the decidability of the reachability problem MTSREACH (see Theorem 2). More precisely,

1. We first define the ordering $\preceq^{\mathrm{conf}}$ on LB configurations (see Lemma 1).
2. We show that, for a configuration $\gamma \in \Gamma$, we can compute a set A such that $\mathrm{Pre}\,(\gamma\!\uparrow) \subseteq A\!\uparrow\,\subseteq \mathrm{Pre}^*\,(\gamma\!\uparrow)$ (see Lemma 2). Hence, the second sufficient condition of Theorem 2 is satisfied.
3. We prove the monotonicity of $\to_{TSO_{lb}}$ wrt. $\preceq^{\mathrm{conf}}$ (see Lemma 3).
4. We then show the first sufficient condition of Theorem 2 and the effectiveness of $\preceq^{\mathrm{conf}}$, i.e., for each pair $\gamma_1, \gamma_2 \in \Gamma$ of configurations, we can effectively check whether $\gamma_1 \preceq^{\mathrm{conf}} \gamma_2$.
5. Finally, we show that the TSO_{lb}-reachability problem can be reduced to the reachability problem MTSREACH (see Lemma 4).

Thus, we can apply Theorem 2 to conclude the decidability of the TSO_{lb}-reachability problem. As a corollary of Theorem 1 and Theorem 2, we get:

Corollary 1. *The state TSO_c reachability problem is decidable.*

Ordering. Let Γ be the set of LB configurations and Γ^{init} the initial LB configurations. In the following, we define an ordering on the set Γ. In the rest of the paragraph, we fix two configurations $\gamma = \langle \mathcal{P}, \mathcal{Q}, \mathcal{B}, \mathcal{M} \rangle$ and $\gamma' = \langle \mathcal{P}', \mathcal{Q}', \mathcal{B}', \mathcal{M}' \rangle$.

First, we define an ordering $\preceq^{\mathrm{proc}}$ on the set of thread states. Let $h : \mathcal{P} \to \mathcal{P}'$ be an injection. In other words, h identifies, for each thread p in γ, a unique image $h\,(p)$ in γ'. We write $\mathcal{Q} \preceq^{\mathrm{proc}}_h \mathcal{Q}'$ to denote that $\mathcal{Q}\,(p) = \mathcal{Q}'\,(h\,(p))$ for every $p \in \mathcal{P}$, i.e., each thread has a state that is identical to the state of its h-image. Notice that the existence of h means that γ' contains at least as many threads as γ (and in general, more threads than γ).

We define an ordering $\preceq^{\mathrm{LB}}$ on the set of lbuffer states. To that end, we use an operation that divides an lb-word to different fragments. We define the set of pivot messages to be the set $\{\langle \mathrm{srd}, \mathcal{N}, x\rangle |\ (x \in \mathbb{X}) \wedge (\mathcal{N} \in [\mathbb{X} \to \mathbb{D}])\}$, i.e., it is the set of all self-read messages. Consider an lb-word $w \in \Sigma^*_{\mathrm{L}}$ we define the *fragmentation* $\mathrm{frag}\,(w)$ of w to be the unique sequence of words $[w_0][v_1][w_2][v_2] \cdots [w_{n-1}][v_n][w_n]$, satisfying the two conditions below. We put the brackets to increase readability; they are not semantically significant. We call $w_0, w_1, \ldots, w_n$ the *fragments*, and call $v_1, v_2, \ldots, v_n$ the *pivot elements*.

- $w_i \in (\{\mathrm{ord}\} \times [\mathbb{X} \to \mathbb{D}] \times \mathbb{X})^*$, for $i : 0 \le i \le n$, i.e., each fragment is a word of other-read messages.
- $v_i \in (\{\mathrm{srd}\} \times [\mathbb{X} \to \mathbb{D}] \times \mathbb{X})$, for $i : 1 \le i \le n$, i.e., each pivot element is a self-read message.

This means that we fragment w around the pivot elements, and the fragments are sequences of other-read messages that occur between the pivot elements. By the definition of lb-words, it follows that the pivot elements in w are all mutually different (i.e., at most one per variable), and hence the number of pivot elements in w is bounded by $|\mathbb{X}|$. This also means that the number of fragments in w is bounded by $|\mathbb{X}| + 1$. However, there is no bound on the length of a fragment.

We define an ordering $\preceq^{\mathrm{LB}}$ on the set of lb-words such that for words w and w' we have $w \preceq^{\mathrm{LB}} w'$ if w and w' agree on the sequence of pivot elements, and each fragment in w is a sub-word (in the sense of $\preceq^{\text{word}}$) of the corresponding fragment in w'. More precisely, let the fragmentations of w and w' be $[w_0][v_1][w_1][v_2] \cdots [w_{n-1}][v_n][w_n]$ and $[w'_0][v'_1][w'_1][v'_2] \cdots [w'_{n-1}][v'_n][w'_{n'}]$ respectively. We write $w \preceq^{\text{LB}} w'$ if (1) $n = n'$ and $v_i = v'_i$ for all $i : 1 \leq i \leq n$, (2) $w_i \preceq^{\text{word}} w'_i$ for all $i : 1 \leq i \leq n = n'$.

We extend the ordering $\preceq^{\text{LB}}$ to lbuffer states. For $\mathcal{B} : \mathcal{P} \to \Sigma_{\text{L}}^*$ and $\mathcal{B}' : \mathcal{P}' \to \Sigma_{\text{L}}^*$, and an injection $h : \mathcal{P} \to \mathcal{P}'$, we write $\mathcal{B} \preceq^{\text{LB}}_h \mathcal{B}'$ to denote that $\mathcal{B}(p) \preceq^{\text{LB}} \mathcal{B}'(h(p))$ for all $p \in \mathcal{P}$, i.e., the content of each buffer of a thread p in $\mathcal{B}$ is smaller, wrt. $\preceq^{\text{LB}}$, than the content of the buffer of the h-image of p in $\mathcal{B}'$.

For an injection $h : \mathcal{P} \to \mathcal{P}'$, we write $\gamma \preceq_h \gamma'$ to denote that the following conditions are satisfied: (i) $\mathcal{Q} \preceq^{\text{proc}}_h \mathcal{Q}'$: each thread p in γ has the same state as its image in γ', (ii) $\mathcal{B} \preceq^{\text{LB}}_h \mathcal{B}'$: the content of each p-lbuffer in γ is smaller wrt. $\preceq^{\text{LB}}$ than the content of the $h(p)$-lbuffer in γ', and (iii) $\mathcal{M} = \mathcal{M}'$: the memories have the same contents. We write $\gamma \preceq^{\text{conf}} \gamma'$ to denote that $\gamma \preceq_h \gamma'$ for some h.

Lemma 1. *The ordering $\preceq^{\text{conf}}$ is a wqo on the set of LB configurations Γ.*

The proof of the above lemma can be done in three steps. First, we need to prove that $\preceq^{\text{LB}}$ is a wqo. Then, we need to extend this wqo ordering to pairs consisting of a state $q \in Q$ and lb-word $w \in \Sigma_{\text{L}}^*$. Finally, we encode each LB configuration as a multiset over pairs of states and lb-words and use Theorem 3 and the fact that $\preceq^{\text{LB}}$ is a wqo over such pairs, to show that $\preceq^{\text{conf}}$ is a wqo.

Predecessors. In the following, we show the following result:

Lemma 2. *Given a configuration $\gamma \in \Gamma$, we show that we can compute a set A such that $\text{Pre}(\gamma\uparrow) \subseteq A\uparrow \subseteq \text{Pre}^*(\gamma\uparrow)$.*

We now explain how to compute the set A. We do this by systematically going through the inference rules (of Fig. 3) that define the transition relation $\to_{TSO_{lb}}$. Each rule contributes a finite (possibly empty) set of elements to A. We give a subset of computation rules $A_w \subseteq A$ in Fig. 4.

We explain hereafter the rules Write(1), Write(2) and Write(3). Let $\gamma = \langle \mathcal{P}, \mathcal{Q}, \mathcal{B}, \mathcal{M} \rangle$ and $\tau = \langle q', \text{w}(x, d), q \rangle \in \Delta$ be a write transition. Let A_w be the set of LB configurations computed by applying to γ the rules Write(1), Write(2) and Write(3) in Fig. 4. It is easy to see that this set is finite. In the case of Write(1) and Write(2), there is one rule per memory value of x. In the

Fig. 4. The rules to compute A_w

case of Write(3), there is one rule for each memory value, minimal *lb-word* pair. Hence A_w is the union of finite sets.

To compute the set A_w, we try to execute the write transition τ in a backward manner. We have two cases to consider, one when the executing thread is in γ (Write(1) and Write(2)), the other when it is not (Write(3)).

In the case of former, let p be the thread that executed the transition. Then the state of p in any configuration in A_w is q' and the states of the other threads remain unchanged. We will also set the memory state of the configurations in A_w such that the values of any variable different from x remains unchanged. However, the value of the variable x in a configuration of A_w can be set to any value. We need to remove the self-read message from the end of the lbuffer of the thread p executing the instruction. By removing it three cases arise: (1) there is no self-read message in the predecessor configuration γ, (2) there is a self-read message in the predecessor configuration which has no corresponding other-read message in γ (both handled by Write(1) rule) and (3) there is a self-read message in the predecessor configuration which got replaced by an other-read message in γ (Write(2) rule). Further, we also need to remove the other-read message of this write, from the end of the lbuffers of the other threads. We simply delete it from any configuration of A_w, if it exists.

In the case when the executing thread is not part of γ, the thread that executed the transition p is added to the existing set of threads. Its state is initialised with q' and lbuffer is initialised to a valid lbword, minimal wrt. $\preceq^{LB}$ ordering. Finally, we remove the other-read message of this write transition, from the end of the lbuffers of all the other threads.

Let $\mathtt{Pre}\,(\gamma\uparrow)$ be the set of LB configurations that can reach $\gamma\uparrow$ through the execution of the transition τ. Then, we show that $\mathtt{Pre}\,(\gamma\uparrow) \subseteq A\uparrow$. The result that $A\uparrow \subseteq \mathtt{Pre}^*\,(\gamma\uparrow)$ follows immediately from $A \subseteq \mathtt{Pre}\,(\gamma\uparrow)$ and the monotonicity lemma (see Lemma 3).

Monotonicity. In the following, we show that the transition relation $\rightarrow_{TSO_{lb}}$ is *monotone* wrt. $\preceq^{conf}$.

Lemma 3. *Given LB configurations* $\gamma_1, \gamma_2, \gamma_3 \in \Gamma$, *where* $\gamma_1 \rightarrow_{TSO_{lb}} \gamma_2$ *and* $\gamma_1 \preceq^{conf} \gamma_3$, *there is a configuration* $\gamma_4 \in \Gamma$ *s.t.* $\gamma_3 \xrightarrow{*}_{TSO_{lb}} \gamma_4$ *and* $\gamma_2 \preceq^{conf} \gamma_4$.

Consider configurations $\gamma_1 = \langle \mathcal{P}_1, \mathcal{Q}_1, \mathcal{B}_1, \mathcal{M}_1 \rangle$, $\gamma_2 = \langle \mathcal{P}_2, \mathcal{Q}_2, \mathcal{B}_2, \mathcal{M}_2 \rangle$, and $\gamma_3 = \langle \mathcal{P}_3, \mathcal{Q}_3, \mathcal{B}_3, \mathcal{M}_3 \rangle$, such that $\gamma_1 \rightarrow_{TSO_{lb}} \gamma_2$ and $\gamma_1 \preceq_{h_1} \gamma_3$ for some h_1. We derive a configuration $\gamma_4 = \langle \mathcal{P}_4, \mathcal{Q}_4, \mathcal{B}_4, \mathcal{M}_4 \rangle$ and an injection h_2 such that $\gamma_3 \xrightarrow{*}_{TSO_{lb}} \gamma_4$ and $\gamma_2 \preceq_{h_2} \gamma_4$. We consider different cases depending on the inference rule used to obtain γ_2 from γ_1. In the following we construct γ_4 and h_2 for the rule write.

Assume that $\gamma_1 \rightarrow_{TSO_{lb}} \gamma_2$ is the effect of the execution of a transition $\delta = \langle q, \mathtt{w}\,(x, d), q' \rangle$ performed by a thread $p \in \mathcal{P}_1$. Define $\mathcal{P}_4 := \mathcal{P}_3$, $\mathcal{Q}_4 := \mathcal{Q}_3\,[h_1\,(p) \leftarrow q']$, $\mathcal{B}_4(h_1\,(p)) = \mathcal{B}_3(h_1\,(p)) \odot \langle \mathtt{srd}, \mathcal{M}_2, x \rangle$, $\mathcal{B}_4(p') = \mathcal{B}_3(p') \cdot \langle \mathtt{ord}, \mathcal{M}_2, x \rangle$ for all $p' \in \mathcal{P}_3 \backslash \{p\}$, $\mathcal{M}_4 := \mathcal{M}_2 = \mathcal{M}_3\,[x \leftarrow d]$. Define $h_2 := h_1$.

Computability of $\preceq^{conf}$. Checking $\preceq^{conf}$ amounts to comparing tuples, multisets, and words so it is trivially computable. The same applies when it comes to checking whether $\gamma\uparrow \cap \Gamma^{init}$ is not empty since this problem is equivalent to checking whether $\beta_{in} \in \gamma\uparrow$ (i.e. $\gamma \preceq^{conf} \beta_{in}$) since $\Gamma^{init} = \{\beta_{in}\}$.

From the LB Reachability Problem to the MtsReach Problem.

Lemma 4. *The state TSO_{lb} reachability problem can be reduced to the reachability problem MtsReach.*

Let us assume a state $q \in Q$. The TSO_{lb}-reachability of q is equivalent to the reachability of the upward closed set U defined as the finite union of the upward closed sets $\gamma\uparrow$ where γ is defined as follows $\langle\{r\}, Q, B, M\rangle$ where $Q(r) = q$ and $B(r) = \epsilon$. Observe that we have one such LB configuration γ for each possible memory state. Let us show the equivalence between the two reachability problems. Suppose first that q is TSO_{lb}-reachable. This means that there is an LB configuration $\beta = \langle P', Q', B', M'\rangle$ such that $\beta_{in} \xrightarrow{*}_{TSO_{lb}} \beta$ and there is a thread $p \in P'$ such that $Q'(p) = q$ and $B'(p') = \epsilon$ for all $p' \in P$. Then, it is easy to see that, by choosing $M = M'$ for γ, we have $\gamma \preceq_h \beta$ with $h(r) = p$. Hence, $\beta \in U$ and therefore U is reachable.

Suppose now that a larger configuration γ' than γ is TSO_{lb}-reachable. Then, we can simply perform a sequence of delete transitions to empty all the lbuffers in order to reach a configuration γ'' (which is larger than γ) but with empty lbuffers. It is easy to see that there is a thread p' (the matching of p) in γ'' that is in the state q (since $\gamma \preceq^{conf} \gamma''$). Hence, the state q is TSO_{lb}-reachable.

7   Conclusion

We have investigated for the first time the reachability problem of concurrent programs with dynamic thread creation running under a weak memory model. An important issue in this case is maintaining causality precedence between threads and their descendants. This issue is not present in the case of static programs where the number of threads can be arbitrarily large but never changes during execution. Dealing with this issue requires nontrivial semantical and algorithmic developments. We prove indeed that in the case of a causality-aware TSO model the reachability problem for programs with unbounded dynamic thread creation is decidable through the introduction of an equivalent dual semantics based on load buffers. More precisely, we prove that this dual semantics is equivalent to the original one (w.r.t. state reachability) and has the desired properties for proving well-structuredness.

For future work, we will consider the reachability problem under other models that are stronger, and more common in existing implementations of the semantics of multithreading under weak memory models. For instance, one simple way to enforce causality is to flush systematically the buffer of a thread right before thread creation it performs.

References

1. Abdulla, P.A.: Well (and better) quasi-ordered transition systems. Bull. Symb. Log. **16**(4), 457–515 (2010). https://doi.org/10.2178/bsl/1294171129
2. Abdulla, P.A., Arora, J., Atig, M.F., Krishna, S.N.: Verification of programs under the release-acquire semantics. In: McKinley, K.S., Fisher, K. (eds.) Proceedings of the 40th ACM SIGPLAN Conference on Programming Language Design and Implementation, PLDI 2019, Phoenix, AZ, USA, 22–26 June 2019, pp. 1117–1132. ACM (2019). https://doi.org/10.1145/3314221.3314649
3. Abdulla, P.A., Atig, M.F., Bouajjani, A., Derevenetc, E., Leonardsson, C., Meyer, R.: On the state reachability problem for concurrent programs under power. In: Georgiou, C., Majumdar, R. (eds.) NETYS 2020. LNCS, vol. 12129, pp. 47–59. Springer, Cham (2021). https://doi.org/10.1007/978-3-030-67087-0_4
4. Abdulla, P.A., Atig, M.F., Bouajjani, A., Ngo, T.P.: The benefits of duality in verifying concurrent programs under TSO. In: Desharnais, J., Jagadeesan, R. (eds.) 27th International Conference on Concurrency Theory, CONCUR 2016. LIPIcs, Québec City, Canada, 23–26 August 2016, vol. 59, pp. 5:1–5:15. Schloss Dagstuhl - Leibniz-Zentrum für Informatik (2016). https://doi.org/10. 4230/LIPIcs.CONCUR.2016.5
5. Abdulla, P.A., Atig, M.F., Bouajjani, A., Ngo, T.P.: A load-buffer semantics for total store ordering. Log. Methods Comput. Sci. **14**(1) (2018). https://doi.org/10. 23638/LMCS-14(1:9)2018
6. Abdulla, P.A., Atig, M.F., Godbole, A., Krishna, S., Vafeiadis, V.: The decidability of verification under PS 2.0. In: Yoshida, N. (ed.) ESOP 2021. LNCS, vol. 12648, pp. 1–29. Springer, Cham (2021). https://doi.org/10.1007/978-3-030-72019-3_1
7. Abdulla, P.A., Atig, M.F., Lång, M., Ngo, T.P.: Precise and sound automatic fence insertion procedure under PSO. In: Bouajjani, A., Fauconnier, H. (eds.) NETYS 2015. LNCS, vol. 9466, pp. 32–47. Springer, Cham (2015). https://doi.org/10.1007/ 978-3-319-26850-7_3
8. Abdulla, P.A., Atig, M.F., Rezvan, R.: Parameterized verification under TSO is PSPACE-complete. Proc. ACM Program. Lang. **4**(POPL), 26:1–26:29 (2020). https://doi.org/10.1145/3371094
9. Abdulla, P.A., Cerans, K., Jonsson, B., Tsay, Y.: General decidability theorems for infinite-state systems. In: Proceedings 11th Annual IEEE Symposium on Logic in Computer Science, New Brunswick, New Jersey, USA, 27–30 July 1996, pp. 313–321. IEEE Computer Society (1996). https://doi.org/10.1109/LICS.1996.561359
10. Adve, S.V., Hill, M.D.: Weak ordering - a new definition. In: Sohi, G.S. (ed.) 25 Years of the International Symposia on Computer Architecture (Selected Papers), pp. 363–375. ACM (1998). https://doi.org/10.1145/285930.285996
11. Atig, M.F., Bouajjani, A., Burckhardt, S., Musuvathi, M.: On the verification problem for weak memory models. In: Hermenegildo, M.V., Palsberg, J. (eds.) Proceedings of the 37th ACM SIGPLAN-SIGACT Symposium on Principles of Programming Languages, POPL 2010, Madrid, Spain, 17–23 January 2010, pp. 7–18. ACM (2010). https://doi.org/10.1145/1706299.1706303
12. Atig, M.F., Bouajjani, A., Burckhardt, S., Musuvathi, M.: What's decidable about weak memory models? In: Seidl, H. (ed.) ESOP 2012. LNCS, vol. 7211, pp. 26–46. Springer, Heidelberg (2012). https://doi.org/10.1007/978-3-642-28869-2_2

13. Batty, M., Owens, S., Sarkar, S., Sewell, P., Weber, T.: Mathematizing C++ concurrency. In: Ball, T., Sagiv, M. (eds.) Proceedings of the 38th ACM SIGPLAN-SIGACT Symposium on Principles of Programming Languages, POPL 2011, Austin, TX, USA, 26–28 January 2011, pp. 55–66. ACM (2011). https://doi.org/10.1145/1926385.1926394

14. Boudol, G., Petri, G.: Relaxed memory models: an operational approach. In: Shao, Z., Pierce, B.C. (eds.) Proceedings of the 36th ACM SIGPLAN-SIGACT Symposium on Principles of Programming Languages, POPL 2009, Savannah, GA, USA, 21–23 January 2009, pp. 392–403. ACM (2009). https://doi.org/10.1145/1480881.1480930

15. Finkel, A., Schnoebelen, P.: Well-structured transition systems everywhere! Theor. Comput. Sci. **256**(1–2), 63–92 (2001). https://doi.org/10.1016/S0304-3975(00)00102-X

16. Kaiser, J., Dang, H., Dreyer, D., Lahav, O., Vafeiadis, V.: Strong logic for weak memory: reasoning about release-acquire consistency in iris. In: Müller, P. (ed.) 31st European Conference on Object-Oriented Programming, ECOOP 2017. LIPIcs, Barcelona, Spain, 19–23 June 2017, vol. 74, pp. 17:1–17:29. Schloss Dagstuhl - Leibniz-Zentrum für Informatik (2017). https://doi.org/10.4230/LIPIcs.ECOOP.2017.17

17. Lahav, O., Boker, U.: Decidable verification under a causally consistent shared memory. In: Donaldson, A.F., Torlak, E. (eds.) Proceedings of the 41st ACM SIGPLAN International Conference on Programming Language Design and Implementation, PLDI 2020, London, UK, 15–20 June 2020, pp. 211–226. ACM (2020). https://doi.org/10.1145/3385412.3385966

18. Liu, F., Nedev, N., Prisadnikov, N., Vechev, M.T., Yahav, E.: Dynamic synthesis for relaxed memory models. In: Vitek, J., Lin, H., Tip, F. (eds.) ACM SIGPLAN Conference on Programming Language Design and Implementation, PLDI 2012, Beijing, China, 11–16 June 2012, pp. 429–440. ACM (2012). https://doi.org/10.1145/2254064.2254115

19. Manson, J., Pugh, W., Adve, S.V.: The Java memory model. In: Palsberg, J., Abadi, M. (eds.) Proceedings of the 32nd ACM SIGPLAN-SIGACT Symposium on Principles of Programming Languages, POPL 2005, Long Beach, California, USA, 12–14 January 2005, pp. 378–391. ACM (2005). https://doi.org/10.1145/1040305.1040336

20. Owens, S., Sarkar, S., Sewell, P.: A better x86 memory model: x86-TSO. In: Berghofer, S., Nipkow, T., Urban, C., Wenzel, M. (eds.) TPHOLs 2009. LNCS, vol. 5674, pp. 391–407. Springer, Heidelberg (2009). https://doi.org/10.1007/978-3-642-03359-9_27

21. Sewell, P., Sarkar, S., Owens, S., Nardelli, F.Z., Myreen, M.O.: x86-TSO: a rigorous and usable programmer's model for x86 multiprocessors. Commun. ACM **53**(7), 89–97 (2010). https://doi.org/10.1145/1785414.1785443

Security

Chromatic and Spatial Analysis of One-Pixel Attacks Against an Image Classifier

Janne Alatalo$^{(\boxtimes)}$ (iD), Joni Korpihalkola (iD), Tuomo Sipola (iD), and Tero Kokkonen (iD)

Institute of Information Technology, JAMK University of Applied Sciences, Jyväskylä, Finland

{janne.alatalo,joni.korpihalkola,tuomo.sipola,tero.kokkonen}@jamk.fi

Abstract. One-pixel attack is a curious way of deceiving neural network classifier by changing only one pixel in the input image. The full potential and boundaries of this attack method are not yet fully understood. In this research, the successful and unsuccessful attacks are studied in more detail to illustrate the working mechanisms of a one-pixel attack created using differential evolution. The data comes from our earlier studies where we applied the attack against medical imaging. We used a real breast cancer tissue dataset and a real classifier as the attack target. This research presents ways to analyze chromatic and spatial distributions of one-pixel attacks. In addition, we present one-pixel attack confidence maps to illustrate the behavior of the target classifier. We show that the more effective attacks change the color of the pixel more, and that the successful attacks are situated at the center of the images. This kind of analysis is not only useful for understanding the behavior of the attack but also the qualities of the classifying neural network.

Keywords: One-pixel attack · Classification · Perturbation methods · Visualization · Cybersecurity

1 Introduction

The use of Artificial Intelligence (AI), including sub-branches Machine learning (ML) and Deep Learning (DL), is continuously increasing as support for decision making in automated image analysis of medical imaging [6, 20]. One enabler for such evolution is that there is the abundance of available data for research and development activities in the medical domain [11]. However, from the cyber security standpoint, this evolution fosters attack surface, and it should be realized that new technologies attract malicious actors and especially medical domain can be seen as a valuable target to gain profit by causing disruptions. It is noticeable that most of the medical data has sensitive nature. For example, Europol has announced that during the ongoing COVID-19 pandemic, the pandemic-themed

M.-A. Koulali and M. Mezini (Eds.): NETYS 2022, LNCS 13464, pp. 303–316, 2022.
https://doi.org/10.1007/978-3-031-17436-0_20

cybercrime activities and campaigns are also targeted to healthcare organizations. [15]. Newaz et al. propose an adversarial attack against ML enabled smart healthcare system [9]. Attacks against new technologies might induce harmful effects: considerable time to recover, mistrust against AI-based models and even fear of misdiagnosis. It is noticeable that Internet of Things (IoT) devices have a remarkable role in the healthcare [2] and there are known security issues with IoT. Several AI models are in risk for adversarial attacks [19] Liu et al. introduce and summarize the DL associated attack and defense methods [7], while Qayyum et al. [10] introduce methods to warrant secure ML for healthcare. Integrity and unauthorized usage of medical image data is important when considering attacks against AI based medical imaging. In that sense, Kamal et al. proposed image encryption algorithm for securing medical image data [3].

One-pixel attack is an adversarial method that changes just one pixel in an image to cause misclassification. The attack is created by using optimization to find the best pixel that flips the classification decisiton made by a classifier [14]. However, its sensitivity to change and effectiveness are not fully understood. A few methods have been proposed to visualize the effect of one-pixel attacks. Wang et al. propose pixel adversarial maps and probability adversarial maps [18]. Vargas et al. go further, and use internal information from the neural network model to create propagation maps to show the influence of one-pixel attacks through convolution layers [16].

In this study, we provide tools to understand the behavior of a neural network classifier targeted by the one-pixel attack. Our present analysis is a natural extension to our prior studies related to the attack method. Earlier, we have introduced a list of methods to fool artificial neural networks used in medical imaging [13]. One-pixel attack appeared to be a comprehensive and realistic attack vector, so we decided to further investigate it as a conceptual framework in the medical imaging domain [12]. When the concept and usability of the attack were understood, we succeeded to implement the technical one-pixel attack against real neural network models used in medical imaging [5]. That first technical attack was a success, but the pixel changes in the images were quite easily observable by a human. It seemed that the attack was not realistic or comprehensive for real-world attackers, so we decided to further develop the attack methodology [4].

The new tools we propose somewhat differ from the earlier studies. All the methods complement each other when investigating the classification effects of one-pixel changes to images. While the other methods are useful when trying to understand the internal state of the classifier (such as Vargas et al. [16]) or mapping attacks against each pixel (such as Wang et al. [18]), our confidence map approach directly addresses the classification result. Wang et al. use *successful attacks generated for each pixel* as a base for their maps [18]. Our periodicity analysis here concerns *successful attack locations of each image* that have been generated earlier. Furthermore, our confidence map analysis iterates over the color space to saturate each pixel in a brute force manner, as we do not use optimization to find attack pixels during the analysis.

The rest of the paper is organized as follows. First, data source and analysis methods, including confidence map computation, are introduced in Sect. 2. Results of chromatic, spatial and periodicity analysis are presented in Sect. 3 with tables and figures. Finally, the study is concluded with final discussion and future research topics in Sect. 4.

2 Methods

2.1 Data Source

In our previous publications we introduced how an artificial neural network image classifier model could be fooled by changing only one pixel in the input image [4,5]. Those studies targeted IBM CODAIT MAX breast cancer detector which uses a modified ResNet-50 model [1]. The model is an open-source convolutional neural network classifier predicting the probability that the input image contains mitosis. The previous studies used a pretrained version of the model that was trained using the TUPAC16 breast cancer dataset [8,17]. We use the same model in this research.

The study used the one-pixel attack to find adversarial images that would make the model predict wrong results for the input images [14]. This method uses differential evolution optimization, where a population of breast cancer images is attacked by randomly choosing one pixel and randomly changing the pixel's colors to new values. The color values are mutated until the lowest confidence score is achieved for the breast cancer image. The method efficiently finds possible one-pixel changes to the image that changes the prediction outcome.

The targeted model can be fooled in two ways. If the model predicts strong probability of mitosis for the input image, then the one-pixel attack is used to find the pixel that lowers the predicted mitosis probability when the pixel color is changed (*mitosis-to-normal*). The other way to fool the model is to try to increase the predicted mitosis probability when the model predicts low mitosis confidence score for some input image (*normal-to-mitosis*). The study explored both possible cases of fooling the model. The study concluded that both *mitosis-to-normal* and *normal-to-mitosis* attacks are possible, but of those two, *mitosis-to-normal* attacks are considerably easier to carry out.

The dataset used in this study contains the one-pixel attack results from the previous study [5], and information of the attacked image, such as the attack pixel's location in the image and the nearby neighboring pixels' color values of the attacked pixel. We were interested in studying attacks that were at least partially successful. We considered *normal-to-mitosis* attacks that raise the confidence score above 0.1 and *mitosis-to-normal* attacks that lowered the confidence score below 0.9 to be potentially dangerous attacks, and included all of them to our visualizations. Using these filters, 3,871 *mitosis-to-normal* attacks and 319 *normal-to-mitosis* attacks were used as a visualization dataset. Although not all attacks in this dataset were successful in flipping the classification result to other class, we consider them to be successful because they change the confidence score perceptually enough that the result is no longer trustworthy.

2.2 One-Pixel Attack Confidence Map Computation

In addition to analyzing the results from our previous paper, we also carried out additional tests for some of the dataset images by brute forcing a subset of all possible attack vectors for the images, producing a one-pixel attack confidence map. This gave us a clearer view how the successful attack vectors were positioned in individual images. The brute force computation was conducted on a few handpicked images that were chosen based on our previous paper results in a way that we had successful and failed examples of both *mitosis-to-normal* and *normal-to-mitosis* attack types.

This research used color images, hence each pixel has three color channels and the color value for each channel has a value between $0 - 255$. This means that the total number of possible colors for a single pixel is $16,777,216$. The images were 64×64 pixels in size, so the total number of all possible attack vectors is $68,719,476,736$ for a single image. We concluded that computing all possible vectors for the images is not worthwhile; therefore, we settled on a subset of all possible attack colors. The selected set of colors C (1) was generated by taking every fifth color value for each channel and taking all their color combinations. In the equation, r, g and b are the red, green, and blue color channels:

$$C = \{(r, g, b) \mid r, g, b \in \{0, 5, 15 \ldots 255\}\}. \tag{1}$$

Even when the brute forced colors were reduced to the set C, there was still $140,608$ different colors for a single pixel, meaning that the total number of attack vectors for a single image was still $575,930,368$. With that many images we could not use the Docker containerized version of the model that was used in our previous study over the HTTP API, because the containerized version of the model does not support GPU computation or image batching. We overcame this problem by deploying the model to our computation server without the containerization layer and implementing a highly efficient GPU accelerated data-pipeline that implemented the one-pixel modifications on GPU without needing to continuously copy the images between CPU and GPU memory. With this setup computing the $575,930,368$ attack vectors for one image took about 5 h on our computation server using one Nvidia Tesla V100 GPU.

The results of the brute force attack vector analysis were reduced to minimum, maximum and average score values for each pixel coordinate.

Let $I_{x,y}$ be the set of all modified images where pixel coordinate (x, y) value is replaced with color value $c \in C$ in the image under brute force computation. Let f be the model that predicts the score for the images. The results of the brute force attacks were processed with method described in Eq. 2 and Algorithm 1.

$$s_{max}(x, y) = \max(\{f(i) \mid i \in I_{x,y}\})$$
$$s_{min}(x, y) = \min(\{f(i) \mid i \in I_{x,y}\}) \tag{2}$$
$$s_{avg}(x, y) = \text{avg}(\{f(i) \mid i \in I_{x,y}\})$$

Algorithm 1. Brute force results processing algorithm

$maxscores \leftarrow$ ARRAY[64][64]
$minscores \leftarrow$ ARRAY[64][64]
$avgscores \leftarrow$ ARRAY[64][64]
for $x \leftarrow 0$ to 63 **do**
    for $y \leftarrow 0$ to 63 **do**
        $maxscores[x][y] \leftarrow s_{max}(x, y)$
        $minscores[x][y] \leftarrow s_{min}(x, y)$
        $avgscores[x][y] \leftarrow s_{avg}(x, y)$
    end for
end for

---

3   Results

3.1   Chromatic and Spatial Analysis

The difference between color values of two different pixels was measured by root mean square error (RMSE).

$$h(\mathbf{x}) = \sqrt{\frac{(c_r - c_{r\mu})^2 + (c_g - c_{g\mu})^2 + (c_b - c_{b\mu})^2}{3}},$$

where c_r, c_b, c_g are the color values of the attack vector and $c_{r\mu}$, $c_{g\mu}$, $c_{b\mu}$ are the means of the attack vector's surrounding pixels' color values. All values were scaled within the range $[0, 1]$.

When the attacks managed to fool the neural network, the error function values were high in *mitosis-to-normal* attacks, as can be observed from Fig. 1, which shows one vertical and one horizontal cluster. This indicates that the attacks which managed to lower confidence score the most had pixel color values noticeably different from the surrounding colors. The positioning of the attack pixel also matters, since some attacks had a higher color difference between neighboring pixels and still did not manage to lower the confidence score by more than 0.2.

In *normal-to-mitosis* attacks the error values were lower than in *mitosis-to-normal* attack, as can be seen in Fig. 2, which shows no clusters; instead, the dots are more evenly distributed between the lower X axis values.

Mean, median and standard deviation numerical measures were calculated for the attacks. In the Table 1, the X and Y mean and median indicate that the attacks were mostly located at the center of the 64 by 64 pixels images. Meanwhile, the color values of red and green were near the maximum value of 255, while blue values were lower with higher standard deviation compared to red and green.

In normal images, the statistical measures listed in Table 2 show that the attack vector is mostly again located at the center of the image, while there is much greater variation in red, green and blue color values, with a standard deviation between 90 and 100 in all of them.

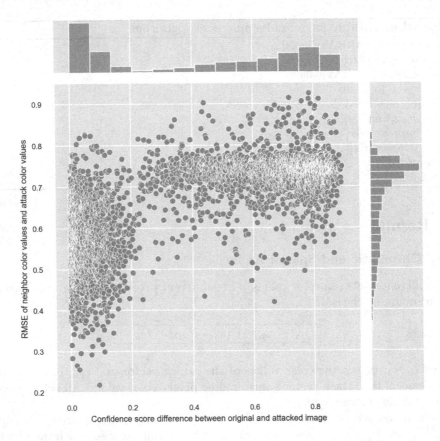

Fig. 1. Scatter plot of error function values between the attack pixel color values and neighboring pixel color values. Notice the vertical cluster at low error values and horizontal cluster at higher error values.

Table 1. Statistical measures for *mitosis-to-normal* attacks ($N = 3871$)

	X	Y	Red	Green	Blue
Mean	32.40	29.30	231.14	227.24	67.07
Median	32	30	255	255	37
SD	8.2	8.59	41.62	45.99	77.85

Table 2. Statistical measures for *normal-to-mitosis* attacks ($N = 319$)

	X	Y	Red	Green	Blue
Mean	31.55	31.15	145.28	153.31	124.29
Median	32	32	154	168	129
SD	10.54	10.77	92.62	93.04	99.53

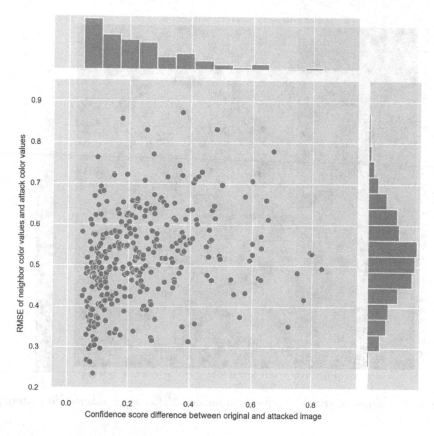

Fig. 2. Scatter plot of error function values between the attack pixel color values and neighboring pixel color values.

The statistical measures show that the dataset is most likely preprocessed in such a manner that the features used by the neural network to classify an image to either mitosis or normal class are located in the center of the image. Higher red and green color values were the key in fooling the neural network in both attacks, while blue color values were closer to zero or in the middle of the color range. In the TUPAC16 dataset, the mitosis activity was low in color range, so the neural network might be fooled by values in the higher color range.

3.2 Periodicity Analysis

The targeted model is a neural network with convolution layers, which shift through the input image in smaller windows and step to the right in steps. To check for biases in the convolutional model, the best attack locations for all the target images is visualized in a heatmap in Fig. 3.

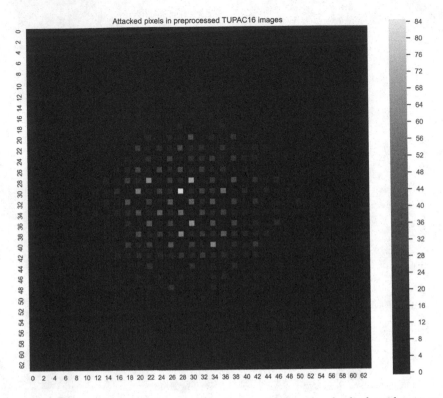

Fig. 3. A heatmap of attack placements in images. Notice the checkerboard pattern at the center.

There was a smaller ratio of successful attacks in *normal-to-mitosis* direction, and the heatmap visualization in Fig. 4 does not show any significant clusters or patterns. There is less periodicity and the center of the image is a more prominent location for the successful attacks.

One of the most remarkable features of the spatial diagrams is the periodicity of the *mitosis-to-normal* attacks. Almost all successful attack pixels have coordinates with even numbers. From all of the 5, 343 *mitosis-to-normal* attacks, the differential evolution algorithm settled on pixel coordinates that had even numbers for both coordinates 5, 334 times. Only 9 times did the algorithm have best success with coordinates where both or one of the coordinates was an odd number. Only 1 of the 9 odd coordinate attack vectors was successful of lowering the score below 0.5 with modified score of 0.387.

For *normal-to-mitosis* attacks the coordinates also preferred even coordinates; however, not so clearly. From all of the 80, 725 attacks 49, 573 or 61.4% settled on even coordinates and 31, 152 or 38.6% settled on odd coordinates.

Our first reaction was to review the attack code for periodic error but after diligent assessment the code was deemed to be working as it should. This led to the conclusion that a periodic process in the classifier itself was causing this

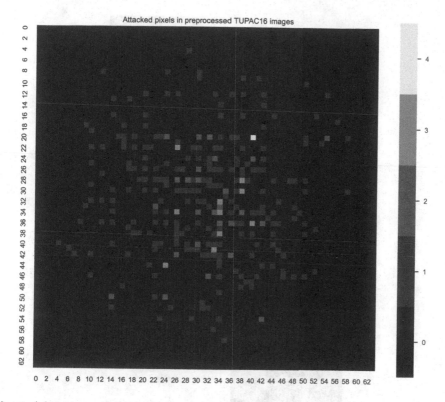

Fig. 4. A heatmap of attack locations in images. The attacks are placed mostly around the center of the image.

noticeable behavior. The behavior was verified after we brute forced the subset of attack vectors using the method described in Sect. 2.2.

Even with the reduced color space the checkerboard pattern was clearly visible when analyzing the results from the brute force computations. Figure 5a shows an example image where the minimum confidence score is visualized for each pixel in the image from all the computed attack vectors. As can be seen in the image, the same checkerboard pattern is clearly visible.

The effect of even coordinates being more vulnerable to pixel modifications might be a side effect of the architecture that the targeted model uses. The model source code shows that the model uses convolutional blocks where convolutional layer stride is set to $(2, 2)$. This could cause the checkerboard pattern. If some filter kernel on a convolutional layer that has the stride of $(2, 2)$ is vulnerable to the pixel modification attack, then that effect would be duplicated to every other pixel while the kernel sweeps across the image dimensions while skipping every other coordinate.

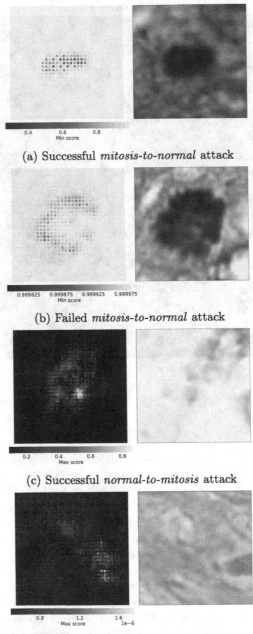

(a) Successful *mitosis-to-normal* attack

(b) Failed *mitosis-to-normal* attack

(c) Successful *normal-to-mitosis* attack

(d) Failed *normal-to-mitosis* attack

Fig. 5. Images showing examples of successful and failed *mitosis-to-normal* and *normal-to-mitosis* brute force attacks. In each subimage, on the right is the original image under brute force attack, and on the left is a heatmap visualization of maxscores or minscores array that are defined in Algorithm 1. The heatmap image shows the pixel locations that had the biggest impact on the output score when the pixel color was changed.

3.3 Brute Force Confidence Map Result Analysis

The brute force computations we performed for some handpicked images for both *mitosis-to-normal* and *normal-to-mitosis* images gave more information about the pixel positions for the successful attacks and a possible explanation why some of the attacks failed.

Figure 5a visualizes the minimum scores for each pixel that were computed for the attack vectors in the executed *mitosis-to-normal* brute force attack for this image. The original score for the image was 0.9874 and the lowest score that one of the pixel modifications achieved was 0.2689. The image shows that all the attack vectors successfully lowering the score in any meaningful way were situated in the middle of the dark spot in the image.

Figure 5b shows a similar mitosis image; however, in this image the dark spot is larger. This is an example of a failed *mitosis-to-normal* attack. The original score for this image was 0.99998 and the lowest score that any of the attack vectors achieved was 0.99979, so the best one-pixel change resulted in practically no change at all. Comparing this image to the successful *mitosis-to-normal* attack in Fig. 5a shows that this time the pixel modifications that were in the middle of the dark spot had absolutely no effect at all, and the pixel modifications that had even the slightest effect to the score were the ones on the edge of the dark spot. This could indicate that the dark spot is so big that the one-pixel modification is not large enough change to fool the model.

Similar to the previously described *mitosis-to-normal* attacks, Fig. 5c and Fig. 5d show successful and failed *normal-to-mitosis* attacks. The successful attack in Fig. 5c increased the score from original 0.09123 to 0.86350, but the failed attack in Fig. 5d had practically no success at all with the original score of 4.29×10^{-7} and the highest achieved score of 1.04×10^{-6}. It seems that the successful *normal-to-mitosis* attacks require some kind of dark spots in the middle of the image that the attack pixel highlights by making the spot look bigger and this way fooling the model. If the image does not have a spot in the middle of the image, then one pixel change is not enough to fool the model to think that there is a spot that would indicate a mitosis.

4   Conclusion

We have presented a way to systematically analyze the quality of one-pixel attacks. The target images were a set of digital pathology images and the target classifier tried to detect cancerous growth in them. We focused our efforts on the color and location of the attacks, as well as periodicity analysis through confidence maps. The tools we have used are able to reveal more information about the vulnerability of the classifier by pointing out the areas where successful attacks are more probable.

Chromatic analysis reveals that there are two clusters of attacks. It seems that the confidence score between the original and the adversarial images either stays low or, in the case of successful attacks, gets a rather big boost towards the wanted classification. Furthermore, the attack seems to be more effective the bigger the color difference is. As expected, this creates conflicting multi-objective optimization goals.

Spatial analysis reveals that the most sensitive areas for the attack are in the middle of the image. This is probably caused by the preprocessing, which produces images that have the prominent feature in the middle. This, in turn, causes the neural network classifier to focus on the middle of the image. Furthermore, combining the spatial and chromatic dimensions, pixels in successful attacks seem to appear inside the dark patches. Another common area is the edge of those dark patches. Taking into account the nature of the target images, this shows that color changes are prominent indications detected by the target model.

Periodicity analysis shows that some rows and columns are more susceptible to the attack. This stems from the features of the target classification model, which uses a neural network. It seems that a brute force mapping of classifier behavior is useful. The confidence maps illustrate that the most successful attacks are clustered around the dark middle areas of the images. It seems that it is difficult to realize a one-pixel attack if there is no clear dark area. This is caused by what the target classifier is trained to detect, and thus, focus on.

The methodology presented in this article is suitable for the analysis of any one-pixel attack, and not confined to the world of medical imaging. Our experiment used one dataset of such images. Therefore, the results may be skewed because of it and the target model used. Further experimentation could show the generalizability of the methods to other domains. The only requirement for the presented tools is to have access to a black-box classifier, which produces confidence scores. Such tools should be useful when assessing the quality of the classifier and its robustness. The need of including robustness metrics and mitigation methods to the toolbox of standard implementations seems like the correct direction in future research.

Acknowledgments. This work was funded by the Regional Council of Central Finland/Council of Tampere Region and European Regional Development Fund as part of the Health Care Cyber Range (HCCR) project of JAMK University of Applied Sciences Institute of Information Technology.

The authors would like to thank Ms. Tuula Kotikoski for proofreading the manuscript.

References

1. IBM code model asset exchange: Breast cancer mitosis detector. (2019). https://github.com/IBM/MAX-Breast-Cancer-Mitosis-Detector
2. Bharadwaj, H.K., et al.: A review on the role of machine learning in enabling IoT based healthcare applications. IEEE Access **9**, 38859–38890 (2021). https://doi.org/10.1109/ACCESS.2021.3059858
3. Kamal, S.T., Hosny, K.M., Elgindy, T.M., Darwish, M.M., Fouda, M.M.: A new image encryption algorithm for grey and color medical images. IEEE Access **9**, 37855–37865 (2021). https://doi.org/10.1109/ACCESS.2021.3063237

4. Korpihalkola, J., Sipola, T., Kokkonen, T.: Color-optimized one-pixel attack against digital pathology images. In: Balandin, S., Koucheryavy, Y., Tyutina, T. (eds.) 2021 29th Conference of Open Innovations Association (FRUCT). vol. 29, pp. 206–213. IEEE (2021). https://doi.org/10.23919/FRUCT52173.2021.9435562

5. Korpihalkola, J., Sipola, T., Puuska, S., Kokkonen, T.: One-Pixel Attack Deceives Computer-Assisted Diagnosis of Cancer, pp. 100–106. Association for Computing Machinery, New York, NY, USA (2021). https://doi.org/10.1145/3483207.3483224

6. Latif, J., Xiao, C., Imran, A., Tu, S.: Medical imaging using machine learning and deep learning algorithms: a review. In: 2019 2nd International Conference on Computing, Mathematics and Engineering Technologies (iCoMET), pp. 1–5 (2019). https://doi.org/10.1109/ICOMET.2019.8673502

7. Liu, X., et al.: Privacy and security issues in deep learning: a survey. IEEE Access **9**, 4566–4593 (2021). https://doi.org/10.1109/ACCESS.2020.3045078

8. Medical Image Analysis Group Eindhoven (IMAG/e): Tumor proliferation assessment challenge 2016 (2016). http://tupac.tue-image.nl/node/3

9. Newaz, A.I., Haque, N.I., Sikder, A.K., Rahman, M.A., Uluagac, A.S.: Adversarial attacks to machine learning-based smart healthcare systems. In: GLOBECOM 2020–2020 IEEE Global Communications Conference, pp. 1–6 (2020). https://doi.org/10.1109/GLOBECOM42002.2020.9322472

10. Qayyum, A., Qadir, J., Bilal, M., Al-Fuqaha, A.: Secure and robust machine learning for healthcare: a survey. IEEE Rev. Biomed. Eng. **14**, 156–180 (2021). https://doi.org/10.1109/RBME.2020.3013489

11. Sasubilli, S.M., Kumar, A., Dutt, V.: Machine learning implementation on medical domain to identify disease insights using TMS. In: 2020 International Conference on Advances in Computing and Communication Engineering (ICACCE), pp. 1–4 (2020). https://doi.org/10.1109/ICACCE49060.2020.9154960

12. Sipola, T., Kokkonen, T.: One-pixel attacks against medical imaging: a conceptual framework. In: Rocha, Á., Adeli, H., Dzemyda, G., Moreira, F., Ramalho Correia, A.M. (eds.) WorldCIST 2021. AISC, vol. 1365, pp. 197–203. Springer, Cham (2021). https://doi.org/10.1007/978-3-030-72657-7_19

13. Sipola, T., Puuska, S., Kokkonen, T.: Model fooling attacks against medical imaging: a short survey. Inf. Secur. Int. J. (ISIJ) **46**, 215–224 (2020). https://doi.org/10.11610/isij.4615

14. Su, J., Vargas, D.V., Sakurai, K.: One pixel attack for fooling deep neural networks. IEEE Trans. Evol. Comput. **23**(5), 828–841 (2019). https://doi.org/10.1109/TEVC.2019.2890858

15. The European Union's Law Enforcement Agency, EUROPOL: How covid-19-related crime infected Europe during 2020, November 2020. https://www.europol.europa.eu/sites/default/files/documents/how_covid-19-related_crime_infected_europe_during_2020.pdf

16. Vargas, D.V., Su, J.: Understanding the one-pixel attack: propagation maps and locality analysis. In: Espinoza, H., et al. (eds.) CEUR Workshop Proceedings, vol. 2640 (2020)

17. Veta, M., et al.: Predicting breast tumor proliferation from whole-slide images: the TUPAC16 challenge. Med. Image Anal. **54**, 111–121 (2019). https://doi.org/10.1016/j.media.2019.02.012

18. Wang, W., Sun, J., Wang, G.: Visualizing one pixel attack using adversarial maps. In: 2020 Chinese Automation Congress (CAC), pp. 924–929. IEEE (2020). https://doi.org/10.1109/CAC51589.2020.9327603

19. Watson, M., Al Moubayed, N.: Attack-agnostic adversarial detection on medical data using explainable machine learning. In: 2020 25th International Conference on Pattern Recognition (ICPR), pp. 8180–8187 (2021). https://doi.org/10.1109/ICPR48806.2021.9412560
20. Zhou, S.K., et al.: A review of deep learning in medical imaging: imaging traits, technology trends, case studies with progress highlights, and future promises. Proc. IEEE **109**(5), 820–838 (2021). https://doi.org/10.1109/JPROC.2021.3054390

Author Index

Printed in the United States
by Baker & Taylor Publisher Services